AFRICAN AMERICAN HISTORY

A JOURNEY OF LIBERATION

ASANTE

by

Dr. Molefi Kete Asante

The Peoples Publishing Group, Inc.

Free to Learn, to Grow, to Change

1-800-822-1080

Editor, Charmaine Harris-Stewart
Copy Editor, Salvatore Allocco
Production/Electronic Design, Doreen E. Smith
Cover Design, Westchester Graphic Group
Design, Doreen E. Smith, Ife Designs
Proofreading, Peggy Dorris
Photo Research, Daniel Ortiz, Jr.
Maps, Mapping Specialist, Doreen E. Smith
Timelines, Troy Allen

Reviewers and Consultants

Asa G. Hilliard, III
Fuller E. Callaway Professor of Urban Education
Department of Educational Policy Studies
Georgia State University
Atlanta, GA

Dahia I. Shabaka
Director of Social Studies & African Centered Education Detroit Public Schools
Detroit, MI

Noma Lemoine
Director, Language Development Program
Los Angeles Unified School District

Catherine H. Head
Alliance of African American Educators
Social Studies Chair
Fairfax High School
Los Angeles, CA

Augusta Mann
Program Director
Center for Applied Cultural Studies and Educational Achievement
San Francisco, CA

Dr. Michael B. Webb
President
International Youth Leadership Fund
Jersey City, NJ

Carol Dean Archer
Professor of Geography/Researcher
Center for Law and Social Justice
Medgar Evers College, City University of New York
Brooklyn, NY

ISBN 1-56256-903-1

The Peoples Publishing Group, Inc.
230 West Passaic Street
Maywood, New Jersey 07607

Printed in the United States of America.

10 9 8 7 6 5 4 3 2 1

DEDICATION

This book is dedicated to those bold school boards and superintendents who have had the courage to ask new questions. They have inspired me and have moved me to write.

ACKNOWLEDGEMENTS

Every book is an authentic collective gift. This one is no different, and I want to thank Jim Peoples and Diane Tapp personally for being the kind of wonderful, caring human beings that they are as publishers. They are truly the future. This book could not have been done without their patience, encouragement, and philosophy.

Each book is unique, and that uniqueness is made so much better by the expert work of editors. My editor, Charmaine Harris-Stewart, has an eye for seeing the invisible, a necessary talent for a good editor. I am very grateful to her for the time she has spent making me sound intelligent.

The Peoples Publishing Group has assembled an outstanding group of professionals, including Doreen Smith, whose knowledge of computers and what they can do truly boggled my imagination. Daniel Ortiz, the research sleuth who is capable of tracking down anything that has ever been recorded or photographed, the insightful copy editor, Sal Allocco, and Ife Nil Owoo, designer.

One of my graduate students at Temple University, Troy Allen, produced some of the timelines. He is sure to become an outstanding scholar.

Finally, I wish to acknowledge the work of Dr. Augusta Mann, Dahia Shabaka, Catherine Head, and Dr. Judylynn Bailey-Mitchell.

I also want to acknowledge Kariamu Asante and Molefi Khumalo Asante for the time they gave me to work on the book. Their understanding is without parallel.

INTRODUCTION BY THE AUTHOR

Molefi Kete Asante

I clearly remember the time I first met Malcolm X. It was August, 1963. It was after I had met Martin Luther King, Jr. The setting was a small restaurant in Washington, D.C. and the great man walked into the crowded space and waited like everyone else to be served. Looking over at my table, he pointed his finger at me and said, "Don't you forget your history."

Not forgetting my history is the reason that I found this book, *African American History, A Journey of Liberation* to be the most exciting project I have ever undertaken. It flows from my belief that the records regarding African Americans must be examined from the inside, from the standpoint of African people being active agents of history, not objects on the fringes of Europe. This book is a new history or historiography, a new way of writing about history.

I have not forgotten my history, but, instead, have worked on ways to improve the transmission of that history to others. African American history is not static, but dynamic, moving us through time transgenerationally and transcontinentally. Students who read this book are introduced to the origins of the African American population, its many cultural streams, and its rich legacy of resistance to injustice and inequality. They find themselves in the presence of the authentic voices of the African people, and, for the first time, see the honest achievements, failures, and victories of a people who were transported across the sea to the Americas and the Caribbean. There is true nobility here. In the United States, that nobility is woven into the tapestry of our nation, stretching from the Atlantic Ocean to the Pacific across a land in which African people have imbedded their own designs.

My task in writing this book was to capture the African agency, the action, the excitement of this marvelous history. Too often, when I conduct workshops for school teachers and we talk about the significant events in our nation's history, the first events that come to teachers' minds are ones created by Europeans rather than Africans or African Americans. After we discuss the need to view African American history from an African center, and then rethink and retalk our knowledge of history, focusing now on an African center, the joy that inevitably swells up is amazing to me. It shouldn't be, I suppose, for it is the joy of ownership, of seeing oneself and one's ancestors as active agents creating and changing the history of this nation, that overflows and stimulates a hunger to know more. It is the same joy your students will know when they see that the ownership of this history belongs to them. It is a strong American voice that has been left out of the other histories students have experienced; it is a history written from inside an African center, in an African-centered voice, praise-singing the ancestors whose lives are the substance of our present and our future as it tells the honest story of the African American in this country.

No, I have not forgotten my history. Join me now on a journey of great anguish and great joy. We have persevered on this journey of liberation, and I hope that, in the telling of this story from an African-centered voice, the journey will come alive in all its nobility and majesty, and will be a liberating experience for every reader.

4.1 million
Australopithecus

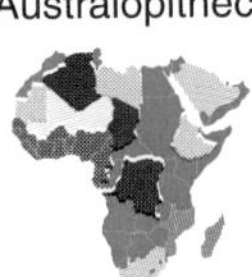

2500
Kemetians compete pyramids

1492
African explorers sail to Mexico

1515
European Slave Trade begins in earnest

1472-1787
Strong African resistance to enslavement

1770
Crispus Attucks killed

1831
Nat Turner's revolt

1850
Harriet Tubman makes her famous journeys

1851
Sojourner Truth's "Ain't I a Woman" speech

1838-1860
Growing numbers of free Africans achieve success in the U.S.

BCE CE

AT LAST! THE COMPLETE STORY IS TOLD:

AFRICAN AMERICAN HISTORY, A JOURNEY OF LIBERATION

1952
Malcolm Little joins Nation of Islam

1954
Beginning of Civil Rights Movement with *Brown v. Board of Education*

1963
March on Washington

1968
Martin Luther King, Jr., assassinated

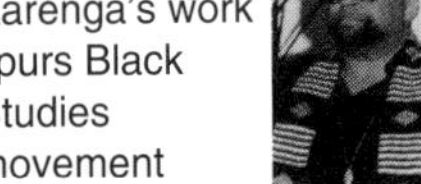

1972
Shirley Chisholm runs for president

1970s
Maulana Karenga's work spurs Black Studies movement

1984
Jesse Jackson runs for president

1995
Dr. Bernard A. Harris, Jr., is the first African American astronaut to walk in space

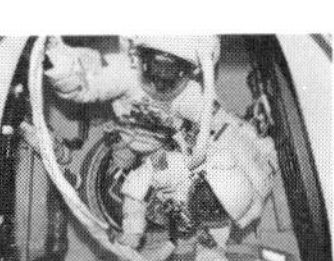

AT LAST!
AN AFRICAN AMERICAN SCHOLAR TELLS THE COMPLETE STORY:

AFRICAN AMERICAN HISTORY, A JOURNEY OF LIBERATION!

" African American History reflects the collective struggle of African people for development and then, because of colonization and enslavement, for liberation and reconstruction.

The book is organized in a way that is pedagogically sound. Especially important is the sophisticated use of maps for orientation. The narrative is inviting and the scholarly foundation is substantial. "

Asa G. Hilliard, III
Department of Educational Policy Studies
Georgia State University

" The perspective and comprehensive scope of African American History, A Journey of Liberation draws the reader into the book and makes you understand the full story, in context, as never before. "

Noma Lemoine
Director, Language Development Program
Los Angeles Unified School District

THE "MISSING" HISTORICAL INFORMATION YOU'VE LONGED FOR, CHAPTER AFTER CHAPTER!

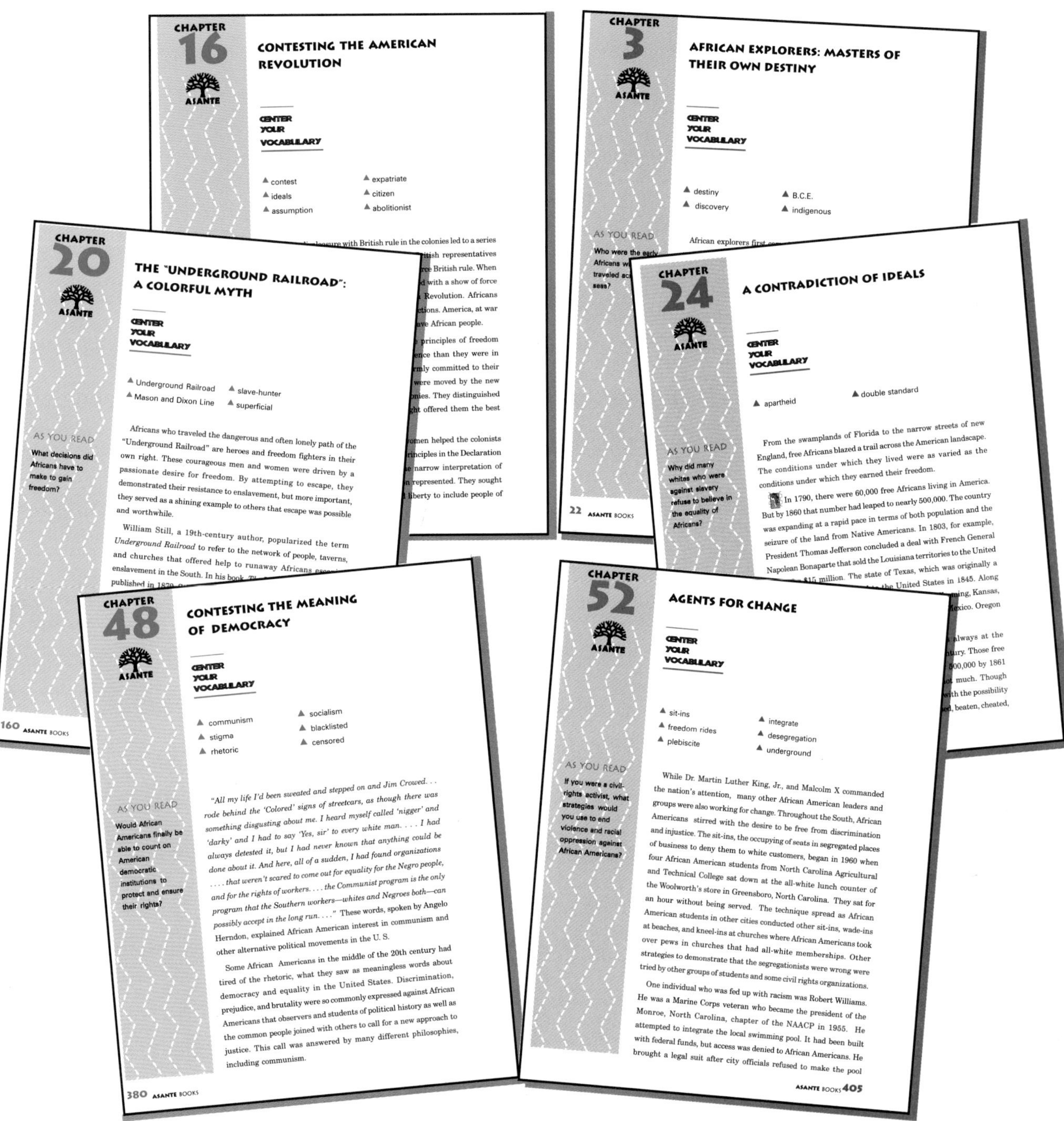

(AND THE ONLY AFRICAN AMERICAN HISTORY SCHOOL BOOK BY AN AFRICAN AMERICAN SCHOLAR—DR. MOLEFI KETE ASANTE—NOT BY A MULTICULTURAL COMMITTEE!)

THIS BOOK *DEMANDS* THAT STUDENTS ACHIEVE, AND IT HAS BUILT-IN INSTRUCTIONAL AIDS TO HELP THEM SOAR, UNIT-BY-UNIT, PAGE-BY-PAGE, STEP-BY-STEP. . .

Each Unit opens by motivating students to learn, think critically, understand timelines, and read for a purpose.The book has 16 Units.

A Timeline Opens Each Unit, showing key events.

UNIT 7

ASANTE

FREEDOM FIGHTERS

C.E.

1739-1841 Africans revolt

1800 South Carolina rules that free Africans will be reenslaved if captured in South Carolina

1808 Britain makes it illegal for their citizens to participate in the European Slave Trade in West Africa and attempts to suppress it across the Atlantic Ocean

1825 Frances Ellen Watkins Harper is born in Baltimore, Maryland

1827 *Freedom's Journal,* first African American newspaper, published.

1829 David Walker publishes his *Appeal to the Colored Citizens of the World*

1843 Henry Highland Garnet publishes *An Address to the Slaves of he United States of America*

1847 Frederick Douglass publishes *The North Star*newspaper

1849 Harriet Tubman escapes enslavement and settles in Philadelphia

1850 Harriet Tubman makes more than 19 trips from the South to free enslaved Africans

1851 Sojourner Truth gives her famous *Ain't I a Woman* speech in Akron, Ohio

1860 Harriet Jacobs publishes her narrative, *Incidents in the Life of a Slave Girl*

1872 William Still publishes *The Underground Railroad*

In small groups, debate both sides of redemptive violence versus nonviolence as though you were 18th-century African freedom fighters. In this unit, the term *redemptive violence* describes violence used in self-defense against enslavement and racism. Some African freedom fighters used redemptive violence, while others believed that Africans could gain freedom through persuasive nonviolence and moral arguments. Time your debate, and let the class vote on the most effective argument.

As you read Unit 7, think about what liberty means to you and your life. How does liberty relate to freedom and self-determination? What do you think of people who are willing to endanger their own lives to fight for liberty?

"Let not those who have never been placed in like circumstances [enslavement], judge me harshly. Until they have been chained and beaten—until they find themselves in the situation I was, borne away from home and family toward a land of bondage—let them refrain from saying what they would not do for liberty."

FREDERICK DOUGLASS

144 ASANTE BOOKS

ASANTE BOOKS 145

A group activity motivates students to work cooperatively and begin the Unit.

As students are ready to begin reading the Unit, an advance organizer help set a purpose for reading critically and comprehending.

ACTIVITIES SUPPORT DIVERSE LEARNING STYLES

Each Unit closes with a Unit Review, which starts with a Summary of the Key Concepts in the Unit.

Each Unit also has a 2-part Personal Witnessing Activity:

Part 1 is *Reflection*—a private journal writing activity.

Part 2 is *Testimony*—a group or individual activity in which students demonstrate to the class what they have learned in the Unit.

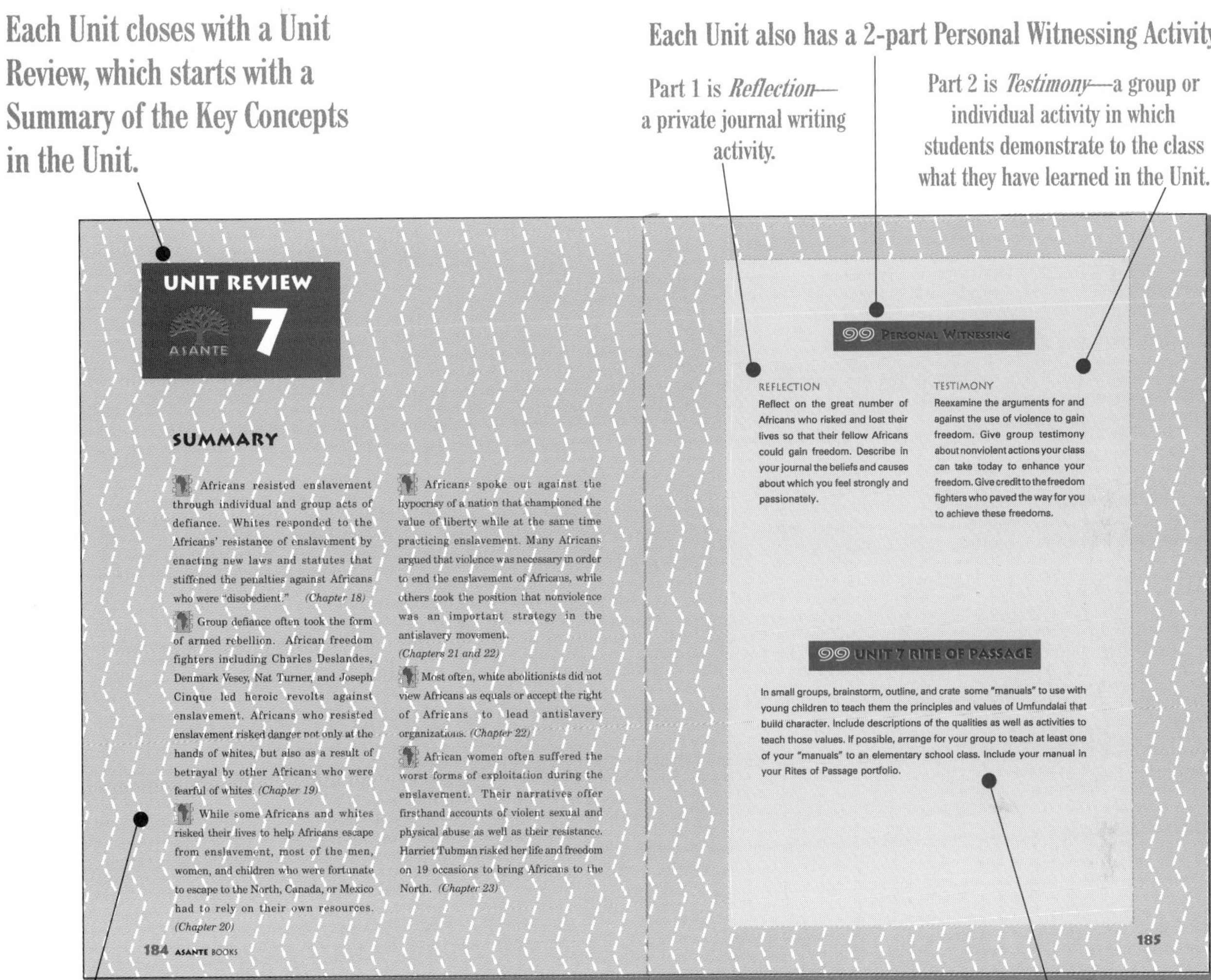

UNIT REVIEW 7

ASANTE

SUMMARY

Africans resisted enslavement through individual and group acts of defiance. Whites responded to the Africans' resistance of enslavement by enacting new laws and statutes that stiffened the penalties against Africans who were "disobedient." *(Chapter 18)*

Group defiance often took the form of armed rebellion. African freedom fighters including Charles Deslandes, Denmark Vesey, Nat Turner, and Joseph Cinque led heroic revolts against enslavement. Africans who resisted enslavement risked danger not only at the hands of whites, but also as a result of betrayal by other Africans who were fearful of whites. *(Chapter 19)*

While some Africans and whites risked their lives to help Africans escape from enslavement, most of the men, women, and children who were fortunate to escape to the North, Canada, or Mexico had to rely on their own resources. *(Chapter 20)*

Africans spoke out against the hypocrisy of a nation that championed the value of liberty while at the same time practicing enslavement. Many Africans argued that violence was necessary in order to end the enslavement of Africans, while others took the position that nonviolence was an important strategy in the antislavery movement. *(Chapters 21 and 22)*

Most often, white abolitionists did not view Africans as equals or accept the right of Africans to lead antislavery organizations. *(Chapter 22)*

African women often suffered the worst forms of exploitation during the enslavement. Their narratives offer firsthand accounts of violent sexual and physical abuse as well as their resistance. Harriet Tubman risked her life and freedom on 19 occasions to bring Africans to the North. *(Chapter 23)*

184 ASANTE BOOKS

PERSONAL WITNESSING

REFLECTION

Reflect on the great number of Africans who risked and lost their lives so that their fellow Africans could gain freedom. Describe in your journal the beliefs and causes about which you feel strongly and passionately.

TESTIMONY

Reexamine the arguments for and against the use of violence to gain freedom. Give group testimony about nonviolent actions your class can take today to enhance your freedom. Give credit to the freedom fighters who paved the way for you to achieve these freedoms.

UNIT 7 RITE OF PASSAGE

In small groups, brainstorm, outline, and crate some "manuals" to use with young children to teach them the principles and values of Umfundalai that build character. Include descriptions of the qualities as well as activities to teach those values. If possible, arrange for your group to teach at least one of your "manuals" to an elementary school class. Include your manual in your Rites of Passage portfolio.

185

The Africa Symbol identifies key concepts. The symbol appears throughout the chapters, and is summarized at the end of the Unit.

Students who complete all 16 Unit Rites of Passage activities for their Rites of Passage Portfolio are eligible for the end-of-book ceremony, demonstrating their growth on personal and intellectual levels, and community service.

SUGGESTED READINGS

Aptheker, Herbert. *American Negro Slave Revolts.* New York: Columbia University Press, 1943.

Bennett, Lerone. *Pioneers in Protest.* Chicago: Johnson Publishing Co., 1968.

Brent, Linda. *Incidents in the Life of a Slave Girl.* New York: Harcourt, Brace, Jovanovich, 1861, 1973.

Douglass, Frederick. *My Bondage and My Freedom.* New York: Johnson Publishing Co., 1970.

Garnet, Henry Highland. *Address to the Slaves of the United States.* New York: Arno, 1968.

Giddings, Paula. *When and Where I Enter: The Impact of Black Women on Race and Sex in America.* New York: Morrow, 1984.

Northup, Solomon. *Twelve Years a Slave.* New York: Miller, Orton & Mulligan, 1855.

Price, Richard. *Maroon Communities.*

Quarles, Benjamin. *Black Abolitionists.* New York: Oxford University Press, 1969.

Walker, David. *Appeal to the Coloured Citizens of the World.* New York: Hill and Wang, 1965.

ASANTE BOOKS 183

Each Unit also ends with an academic and professional bibliography of resources on which the Unit is based.

Turn! You'll Want to See the Built-In Chapter-by-Chapter Instructional Aids, too! . . . ☛

CHAPTER-BY-CHAPTER, COMPLETE HISTORY, GOOD SOLID INSTRUCTION, **PLUS** CULTURALLY-BASED LEARNING STRATEGIES

AS YOU READ opens each chapter with purpose-setting questions to guide students.

Key Vocabulary is listed at the beginning of each chapter. Words are in the glossary.

CHAPTER 20

ASANTE

THE "UNDERGROUND RAILROAD": A COLORFUL MYTH

CENTER YOUR VOCABULARY

▲ Underground Railroad ▲ slave-hunter
▲ Mason and Dixon Line ▲ superficial

AS YOU READ
What decisions did Africans have to make to gain freedom?

Africans who traveled the dangerous and often lonely path of the "Underground Railroad" are heroes and freedom fighters in their own right. These courageous men and women were driven by a passionate desire for freedom. By attempting to escape, they demonstrated their resistance to enslavement, but more important, they served as a shining example to others that escape was possible and worthwhile.

William Still, a 19th-century author, popularized the term *Underground Railroad* to refer to the network of people, taverns, and churches that offered help to runaway Africans escaping enslavement in the South. In his book, *The Underground Railroad*, published in 1872, Still described the routes that were taken most often by runaway Africans. These routes followed the Mason and Dixon Line, an imaginary boundary created in 1763 to divide Pennsylvania and Maryland. The Mason and Dixon Line came to represent the division between the slaveholding states and the free states. The line cut through Quaker territories in Ohio and Pennsylvania. The Quakers were a religious society that showed an early moral interest in freeing Africans from enslavement.

The Underground Rail[...] was a colorful way to characterize the men and women, African[...]

160 ASANTE BOOKS

THE UNDERGROUND RAIL ROAD.

WILLIAM STILL.

▲ William Still included real stories and letters about many men and women who escaped enslavement in his book, *The Underground Railroad*, published in 1872.

help Africans escape to the North. But in reality, the Underground Railroad was not very effective. Most of the Africans who escaped from enslavement did so on their own and by their own bravery and intelligence. Courageous Africans—men, women and children who were fortunate in escaping enslavers—had to rely largely on their own resources and skills to find their way to safety. They had no maps, food, or clothing. Their only guide was the lone North Star on the distant horizon. They were often tired, lonely, and scared as they tried desperately to cover their tracks from the keen scent of the bloodhounds and the more dangerous pursuit of the slave-hunters.

Free Africans and some whites in the North provided safe houses along the way for the runaways. But many Africans could not take advantage of these houses because they did not know where they were located. Only in the cases where there had been routine trips, as was the case with Harriet Tubman who made 19 trips to Maryland and Delaware to escort enslaved Africans to freedom, could there be a series of safe houses usable by the escaping Africans. Other Africans seeking to escape to Canada or to Mexico, had to find their own way.

ASANTE BOOKS 161

Key information is noted with a symbol—a study aid for students. (Key information is summarized in the Unit Review, too.)

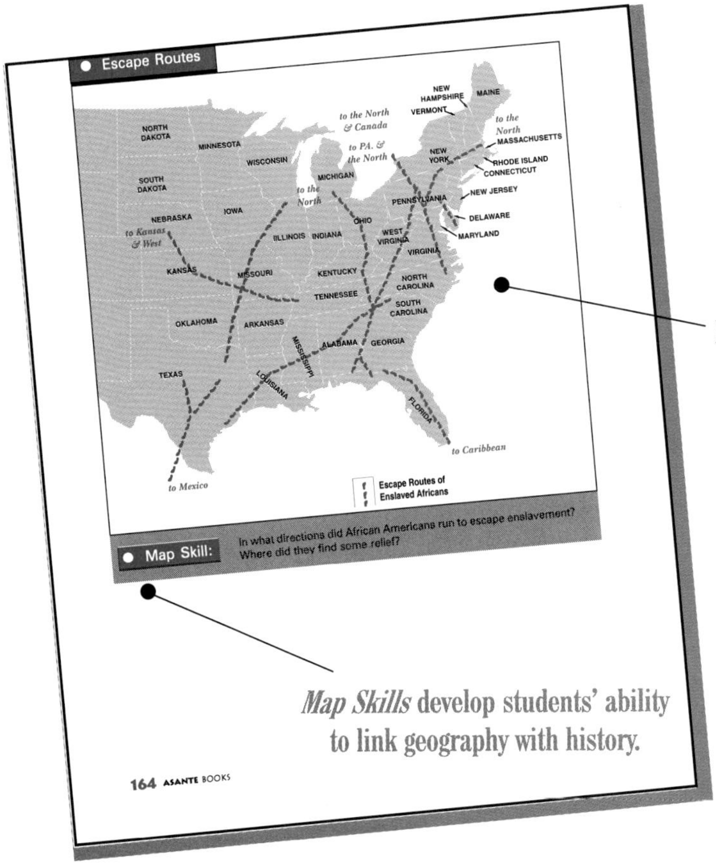

Escape Routes

Map Skill: In what directions did African Americans run to escape enslavement? Where did they find some relief?

164 ASANTE BOOKS

Maps are based on Peters's Projections, which give a true representation of land mass and relative sizes.

Map Skills develop students' ability to link geography with history.

◆ CENTER YOUR THINKING

1. What is a narrative?
2. Name two famous African American women who were antislavery activists, and tell what they did.
3. Do you agree with the statement that women were exploited in ways that men were not? Explain why.
4. Explain what Sojourner Truth meant when she said, "Ain't I a Woman?"
5. HOLISTIC ACTIVITY Students as Journalists
Your group will interview the 19th-century antislavery activists in this chapter. Write a list of questions to ask them. Now write a script of the interview, and present it for the class.

Each chapter ends with 4 questions which reinforce comprehension, interpretation, analysis, and critical-thinking.

A Holistic Activity supports diverse learning styles.

A Complete Activity Book and Teacher's Activity Guide Are Available!

Also, Unit and End-of-Book tests, vocabulary activities,comprehension and study skill activities, complete answer key, and much, much more!

3 PORTFOLIOS SUPPORT ALTERNATIVE LEARNING STYLES:

- **Alternative Assessment Portfolio** activities in the Teacher's Activity Guide.
- **Writing Portfolio** activities for each Chapter and Unit in the Activity Book.
- **Rites of Passage Portfolio** activity for each Unit in the student book.

AFRICAN AMERICAN HISTORY

A JOURNEY OF LIBERATION

ASANTE

CONTENTS

UNIT 8 THE POLITICS OF OPPRESSION: FREE AFRICAN AMERICANS 186

UNIT 9 THE CONFLICT DEEPENS 208

UNIT 10 STRIKING FOR LIBERTY AGAIN! 238

UNIT 11 RECONSTRUCTION 264

UNIT 16 THE AFROCENTRIC FUTURE 440

MAPS AND MAP SKILLS

**EACH CENTERED PERSON
BECOMES AN OWNER,
NOT A RENTER, OF KNOWLEDGE.
CENTER YOURSELF.**

Molefi Kete Asante

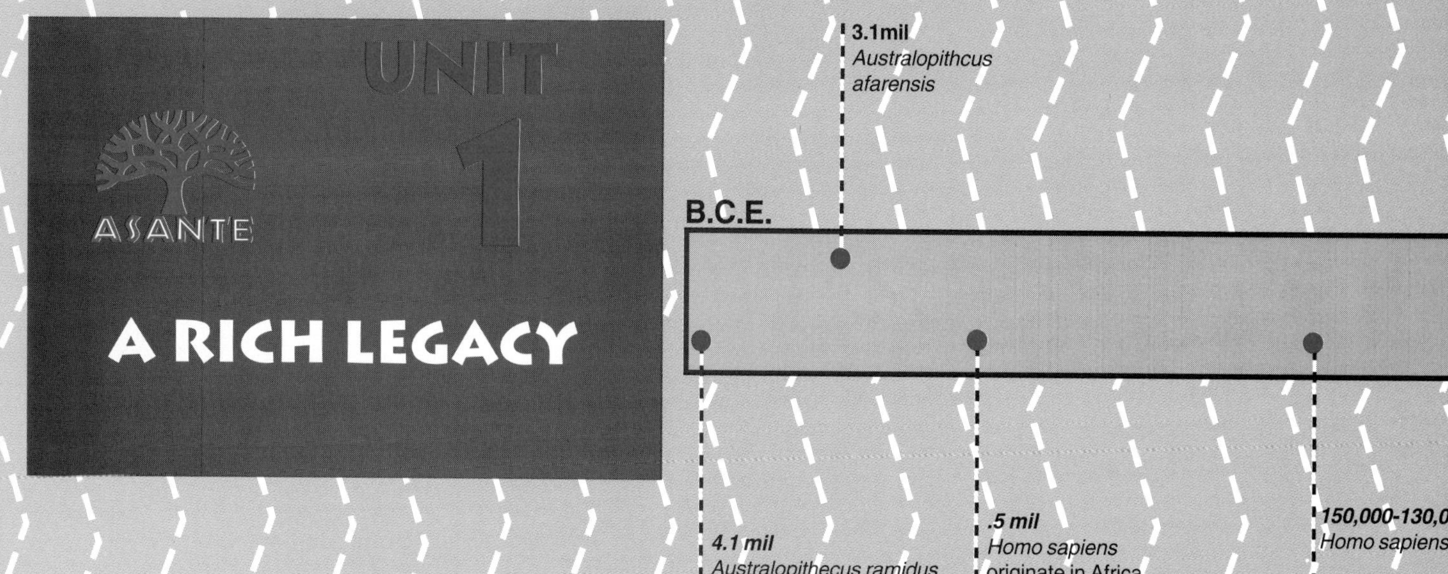

Work in small groups. Close your eyes and let your imagination take over. Envision your ancestors from 400 years ago. Create a group story about them. How do they look? What are their homes and families like? their education systems? their spiritual beliefs? their recreation?

Ancestors play an important role in the personal history of each of us. How have your ancestors influenced your life? In this unit, you will read about the African ancestors of African Americans and their great gifts to the world.

> *"Just like moons and like suns,*
> *With the certainty of tides,*
> *Just like hopes springing high,*
> *Still I'll rise."*
>
> MAYA ANGELOU, STILL I RISE

An African-centered World

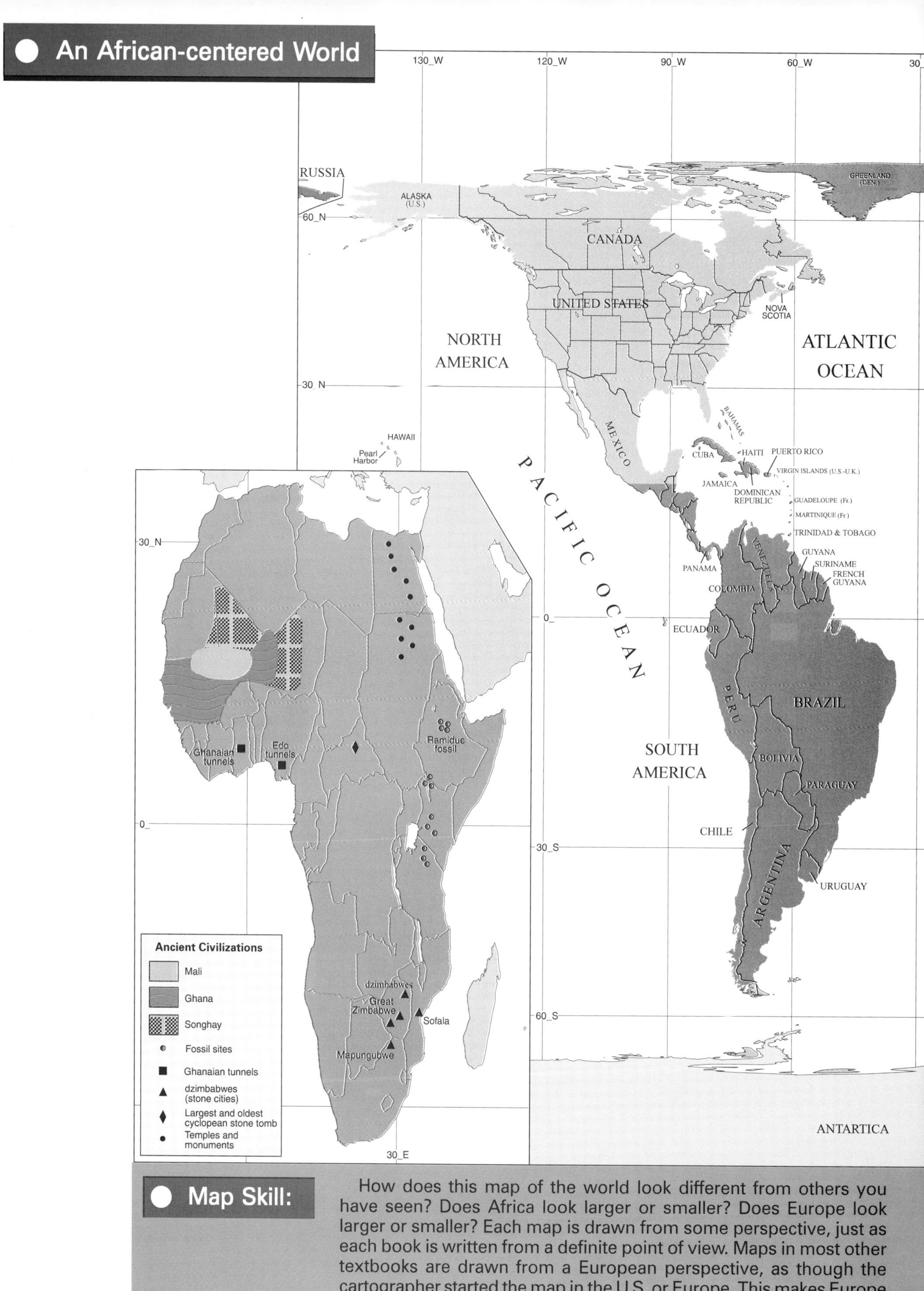

Map Skill:

How does this map of the world look different from others you have seen? Does Africa look larger or smaller? Does Europe look larger or smaller? Each map is drawn from some perspective, just as each book is written from a definite point of view. Maps in most other textbooks are drawn from a European perspective, as though the cartographer started the map in the U.S. or Europe. This makes Europe and the U.S. look larger, and changes the shape of Africa and the

other continents. Maps drawn from a European perspective are called Mercator Maps.

The maps in this textbook are drawn starting from the equator, and then created moving both up (north) and down (south), with the goal of giving you a more unbiased view. Of course, as the perspective changes away from Europe and to an even view, the shapes of the continents and countries changes. The maps in this book are Peters Projection Maps, and they were created to accurately represent all land masses, especially as they relate in size to each other.

▲ A 300-year-old mosque near Damongo in Northern Africa

▲ The ancient city of Timbuktu was a major trade and intellectual center in the 15th and 16th centuries.

CHAPTER 1

POWERFUL ANCESTRAL BONDS

CENTER YOUR VOCABULARY

- ▲ empire
- ▲ C.E.
- ▲ eminent
- ▲ legacy
- ▲ cultural patterns
- ▲ entrepreneurs
- ▲ industrialization
- ▲ Americas

AS YOU READ

What was life like for the people of West Africa prior to the invasion of Europeans?

The day the Moroccan army stormed into the ancient city of Timbuktu, it was hot and dry. Despite the heat, scores of students listened to the eloquent professor, Ahmed Baba, as he lectured outside the mosque, or temple, at the wall of his 1,600-book library. He was teaching his students at the University of Sankore about the origins of the Songhay Empire. The year was 1594 C.E. (in the Common Era) and the University of Sankore was among the greatest centers of learning in the world. The students who had gathered to hear Baba speak were thrilled at the opportunity to learn from the most eminent professor in Sankore's history.

As the Moroccans drew closer to the university, the scene for the Songhay people was frighteningly similar to an earlier attack. In 1590, some 5,000 Moroccans had invaded the empire hoping to seize control of the wealth of Songhay, particularly its rich gold and salt mines. Although the Moroccans never succeeded in discovering where the gold mines were, they took complete control of the salt mines at the town of Taghaza, which is now part of southern Morocco.

But on this hot, hazy day in 1594, the Moroccans were after more than gold and salt. Forcing their way quickly through the streets, the Moroccan soldiers could smell the sweet success of victory. They could hear Ahmed Baba's calm voice as he lectured, completely unaware that danger was just around the corner. Within minutes, Ahmed Baba, the last great professor of the University of Sankore and author of more than 40 books on astronomy, law, science, theology, rhetoric, and logic, was grabbed from behind, shackled in chains and carried away by the invading Moroccan Army. Ahmed Baba's arrest brought to an end one of the many glorious periods in African history. Songhay's defeat signaled the beginning of one of the stormiest and most traumatic periods in the history of African people.

STRONG CONNECTIONS

The Moroccan Africans plundered Songhay, taking over the wealth of the land and the rich culture of their fellow Africans. However, they were unable to control the vast Songhay Empire which lay shattered and broken into tiny pieces, never to regain its former glory. (See *Classical Africa*, Chapter 30.) Tiny splinters of this great empire traveled in the collective memories of those Africans who were scattered to the west during the European Slave Trade.

From that time until today, Africans all over the world have set out on a long, difficult journey to reclaim the legacy of their cultural heritage and rightful place in human history. Travel with us now as we embark on a truly exciting journey with a people ripped apart by enslavement but connected by the much stronger bonds of a shared past.

THE IMPERIAL THREESOME: GHANA, MALI, SONGHAY

The Empire of Songhay rose to prominence as the Malian Empire went into decline in the late 15th century. Mali was the most famous empire of West Africa. In 1255 C.E., the kingdom of Mali, at the center of Mali's vast empire of smaller kingdoms, was the richest kingdom in all of West Africa. Mali was a major trading center and intellectual attraction for Arabs and Portuguese, among others. It also had the strongest army in the empire. Mali owed its military might to the Ghanaian Empire's legacy, which as early as the 7th century C.E. had developed strong cultural patterns, distinctly African principles, and traditions that united the entire coast of West Africa. The Malian Empire declined in the 15th century because it was unable to keep the various nations that constituted the empire from revolting against the taxes they had to pay. The kingdoms on the fringes of the empire often refused to pay their taxes, and the emperor, the paramount king of Mali, had to send troops to keep them in line.

Ancient Empires

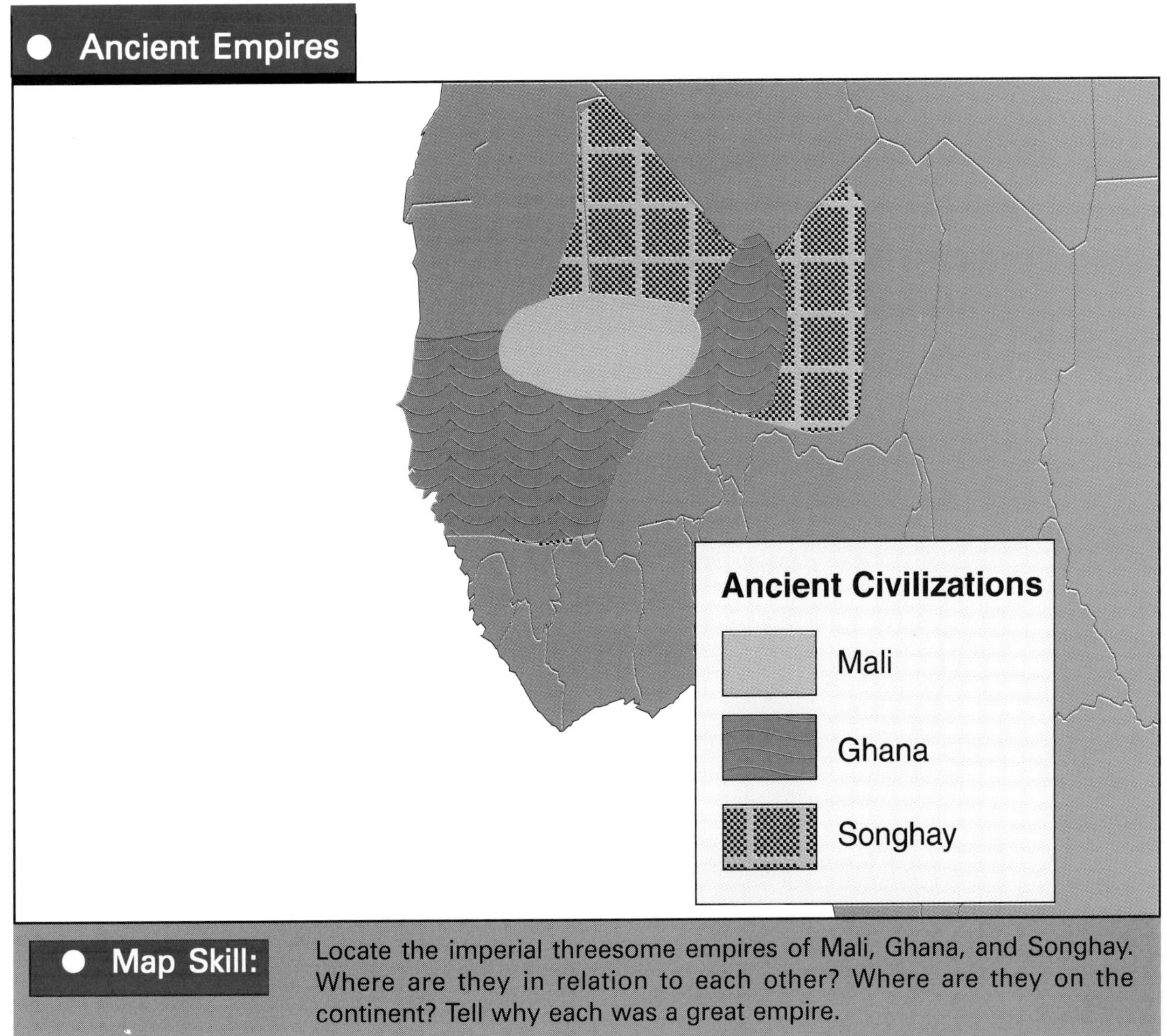

Map Skill: Locate the imperial threesome empires of Mali, Ghana, and Songhay. Where are they in relation to each other? Where are they on the continent? Tell why each was a great empire.

When Sunni Ali Ber came to power as a minor king in 1464 in the small kingdom of Gao, Mansa Musa was emperor of all of Mali. Bit by bit, the revolt of the kingdom of Gao and other small kingdoms wore down the mighty Malian Empire. When the Songhay Empire emerged to take over, it had at its core the kingdom of Gao ruled by Sunni Ali Ber.

The power and dominance of Ghana, Mali, and Songhay controlled western Africa from 300 B.C.E. to 1594 C.E. This imperial threesome ruled for almost 2,000 years and formed the high point of political, cultural, and military might from the earliest time of Ghana, around the 4th century B.C.E., to the end of Songhay in the late 16th century C.E. Names of the emperors sparkle in human history like diamonds in the desert, so vast and glorious is the scope of African history during this period. Sumanguru, Sundiata, Mansa Musa, Askia Mohammed, Sunni Ali Ber, and Abubakari are just a few of the names of the greatest emperors of West Africa.

With the collapse of Songhay in 1594 C.E., the entire western region of Africa was left unprotected. Only small kingdoms with weak armies remained to defend the vast coastal borders. This made it easy for the European nations to occupy some sections of the African coast. One hundred years after the first European invasion in 1441 C.E., Africans would be found in every part of the Western Hemisphere as indentured servants or enslaved people. So profitable and valuable would Africans become to European entrepreneurs, whose main concern was making money, that the enslavement of Africans would become one of the keys to industrializing Europe and America.

When the first Africans arrived in Jamestown, Virginia, in 1619 aboard a Dutch ship, they were not the first Africans to grace the American shore. Africans had already visited the Americas—North, Central, South America, and Mexico, as well as the Caribbean—500 years earlier. But who were these Africans? Where had they originated? What cultural legacies, heritage, and traditions did they bring with them?

◆ CENTER YOUR THINKING

1. Why did the Moroccans try to conquer the Songhay Empire?
2. How did African culture survive in North and South America and the Caribbean despite enslavement?
3. Using information in Chapter 1, give examples of how a people's culture influences the way they live, their social relationships, and their behavior toward one another.
4. According to many scholars, West Africa prior to the European slave trade had a common culture. Are there groups that you can observe around you who share a common culture? Give reasons to support your answer.
5. HOLISTIC ACTIVITY Student As Teacher

   Using large poster paper or a computer graphics program, create a pictorial chart to use in teaching young children about the three great kingdoms of Ghana, Mali, and Songhay. Read more about these kingdoms in *Classical Africa*. Include information on rulers, trade, natural resources, dates, military stength, and other areas of interest to you.

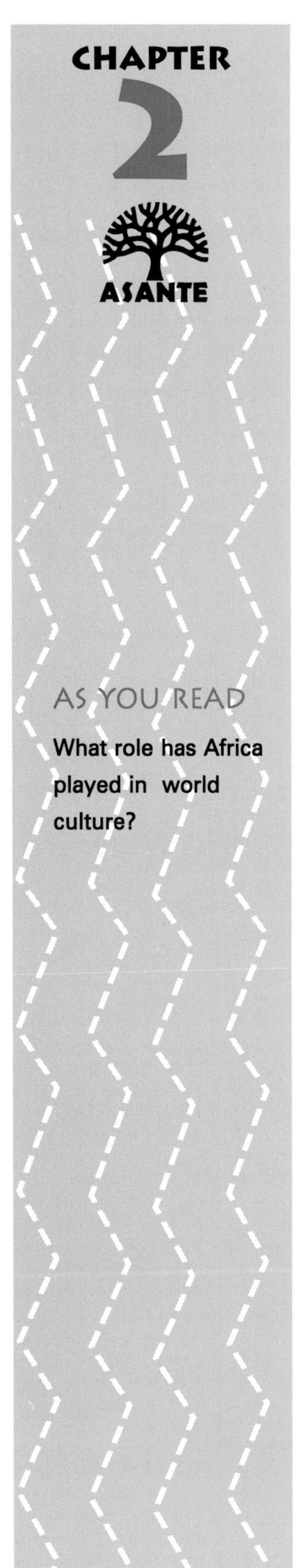

THE AFRICANS

CENTER YOUR VOCABULARY

- continent
- ancestors
- Kemet
- oral tradition
- architecture
- extended family

Africans are people whose origins are on the continent of Africa. The continent itself is four times the size of the United States of America. It has a total area of 30.2 million square kilometers (11.7 million square miles) and encompasses more than 50 countries. There are many rivers, lakes, and waterfalls on the continent. Three of the world's great rivers cut through the landscape. The Nile, the world's longest river at 6,695 kilometers (4,151 miles), is in Northeast Africa. In Central Africa, the Zaire (Congo) River carries one of the largest volumes of water in the world. The Niger, the fabled river of West Africa, is known for the variety of trade it enables, with merchants buying and selling cotton, salt, gold, ivory, bronze statuettes, and textiles. There are colorful villages along its banks. Two powerful deserts, the Sahara, the world's largest, and the Kalahari, are major features of the continent. It is from this beautiful and diverse continent, with its vast rain forests and mountains serving as belts and buckles on the map of Africa, that Africans, now located all over the world, originated.

Humans first learned how to tame animals, build bridges, plant and harvest foods, organize communities, and paint records of their activities on the continent of Africa. In fact, human beings originated

● Climate and Physical Features

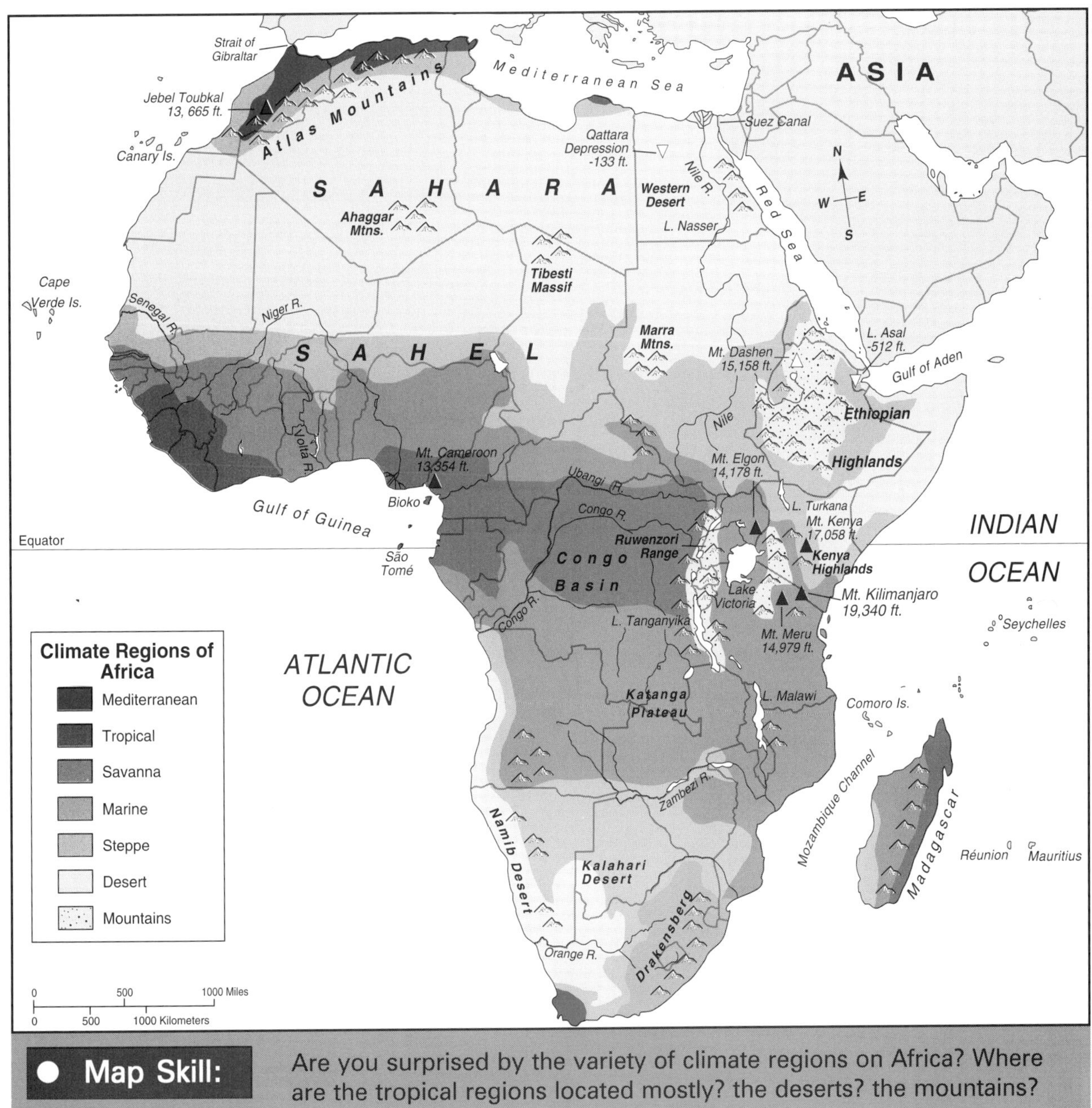

● Map Skill: Are you surprised by the variety of climate regions on Africa? Where are the tropical regions located mostly? the deserts? the mountains?

on that continent and traveled from Africa to various other parts of the earth. Africans are the ancestors, the peoples from whom we are descended.

MOTHER AFRICA

Only recently, Ethiopian and American paleontologists discovered an exposed fossil tooth, partially hidden in the pebble-covered desert of north central Ethiopia. The tooth, along with other fossils found in the area, belongs to a previously unknown species of small, humanlike creatures who walked the Earth some 4.4-million years ago. The researchers named the new creature *Australopithecus ramidus*. Africalogists, those who teach about ancient Africa, and anthropologists have not found anything as revolutionary as this since 1974 when the famous fossil skeleton known as *Australopithecus afarensis*, referred to by the Ethiopians as *Dinqnesh* (Deenk-NESH) and by the Americans as Lucy, was discovered. *Dinqnesh* or Lucy, a 3.2-million-year-old female, had some human characteristics. Researchers believe that *Dinqnesh* walked on two legs, not four. However, the skull and tooth fragments indicated that she was more apelike than human.

Modern comparisons between the genetic makeup of humans and apes suggest that the split between the two occurred 4-million to 6 million years ago. Paleontologists predict that older fossils will be more apelike, while fossils that are dated after *Dinqnesh* will be more humanlike.

As scientists continue to debate whether *ramidus* is really the common ancestor of humans and apes or whether it is the first species to appear on the human side after the split, one thing is certain: Africa is the birthplace of all humans. It is also the key to unlocking many of the mysteries of the past.

GREAT GIFTS

African contributions to human civilization, geology, archaeology, architecture, astronomy, mathematics, and literature assist us in a full understanding and appreciation of the great gifts Africa gave to the world. Europeans traveled to Africa to study art, measurement, philosophy, and religion with the outstanding intellectuals of the world. In fact, Africans created the first calendar, and the names of nearly all the Greek gods came from Africa.

Africans have had a long, respectful association with nature. African philosophy is based upon a harmonious relationship with nature. This means that trees, mountains, rivers, and meadows are respected as one with human beings. Humans, whether dead, living, or unborn, are equally respected. Thus, Africans have always held a belief in the sanctity of human beings and of the earth. No wonder then that Africans approached the sky, the earth, and water with wonder and found inspiration in the lessons of those elements. African people studied the sky for clues to the weather, nature, and the destiny of human beings. For example, in the 11th century C.E., the Dogon people of Mali discovered Sirius B, one of the rarest and brightest stars in the Dog Star constellation, more than 700 years before any other people. Ancient Africans in Kemet (Egypt) would climb to the roof of the temples to watch the night sky for hundreds of nights and record their observations.

KEMETIC AND GREEK GODS

KEMETIC	GREEK	CHARACTERISTICS
Amen	Zeus	Supreme god (ruler)
Bes	Dionysus	God of wine
Djehuty	Hermes	God of science and knowledge
Hathor	Aphrodite	Goddess of love and beauty
Horus	Apollo	God of light and sun
Imhotep	Asclepius	God of healing and medicine
Neith	Athena	Goddess of war, wisdom and crafts

As you read this book on the African Americans, consider a recent discovery in Nigeria, West Africa, confirming that a network of tunnels, 16,092 kilometers (10,000 miles) long, was constructed by the Edo people around the 8th or 9th century C.E. The discovery, made public for the first time in 1994, is so new that scholars have not been able to date the tunnels accurately. Furthermore, this huge public works project is just one of many indications that there is much more to find. Not very far from this area of Nigeria, the Akan elders of Ghana recite the story of the construction of royal tunnels that connected several villages. The presence of several tunnels in central Ghana suggest that the Akan elders and others who keep

Archaeological Sites

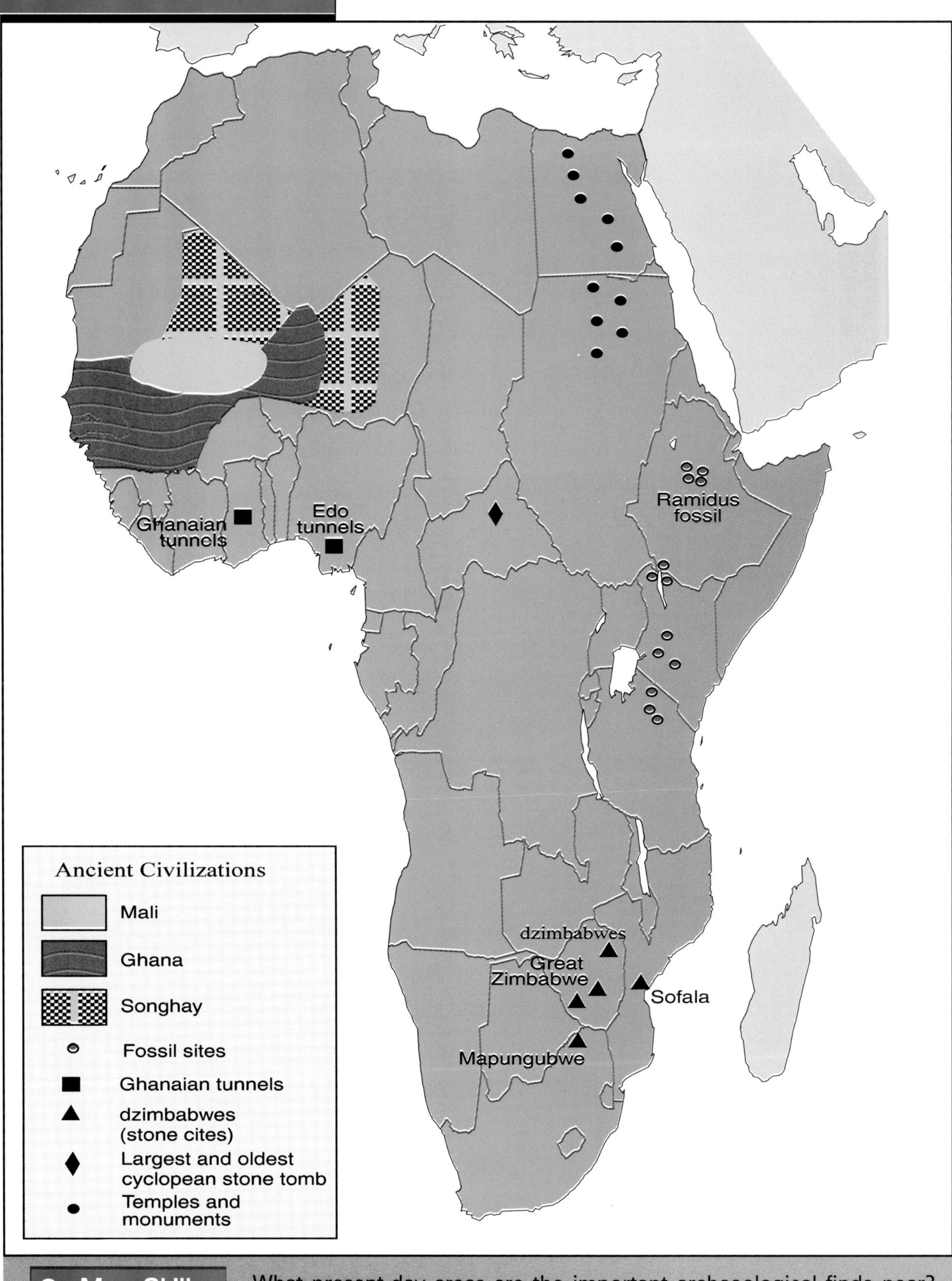

Map Skill: What present-day areas are the important archaeological finds near? What continent are they on?

oral traditions alive hold key information to these discoveries. The Ghanaian tunnels, which historians believe were constructed in the 17th century C.E., precede the construction of public tunnels in Europe and the United States by more than 200 years.

In the south of the continent, ancient Africans demonstrated their own brand of creativity in the world of architecture, or the science of designing and building. The Zimbabweans, Mozambicans, and South Africans have inherited more than 800 stone cities, called dzimbabwes, built between the 9th and the 15th centuries all over the southern region of Africa. As you study and learn more about great architecture, you will develop a greater appreciation for many of the early contributions that ancient Africans made to the modern world.

A GLIMPSE AT 16TH CENTURY AFRICA

As they gathered in the forest, the seven kings of adjacent villages wondered aloud if the priest would make it to the meeting. Okomfo Anokye, the supreme priest, had called a conference of kings in order to create a confederation. The youngest king, Osei Tutu, had brought his royal paraphernalia and had already taken his seat in his great chair when the priest arrived. He stood, however, and greeted the great priest. Soon after, Okomfo Anokye commanded a golden stool to come out of the sky. Within seconds, a golden stool descended from the sky and landed on the knees of the young king, Osei Tutu. The priest then told the other six kings that Osei Tutu and those who would reign on his throne will forever be given the title Asantehene, paramount king of the Asante people.

As in other African nations at this time, everything seemed to turn on religion. The people's religion was named after the people. The people's language was named after the people. The art, music, and agriculture—even the royal reign of the people—was tied to the concept of the sacred, the holy, the mysterious. Africans, past and present, approach life with a high respect for others because all relationships depend upon being in harmony with the ancestral spirits.

Ethnic Groups of West Africa

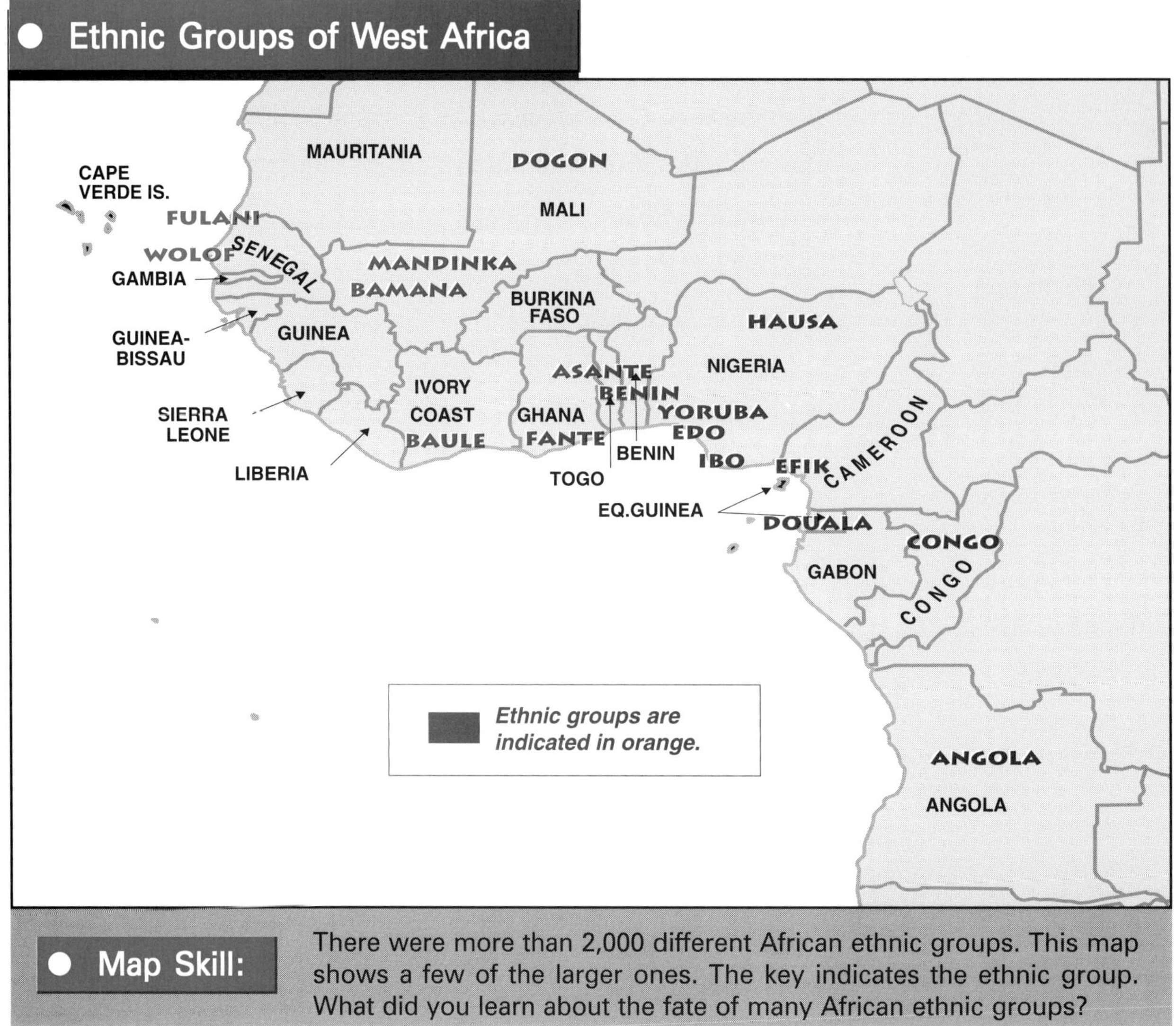

Map Skill: There were more than 2,000 different African ethnic groups. This map shows a few of the larger ones. The key indicates the ethnic group. What did you learn about the fate of many African ethnic groups?

Among the 2,000 different African ethnic groups, one can find a common thread in the approach to rites of passage. Almost every African ethnic group has a ritual for the passage of a child from girl to womanhood or boy to manhood. There are certain things one has to learn and certain ideas one has to master, and in some cases a young boy has to achieve physical mastery over an animal or a natural barrier, such as a river, to demonstrate his lack of fear and the attainment of manhood. Girls often have to master the preparation of medicines, and learn about childbirth and housebuilding. While each African ethnic group has its own rites of passage, all Africans believe that it is necessary to pass down the knowledge gained from the ancestors to the next generation. This knowledge is passed down from generation to generation as oral tradition by speaking and telling stories of the past.

▲ Statue of a royal head from Ife, Nigeria

Today, there are many diverse communities and cultures on the African continent. Along the great western shore of Africa, for example, the people are largely farmers, artisans, and fishers. The soil is fertile, the sunshine is brilliant, and the rain is plentiful. Colorful customs and traditions are a rich legacy here. One can find evidences, ancient and contemporary, of the elaborate style and vibrant color in the art forms of the Yoruba and Benin ethnic groups of Nigeria. Among the Akan people of Ghana, complex rites of royal accession for both the queen mother and the king are similar to the rites held for the ancient pharaohs of Kemet. The land, the people, and the culture of Africa are all closely woven together.

Cultural bonds among Africans of diverse groups are strong, even though each group has its own history. One unifying bond is the emphasis on ancestral relationships with the living. Almost all African cultures show a deep respect for their ancestors. Today, this

▲ Ghanaian women in the community decorate houses with traditional patterns.

can be seen in the strong bond many African Americans have toward their extended family—grandparents, great "aunts" and "uncles," and "cousins." Close family friends, ministers, and other respected non-family members are given family titles such as "aunt" or "uncle."

African music is dramatic, contagious, and polyrhythmic, giving it a unifying characteristic that is essentially African. The percussive, steady beat of African American rap music and the pulsating sound of Jamaican reggae are undeniably tied to the rhythmic beat of the African drum, even though each musical form developed independently in different areas of the world.

In the midst of this bond of family and culture, imagine that a horrible thing happens. Imagine now that a great catastrophe shatters your life. Everything that you have around you and for your future disappears. Your music is not heard, your clothes are not worn, your language is forbidden, your ancestors' graves are destroyed, and you are left with nothing, not even a name of your own. This is the way it was for those Africans who were uprooted from the continent, kidnapped and taken against their will by Europeans across the ocean to the Americas and the Caribbean.

◆ CENTER YOUR THINKING

1. What were some early African contributions to architecture?
2. What is meant by the statement, "Africa is a rich continent"?
3. If the remains of the earliest ancestors of humans are found in Africa, are all people descended from Africans? You may use the suggested reading list at the end of this unit for further research to support your view.
4. What are the most important aspects of African culture, in your view? How are these similar or different from your own culture?
5. HOLISTIC ACTIVITY Students as Musicologists

   Listen to some traditional African music, and compare the rhythms, instruments, singing, and use of the drum with African American forms of music, for example, jazz, rap, reggae, and rhythm and blues. Write your comparison or perform it. You may find traditional African recordings in your library or with family and friends.

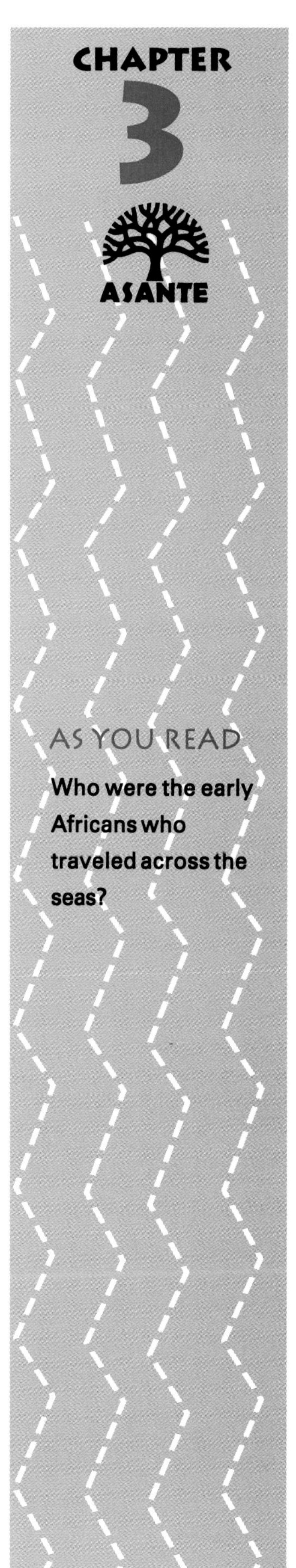

AFRICAN EXPLORERS: MASTERS OF THEIR OWN DESTINY

CENTER YOUR VOCABULARY

- ▲ destiny
- ▲ discovery
- ▲ B.C.E.
- ▲ indigenous

African explorers first came to the Americas as captains of their own ships and masters of their destiny, or fate. The African and North and South American continents are not as far apart as you might think. Senegambia, on the west coast of Africa, is only about 2,413 kilometers (about 1,500 miles), as the crow flies, from the South American coastal countries of Guyana and Suriname. As early as the 8th century B.C.E. (Before the Common Era), African voyagers sailed to Mexico, one of several countries connecting the North and South American continents. The Olmec sculptures, located in the Mexican towns of Tres Zapotes, La Venta, and San Lorenzo, indicate that some of these early travelers settled in Mexico and had a positive influence on the Olmec people.

The Olmec civilization is one of the earliest civilizations we know of in Mexico and the neighboring area. The similarities between the Olmec culture and African culture is striking. The Olmec culture, like the Kemetic culture (See *Classical Africa*, Chapter 6) is known for its majestic pyramids, elaborate carved figures, elegant plazas and colonnaded courts, and its own form of hieroglyphic writing. Eleven colossal African heads, sculpted in stone, with heavy lips,

▲ This Olmec Head shows the African influence.

full cheeks, broad nostrils, and braided hair are among some of the most visible signs of African presence in ancient Mexico. These African sculptures, each standing about 2.7 meters (9 feet) and weighing about 13,699 kilograms (9 tons) are cited in the works of several modern scientists as evidence of the African presence in the Americas in ancient times. The "discovery" of America by Columbus would be surprising news to the ancient Africans who visited these lands long ago.

Africans visited the Americas again in 1311 and 1312 C.E. in Abubakari II's Malian fleet. Abubakari was a leader of Mali who sent 100 large fishing boats, each seating 40, across the Atlantic Ocean in 1311 C.E. The next year, according to the African historian, Al Omari, he resigned his throne and crossed the ocean himself with 200 ships and 200 supply boats. Did he make it? Scholars have used modern scientific techniques to demonstrate that is quite possible that Abubakari did make the journey and also introduced African cotton to Mexico. Today, many aspects of the Malian culture are quite visible in the folk stories and dances of the indigenous, or native, people.

These long fishing boats reflect Africans' love for the sea. ▶

DID YOU KNOW?

Christopher Columbus notes in his diary that he found a dark-skinned people whom he assumed to be traders from Guinea, West Africa, trading with the native Caribbean people. On his third voyage to the Americas in 1498 C.E., while he was in the Cape Verde Islands just off the coast of Africa, Columbus wrote that Africans had been known to sail west in boats filled with goods for trade.

OTHER AFRICAN TRAVELS

Besides their voyages to the Americas, Africans traveled to many other parts of the world. The Nubian and Kemetic people in eastern Africa, for example, built large boats with sails as far back as 3100 B.C.E. This capability gave seafaring Africans all along the coastline plenty of opportunity to explore the high seas. When Spanish voyagers Bartolomeu Dias and Vasco da Gama explored the Indian Ocean, they found Africans trading with the people of India and China. When Christopher Columbus reached the Cape Verde Islands in the Atlantic Ocean, he found that a "dark-skinned" people had been trading with them for more than 100 years. Africans continued to explore and locate other cultures during enslavement and well into the 19th and 20th centuries.

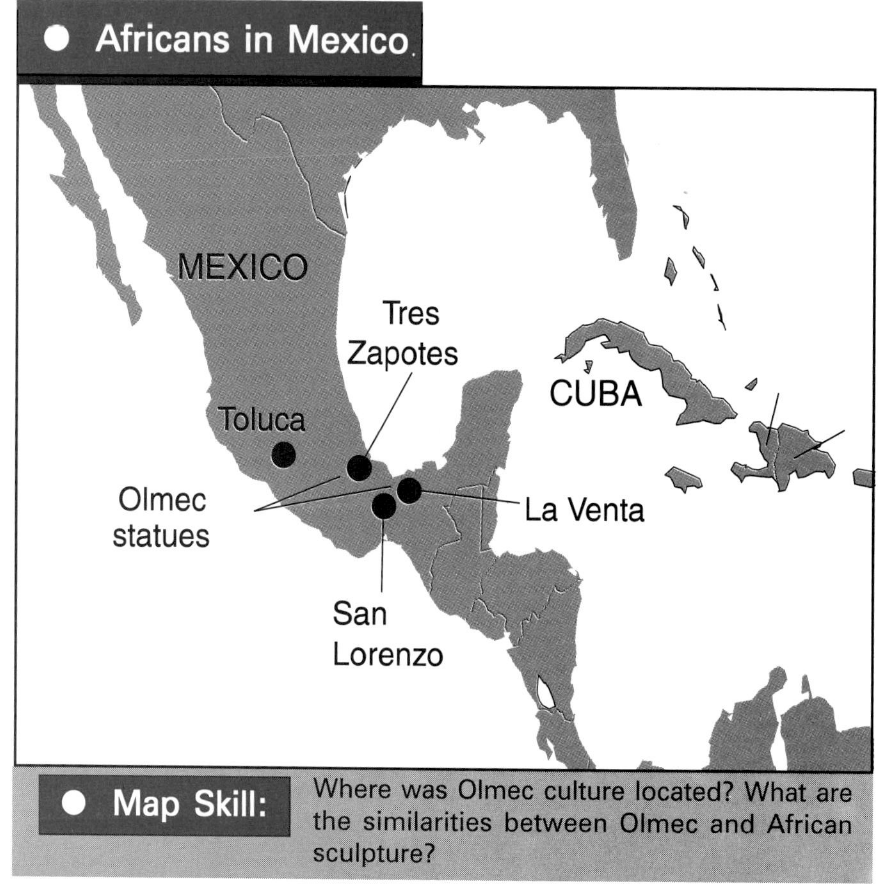

Map Skill: Where was Olmec culture located? What are the similarities between Olmec and African sculpture?

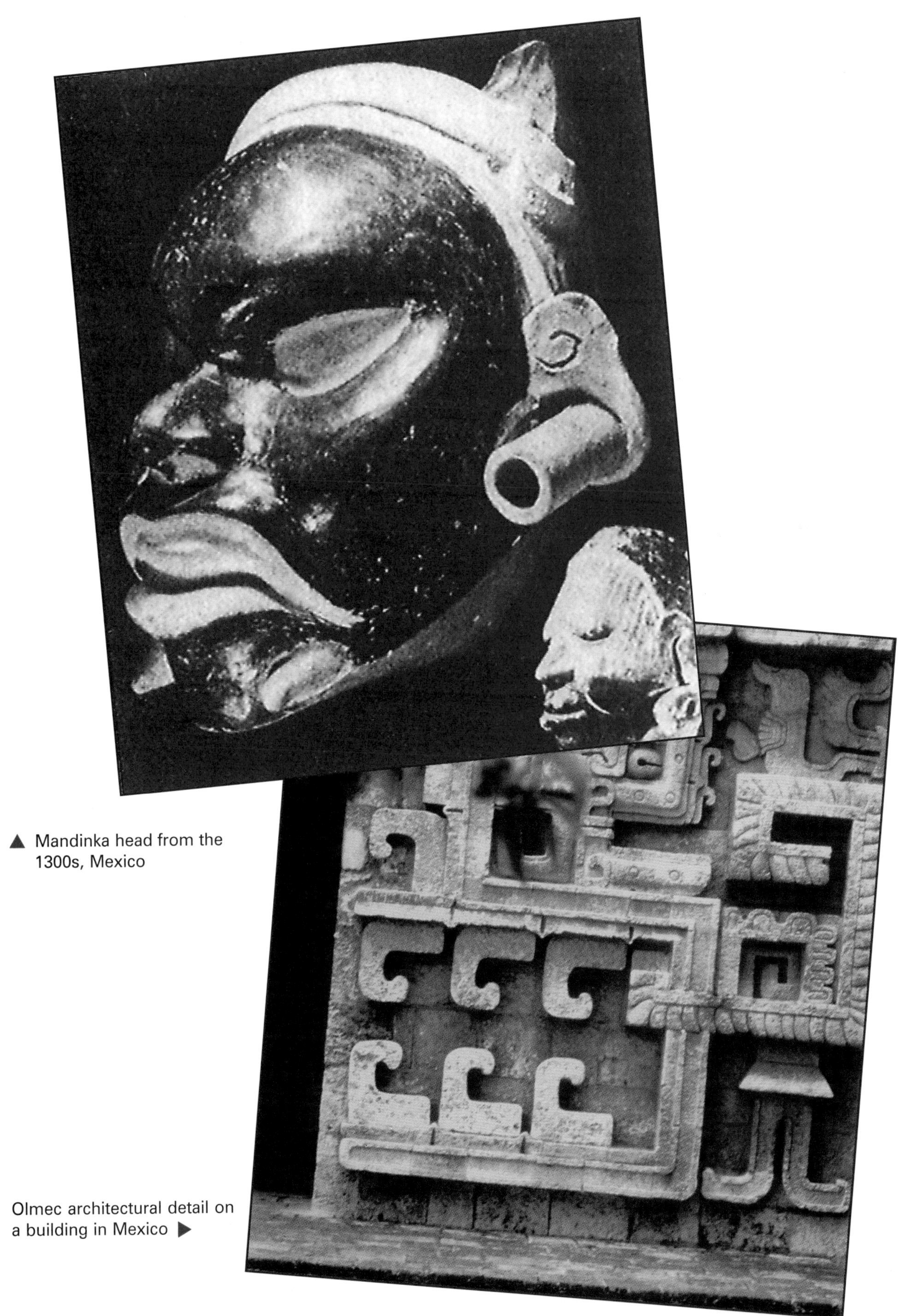

▲ Mandinka head from the 1300s, Mexico

Olmec architectural detail on a building in Mexico ▶

African Explorers

1450-800 B.C.E.	Olmec voyages to Mexico
1305-1312 C.E.	Abubakari II sends ships across the Atlantic
1310-1491	Mandingo merchant explorers and fishers
1492	Pedro Alonso Niño, an African, accompanies Columbus on voyage to America
1513	Nuflo de Olano, an African, journeys with Vasco Nuñez de Balboa
1514	A group of Africans travels with Spanish voyager Pedro Arias Dàvila in Panama
1523	A group of Africans travels with Spanish explorer Alvarado
1527-1539	Estevanico, an African, explores New Mexico
1539	Hernando De Soto, a Spaniard, travels with Africans through Georgia and Florida

◆ CENTER YOUR THINKING

1. What are some comparisons that can be made about the classical Olmec and African cultures?
2. What is some of the evidence that Africans were seafarers?
3. What evidence can you give to determine why Africans journeyed across the ocean to visit North and South America and the Caribbean?
4. Based upon the information in Chapter 3, tell how Africans might have adapted to living in North and South America and the Caribbean. How do you think the contact between Africans and Olmecs might have changed both cultures?
5. HOLISTIC ACTIVITY Students as Mathematicians

   In small groups, list the voyages to America by African explorers and traders. Using maps, globes, calculators, and computers, calculate the approximate total mileage of the explorers' voyages between African countries and the Americas. Are you surprised at the number? Why?

SUGGESTED READINGS

Asante, Molefi K. *Classical Africa.* Maywood, NJ: Peoples Publishing Group, 1993.

Asante, Molefi K. *Kemet, Afrocentricity, and Knowledge.* Trenton, NJ: Africa World Press, 1990.

Asante, Molefi K., and Mark Mattson. *Historical and Cultural Atlas of African Americans.* New York: Macmillan, 1991.

Ben-Jochannon, Y. *Black Man of the Nile.* Trenton, NJ: Africa World Press, 1990.

Diop, Cheikh Anta. *The African Origin of Civilization.* New York: Lawrence Hill, 1974.

Diop, Cheikh Anta. *The Cultural Unity of Black Africa.* Chicago: Third World Press, 1978.

Harding, Vincent. *There is a River.* New York: Harcourt Brace Jovanovich, 1981.

Sertima, Ivan van. *They Came Before Columbus.* New York: Random House, 1976.

Williams, Chancellor. *The Destruction of Black Civilization.* Chicago: Third World Press, 1974.

SUMMARY

Africa is a beautiful and vast continent of 30.2 million square kilometers with more than 50 countries and a diverse variety of landforms, including rivers, deserts, lakes, mountains, and forests. Along the western shore, the people are mainly farmers, artisans, and fishers. The land, people and cultures of Africa are closely interrelated. *(Chapters 1 and 2)*

The collapse of the Songhay Empire at the end of the 16th century C.E. devastated West Africa. With no strong central power, the region was unprotected, and European nations set up strongholds in coastal areas. The cultural legacies of the great West African kingdoms and empires were carried to the West by Africans who were enslaved by Europeans. *(Chapters 1 and 2)*

Our earliest human ancestors come from Africa. African contributions to civilization are reflected in almost every field. Africans were great seafarers and explorers and, from as early as 3100 B.C.E., made ocean voyages. In the 8th century B.C.E., Africans traveled to North and South America, the Caribbean, and Asia. *(Chapters 2 and 3)*

Personal Witnessing

REFLECTION

Reflect on ways you can help educate the people in your family, school, and community about the rich African heritage that is centuries old in every field. In your journal, write about the contributions that you especially admire, how you feel about these contributions, and how they relate to all humans today and especially to African Americans. You may wish to read more about these contributions. The suggested readings for this unit will give you books that are recommended.

TESTIMONY

Give your personal testimony, or opinions, about the contributions of the great continent of Africa to humankind. With a small group, prepare a panel discussion as if you were going to participate in a television panel to express student opinions about important topics. Your panel topic is AFRICAN AMERICAN STUDENTS SPEAK OUT: HOW AFRICAN ANCESTORS INFLUENCE OUR LIVES. Share your knowledge and personal opinions. Be sure that everyone has equal time to speak. If possible, present your panel to the class.

◆ RITES OF PASSAGE UMFUNDALAI

All African people have ceremonies to celebrate different steps in a young person's passage to adulthood. These ceremonies are called *rites of passage*. In this book, you will learn about a *rite of passage* originally created by and for African Americans. Its African name is *umfundalai*. In this book, the rites of passage extend to all students who wish to center themselves within African and African American history and culture.

This book and your study of it are but one important step in your passage to adulthood. If you successfully complete each of the 16 rites in this book, you can feel proud that you have grown and achieved a level of excellence, understanding, and centeredness that many people never reach. You will also have earned the right to be presented as an adult at the *rites of passage* ceremony that we hope you will hold after completing your study. To become an adult and to be the best man or woman you can be is a worthy goal, but not one that is reached easily or quickly. You are challenged to complete all these activities with excellence and to center yourself in Africa. If you do so, you join the author and other wise men and women on a joyous journey to understanding.

To evaluate your progress and your worthiness, keep a Rites of Passage portfolio with your Rites of Passage activity from each Unit. If your portfolio of 16 Rites of Passage activities exhibits excellence at the end of your study, you are eligible for the rites of passage ceremony.

UNIT 1 RITE OF PASSAGE

If you complete the rites of passage successfully, there are 12 qualities that you must master and exhibit. For your Unit 1 Rite of Passage activity, make a portfolio with 12 sections. Your portfolio could be a notebook. Write in each section *every week*, recording one action you have taken or one item of new knowledge that demonstrates your progress and growth. Every month, review the 12 sections of your portfolio to evaluate whether or not you are pleased with your progress and whether you wish to change your behavior. As you continue your study, you will also add sections to your portfolio.

The 12 sections of your portfolio are:

- Naming your family ancestors as far back as you are able to research;
- Practicing self-discipline in speech and action;
- Completing good school work;
- Applying energy to your creative work;
- Showing respect and good manners to all, especially the opposite sex;
- Assisting those less fortunate than you;
- Respecting and assisting your elders;
- Obeying and respecting your parents;
- Taking proper care of yourself physically by staying drug-free, and getting proper exercise and rest;
- Learning the practical information needed to exercise leadership in your school and community;
- Giving an oral presentation of a poem or song in the African oral tradition;
- Learning the Nguzo Saba, or seven principles of Kwanzaa: Umoja, unity; Kujichagulia, self-determination; Ujima, collective work and responsibility; Ujamaa, cooperative economics; Nia, purpose; Kuumba, creativity; and Imani, faith.

SCATTERED TO THE WEST: THE EUROPEAN SLAVE TRADE

Without warning, a new government with new laws divides the students in your school into groups and forces each group to go to boarding school in a different country. You may take nothing with you and may not wear your own clothes, speak your own language, sing your own music, or have any contact with your family. As a group, make a list of how you might feel.

As you read this unit, think about the effects on humans when, to survive, they must bury their pain and suffering deep in their souls. What strengths grow from this experience? After you finish this unit, make a list of how you think the Africans felt. Compare your two lists.

C.E.

1449
Estimated 900 Africans in Portugal

1482
Portugese build Elmina Castle, a mine located in present-day Ghana that became the largest slave dungeon on the west coast of Africa

1492
African voyagers sail to Mexico

Moors expelled from Spain

Sunni Ali Ber dies

Western kingdoms of Songhay are left unprotected

Alonzo Pedro Nunez navigates Columbus's voyage to Hispaniola

> "What I come through in life, if I go down into myself for it, I could make a book."
>
> J.W. WHITE
> **(a former enslaved African)**
> **Bullwhip Days**

1493
Pope Alexander VI issues Papal Bull of Demarcation

1501
Queen Isabella sends Africans to Hispaniola

1510
Ovando readmits Africans to Hispaniola

1515
European Slave Trade begins in earnest

1519
Henrique leads a maroon revolt against the Spaniards

1522
Africans stage more revolts against the Spanish in Hispaniola

1527
Africans revolt in Puerto Rico

1528
The African Estevanico lands near Tampa Bay with a party of 400 explorers

1538
Estevanico leads expedition to New Mexico

1546
Juan Lantino, an African from Guinea, receives a Bachelor's degree from University of Grenada

1594
Ahmed Baba, the great African scholar, is captured by the Moroccans

CHAPTER

4

ASANTE

ENSLAVEMENT BEGINS

CENTER YOUR VOCABULARY

- *mfecane*
- slavery
- enslavement
- exploit
- maroon
- *Asiento*

AS YOU READ

How was the enslavement of Africans by Europeans different from other instances of slavery?

The forced removal of African people from their own communities in Africa and their dispersion over most of the Americas and the Caribbean form what is known today as the *African mfecane* or *diaspora*. *Mfecane* is a southern African word meaning "great scattering." Because of the European Slave Trade, Africans were scattered to the West with the force of a strong wind blowing millions of seeds across a vast plain. Enslaved Africans had little choice but to put down new roots or perish in the harsh climate of enslavement.

African people such as the Ibo, Efik, Hausa, Asante, Bamana, Yoruba, and Mandinka were removed forcefully from the continent of Africa. They were taken to places such as Jamaica, Cuba, Haiti, Brazil, Guyana, Mexico, and what became the United States. Although Africans were brought to the North and South American continents and the Caribbean islands, we are concerned principally with those Africans who are found in what is now the United States.

The brutal enslavement of Africans by Europeans for the sole purpose of financial gain was one of the lowest points in human history. Slavery was not new, but the idea of humans being treated like chattel, or personal property, was radically different from the slavery that had existed in other places in the world, including the continents.

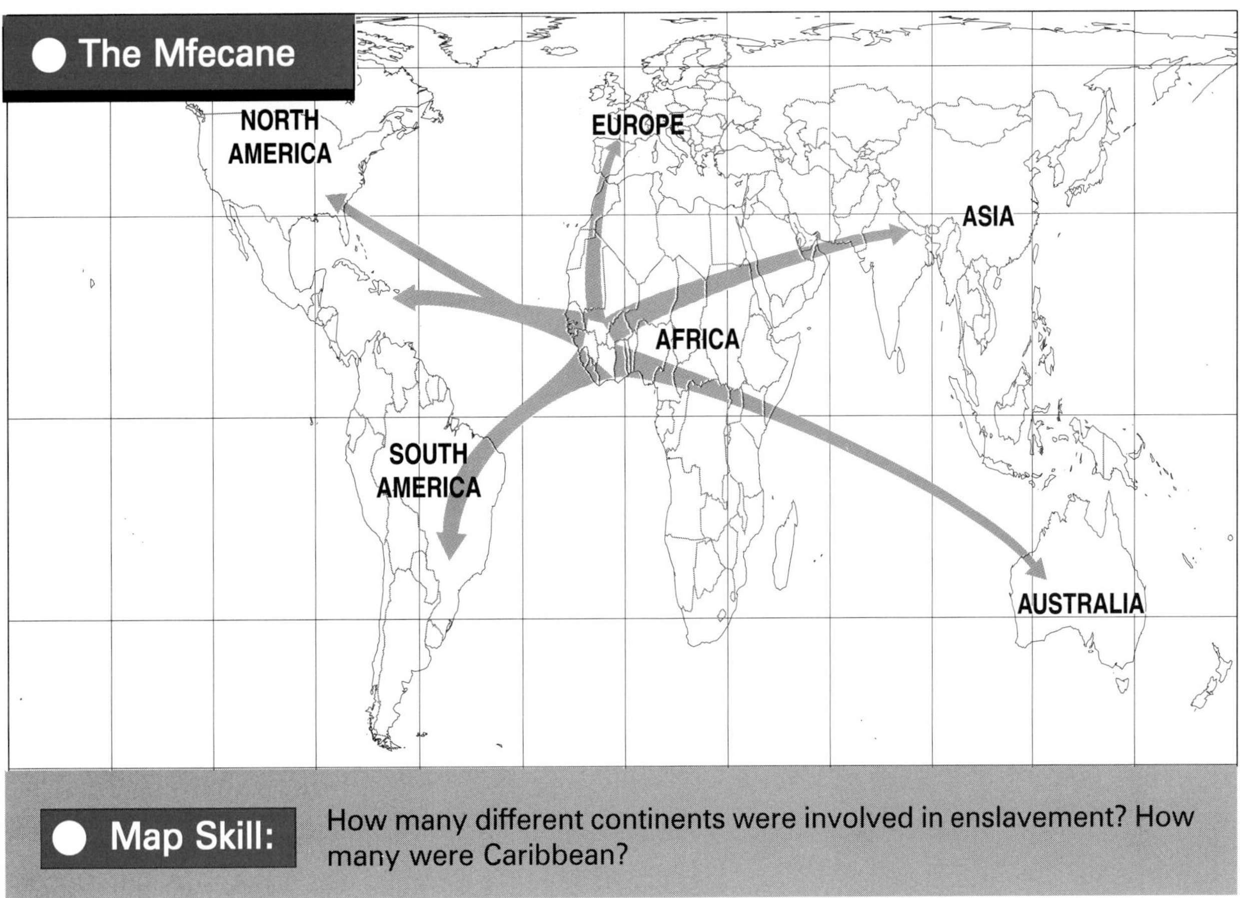

The Mfecane

Map Skill: How many different continents were involved in enslavement? How many were Caribbean?

Before the enslavement of African people, the conditions of slavery and the social standing of slaves varied greatly from one culture to another. In some cultures, slavery was used to punish people for breaking the law or for not paying their debts. In other cultures, people could voluntarily sell themselves and their families into slavery for financial gain or to repay a debt. In still other societies, those who could not provide for themselves often became slaves to the wealthy. Prisoners of war were sold as slaves, becoming part of the lower classes in the victor's society.

The new enslavement in the Caribbean and North American colonies, had three distinct differences from slavery in other cultures:

- African people were singled out for enslavement on a scale that had never been seen before. The European Slave Trade began the largest forced migration in the history of the world. From 1515 C.E. to 1888 C.E., European traders raided the coastal villages of West Africa, capturing 15 to 50 million Africans for the trade.

Europeans engaged in the immoral and ruthless enslavement of African people for one single purpose—financial profit. To justify the dehumanizing system of enslavement, Europeans invented the false argument that Africans were inferior and deserved this cruel and unrelenting enslavement.

African enslavement and oppression became the most prolonged, nonreligious instance of inhumanity ever practiced against any race of people. The effects of enslavement and racism are still with us today.

THE PORTUGUESE IN AFRICA

The 15th century C.E. was a historic period for the African world. By 1401, Africans had founded the University of Salamanca in Spain. There had been achievements in science, literature, and architecture. By 1492 they were expelled from Spain. This was also the century when Sunni Ali Ber, the great king of Songhay, died, leaving a vast and magnificent empire unprotected from Arabs and Europeans. Seizing this moment of African weakness, the Portuguese, a nation that shares the Iberian Peninsula with Spain, began its own exploitation of the African coast.

At first, the Portuguese came looking for gold because of the stories of African wealth that Arab traders and others had told about the grand empires of the Sudan. Now that the area was relatively unprotected, Portugal was free to exploit, or use, Africa for its own purpose.

Quite by accident, Portugal became the country to start the European Slave Trade. It led the European nations in the trade, but its intentions at first were not international. When the Portuguese first began to sail down the coast of West Africa, Christopher Columbus (1451-1506 C.E.), credited with opening up the Americas and the Caribbean for European exploitation, had not even been born.

In 1441, Portuguese sailors, under the sponsorship of Prince Henry the Navigator, sailed down the coast of West Africa. They returned to Portugal with ten African people as "gifts" to Prince Henry. The African people were considered novelties by the Portuguese, who at that time in history had had very little contact with other cultures. The Portuguese were ignorant of other cultural traditions that were different from their own. From this point onward, Africans became a part of the Portuguese society. Some Africans traveled to Portugal under their own power as diplomats, workers, and students of Christianity. Others were captured and forcibly taken to the royal courts in Portugal and later, Spain, where they worked alongside Portuguese and Spanish peasants.

By 1444, the Portuguese were bringing Africans regularly to Europe. Soon, Spain followed, also bringing Africans. A dangerous system was beginning. Portuguese and Spanish sailors began frequent raids of West African coastal countries such as Senegal, Guinea, Ghana, and the Ivory Coast to capture Africans and sell them to the wealthy. The number of Africans forced into Europe skyrocketed. By 1449, there were an estimated 900 Africans living in Portugal alone.

In the 16th century, Spain sent Portuguese Africans to its colonies in the Caribbean to replace the enslaved Native Americans who were dying from overwork and mistreatment. The Native Americans were the indigenous people or original inhabitants of these Caribbean islands. Their culture of trust, nonviolence, and respect clashed with the Spanish, making it easy for the Spanish invaders to exploit them. Overworked and weakened by new European diseases, the indigenous people were being killed at an alarming rate. Africans were forced to go to the Spanish colonies as Spain's solution to its labor problems. This policy set the inhuman principle for African enslavement in North America.

ENSLAVEMENT IN HISPANIOLA

The European immigrants, or "foreigners," in the Spanish colony of Hispaniola (Haiti and the Dominican Republic today) learned quickly that Africans were violently opposed to their enslavement. The Africans who were supposed to replace the dying Native Americans were difficult to control. They revolted often and forcefully. Those who escaped joined forces with the Native Americans and formed maroon communities deep in the hills of Hispaniola. The hills were not easily accessible to Spanish overseers who did not know the land. From their advantage, the Hispaniola Maroons, or runaways, raided the European sugar plantations, freeing other enslaved Africans and taking the supplies they needed. Slavery in the Americas and the Caribbean would be rapidly transformed from the idea of servitude and indentureship to one of permanent enslavement. Africans would become victims of the most brutal form of human forced labor with no rights and no possibility of freedom. Thus, by 1515 when the trans-Atlantic slave trade began, Spain and Portugal had become the major transporters of Africans into the inhuman system in North and South American and the Caribbean.

Hispaniola, under the control of the Spanish Governor, Nicolas de Ovando, was in crisis. He was desperate to provide a work force for the plantations and mines. Ovando was outraged by African resistance to enslavement. He adamantly refused to accept any more Africans into the island because he could not control them. At wit's end, Ovando asked Spain to send Spanish slaves to Hispaniola. Spain's Queen Isabella responded with a proclamation in 1501 that allowed Spanish peasants to be sent to Hispaniola to work as slaves. In addition, Ovando began to import Native Americans from the nearby Bahamas. But the Bahamians suffered the same fate as the indigenous people of Hispaniola and died at an alarming rate.

▼ Africans were forced to work in the gold mines and sugar plantations in Hispaniola.

By 1510, Ovando had changed his mind. He decided to risk importing Africans into his colony once again to solve his labor problems. Africans began to appear in the Caribbean in greater numbers. Spain issued another royal order permitting the transport and sale of 50 more Africans to Hispaniola. A third royal order for

▲ During the 1500s, enslaved Africans in Hispaniola were forced to carry wealthy Spaniards in a vehicle called a *litera*.

200 Africans followed the same year. This process of importing Africans into the colonies for their labor became a cruel model, establishing the European Slave Trade on a grand scale of economic and dehumanizing proportions.

THE ASIENTO

Conflict was inevitable. Spain, Portugal, and later other European countries wanted African labor to develop the valuable natural resources of the Americas. You can imagine what would happen if both Spain and Portugal sent ships to the same area of Africa to capture Africans. There would be a contest, perhaps even a battle, to decide who had the right to capture those Africans. Then there would be another contest or battle to decide which nation had the right to "sell" Africans and where they could be sold.

Because this type of conflict happened so often, the Europeans came up with a way to negotiate the claims. To settle such disputes, the Spanish rulers created a contract called the *Asiento*. The Asiento gave traders the exclusive right to take Africans from Africa to the Spanish colonies for a period of 30 years. Private as well as government-supported trading companies competed fiercely for the Asiento. The Asiento was sold to the highest bidder.

The Asiento was bought and sold many times throughout the 17th and 18th centuries. Sometimes, it was held by Dutch traders; at other times, it was held by Portuguese, French, or English merchants. In 1621, Holland created the Dutch West India Company. The company immediately challenged Portugal's control of the trade in Africa. By the mid-17th century, the Dutch had taken control of the major trading routes in the Americas and the Caribbean. By the end of the 17th century, Dutch traders were active in the ports of almost all the American colonies. They also brought the first Africans to the French Caribbean islands of Martinique and Guadeloupe.

In 1713, a group of British merchants purchased the Asiento. They contracted with Spain to provide 144,000 enslaved Africans to the Spanish colonies in the Americas for the next 30 years. The British merchants were required to pay the Spanish and British royal treasuries 25 percent of all their trading profits for the entire 30 years of the Asiento.

The Europeans, hungry for profit, also fought over control of the land in the Caribbean and the Americas. Principally, these disputes were between the Portuguese and the Spanish. To settle these disputes, the Spanish pope, Alexander VI, issued a Papal Bull of Demarcation in 1493. It arrogantly divided the Americas and all the other countries east of Spain, giving some to Spain and some to Portugal. The Papal Bull of Demarcation did not regard the rights of the people who owned the land.

One of the many slave forts in Africa built by the Europeans as a holding pen for Africans before the Middle Passage. ▶

THE BRITISH SLAVE TRADE

Britain dominated the European Slave Trade in the 18th century. Although the British were not part of the early development of slave-trading practices in Africa, their extensive participation in the trade made them a dominant player. During the Seven Year's War (1756-1763), Britain transported more than 10,000 Africans to Cuba and approximately 40,000 to Guadeloupe. By 1788, more than 60 percent of Africans brought by Britain to the Americas were sold to colonies controlled by other countries.

Britain's economy flourished. British colonies in the Caribbean and the Americas were heavily taxed. The British government also charged a 10 percent duty on all private companies participating in trade. The duties and taxes that were collected gave Britain unlimited resources and capital for investment. The profits generated by this activity made the cruel trade in humans an important factor in Britain's economic life. Britain's economic success set in motion an even more dangerous pattern for exploiting African people.

◆ CENTER YOUR THINKING

1. How did Africans in the European colonies of the Americas and the Caribbean respond to their brutal enslavement by Europeans?
2. How did the European Slave Trade differ from any forms of enslavement practiced by Africans?
3. How was it possible for Europeans to enslave millions of Africans?
4. How has the myth of African inferiority influenced the way that African people are viewed today?
5. HOLISTIC ACTIVITY Students as Graphic Artists

   Graphic artists use devices such as maps, time lines, charts, and various graphics and pictures to summarize and clarify information for readers. In a small group, work together to design and create examples of additional pictorial and graphic devices to summarize the information in Chapter 4. Share your designs with the other small groups in your class.

CHAPTER

5

ASANTE

AS YOU READ

How did the European Slave Trade impact West Africa?

TRIANGULAR TRADE

CENTER YOUR VOCABULARY

- ▲ labor
- ▲ bribes

The Triangular Trade is the name most history books give to the export/import component of the European Slave Trade. On a map, the European Slave Trade made a triangular route connecting the Americas to Europe and Africa. The trade started in a harmless enough way. Europeans exported goods and guns manufactured in Europe to African merchants. Africans supplied Europeans with gold, silver, bronze, nuts, and ivory in return. By the time the Americas had become the new frontier for European expansion, Europeans had a critical need for labor to clear the land for farming and industry.

How do you get labor? You either pay people wages for it, or you do not. If you do not pay for labor, there are several other ways to get it. Human labor can be volunteered, or it can be taken by cunning or force. If you choose to take it, as many Europeans did, there are several ways to proceed.

First, you could steal the labor. Imagine yourself hiding in the bushes, watching a young man tending cattle. You creep up behind him, capture him, and throw him into your slave fort or holding pen. When your holding pen is full, you load your ship with captives and transport them to the Americas.

Second, you could promise to pay the people for their labor to trick them into boarding your ship. Then you can sail away, kidnapping the people. Or you might attack other ships on the high seas, take their enslaved Africans, and sail to the Americas.

▲ Enslaved Africans are chained in a coffle and forced to march to the slave forts on the coast.

Many European traders used a combination of these methods. Others found it easier to pay African kings for their war captives. When the supply of war captives wasn't enough, some Africans who were as greedy as the Europeans raided enemy villages for a fresh supply of prisoners to sell to the European traders. All of these methods were used to capture Africans for the European Slave Trade. When the ships reached the Americas, the enslaved were sold again for profit. With their profit, the European traders purchased the raw materials (sugar, tobacco, coffee) produced in the Americas and took them back to Europe to be manufactured into other goods.

AFRICAN PARTICIPATION IN TRIANGULAR TRADE

African nations did not benefit from the European Slave Trade or the Triangular Trade. Some Africans took bribes, or valuable goods, offered by the European slave traders to kidnap Africans for the trade. But as word spread across the continent about the horrible abuse and intense suffering the enslaved endured at the hands of Europeans, most Africans stopped participating in the European

●The Triangular Trade

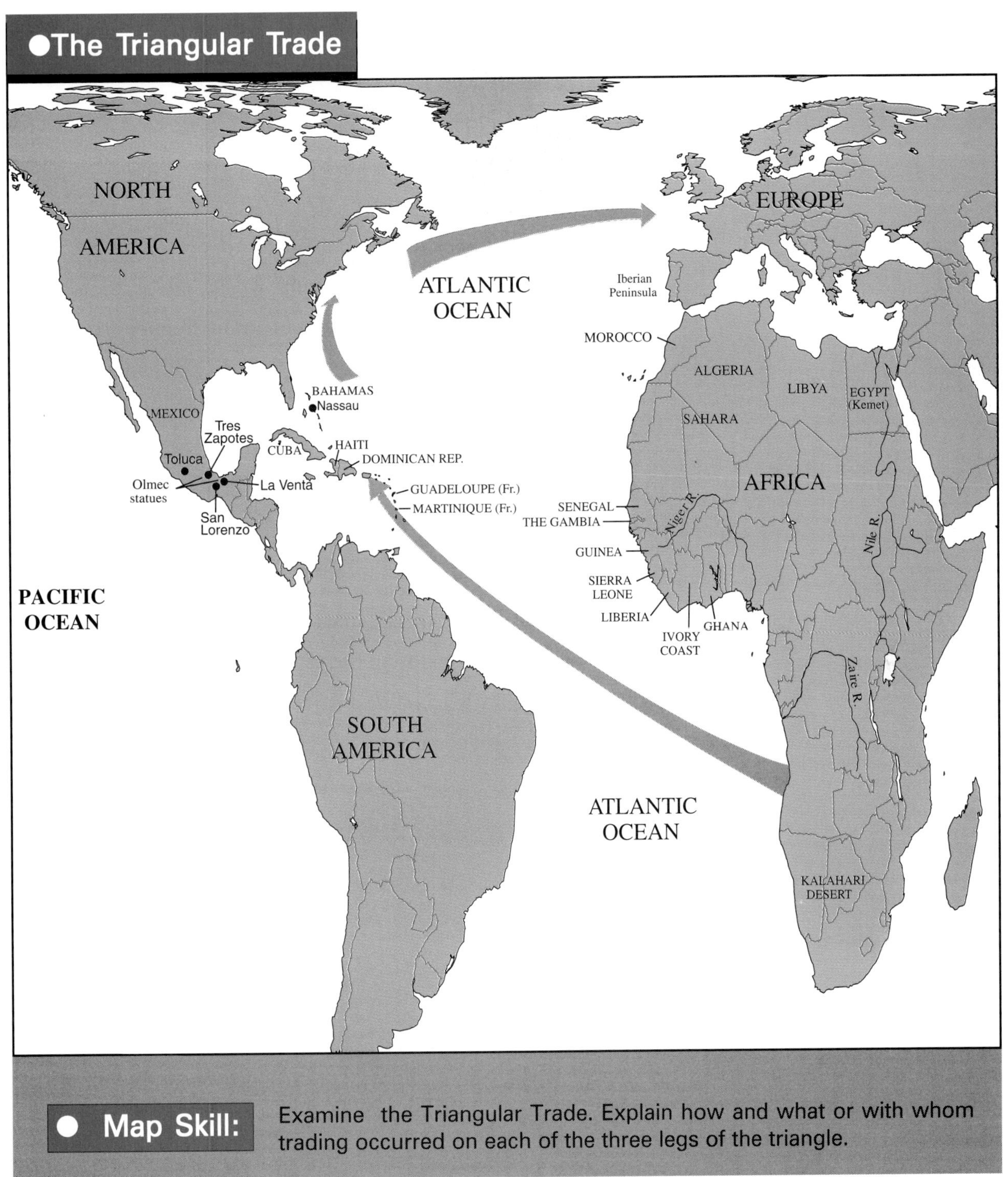

● Map Skill: Examine the Triangular Trade. Explain how and what or with whom trading occurred on each of the three legs of the triangle.

Slave Trade. Africans began to see that there was a big difference between slavery as it was practiced in Africa and the system of dehumanizing enslavement practiced by the Europeans.

Olaudah Equiano was an African who was kidnapped from his home in Iboland, Nigeria, in 1756. He was sold twice, once in Virginia and later in England. Equiano survived his enslavement and

▲ Olaudah Equiano

eventually bought his own freedom. In his writings, he tells much of the nature of African slavery:

"Sometimes indeed we sold slaves . . . but they were only prisoners of war, or such among us as had been convicted of kidnapping, or adultery, and some other crimes, which we esteemed heinous. . . With us they do no more work than other members of the community, even their master; their food, clothing, lodging were nearly the same as theirs, (except they were not permitted to eat with those who were freeborn), and there was scarce any other difference between them. . . . Some of these slaves have even slaves under them as their own property and for their own use."

The enslavement that Equiano and other Africans endured in the Americas was, of course, brutally different from the slavery Africans were familiar with in West Africa. Africans did not use slaves as a principal means of economic production and profit as Europeans did. In the communities along the West African coast, slavery did not support the livelihood of the entire society, as it did in Europe and the Americas.

◆ CENTER YOUR THINKING

1. Why did Europeans desire African labor?
2. Why did most Africans stop participating in the European Slave Trade?
3. What role did Africans play in the Triangular Trade?
4. What effects did the European Slave Trade have on European and African economies?
5. HOLISTIC ACTIVITY Students as Researchers

   The writings of Olaudah Equiano are published in various books that are available today. Go to your school and your neighborhood libraries. Ask a librarian to assist you in finding books about Equiano and his writings in collections of slave narratives, biographies, and children's books.

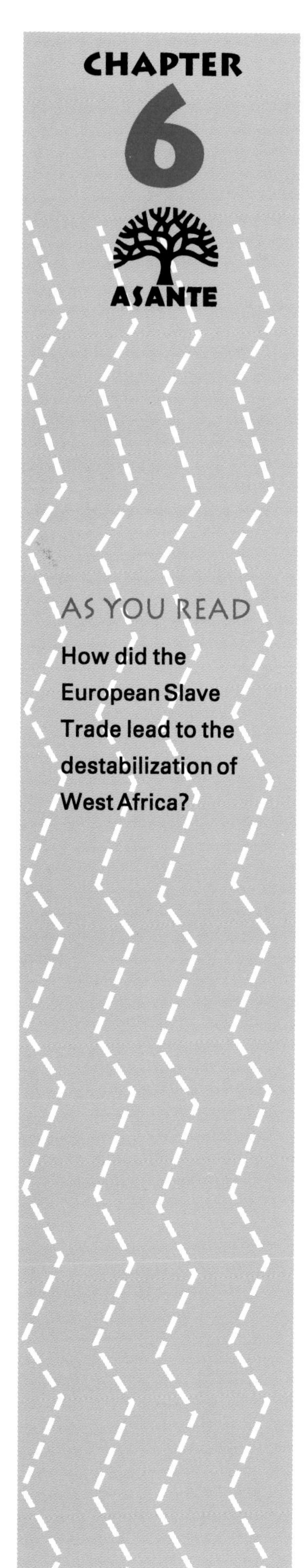

ECONOMICS OF THE TRADE

CENTER YOUR VOCABULARY

▲ economics
▲ leased
▲ values
▲ consumption

The free labor of Africans drove the economies of Europe and North America. Almost all the major industries in Europe and North America profited from the cruel enslavement of Africans. The African system of government, economy, culture, family life, education, artistic life, music, and dance, on the other hand, were devastated by the ruthless raids led by the European slave traders. Men, women, and children were kidnapped at gunpoint and forced to leave their home and loved ones.

Economics refers to the principles by which a society produces goods and services and then distributes and consumes those goods and services. Governments and other political institutions are designed to create stability so that people can work proudly, produce goods and services, and be able to lead a comfortable life. All of this is possible when the economic patterns are well established and the conditions of trust exist between the various parts of a community that perform the different economic activities. Some people make things, others distribute those things, and everyone puts those things to use. Their activity puts in motion the key principles of economics: production, distribution, and consumption or use.

Many African societies became politically and economically unstable as a result of the European Slave Trade. Entire nations were disrupted. More than 100 small ethnic groups were completely

▲ African chiefs and elders gather in Anna Village, Ivory Coast, 1972. Think about the elders and artisans who were kidnapped by Europeans 400 years ago.

destroyed. Small, village-based industries vanished overnight when tradespeople such as the village blacksmith or the weaver were kidnapped by Europeans. Most African societies operate on the basis of hereditary artisan guilds or trades. Artistic techniques and trade skills are handed down from family to family, generation to generation, through a long line of ancestors. The entire society was structured to support each other economically, with each family playing an important part. You can imagine what would happen if architecture were a hereditary occupation and the only family in your city practicing it was kidnapped and enslaved.

On a grander scale, consider the Songhay Kingdom in West Africa. Songhay and other African kingdoms suffered acutely when their best and brightest citizens were kidnapped by profit-hungry Europeans. African royalty, herbalists, astronomers, teachers, elders, priests, and young soldiers disappeared. Specialized trades, such as pottery and masonry, vanished with their owners. Songhay was left with a disrupted system for producing goods and disrupted trade

▲ An Asante man weaving with a loom

routes for the distribution of goods because of the slave trade. Suppose you were like Diallo, the goldsmith, who worked in a small village and could no longer depend upon the caravans to reach you with the supply of gold you needed for your business. What would you do? Perhaps to so many of these African producers in Songhay, it was as though the world had stopped or someone had put a dead cat in the well and the water had become foul. The women who went to market at certain places could no longer go on their own without soldiers to protect them because they might be kidnapped by slave-raiders. The entire economy of Songhay was hurt by the presence of foreign invaders in the countryside.

A GROWING DEPENDENCE

As the demand for Africans in the West grew, Europeans used their manufacturing novelties and guns to bargain with African rulers into turning over not just gold and ivory, but also their prisoners of war as well. Power struggles between African nations intensified. Many of these battles were won or lost with European guns, creating a dependence, or strong need, on this deadly European invention.

Values such as cooperation, collective work, unity, and harmony with nature and religion were corrupted by the European Slave Trade. People who had willingly assisted others before the trade were now frightened and suspicious of their neighbors. Africans feared that even their closest neighbors might be working with the European slave-raiders. Entire villages were covered by the gloomy shadow of enslavement. During the next 400 years, the countries on the entire continent of Africa would have great difficulty molding stable economies. An unhealthy dependence on Europe would drive the African economy as the European invaders turned the interests of Africa away from Africans.

In the West, the European Slave Trade generated entrepreneurs, people who organized and managed businesses connected to the trade, in Europe and the Americas. The Europeans often leased or rented ships and borrowed money to finance their trade in human beings. Sailors had to be paid. Insurance had to be arranged. Crews had to be outfitted with compasses and other equipment, medical supplies, food, and guns to protect themselves from attack. Duty and taxes had to be paid to the European governments to participate in the trade. Goods had to be purchased with which to bargain with African kings. All the positive qualities of entrepreneurship were turned to a horrible and inhumane use against Africans.

The slave trade created such huge profits that the Europeans closed their ears and hardened their hearts to the plight of Africans caught at the center of this barbaric practice.

Out of this condition, many Africans in America would be able to echo the words of J.W. White, a former enslaved African, who said, "What I come through in life, if I go down into myself, I could make a book." Africans who survived the grueling trip aboard the cramped slave ships endured such horrors that, for their own sanity, many buried their pain and suffering deep in their souls.

The European Slave Trade benefited the economies of Europe and the Americas. It did irreparable harm to Africa's economy. ▶

◆ CENTER YOUR THINKING

1. Why did Europeans continue the slave trade for centuries?
2. What effect did the introduction of guns by Europeans have on Africa?
3. How did the European Slave Trade corrupt traditional African values?
4. What effects did the European Slave Trade have on the development of African societies?
5. HOLISTIC ACTIVITY Students as Artists

   In a small group, create a small, two-panel mural that can be displayed in the classroom or in the school hallway. In one panel, illustrate life in West Africa before the European slave-raiders came to the continent. On the other side, illustrate life after the European raids for slaves had become an ongoing occurrence. From your reading of Unit 2, include in the mural depictions with labels of West African men and women at work in various occupations before and after the invasions. Depict the fear and suspicion Africans had of their fellow Africans during the time of the European Slave Trade as opposed to the traditional African values such as cooperation, collective work, unity, harmony with nature, and religion that were corrupted by the slave trade.

SUGGESTED READINGS

Bennett, Lerone. *Before the Mayflower.* Chicago: Johnson Publishing Company, 1990.

Cronon, Edmund. *Black Moses.* Madison: University of Wisconsin, 1968.

Fisher, Miles Mark, *Negro Slave Songs in the United States.* Secaucus, NJ: Carol Publishing Group, 1990.

Raboteau, Albert. *Slave Religion.* New York: Oxford University Press, 1981.

Reddings, J. Saunders. *They Came in Chains: Americans from Africa.* New York: Doubleday, 1950.

Redkey, Edwin. *Black Exodus.* New Haven, CT: Yale University Press, 1969.

SUMMARY

The *mfecane*, or forced removal of African people from their homes to other parts of the world, was cruelly hastened by the European Slave Trade. Although slavery had existed in Africa and most other societies before, the enslavement in the Caribbean and North American colonies by Europeans was horribly different in three ways: (1) the scale on which African people were singled out for enslavement was huge; (2) Europeans enslaved Africans solely for financial gain and invented a dehumanizing system to justify their brutal actions; and (3) African enslavement and oppression has been the most prolonged nonreligious example of enslavement ever, and its effects are still with us today. *(Chapter 4)*

The Asiento, or contract for slave trade in the 17th and 18th centuries, and the British Slave Trade in the 18th century made the European Slave Trade flourish and set a pattern for exploitation and dehumanization of African people. The Triangular Trade is a part of the European Slave Trade, describing the triangular route taken from Europe to Africa to the colonies. African nations did not benefit from the Triangular Trade, and although some African rulers participated initially, they soon ceased. *(Chapters 4 and 5)*

The economics of the European Slave Trade benefited European countries and devastated the economies of African nations and groups. Political and economic instability in many African societies and the wholesale destruction of more than 100 small ethnic groups resulted. African values were corrupted by the slave trade, as were values such as cooperation and collective work. *(Chapter 6)*

Personal Witnessing

Reflection

Imagine that you live in West Africa during the European Slave Trade. You and your family were never captured, but many of the people in your village were, including some of your friends. Give yourself an African name and then, using that name, write in your journal a brief account of what you saw of the slave trade and your feelings during those days.

Testimony

You can read the actual words of Africans telling about their experiences during the enslavement in a large collection of writings that are referred to as *slave narratives.* In a small group, select one or more slave narratives from the library. Find one that you find especially touching. Prepare a dramatic reading for your class or school assembly of a part or parts of the narrative. Practice until you feel it is realistic. You might do a choral reading with a lead person and a chorus of background speakers. Everyone in the group should take part in some way. Use your creativity and make the presentation one of grace and feeling.

Unit 2 Rite of Passage

One principle of the Umfundalai process is your physical well-being. In small groups, cooperate to create a presentation of the different aspects that each individual in your group feels is important in maintaining physical well-being. Your presentation may include oral presentation, a physical dance or workout, and any other creative presentation your group feels is important. Add a description of your presentation to your Rites of Passage portfolio.

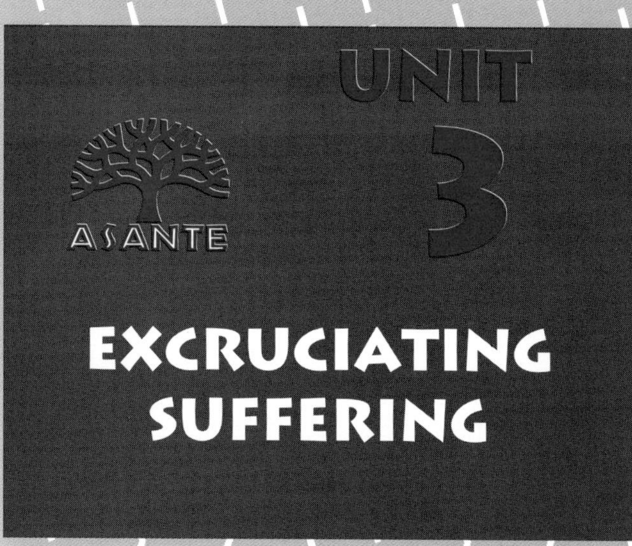

EXCRUCIATING SUFFERING

You and your classmates have been asked to produce a TV documentary on the inhumanity of humans. In small groups, write a plan of what your documentary would include. What historical information would you need? what interviews? what photographs and film clips? What will be the conclusion of your documentary, the one idea you want people to learn from it?

In this unit, you will read about how the European Slave Trade inflicted incredible suffering on African people and how dehumanization was an important weapon. What is dehumanization? Why would men and women work to dehumanize people? How can it be avoided today?

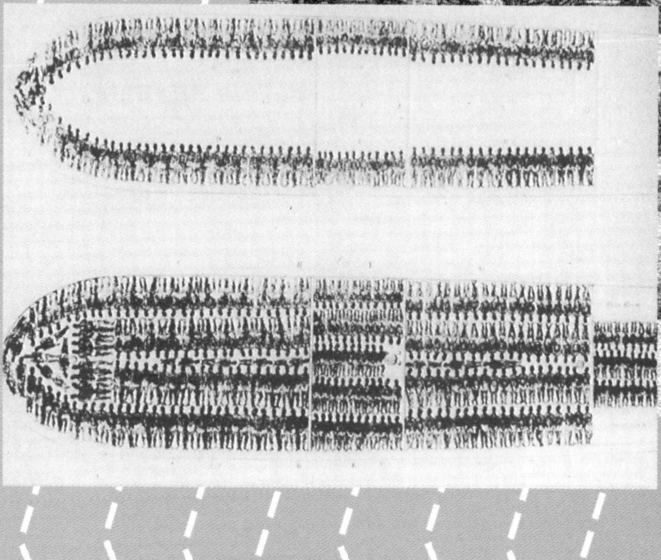

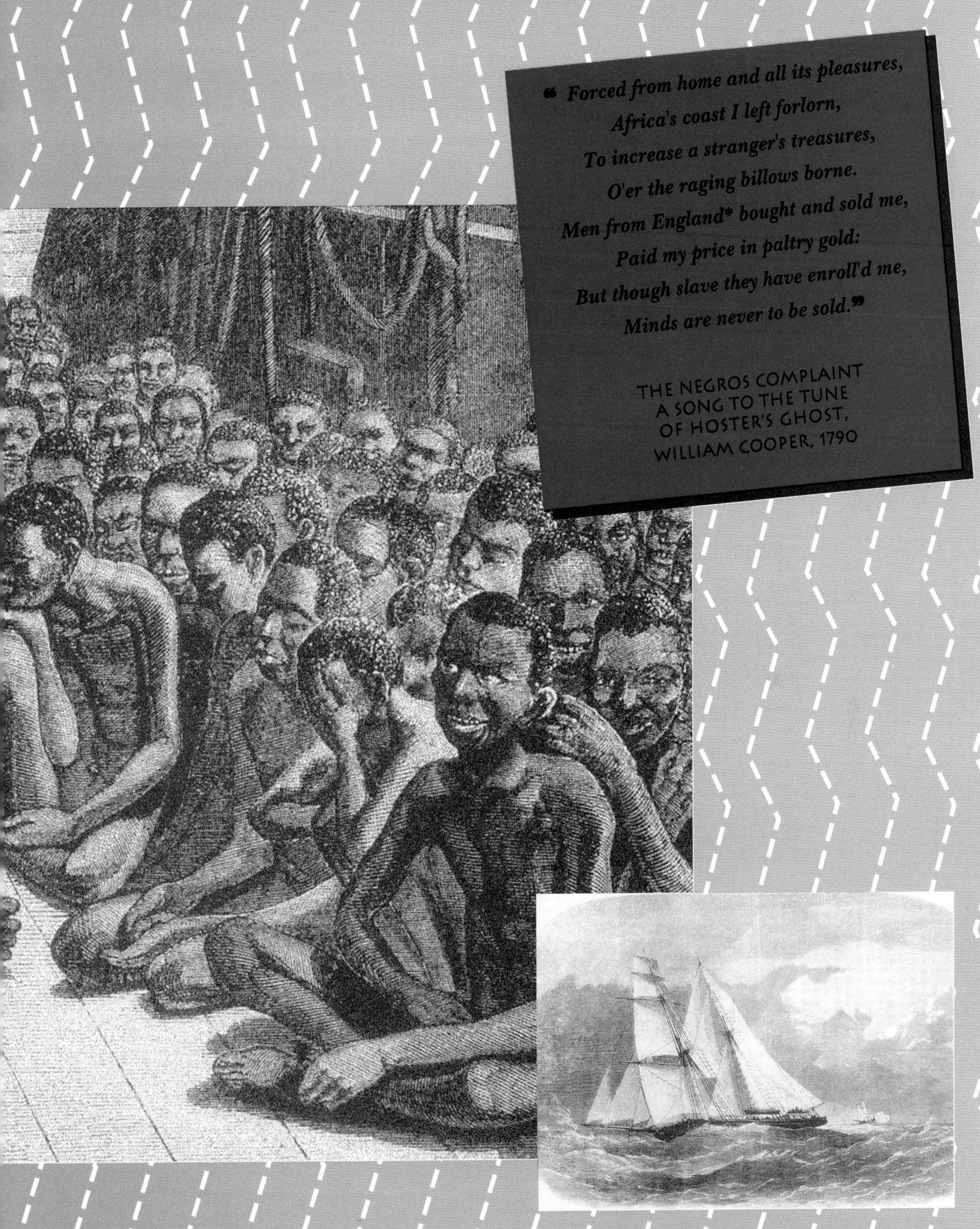

❝ Forced from home and all its pleasures,
Africa's coast I left forlorn,
To increase a stranger's treasures,
O'er the raging billows borne.
Men from England bought and sold me,*
Paid my price in paltry gold:
But though slave they have enroll'd me,
Minds are never to be sold.❞

THE NEGROS COMPLAINT
A SONG TO THE TUNE
OF HOSTER'S GHOST,
WILLIAM COOPER, 1790

▲ Enslaved Africans aboard the deck of a slave ship off the coast of Florida in 1860.

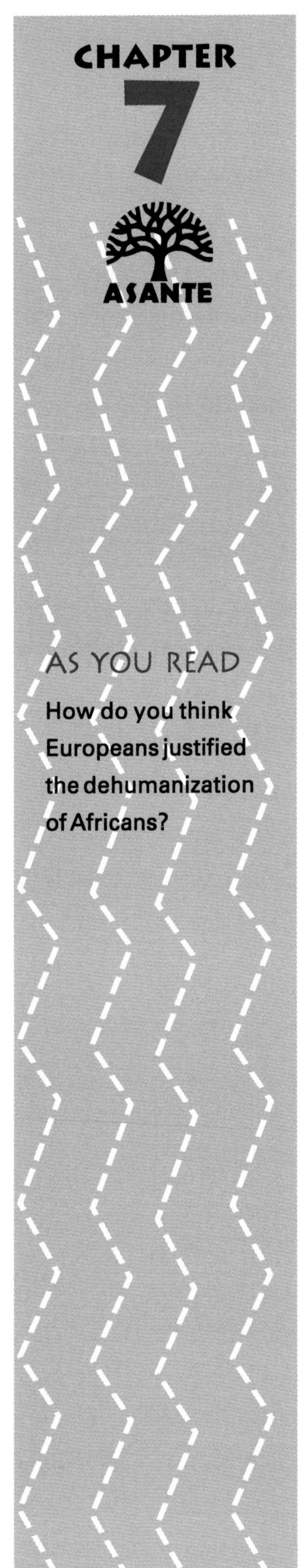

THE DREADED MIDDLE PASSAGE

CENTER YOUR VOCABULARY

- ▲ tragedy
- ▲ Middle Passage
- ▲ narratives
- ▲ dehumanization
- ▲ oppressor
- ▲ racism

To get even a modest understanding of enslavement, you must feel the pain and experience the horror of millions of human beings torn from their homeland, packed into overcrowded ships, and shipped halfway around the world. Uprooting Africans from their homes and forcing them to sail across the sea to a strange land was a terrible crime against humanity. For 300 years, European ships became chambers of horror for millions of Africans. The separation, pain, brutality, and death that resulted from this barbaric practice is perhaps truly impossible to comprehend.

Imagine crossing the ocean aboard a small ship made to hold 200 people but packed with 1,000 weeping and crying men, women, and children. Each African was forced to fit into a space no more than 55.9 centimeters (22 inches) high, roughly the height of a single gym locker, and 61 centimeters (24 inches) wide, scarcely an arm's length. There were no lights aboard the ships, little food, and no toilet facilities. Sarah Weldon, a former enslaved African, said that the horror was so dreadful that when an African died, others cried aloud, "Gone she to her own country, gone she to her own friends."

Imagine the pain of African mothers as their babies were torn from their protective arms and their young children were whipped and forced to eat so that they could be healthy and ready for sale when the ship docked. Imagine the strain on the men when they could not defend the honor of their own mothers, wives, or daughters. Imagine the terror the women must have felt, knowing they had no one to protect them from the cruelty of their captors.

Many times, brave Africans would escape and leap overboard, preferring death to the inhuman indignities aboard the ships. The tragedy of the European Slave Trade, the useless destruction of life, could never destroy the dignity of Africans. Some survived. Those who did would call this horrible voyage the dreaded Middle Passage.

COURAGE AND VALOR AMID DESPAIR

The Middle Passage was the journey across the Atlantic to the Americas. For Africans, it was an excruciating journey that lasted 35 to 90 days, depending on the weather. The narratives, or true-life stories, of enslaved Africans as well as the logs, diaries, and journals of slave-ship captains tell of the horrible Middle Passage in graphic detail. In his narrative, Olaudah Equiano described his Middle Passage, a voyage he knew firsthand as a captive.

"The stench of the hold while we were on the [African] coast was so intolerably loathsome. . . . The closeness of the place, and the

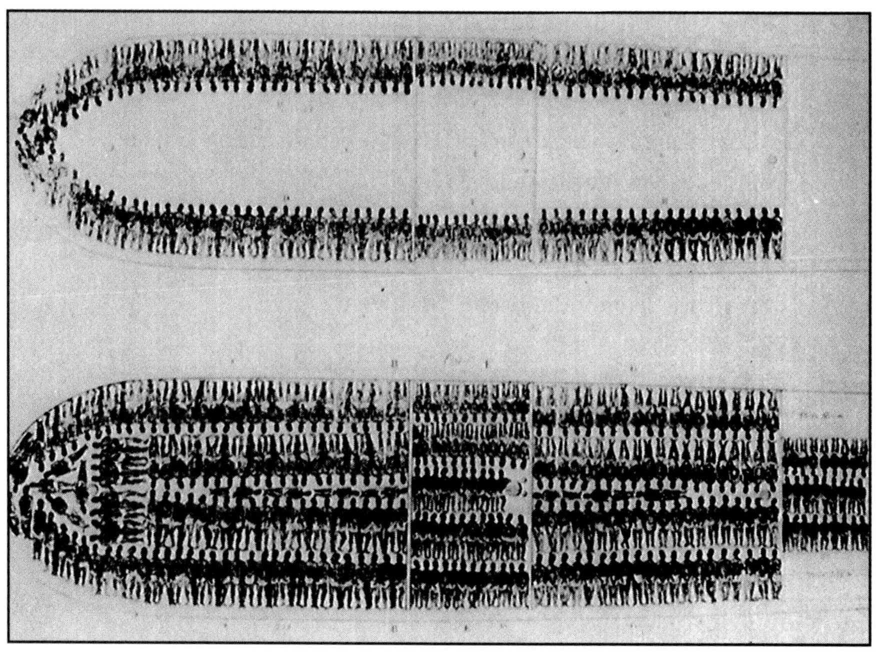

▲ Diagram of the lower deck of a slave ship packed with men, women and children, chained by the neck and legs and squeezed in for maximum profit.

heat of the climate, added to the number in the ship, which was so crowded that each had scarcely room to turn himself, almost suffocated us. This produced copious perspiration, so that the air soon became unfit for respiration, from a variety of loathsome smells, and brought on a sickness among the slaves, of which many died. . . . This wretched situation was aggravated by the [chafing] of the chains, now became unsupportable, and the filth of the necessary tubs (outhouses), into which the children often fell. . . ."

It is no wonder that Equiano tried to starve himself to death to escape the Middle Passage. He was whipped and forced to eat.

Belinda, another captive, described the terror of her Middle Passage:

"Three hundred Africans in chains, suffering the most excruciating torments, and some of them rejoicing that the pangs of death came like balm to their wounds."

Broteer, who was renamed Venture Smith by his enslaver, was stolen from Guinea when he was eight. In his narrative, he tells of his capture and of the loss of 25 percent of the Africans on his Middle Passage.

Sadly, many of the captives aboard the overcrowded slave ships were children. An African slave trader says:

"I returned on board to aid in stowing [on the slave ship] one hundred and eight boys and girls, the eldest of whom did not exceed fifteen years [old]. As I crawled between decks, I confess I could not imagine how this little army was to be packed or draw breath in a hold but twenty-two inches high!"

A slave ship's captain states in his log that he made the most of the room available in the hold, or below deck, when he was stowing captives. The captain admits to wedging Africans in as tightly as possible:

"They had not so much room as a man in his coffin, either in length or breadth. It was impossible for them to turn or shift with any degree of ease."

A slave ship's doctor tells how the area below decks in which the Africans were held was "so crowded . . . that it is impossible to walk through them, without treading (stepping) on them. Those who are out of irons (chains) are locked spoonways to one another."

The captives were chained below deck for about 16 hours each day, causing raw sores or blisters on their ankles. They suffered from seasickness, dysentery, yellow fever, malaria, smallpox, and other ailments. To make matters worse, they were forced to lie in their own filth because they were only allowed up on deck for a very short time. When they were brought up on deck to exercise, the captives were "made to jump in their irons," even if their ankles were blistered and sore. The slave dealers mockingly referred to this exercise as "dancing." Those who refused to "dance" were flogged.

Theodore Canot, a slave trader, documents the high death rate associated with the trade. During one voyage, he lost nearly 50 percent of the Africans on board to disease: "The eight hundred beings we had shipped in high health [from Africa] had dwindled to four hundred and ninety-seven skeletons."

From the records and testimony of several captains of slave vessels, it appears that millions of Africans lost their lives in this routine manner. By 1781, the system of dehumanization that enslavement produced was so ingrained that one ship's captain threw 132 of the 440 enslaved Africans overboard so that he could collect the insurance money!

NAMELESS AND STATELESS

It was here on these ships during the dark and sometimes stormy nights on the ocean that African captives became nameless, stateless, and countryless people. Few people have shown the courage of the Africans who refused to die in the midst of the horrifying experiences of the Middle Passage.

When Africans landed in the Americas after weeks at sea, they believed that nothing could be so dehumanizing as the trip across the ocean had been. But they were wrong. The process of dehumanization had only begun.

Dehumanization, the idea of reducing humans to things, became the special weapon of the slave-ship captains. This practice was soon adopted by the colonists. Perhaps the colonists were comfortable dehumanizing Africans because it eased their own consciences. Europeans who participated in the trade had to make themselves believe that Africans were inferior and uncivilized in order to justify their cruel treatment of Africans. To dehumanize another person, you have to believe in your own superiority and the other person's inferiority and be willing to inflict pain and suffering to such a degree that it separates the sufferer from the oppressor. An oppressor is a person or a group who keeps others down by cruel or unjust use of power. This contrived separation, based at best on arrogance and ignorance, has been used to justify many insufferable

▲ During the Middle Passage, enslaved Africans became a nameless, stateless, and countryless people aboard these ships of horror.

racial crimes against humanity. Underlying racism is an ignorant, sick hatred of another entire race of people. Racism cannot be explained logically. In every instance where human beings define others as inferior or bad because they are "different," racism abounds. Can you think of any examples? How can racism be stopped?

◆ CENTER YOUR THINKING

1. What were conditions like in the slave ships during the Middle Passage? How do we know about what took place on slave ships during the Middle Passage?
2. How did brave Africans resist enslavement and the Middle Passage?
3. How did Europeas justify their cruel treatment of Africans?
4. Contrast and compare the meanings of the terms *dehumanization* and *racism*.
5. HOLISTIC ACTIVITY Students as Storytellers

   Oral storytelling is a strong tradition of African people. In each group, there are older people who are storytellers called *griots*. Griots record the past of the people as oral history. Whenever the people needed to hear about their history during ceremonies, rituals, and holidays, they called on the griot to remember and recite the experiences of the past. This chapter is about the despair of African people during the European Slave Trade. In small groups, practice telling this tragic story to a group of young people. Tell the story with the wisdom and style that you think an African griot would have used.

SUGGESTED READINGS

Ball, Charles. *Fifty Years in Chains*. New York: Dover Publications, 1970.

Blassingame, John. *The Slave Community*. New York: Oxford University Press, 1972.

Franklin, John Hope. *Emancipation Proclamation*. Garden City, NY: Doubleday, 1963.

Hodges, Norman. *Breaking the Chains of Bondage*. New York: Simon and Schuster, 1972.

Karenga, Maulana. *Introduction to Black Studies*. Los Angeles, CA: University of Sankore Press, 1990.

Levine, Lawrence. *Black Culture and Black Consciousness*. New York: Oxford University Press, 1977.

SUMMARY

Africans were forced to embark on the Middle Passage aboard ships built to hold 200 people but packed with as many as 1,000. They were forced into spaces 55.9 centimeters (22 inches) high and 61 centimeters (24 inches) wide, with little food and no toilet facilities, and were forced to lie in their own filth. During the voyage, which lasted 35 to 90 days, as many as half of the Africans died of disease, hunger, and illness. *(Chapter 7)*

The personal narratives of Africans who survived and the descriptions of slave-ship crews provide chilling accounts of the savagery of Middle Passage voyages. Slave-ship crews often justified their actions by convincing themselves that African people were not human and were racially inferior. We are still dealing with this racist attitude against people of African descent today. *(Chapter 7)*

Personal Witnessing

REFLECTION

When you read or hear about people in despair, it usually brings out strong feelings in you. What feelings did you experience as you were reading about the Middle Passage? Use your journal to record some of the strongest feelings you experienced. Remember, as you learn about the despair, the incredible strength of the Africans to survive and flourish in the Americas and the Caribbean against enormous odds.

TESTIMONY

Book reviewers read books and then inform and influence the public by writing critiques of the books' content as well as quality. Go back to your collection of slave narratives. Act as a book reviewer and write a short review focusing on your opinion on the effectiveness of these accounts in recording the nobility of a people and their survival despite the inhumanity of their treatment.

UNIT 3 RITE OF PASSAGE

Umfundalai emphasizes good school work. Building on the tradition of African people for communal and cooperative work, form study groups that meet after school and on weekends. Your group's goal is to guarantee that all members of the group succeed in their school work and to help each other improve. Create a logo and slogan for your group. As you study together, record in your Rites of Passage portfolio a summary of your study sessions and how they helped you improve. Of course, you must remember that you will still have to study alone, as well.

LOST IN AMERICA

C.E.

1607-1641
Yanga and a group of Africans take control of a major trading route between Veracruz and Puebla during the Spanish occupation of Mexico

1619
First Africans arrive in Jamestown, Virginia

In small groups, discuss and list some situations that you feel need to be changed because of human suffering. If your group could enact laws to improve these situations, what would the laws be? Why? Consider writing letters to your elected officials to explain your group's thinking.

In this unit, you will read about laws that were passed to make the brutal mistreatment of enslaved Africans legal and about the thinking of the people who made those laws. How could such thinking occur? What can be done to ensure that such laws are never made again in this country?

1631
British merchants enter the trade

1640
Arab invasion of Africa, initiating the spread of Islam

1641
Massachussetts becomes the first colony to enslave Africans for life

1662
European Slave Trade is officially sanctioned by the British Crown

"The African did not see America as a mountaintop of possibility; the African saw America as a valley of despair."

C.L. FRANKLIN
Sermon
"Dry Bones in the Valley"

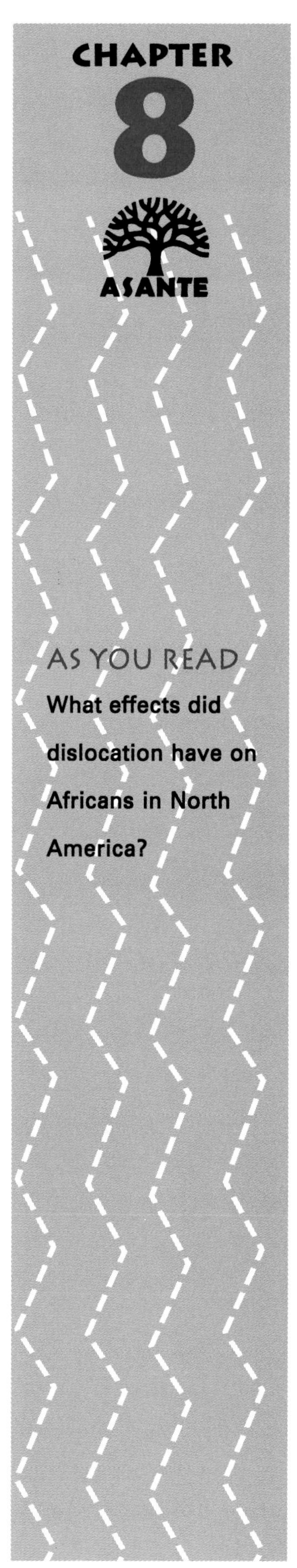

DISLOCATION

CENTER YOUR VOCABULARY

- ▲ dislocation
- ▲ queen mother
- ▲ Ebonics
- ▲ pagan
- ▲ stereotype
- ▲ homogenous

Africans, who came to North America with their own distinct languages, customs, religions, and values, were confronted with European values and customs that were very different. The new arrivals were reminded at every turn that their traditions and culture were not welcome in North America. They experienced dislocation because they could no longer hold onto their African values and traditions. This psychological and physical shift from their African center is called *dislocation*.

What would have happened to the Queen Mother Boah Tafo of Ghana had she been among the first Africans brought to Virginia? Except for the king, the queen mother in Ghana is the most powerful person in the kingdom. In Ghana, she would have been in charge of selecting the new Akyem (ah-KEHM) king, verifying his ancestral lineage, and settling disputes in the royal cabinet.

But in America, this woman of noble birth and royal character would have been reduced to a person without power or influence and dominated by white rule. As an indentured woman, she would never have been given the same protection as white women from the unwelcome advances of European men. Under enslavement, the queen mother—enslaved, African, and female—could not have defended herself from her attackers. In the comfort and security of

Africa, the queen mother is a highly respected leader of men and women. Here in the fertile river country of Virginia, the queen mother would have been helpless.

Because Africans were forced to the Americas to perform specific tasks, the Europeans did not care that they had been members of royal families, blacksmiths, diplomats, educators or priests. What the Europeans really needed were Africans to do manual labor. Consequently, Europeans believed there was no need to respect the identity, names, traditions, values, religion, or languages of African people.

During the first 100 years of African existence in North America, there was a strong attempt to stamp out any trace of African culture that might have survived. Among the first things to go were African names. The Africans who waded ashore in 1600 C.E. had names like Diallo, Nwonko, Awolowo, Obenga, Nyang, Owusu, Asare, Kasavubu, and Amachie. Their names were changed before their feet ever touched solid ground. The colonists gave them European names such as Smith, Coleman, Williams, Wilson, Hopkins, Johnson, Taylor, Anderson, and Simpson.

▼ Africans who landed in America in the 1600s were dislocated.

African languages disappeared with the same lightning speed as African names. Africans were punished severely if they were caught speaking their own languages. Consequently, Africans were forced to learn English or whatever language was spoken by the Europeans. In just a few generations, more than 100 African languages were erased from the memories of the majority of Africans who came to the Americas. A new language, Ebonics, a mixture of English words and African structure and syntax, evolved to serve the African population in communicating with each other and with whites.

Africans survived, but they were devastated in almost every way by this initial separation from their cultural roots. When the colonists outlawed drumming in an attempt to control African revolts, enslaved Africans lost another key cultural element. Music is central to African culture. African drums were used as a communication tool to send and receive short messages. The drum is used on its own or combined with other instruments to produce many different sounds. The sounds are as unique as the African ethnic groups and co-cultures that produce them, but the drum also has a unifying quality that brings all Africans together. African music gives birth to dance, and dance is the calling forth of the spirits of the ancestors, a ritual prayer for support and strength.

Enslaved Africans were robbed of every aspect of their lives that defined them as a people with a distinct culture and traditions. This means that if you were African and enslaved, your name could be changed from Molefi to Mike. You would be forbidden to speak your African language ever again. You would be forced to give up your religion and accept Christianity. The enslavement would steal every personal right that you considered to be yours, including something as important as a rite of passage for girls and boys! What are some of the traditions practiced in your family that makes your family life different from others? These traditions may be simple or they may be elaborate, but they help to define you. In colonial America, Africans were forbidden to be themselves.

What was created in Africans during this early period of American history was a dislike for things African, even a dislike for how Africans themselves looked. This was the beginning of a self-hatred or decentering among Africans that had never occurred in Africa. Africans on the continent did not make judgments about each other's skin color, eyes, hair, or other physical features. They did not consider themselves pagans (non-religious) for not practicing Christianity. They certainly did not think they needed the kind of refinement that

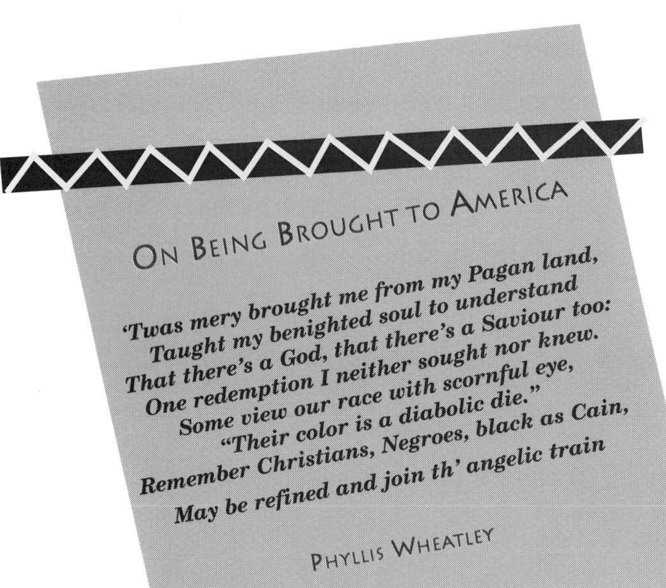

Phyllis Wheatley refers to in her poem, "On Being Brought to America." However, in North America, the colonists recognized only white Christians as their human equals and European values as worthy of their attention. The colonists' antagonism toward African culture created a negative stereotype and therefore a bias against Africa and Africans.

Fortunately, because all people do not react the same way to oppression, there were many Africans who managed to hold onto some aspect of their self-esteem and keep a positive image of their African heritage. But this was difficult. It was even more difficult to instill African pride in the generations that followed the first African arrivals in 1619. However, in each generation of Africans, there were always a few strong, independent men and women who believed in themselves. They were the ones who tried to center themselves by respecting their ancestors, keeping African traditions alive, and vowing to keep their dignity under impossible conditions. Without a culture to hold on to, the majority of Africans were decentered and lost in America, a modern tragedy.

African American preachers would rise up with the same eloquence of the West African *jales*, the praise singers, storytellers, and historians. They would use their oratory and their imaginations to relieve the boredom of life in enslavement. Other people would not be preachers but word-magicians, spreading joy, wonder, and excitement in the stories they told. Occasionally, however, there were responses to enslavement that seemed to parallel cultural images from the distant past. It was easy to see the strength and courage of early African warriors on the continent in the wrestling and boxing matches among the enslaved on the plantations. The fiery spirit of African resisters was reminiscent of the proud fighting spirit of great West African conquerors such as Sundiata and Mansa Musa who helped to make Mali powerful from the 13th to the 15th centuries. The skill with which colonial Africans cleared and prepared the land for planting and harvesting echoed the harmony with nature that had been treasured by their African ancestors on the continent. Runaway Africans heading north to freedom studied the skies with the same keen interest that the Dogon people of West Africa studied the stars. Perhaps it was these spiritual bonds that held enslaved Africans together when the cultural bonds were stripped away.

ETHNIC DIFFERENCES

The African condition of servitude has led many people to believe mistakenly that enslaved Africans were homogenous, a single group with the same ethnic background and reactions to their enslavement. To be sure, enslaved people shared many of the emotions that came with being physically and emotionally separated from their mother countries in Africa and their particular ethnic communities. Without a translator, these various ethnic groups who were forced together on the plantations were often unable to speak to each other. But African ethnic groups also had distinct characteristics that made their responses to enslavement vary from group to group. The Yoruba, for example, were deeply philosophical and used their culture as an anchor against enslavement. The Asante and Mande were experienced fighters and were often engaged in plots against the enslavers.

On the plantations, some Africans were so terrified of the enslavers that they soon accepted their enslavement and informed on other Africans who resisted. They informed to survive. However, the vast majority of Africans found other ways amounting to genius to survive the enslavement. They told the whites what they knew the whites wanted to hear. Later, they would laugh with each other about how they had fooled the enslavers. This was a learned response for survival that developed after many Africans had been killed for daring to speak out or resist their enslavement. Frederick Douglass, a former enslaved African, once warned enslaved Africans to speak to whites with the fronts of their heads. He believed that a person's emotions and higher-level thinking began in the back of the head before moving forward to the front of the head where they were then voiced as words through the mouth. He believed that if the enslaved spoke from the front of the head, they would be able to hide their real emotions and thoughts from whites. Enslaved Africans saw daily examples of the danger of speaking up for themselves. Whites did not want honesty. They did not want to hear the truth.

The great poet Paul Laurence Dunbar was moved to say in one of his poems:

> ***We wear the mask***
> ***that grins and lies***
> ***It hides our cheeks and***
> ***shades our eyes.***
> ***This debt we pay***
> ***to human guile***
> ***with torn and bleeding hearts,***
> ***we smile,***
> ***and mouths with myriad subtleties.***

Africans learned many other necessary skills for survival among hostile whites. They had to appear obedient, humble, and ignorant. If an African refused to show obedience and ignorance, he or she might be killed. In 16th-century America, enslavement and racism created three distinct groups: Native Americans who owned the land, Europeans who captured the land, and Africans who were forced to develop the land. It seemed essential to the whites to believe in their superiority over all others.

NOBILITY AND PURPOSE

Africans displayed a sense of nobility and high purpose in the way they approached their lives under duress. Colonial Africans took their culture inward when they were prevented from expressing any positive, outward signs of their African values and styles. Africans triumphed, even as their African names were torn from them and replaced by new ones, because they knew the essence of their forefathers could not be stamped out by the cruelty of their oppressors. When enslavement ripped apart ethnic bonds by forcefully separating ethnically similar African groups, dislocated

Africans forged new bonds with each other to minimize the oppressive conditions of their enslavement.

Many African Americans are unable to trace their roots to one specific African ethnic group. Furthermore, today's African American community is a composite of many different African elements and some Native American and European elements. There are also a growing number of African Americans who have Chinese, Indian, Japanese, Korean, Filipino, and other cultural backgrounds. Given this diversity, skin color and other physical characteristics are unreliable methods for identifying and classifying African Americans.

As we move toward the 21st century, culture—not color—may be the determining factor to defining race.

◆ CENTER YOUR THINKING

1. How did the enslavers try to destroy the traditions, values, and culture of Africans?
2. How did Africans respond to the efforts of the enslavers to destroy their culture?
3. What is Ebonics and how was it created?
4. Compare and contrast *immigration* and *dislocation*.
5. HOLISTIC ACTIVITY Students as Graphic Artists

   Work in small groups. Fold a large sheet of drawing paper in half lengthwise. Label one column BEFORE and the other AFTER. In the BEFORE column, depict African people before enslavement. In the AFTER column, depict the same people after being enslaved in America. You may use any art materials to construct a collage, poster, or any other creative expression. Add written descriptions and poetry, dialogue, or labels. Display your completed work.

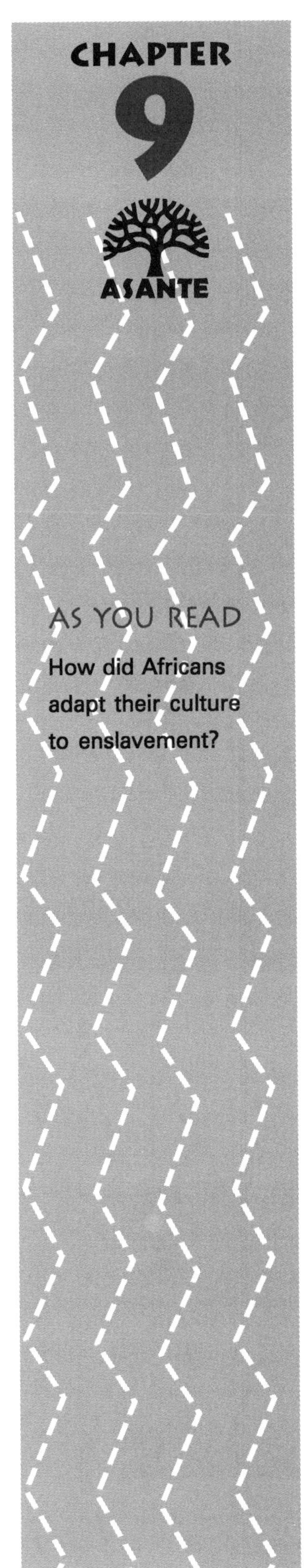

INDENTURED, NOT ENSLAVED

CENTER YOUR VOCABULARY

- ▲ indentured Africans
- ▲ indentureship
- ▲ valor
- ▲ deceit

One early morning in August 1619, a Dutch ship came up the James River and docked at Jamestown, Virginia. The captain of the ship traded 20 Africans for goods to the English colonists. They were the first indentured Africans in an English colony. These early indentured Africans were probably servants in Spain or Portugal prior to their arrival in America. Indentureship was a European practice that allowed a person to enter into a contract or bond to work for someone else, usually for a period of seven years. At the end of this period, the indentured servant or bondsperson was released. However, for Africans, indentureship gradually became indentureship for life.

Indentured Europeans often chose to come to the Americas. Many of them were poor people looking for a better way of life. Some were criminals. A few were kidnapped and forced into indentureship, much like the Africans who came from Portugal and Spain. Regardless of their reasons for leaving Europe, the majority of Europeans became indentured workers to earn money to buy land in the Americas. Only the very wealthy could afford land in Europe. Indentured Europeans hoped to build their fortunes growing cotton and tobacco for export.

The first African arrivals who sailed up the James River had similar goals and ambitions. Only a few were able to realize their dreams and secure a financial future in the new land. Enslavement stripped

Africans of all their human rights, making them, by law, the property or chattel of the Europeans.

BORN IN FREEDOM

Less than five years after Africans first came to the Jamestown colony, some of them had adapted to the English way of life. Others found the colony much too foreign for their own taste and could not totally adapt. Those who found it possible to accept the Christian religion, change their names, and participate in the general structure of the society as established by the English were soon adopting English behaviors and culture and denying their own.

In 1624, Isabella and Anthony Johnson, who were indentured, became the parents of the first African American child born in the British colonies. William was born free because his parents were not enslaved.

The Johnsons were among the first economically successful Africans in Virginia. They established a community on the Pungoteague River in Northampton County in 1651, after receiving about 1 square kilometer (250 acres) of land from the local government for agreeing to import and hire five indentured servants. This type of arrangement was quite common and often used to encourage the colonists to expand and develop the colonies. However, Africans who had worked off their indentureship and could save enough money to hire their own indentured servants had the right to do so.

▼ From 1619 to 1650, African people who came to the English colonies in America were indentured servants, not enslaved people.

When their indentureship ended, a few Africans, including several of Anthony Johnson's relatives, also received land in Northampton County for hiring indentured servants. John Johnson received 2 square kilometers (550 acres)

in 1652 for hiring 11 bondspeople. Richard Johnson obtained nearly half a square kilometer (100 acres) for bringing in two indentured servants. Like the Johnsons, indentured Africans throughout the colonies found ways of adapting to new values and customs in a new country. Both indentured and free Africans attempted to make new lives for themselves.

Think about what the American landscape would have been like if the enslavement never existed. There would have been far fewer Africans in this country. It is unlikely that Africans on the continent of Africa would have traveled to America for land, religious freedom, or wealth because they already had those things in their own countries. Perhaps the Africans who wanted to come to America would have had the same opportunity for personal and financial success that the other colonists had. We will never know.

The freedom of Africans to pursue a new life would be short-lived as the Europeans claimed new colonies and color prejudice became associated with enslavement. Soon, enslavement was specific to Africans. Whites who had been poor indentured servants were eventually just poor, but they could not be enslaved. Enslavement was reserved in the law for Africans. Gradually, those Africans who had been indentured when the laws were passed legalizing enslavement in certain states lost their chance to become free. There was no longer any opportunity for Africans to become the kind of entrepreneurs that whites were to become in the new colonies. Africans were no longer to own their own labor or their own bodies. What had started out in the English colonies as a form of indentureship for both races had gradually become a system of oppression for only one race of humanity. It would be this tremendous social and legal flaw in the American system that would inspire resistance and valor in the African people for the next 250 years.

ENSLAVEMENT SPREADS

In addition to the Virginia colonists who founded Jamestown in 1607, there were small groups of colonists all across the eastern seaboard. Many of them were emigrating from Europe to escape political or religious persecution. When they landed in America, they immediately created their own communities or colonies along the eastern coast. At first, these colonies had no laws permitting the enslavement of Africans. The process of enslaving Africans was accomplished gradually through deceit, dishonesty, and trickery. Throughout North America, the European colonists found ways of extending the service of indentured Africans until laws were passed making Africans and their children servants for life!

◆ CENTER YOUR THINKING

1. How did indentureship differ from enslavement?
2. How did Africans manage to keep some aspects of their culture?
3. What are some of the factors that caused self-hatred among Africans?
4. Discuss whether you think some of these factors are present today.
5. HOLISTIC ACTIVITY Students as Writers

   Working in small groups, write a series of four letters that indentured Africans in the 18th century might have written. Describe how you came to America as a free person, your plans and dreams for the future, and your reactions to the laws that did not allow you to ever end your indentureship. Share your letters with the class.

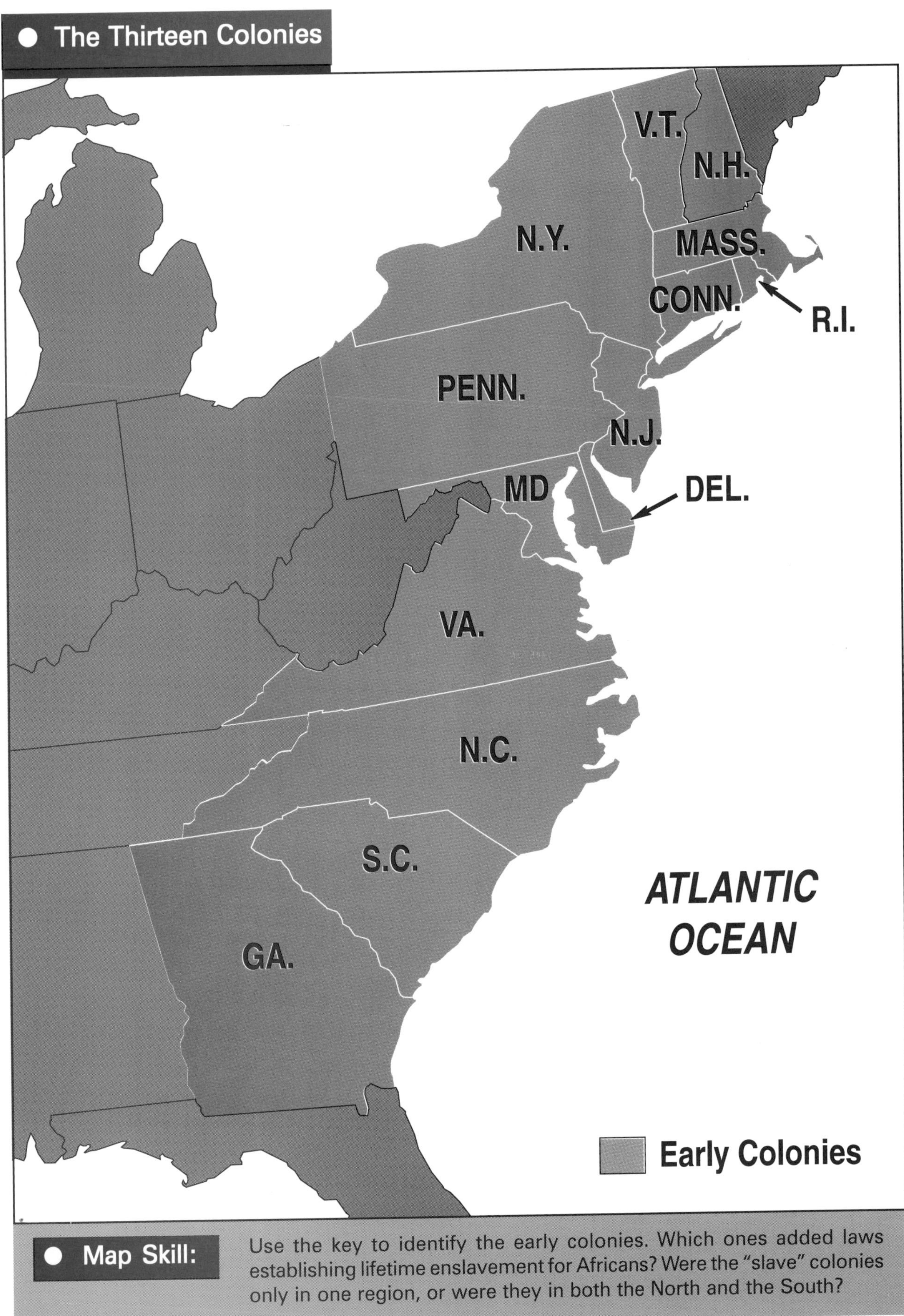

Map Skill: Use the key to identify the early colonies. Which ones added laws establishing lifetime enslavement for Africans? Were the "slave" colonies only in one region, or were they in both the North and the South?

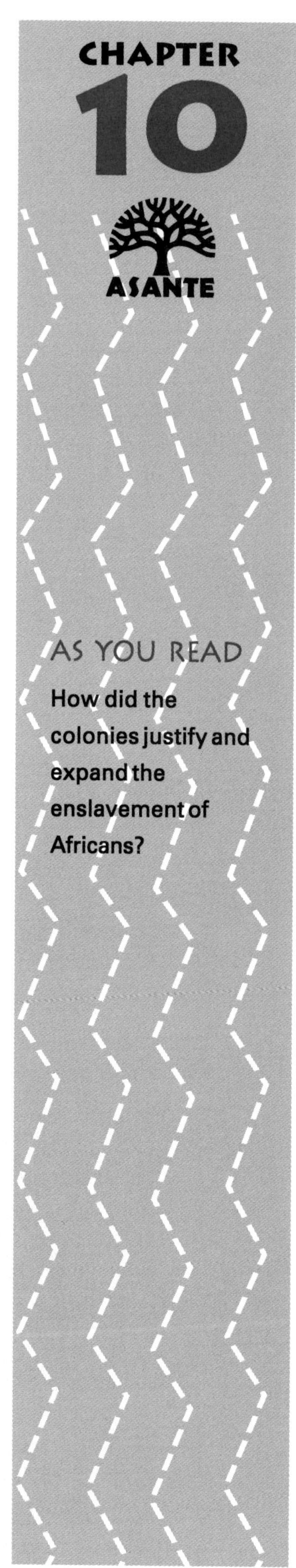

SIGNED INTO LAW

CENTER YOUR VOCABULARY

- ▲ de facto
- ▲ common labor
- ▲ statute
- ▲ civil libertarian
- ▲ *durante vita*
- ▲ racial discrimination

Various colonies began to justify the enslavement of Africans by writing into their laws principles that would support enslavement. Massachusetts, founded by the Pilgrims who traveled from the Netherlands to America in search of their religious freedom, became the first colony to legalize the enslavement of Africans in 1641. The enslavement of Native Americans was already legal in the colony. During the next 30 years, several other states passed laws legalizing enslavement, among them Virginia, which placed Africans into perpetual bondage.

In 1662, Virginia added a law that declared that all African children born in that colony would be free or enslaved, based on the status of the mother. The law was enacted to deal with the numerous children produced from unions between white colonists and enslaved African women. The law read: "Whereas some doubts have arisen whether children got by any Englishman upon a negro woman should be slave or free, be it enacted . . .: that all children borne in this country shall be held bond or free only according to the condition of the mother."

Of course, by this time, the enslavement of Africans was de facto, the accepted practice in all the colonies. Most African women were enslaved, which made most African children slaves as well. The new law, making the status of the mother determine the status of the child, was the opposite of the established British common law

EARLY COLONIES

1623	New Hampshire was established.
1624	The Dutch founded New Netherlands, which was renamed New York.
1633	Connecticut was settled.
1634	Maryland was settled.
1636	Rhode Island was settled.
1638	Delaware was settled.
1643	Pennsylvania was settled.
1660	New Jersey was settled.

practiced by white colonists. British common law said that the father's condition determined the status of the child. British colonists created a different set of laws for Africans. With these laws, a white father was not responsible for his "black" children.

In 1663, Maryland passed its own law enslaving Africans *durante vita,* or for life. At first, lawmakers ruled that the status of an African child born into that colony was dependent upon the status of the father, not the mother. However, this soon changed to reflect the American custom of using the mother's status to determine the status of an African child.

North Carolina followed with a statute, or law, in 1669 giving enslavers absolute power and authority over the Africans they enslaved.

LEGALIZING ENSLAVEMENT

1650	Connecticut passes a law allowing the enslavement of Africans.
1661	Virginia passes a law that places Africans into perpetual bondage.
1663	Maryland passes a law that enslaves Africans in its colony *durante vita,* or for life.
1669	North Carolina gives enslavers absolute power and authority over Africans they enslaved.
1682	Virginia declares that all servants brought into the colony from non-Christian or nonwhite countries would be slaves.
1682	Pennsylvania legalizes the enslavement of Africans.
1708	Rhode Island allowed the enslavement of Africans.
1740	South Carolina passes a law allowing the enslavement of Africans and Native Americans.
1749	Georgia permits the importation and use of enslaved Africans.

EARLY ATTEMPTS TO JUSTIFY ENSLAVEMENT

Goal: Free Labor *Solution: Enslavement* *Outcome: Oppression and Racism*

QUOTE	COLONISTS' REASONING	COLONISTS' ASSUMPTION	OUTCOME	REFLECTION
"The African is the most degraded of human races and whose form approaches that of the beast." **George Curvier**	Enslaved Africans are physically and culturally different from whites; therefore, they should not be treated the same as whites.	Enslaved Africans are not human.	Dehumanization	Physical characteristics and culture are only part of what makes us human. What are some other factors the European colonists neglected to take into account?
"Let us forget Africa never to return to it for Africa is no part of the historical globe." **Georg Hegel**	Africa has never made any worthwhile contributions to world history.	Enslaved Africans do not belong to any distinct culture, civilization, or race worthy of our attention.	Based on their dark skin, enslaved Africans are renamed *Negroes*, a term which comes from the Spanish word *negro* which means "black."	European scholars were certainly aware of early European and Arab accounts of the flourishing civilizations they encountered when they traveled to Africa. However, this information conflicted so much with whites' perception of Africa and Africans that the scholars found it easier to ignore it. Had this information been more accepted, how might it have changed history?
"I am apt to suspect that the Negroes in general are naturally inferior to the whites. There has never been a civilized nation of any other complexion than white." **David Hume**	Negroes are not white; therefore, they must be uncivilized.	Enslavement is a natural condition for Africans.	Enslavement is legalized.	Enslavement is linked to race and color. Africans are viewed as "naturally inferior" to whites, and enslavement is deemed to be in the best interest of African people. If enslavement was such a good thing for Africans, why did so many Africans protest and rebel against it for more than 250 years?
"They break, waste, and destroy everything they handle." **Dr. Samuel Cartwright**	Africans are not clever enough to have hidden reasons for destroying enslavers' property.	Africans cannot be trusted with important tasks.	Africans are restricted to physical labor and are prevented from doing jobs that demonstrate their intellect.	Many African Americans in positions of authority are quite familiar with the experience of having their judgment second-guessed by whites who still believe this myth. Why do you think this myth still persists today?

Interestingly, John Locke, the famous white civil libertarian who wrote about the state's obligation to protect and ensure the God-given rights of men, authored this law. A civil libertarian is an advocate for individual rights. Locke was one of the leading thinkers of his time. His philosophy greatly influenced Thomas Jefferson and the thoughts Jefferson expressed in the Declaration of Independence. Locke did not consider Africans "men" and so did not include them in his call for civil liberty. This omission gave the white colonists a reason to deny enslaved Africans their most basic human rights.

In 1682, Virginia declared that all indentured servants brought into the colony from non-Christian or nonwhite countries would be enslaved. This included Africans and Native Americans. The law was simply a legal measure to enslave Africans because they were obviously not Christian and definitely not white.

Some 50 years later, South Carolina legalized enslavement. By then, Britain's King George I had divided the colony of Carolina into North and South Carolina. Two years later in 1732, the southern portion of South Carolina became the colony of Georgia. In 1740, South Carolina passed a law declaring Africans and Native Americans "absolute slaves" who "shall be claimed, held, taken, reputed, and adjudged in law to be chattels personal." The same attitudes that allowed the passage of such a horrendous law were to persist, leading to much of the racial hatred that would occur later in the United States.

THE DILEMMAS OF ENSLAVEMENT

The laws that were passed legalizing the enslavement of Africans reflected the racial attitudes of the times. Many of the colonists had made themselves believe that Africans were not human and therefore were "inferior," not only to themselves, but also to the entire white race.

The colonists justified their enslavement of Africans by denying that Africans were a highly civilized people with traditions and customs that were greatly admired thousands of years before Europe existed. The colonists also chose to ignore early European and Arab accounts of the flourishing civilizations they encountered when they traveled to Africa. The suppression of information about Africa became an active habit among European writers who could not reconcile Africa's glorious past with the European myth of African inferiority. Kept ignorant of African achievements, the masses of white people went along with the opinions of the leading political, religious, and academic authorities, and believed in African inferiority.

As long as European immigrants held to their own racial "superiority" myth, they could dismiss their guilt for enslaving Africans. In fact, they could argue that because they were "superior" they had a right to enslave Africans. Of course, this was a false notion, but it worked in the minds of whites who believed it.

The physical differences between both races, particularly skin color, was an easy point of distinction and racial discrimination. Racial discrimination is an act of prejudice directed at a particular group of people because of their race. Africans were referred to as *Negroes* and later *blacks*. Europeans were called *whites*. Such vivid imagery allowed whites to associate themselves with all that they considered good and worthwhile, while conjuring up negative images of darkness, evil, and general unworthiness about Africans. Europeans called Africa *the Dark Continent*. With a label like this for Africans' homeland, what contributions would you expect from Africans? Probably not much, if you were David Hume, a respected Scottish philosopher who believed that Africans and other dark-skinned people of color were "inferior" to whites.

Hume said in 1748:

"I am apt to suspect the Negroes and in general all the other species of men to be naturally inferior to whites. There never was a civilized nation of any other complexion than white, or even an individual eminent either in action or speculation, no ingenious manufacturers among them, no art, no sciences."

By calling Africans *Negroes*, the European colonists further separated Africans from their African culture. Even the renowned

Thomas Jefferson, one of the authors of the Declaration of Independence and the third president of the United States, doubted whether Africans were part of a distinct civilization, much less a flourishing one. Jefferson, an enslaver, wrote in his *Notes on Virginia* in 1790: "I advance it, therefore, as a suspicion only, that the blacks, whether originally a distinct race or made distinct by time and circumstance, are inferior to the whites in the endowments of both body and mind."

Jefferson was challenged by Benjamin Bannaker, an African astronomer, clockmaker, farmer, almanac writer, and surveyor, who lived in the colonies and whose long list of accomplishments contradicted Jefferson's theory of white supremacy. In a 1791 letter that was published widely, Banneaker told then Secretary of State Jefferson that it was absurd to think of Africans as an inferior race. By the very nature of his letter, Bannaker demonstrated that, at the very least, enslaved Africans possessed the same reasoning powers and literary skills as their colonial oppressors. In his letter to Jefferson, Bannaker challenged the religious principles of the colonists by pointing out that if they believed in God and His equal and impartial distribution of life, liberty, and the pursuit of happiness for all men, then the colonists were in direct contradiction of God's law in their use of fraud and violence to enslave Africans. Bannaker further argued that the colonists were "guilty" of a most criminal act in their continued enslavement of Africans.

▲ Benjamin Bannaker, a free African and a brilliant scientist, created one of the first series of almanacs in the United States.

It was impossible to think of Africans as inferior when they continued to resist enslavement. A well-known Southern doctor, Samuel Cartwright, decided that resistance to enslavement was a sign of mental illness. He named several so-called diseases associated with enslaved Africans. One of them was *Dyasthesia aethiopica* which he described: "From the careless movements of the individuals affected with this complaint they are apt to do much mischief. Thus they break, waste, and destroy everything they handle." Dr. Cartwright saw resistance to enslavement was a disease, rather than a natural reaction to oppression.

◆ CENTER YOUR THINKING

1. What were some of the justifications for slavery?
2. How did Benjamin Bannaker challenge Thomas Jefferson?
3. In what ways did Africans resist enslavement?
4. How was the myth of African inferiority created, and what effect did it have on Europeans? Africans?
5. HOLISTIC ACTIVITY Students as Chart Makers

   Working in small groups, choose a quotation from another chapter or book, and make your own chart titled EARLY ATTEMPTS TO JUSTIFY ENSLAVEMENT. Choose your columns or rows carefully. Samples include: Colonists' Reasoning, Colonists' Assumptions, Outcomes, Reflections/ My Conclusions.

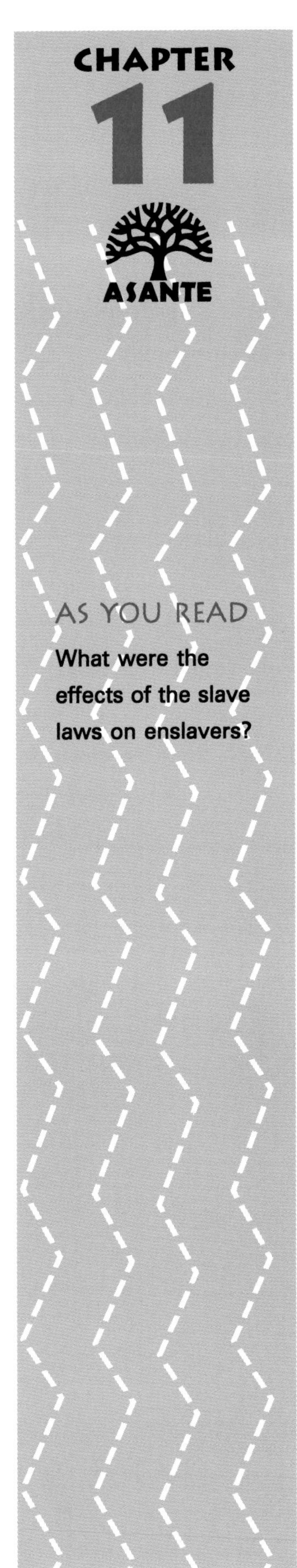

THE LEGAL IMPACT OF ENSLAVEMENT

CENTER YOUR VOCABULARY

- ▲ mandate
- ▲ thieves
- ▲ recourse
- ▲ manumission

There were many laws governing the conduct of the enslaved person. There were not many laws governing the enslaver's behavior. Africans learned quickly that their survival depended on finding new ways to get around the law. If the law said that an African could not testify in court against a white person, then the African had to make the white person's crime visible and public. This meant that Africans with special knowledge and special skills were highly valued among the enslaved. Although the law prohibited Africans from learning to read and write, there were always some Africans who managed to acquire the skills they needed to function in a white world. As legislators handed down new laws cementing the institution of enslavement, the enslaved created their own codes of conduct to lessen the impact.

LEGAL DEFINITIONS

The law determined the definition of the enslaved. For example, in Louisiana the civil code said, "A slave is one who is in the power of a master to whom he belongs. The master may sell him, dispose of his person, his industry, and his labor: he can do nothing, possess nothing, nor acquire anything, but what must belong to his master." Like chattel, or personal property, an enslaved person had no rights or recourse whatsoever. A young woman could not protect herself from the advances of the enslaver. A mother's child could be sold away from her to another plantation in a distant state. A man could have his fingers cut off or his foot cut off with no recourse to the law; the only rule on the plantation was that the enslaver owned the African person and could take any liberties he or she saw fit to take. It was a dangerous and uncertain time both for the whites who perpetrated enslavement and the Africans who were its victims. Violation of the law meant swift and certain punishment for the enslaved. The danger for the whites resided in the fact that Africans had experienced so much cruelty that there was no telling when they would erupt in rage.

The conditions of chattel slavery were also mandated by law. Most states regulated how much and what type of food and clothing the enslaver was to provide. A typical diet consisted of fatback (pork), cornmeal, and molasses. Clothing consisted of a single shirt or pants for the men, a dress for the women, overcoat, and shoes. But because the law was not strictly enforced, the enslaved's diet and clothing was really determined by how the enslaver felt about the Africans on his or her plantation. There is no evidence, for example, that enslavers were ever punished for underfeeding the Africans who worked for them. There is, however, overwhelming evidence that

▼ Enslaved Africans picking cotton on a plantation in the South

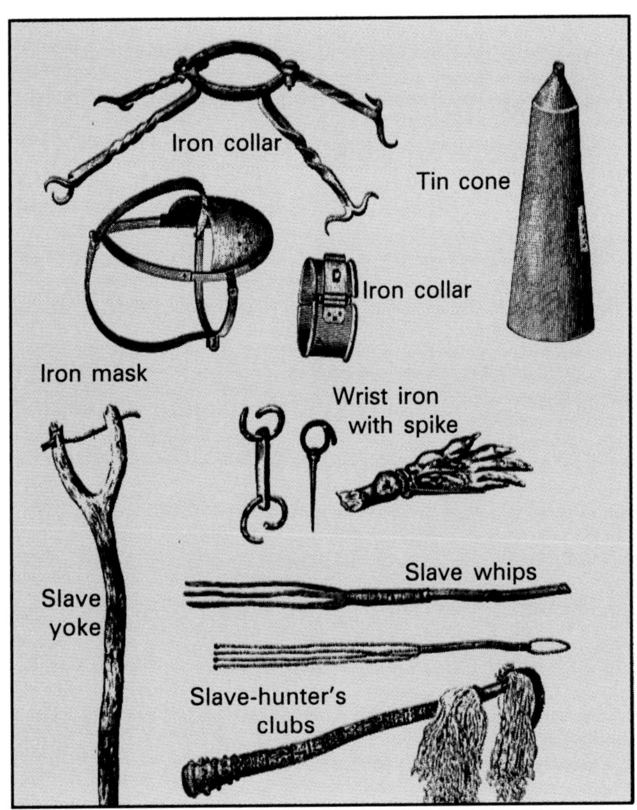

▲ Instruments of torture

enslavers mistreated Africans. The minimum standards outlined in the law were simply an unenforced legal guide.

When enslaved Africans were given insufficient food, they resorted to taking what they needed from the storehouses. Charles Ball, an African who escaped enslavement, said, "I was never acquainted with a slave who believed that he violated any rule of morality by [taking] anything that belonged to his master, if it was necessary to his comfort." However, the enslavers considered this stealing and passed harsh laws to deal with it. It became an accepted belief that Africans, by nature, were thieves. The enslavers did not consider themselves thieves even though they used the forced labor of Africans to provide themselves with fine clothes and fancy food.

PUNISHMENT

The physical punishment of the enslaved was also a matter of law. An enslaver could inflict any punishment he or she saw fit. Burning, cutting off feet or hands, branding, starvation, crucifixion, whipping, and other acts of cruelty were all legal punishments. In 1723, Virginia decided that "Manslaughter of a slave (death resulting from corrective punishment) is not deemed to be a punishable offense."

This meant that in the 18th century, it was legal for Alfred Rackley, an enslaved African from Dooly County, Georgia, to be whipped mercilessly to death. Under the law, the enslaver was not guilty of a crime. There were numerous examples of Africans like Rackley who died under punishment and whose murderers went unpunished.

▼ Stocks were used to hold the enslaved's hands and feet in a viselike grip.

MANUMISSION

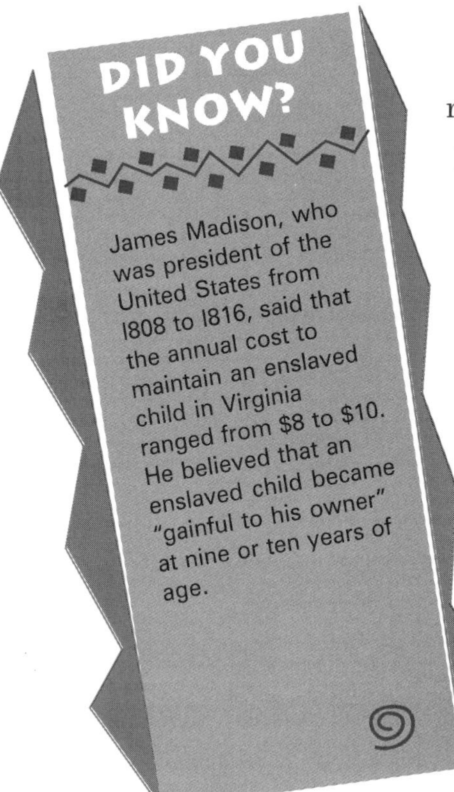

The conditions under which an enslaved person could receive manumission, or freedom, were also spelled out by law. In some states, enslaved Africans could only be freed by the state. Virginia, for example, decreed in 1723, that enslaved Africans could not be set free "except for some meritorious service, to be adjudged and allowed by the governor and council." Enslaved Africans knew that this kind of freedom was very temporary because it could be taken away much easier than it was given. In such states as Virginia, Mississippi, Alabama, and Arkansas, enslaved Africans who were freed could be reenslaved for debts owed by their former enslavers. As a result, many freed Africans fled north as quickly as possible to avoid being captured and reenslaved.

OTHER ASPECTS OF ENSLAVEMENT

- Enslavement was perpetual and hereditary.
- The enslaved was property and could be sold, mortgaged, or leased at any time.
- The enslaved could not legally marry in most states.
- The enslaved could be punished for standing up straight and looking a white man in the eye.
- The enslaved could not hold meetings or religious services without a white witness.
- The enslaved could not gather away from the plantations in groups of more than two or three.
- The enslaver determined the type, time, and degree of labor the enslaved person must perform.
- The enslaver could designate an agent to oversee the enslaved.
- If an enslaved person was injured by someone other than the enslaver, the enslaver could bring a lawsuit to recover damages for the injury.
- The enslaved could not charge the enslaver with cruel or inhumane treatment, testify, or bring a lawsuit against the enslaver.
- The enslaved could not be taught to read or write.
- The enslaved person had to have a pass from the enslaver to leave the plantation.

◆ CENTER YOUR THINKING

1. Explain why there weren't any laws to govern the conduct of enslavers.
2. Tell why Africans with special knowledge and special skills were highly valued among the enslaved.
3. Why were slave laws so harsh? How did these laws affect the colonists? How did they affect enslaved people?
4. Define the term *manumission*. Tell how enslaved Africans could receive manumission. Describe one problem associated with manumission.
5. HOLISTIC ACTIVITY Students as Researchers

   Do a literature search to identify laws that governed the enslavement of African people in America. Rely on your librarian for help, and use computer searches. Have each person in your group describe one law to the group, and then discuss and write down the group's ideas on how Africans might have avoided or lessened the impact of that law.

CHAPTER

12

ASANTE

IN OUR OWN WORDS

CENTER YOUR VOCABULARY

- poignant
- overseer
- supplement
- sanction

AS YOU READ

How was the European system of enslavement so horrible and dehumanizing to African people? How did they describe their experiences?

The narratives of enslaved and free Africans are some of the best sources for learning firsthand about the conditions of enslavement. In their narratives, we read the Africans' own poignant, touching, words about what they ate, how they lived and worked, the enslavers, punishments, methods of resistance, and, most important, how they saw themselves and their position in this country.

The enslaved said that they worked from "can't see in the morning till can't see at night." Enslavement meant that they could not marry or live with the person they fell in love with without the approval of the enslaver. It meant that the children they bore did not belong to them, and that these children could, at any time, be forcibly taken away and sold. It meant possibly never seeing a sister, brother, daughter, father, mother, or son ever again. It meant being at the mercy of a cruel enslaver. It meant that enslaved women did not own their own bodies, that they could be raped and had no legal means of protest. It meant seeing a mother, son, daughter, sister, father, or brother whipped and horribly abused and not be able to do anything about it.

Enslavement in the Deep South (Georgia, Alabama, South Carolina, Mississippi) was considered worse than enslavement in

▲ An enslaver watches as an enslaved African is forced to whip a fellow African.

Iron masks are bolted in place and used in combination with an iron collar. ▶

▲ Five generations of this family lived on a South Carolina plantation together.

the upper Southern states such as Virginia, Maryland, and Delaware because of the hard, backbreaking work required on the cotton and sugar plantations. The worst was to be enslaved in the Caribbean. The narratives given by the enslaved show that as punishment for resisting, Africans in the North were sometimes threatened with enslavement in the Deep South or in the West Indies. The overseers, or managers, on the sugar plantations in the West Indies were well known for their extreme cruelty to enslaved Africans.

In their memoirs, Africans recorded the ordinary and the extraordinary, misery and victory that touches the human spirit in its simplicity and quiet dignity.

Josiah Henson, on whom the Uncle Tom character in Harriet Beecher Stowe's book, *Uncle Tom's Cabin,* is based, described his living conditions:

"We lodged in log huts and on the bare ground. Wooden floors were an unknown luxury. In a single room were huddled, like cattle,

The sale began—young girls were there,
Defenseless in their wretchedness.
Whose stifled sobs of deep despair
Revealed their anguish and distress.
And mothers stood with streaming eyes,
And saw their dearest children sold;
Unheeded rose their bitter cries,
While tyrants bartered them for gold.
And woman, with her love and truth—
For these in sable forms may dwell—
Gazed on the husband of her youth,
With anguish none may paint or tell.
And men, whose sole crime was their hue,
The impress of their Maker's hand,
And frail and shrieking children, too,
Were gathered in that mournful band.
Ye who have never laid your love to rest,
And wept above their lifeless clay,
Know not the anguish of that heart,
Whose loved are rudely torn away
Ye may not know how desolate
Are husbands rudely forced to part,
And how a dull and heavy weight
Will press the life-drops from the heart.

FRANCES WATKINS HARPER
THE SLAVE AUCTION

ten or a dozen persons, men, women and children. . . . There were neither bedsteads, nor furniture of any description. Our beds were collections of straw and old rags, thrown down in the corners and boxed in with boards, a single blanket the only covering. . . . The wind whistled and the rain and snow blew in through the cracks, and the damp earth soaked in the moisture till the floor was miry as a pigsty."

According to Henson, his meals consisted of cornmeal and salt herrings, with a little buttermilk, and a few vegetables in the summer. A few fortunate Africans were given a patch of land to plant vegetables and other produce to supplement their meal. Others barely had enough to eat.

Henson's clothing was made from coarse cloth. Children wore nothing but a shirt. As they grew older, they were given used linsey, a coarse cloth of cotton and wool. In the winter months, enslaved men were given an old waistcoat or a frock coat and a woolen cap every two to three years. Shoes were handed out yearly.

In her narrative, Sojourner Truth, a strong supporter of women's rights, recorded the many beatings she received from English-speaking enslavers because she could not speak English. Previously, she had worked for enslavers who only spoke Dutch, but in her new owners' eyes, that fact was not sufficient to stop the beatings.

▲ Overseers on the sugar plantations in the Caribbean were well known for their cruelty to Africans.

Ella Wilson also told of being whipped and of the humiliation she felt at being stripped of her clothing and dignity:

"My master used to throw me in a buck and whip me. He would put my hands together and tie them. Then he would strip me naked. Then he would make me squat down. Then he would run a stick through behind my knees and in front of my elbows. My knee was up against my chest. My hands was tied together just in front of my shins. The stick between my arms and my knees held me in a squat. That's what they call a buck. . . . He would whip me on one side till that was sore and full of blood and then he would whip me on the other side till that was all tore up. . . ."

At age five, Harriet Tubman was whipped four times before breakfast one morning because her mistress thought she was being rude. At age seven, she was flogged for tasting sugar for the first time. An overseer hit her in the head with a 2-kilogram (2-pound)

▲ Sojourner Truth

iron weight when she was 16, causing her to have "spells" the rest of her life. She received many other beatings while she was enslaved.

Under these difficult conditions, Africans were still able to express affection and devotion to each other. There are heroic stories of love and romance that overcame, at least for a time, the cruelty Africans endured under enslavement.

In her memoir, Bessie, an enslaved woman in 19th-century Alabama, tells a moving story of undying love. John Harper, an enslaved African who worked on the same plantation, fell in love with Bessie, who was blind and so short that she had to stand on a box to wash dishes in the enslaver's kitchen. They married, but their happiness ended as quickly as it began. John was sold to another plantation owner many miles away in Louisiana.

When the Civil War began in 1861, Bessie gave up all hope of ever seeing John again. She was freed at the end of the Civil War in 1865, but Bessie had nowhere to go and no one to turn to. She asked her former enslaver for permission to remain on the plantation as a dishwasher. Many years went by, but John had not forgotten his true love. He suffered many years of hardship, moving from one plantation to another. Each time he was sold, he asked the other

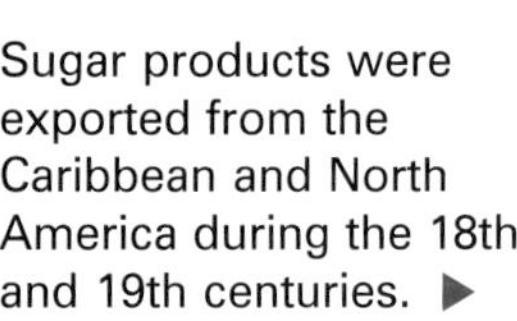

Sugar products were exported from the Caribbean and North America during the 18th and 19th centuries. ▶

Africans on the plantation if they had heard of or seen Bessie. When he was freed, he spent many years trying to find Bessie. In desperation, he decided to go back to Alabama on the slim chance that Bessie might still be there. John and Bessie were finally reunited. He took her off the plantation to a home he had built for them in Mississippi.

John and Bessie were certainly not a typical example: many lives and family ties were heartlessly severed. Enslavement, sanctioned as right by law and by whites, weighed heavily on enslaved Africans. Who could they turn to? What could they do to rid themselves of this cruel burden?

◆ CENTER YOUR THINKING

1. What do the slave narratives tell you about enslavement in the Deep South and in the West Indies?
2. Explain why enslavement was so cruel.
3. What are the slave narratives?
4. Give at least one example of strength and endurance that you have learned from the slave narratives.
5. HOLISTIC ACTIVITY Students as Poets

   Write a long poem in your group, with each person creating a stanza or with the group participating in the entire poem, on the subject of European treatment of African people. Work together to edit and revise the poem to the satisfaction of the entire group. Present it as an oral reading to the class.

SUGGESTED READINGS

Aptheker, Herbert. *American Negro Slave Revolts*. New York: International Publishers, 1963.

Blassingame, John. *The Slave Community: Plantation Life in the Antebellum South*. New York, 1972.

Davis, David Brion. *The Problem of Slavery in Western Culture.* Ithaca, NY: Cornell University Press, 1966.

Du Bois, W.E.B. *The Souls of Black Folk*. New York: Bantam Books, 1989.

Harris, J. William. *Society and Culture in the Slave South*. London: Routledge, 1992.

SUMMARY

Enslaved Africans found that they were forced into a brutal system that stripped away their previous status in society with complete disrespect for their identity, names, traditions, values, religion, and language. The narratives of Africans during enslavement describe the horrors of their condition. Still, many Africans drew strength from the values and traditions of their faraway homes. Africans found ways to adapt and preserve their culture, and, with incredible strength, they survived.
(Chapters 8 and 9)

The condition of enslavement created a lack of respect for anything African. The dehumanization of Africans because of enslavement was the beginning of a self-hatred among Africans that had never occurred in Africa. Europeans justified their treatment of Africans by denying their status as equals or even as humans. Knowledge of the contributions that Africans had made to world civilization was suppressed. Skin color and other characteristics of Africans were made into false symbols of inferiority.
(Chapter 10)

Among the first Africans who arrived in the new European colonies were indentured workers, many of whom were able to purchase their freedom. However, by the end of the 17th century, a series of laws had been enacted to expand slavery and to make it possible for Africans who had been mamumissioned to once again be enslaved. *(Chapters 10 and 11)*

99 Personal Witnessing

REFLECTION

Reflect and write about your feelings in reaction to the system of enslavement and the narratives you have read. Include your thoughts and feelings on the incredible strength of Africans to survive this experience and build new lives.

TESTIMONY

Working in small groups, write your own slave narrative. Include your dreams and determination to survive and overcome enslavement eventually. Discuss ways to include the thoughts and themes that you have learned from this painful history and that apply today.

99 Unit 4 Rite of Passage

Umfundalai emphasizes self-discipline in speech and action. Either individually or in your small group, make a list of actions to take to discipline yourself in speech and action. In what situations is self-restraint needed? In what areas are you in need of practice to improve yourself? What examples of self-discipline can you point to in role models you have? Next, make a list of the actions you or your group will take, and create a class poster to communicate your list. In your group or with a partner, give each other constructive feedback on ways to discipline yourselves. Put a copy of your group's poster in your portfolio, and also, continue recording in your portfolio the actions you take personally throughout the year.

RESISTANCE TO ENSLAVEMENT

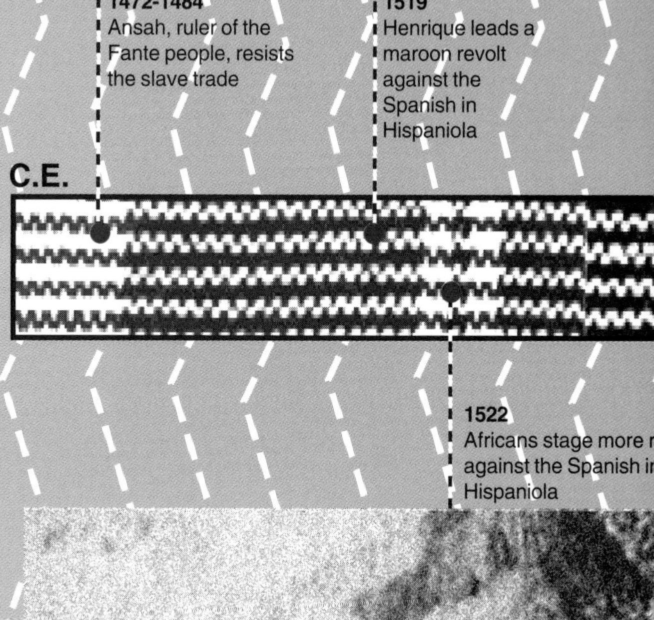

The resistance of Africans to enslavement never stopped and was highly spirited. Before you read this unit, work in small groups to predict some of the ways that Africans resisted enslavement during three periods: first, in Africa; second, on the slave ships; and last, in the United States. Make a group chart and compare your predictions with what you learn in this unit.

As you read Unit 5, consider whether you think that the pursuit of freedom and resistance to control by others is inborn in all humans.

1526
Africans revolt in the Spanish colony of South Carolina

1527
Africans revolt in Puerto Rico

1529
Africans revolt in Colombia

1530
Africans revolt in Mexico

1531
Africans revolt in Panama

1533
Africans revolt in Cuba

1626-1656
Queen Nzingha of Angola declares war against all slave traders

1642-1779
Africans stage numerous revolts in America

1787
The King of Almammy, a Senegales ruler, outlaws the slave trade in his kingdom

"The role which the great Negro Toussaint called L'Ouverture played in the history of the United States has seldom been fully appreciated. Representing the age of revolution in America, he rose to leadership through bloody terror, which contrived a "Negro" problem for the Western Hemisphere, intensified and defined the anti-slavery movement, became one of the causes, and probably the prime one, which led Napoleon to sell Louisiana for a song, and finally, through the interworking of all these effects, rendered more certain the final prohibition of the slave trade by the United States in 1807."

W.E.B. DU BOIS

CHAPTER 13

ASANTE

RESISTANCE ON THE CONTINENT

CENTER YOUR VOCABULARY

▲ resistance

▲ collateral

AS YOU READ

Who were the leaders in the fight against the enslavement of Africans?

African leaders showed their resistance, or opposition, to the European Slave Trade in many different ways. Some kings, such as Ansah, ruler of the the Fante people of Ghana (1472-1484), monitored the numbers of European ships along the African coastline and tried to prevent them from coming ashore. Others did not permit Europeans in their kingdom, whereas in Benin, where they thought the Europeans were coming with evil intentions, the kings killed them on the spot. Still other kings, who initially welcomed the trade, later tried to stop it after they saw the problems it created in their kingdoms. These strong African leaders were able to discourage the European Slave Trade, though they were not able to stop it. The greed of the European slave traders and the greed of Africans who accompanied them on slave raids could not be stopped entirely.

Because most of the information we have about the resistance of Africans comes from European writers, it is certain that we do not know the full story of African resistance to the European Slave Trade. Yet, enough examples of displeasure and resistance on the part of Africans exist to demonstrate that enslavement was never universally accepted by Africans.

Nzenga Meremba, an African king who took the Christian name Affonso, tried to stop the trade in the Congo. Affonso had originally participated in the trade to receive technical and military support from Portugal for his nation. In exchange, he agreed to turn over his African prisoners of war to the Portuguese. The Portuguese demanded that Affonso send some of his most promising young men to Portugal as collateral, or a pledge, to guarantee his cooperation. Affonso believed that the young men would be educated as priests in Portugal and returned to the Congo to teach the Catholic doctrine. He kept his end of the agreement by supplying the Portuguese with African prisoners of war. He also allowed the Portuguese to set up churches in the Congo to convert the Congolese people to Catholicism. The Portuguese did not keep their end of the agreement. When Affonso wrote to Portugal asking for "two physicians and two apothecaries (pharmacists) and one surgeon." his request was denied. Repeated requests for aid in shipbuilding and carpentry were also turned down. Affonso later learned that the young men had been captured and sold as slaves in Portugal.

By 1526, Affonso began to realize the damage that the European Slave Trade was doing to his kingdom. He wrote to John III, who had succeeded King Manuel as ruler of Portugal, asking him to put an end to the slave trade in the Congo.

"Sir [you] should know how our Kingdom is being lost in so many ways. . . . This is caused by the excessive freedom given by your . . . officials to the men and merchants who are allowed to come to this Kingdom to set up shops with goods and many things which have been prohibited by us and which they spread throughout our Kingdoms and Domains in such an abundance that many of our vassals [servants], whom we had in obedience, do not comply because they have the things in greater abundance than we ourselves. . . . So it is doing a great harm not only to the service of God, but the security and peace of our Kingdoms and state. . . . We cannot reckon how great the damage is, since the above-mentioned merchants daily seize our subjects, sons of the land and sons of our noblemen and vassals and our relatives. . . . *It is our will that in these Kingdoms there should not be any trade in slaves nor markets for slaves.*"

In 1727, a Dahomean monarch, King Agadja (ah-GAH-jah), captured an Englishman who entered his kingdom with a slave-raiding party eager to capture Africans for the trade. After holding

Resistance In Western Africa

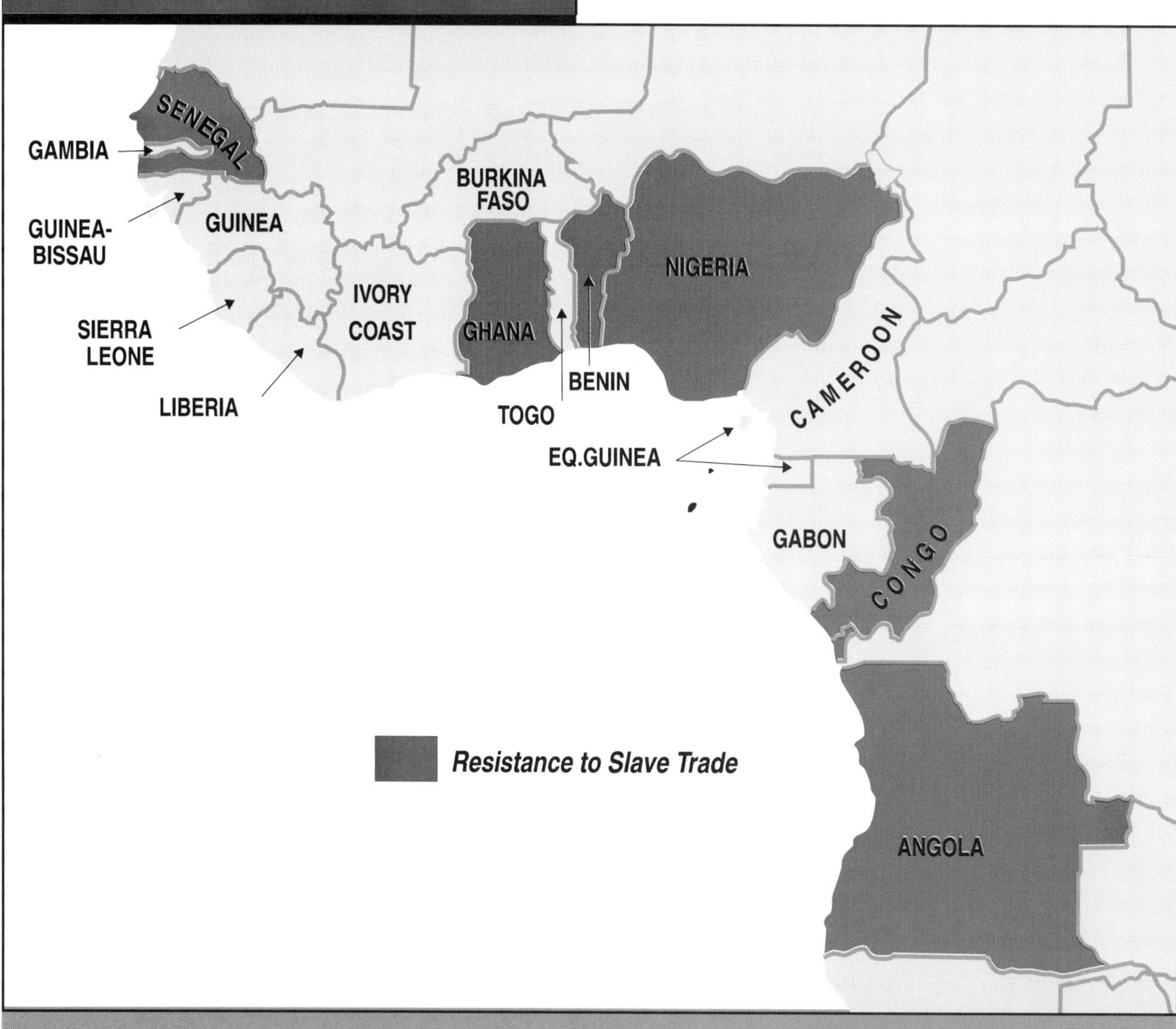

Map Skill: Resistance occurred throughout the continent. But which kinds of areas were hardest hit by slave traders? What impact do you think geography had on the trade and enslavement? Locate the areas of resistance. Where would you rather live, on the western coast of Africa or farther east?

the Englishman for several weeks while his crew pleaded for his life, Agadja released him on the condition that his crew return all of the Africans they had captured. Agadja also instructed the Englishman to warn the rulers of England that if any more slave-raiders were sent to his kingdom, they would be captured and killed.

A Senegalese ruler, the king of Almammy, passed a law in 1787 that made it illegal to take enslaved Africans through his kingdom. To emphasize his determination, he returned the presents French slave traders had sent to him as bribes.

Queen Nzingha of Angola waged a 30-year war against slave traders until the Portuguese negotiated a treaty with her in 1656. The treaty stayed in effect until her death in 1663.

▼ The army was prepared to capture and kill slave raiders who came to their kingdom.

◆ CENTER YOUR THINKING

1. Describe at least two ways that African leaders opposed the European Slave Trade.
2. Why did King Affonso support the European Slave Trade at first?
3. What were some of the tactics that European slave traders used to achieve their purposes?
4. Summarize the attitude of Africans in Africa to the European Slave Trade. Was enslavement widely accepted by Africans?
5. HOLISTIC ACTIVITY Students as Leaders

   In your small group, brainstorm a list of terms that describe true leadership. Discuss how the African rulers demonstrated their leadership during the years of the European Slave Trade. Finally, discuss and debate whether you think these same leadership qualities are as important today. Defend your group's thinking to the other groups.

CHAPTER 14

ASANTE

RESISTANCE AT SEA

CENTER YOUR VOCABULARY

- ▲ suicide
- ▲ revolt
- ▲ infanticide
- ▲ reconcile

AS YOU READ

What were the reasons that Africans practiced suicide and infanticide?

Enslaved Africans held in bondage on slave ships used whatever means they could to resist their captivity including escape, suicide, infanticide, and armed revolt. They did not reconcile themselves to the idea of enslavement.

One European slave trader, Theodore Canot, notes the measures that had to be taken to prevent suicide by starvation, a common means of resistance. "It is the duty of the guard to report immediately whenever a slave refuses to eat." Many Africans refused to eat in spite of being whipped and forced to eat. They preferred to starve themselves to death rather than be enslaved.

It is always a tragedy when someone chooses death over life. The Africans who took their own lives (suicide), killed their own babies (infanticide), or turned on their captors with weapons felt they had no choice.

Today, the circumstances under which people commit infanticide or suicide are different. There are many avenues available for help. In the 1800s, the Africans did what they could to resist enslavement. They were always looking and waiting for that one moment when they could strike out against their captors and escape.

A slave-ship's captain recalls other means of suicide. "A few days after departure, a slave leaped overboard . . . and another choked himself during the night." Another captain tells of a young woman who hung herself rather than submit to enslavement. Still another captain tells of the instance in which 20 Africans jumped overboard to their deaths, rejoicing that they had escaped enslavement as they slowly drowned.

With little more than makeshift weapons, African captives staged numerous revolts. John Cassuneuve, a slave-ship captain, tells of a revolt on his ship, the *Don Carlos*:

"About one in the afternoon, after dinner, we according to custom, caused them, one by one, to go down between decks, to have his pint of water; most of them were yet above deck, many of them provided with knives, which we had indiscreetly given them two or three days before . . . Others had pieces of iron they had torn off our forecastle door, as having premeditated a revolt. . . . They had also broken off the shackles from several of their companions' feet, which served them, as well as billets (wooden pillows) they had provided themselves with, and all other things they could lay hands on, which they imagined might be of use for their enterprise. Thus armed, they fell in crowds and parcels on our men, upon the deck unawares. . . . We stood in arms, firing on the revolted slaves . . . many of the most mutinous, leapt overboard, and drowned themselves in the ocean with much resolution."

John Newton, a slave-ship captain and author of many hymns including "How Sweet the Name of Jesus Sounds," noted that ". . . The men slaves are not easily reconciled to their confinement and treatment; and if attempted, they are seldom suppressed without considerable loss; and sometimes they succeed, to the destruction of a whole ship's company (Europeans) at once. . . . One unguarded hour, or minute, is sufficient to give the slave the opportunity they are always looking for."

Theodore Canot describes a revolt on his slave ship. "From the beginning there was manifest discontent among the slaves. . . .

▲ Africans revolt against the crew aboard a slave ship.

Suddenly . . . one fair afternoon . . . a simultaneous rush was made by the confined slaves at all the after-gratings, and amid the confusion they knocked down the guard and poured on deck. . . . The women . . . seconding the males . . . rose in a body, and the helmsman was forced to stab several with his knife before he could drive them below again. . . . The rebels were hot for fight to the last, and boldly defended themselves with their staves (sticks) against our weapons. . . .Their resistance was so prolonged and perilous, that we were obliged to disarm them (kill them) forever."

Nicholas Owen, another slave trader, recorded in his journal an attempt to recapture a ship after the Africans had revolted. He recalls "fighting a French ship who was taken by slaves, all the people killed save the captain and doctor who was ashore, but without success, for the slaves behaved so as to make us give over the attempt [to recapture the vessel] with loss on our side."

◆ CENTER YOUR THINKING

1. Tell at least three ways Africans resisted enslavement.
2. What is the author's opinion of forms of resistance that result in death, such as infanticide and suicide?
3. Retell, in your own words, the story of one of the slave revolts.
4. In your opinion, under what situations, if any, is suicide or infanticide a justifiable act?
5. HOLISTIC ACTIVITY Students as Researchers

   In the United States during the late 1800s, African American newspapers were published in major Northern cities such as New York City. With assistance from your school or local librarian, find and read examples of these, searching for articles on the Middle Passage. Report your findings to the class by making a group poster and adding your group's commentary.

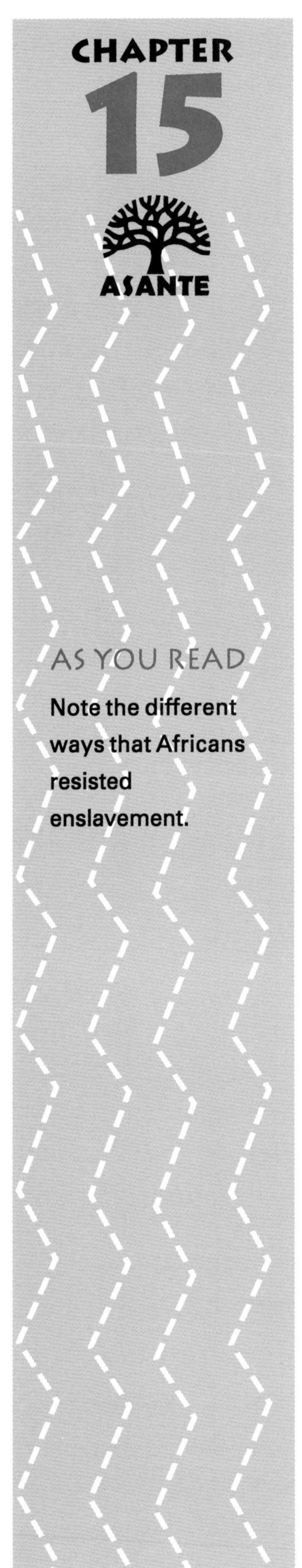

RESISTANCE IN THE AMERICAS

CENTER YOUR VOCABULARY

- ▲ insurrection
- ▲ uprising
- ▲ rebellion
- ▲ accord
- ▲ conspire
- ▲ redemption

African resistance to enslavement intensified when enslaved Africans landed in the colonies. No longer confined to the slave ships, the enslaved found greater opportunities for resistance and revolt. Between 1517 and 1533, enslaved Africans throughout the Americas staged frequent insurrections. By 1532, the Spanish even established a special police force, called *Cimarrones*, to try to recapture Africans who had run away to escape enslavement in the Americas. The African successes in escaping and avoiding recapture resulted in many new laws restricting the movements and actions of Africans in the Americas.

History records that Africans resisted enslavement regardless of the laws that were passed and the severe physical abuse. Revolts, insurrections, uprisings, rebellions—all terms that describe African resistance—signaled the extent of the Africans' desire to be free. Africans in Venezuela in 1517 felt the same human stirrings of resistance to enslavement that the Africans in Hispaniola, South Carolina, Puerto Rico, Colombia, Mexico, Panama, and Cuba felt when they mounted their attacks on the enslavers.

A proud group of Africans in the Danish Virgin Islands (purchased in 1917 by the United States for $50 million) demonstrated their courage in 1733 by revolting on the island of St. John and holding the island for several months before the rebellion was put down. The Danish abolished the slave trade in 1802 but refused to abolish enslavement until forced to do so by the brilliant rebel General Moses Buddhoe Gottlieb. He rode his horse up to the capital at around noon and demanded that the enslaved Africans be freed by 4 o'clock in the afternoon or else all whites would be killed. The governor of the Virgin Islands, Peter von Scholten, immediately proclaimed freedom for the enslaved Africans. Africans would continue to protest the conditions of the labor accords even after the end of the enslavement. One of them, Queen Mary Thomas, led a revolt in 1878 on the island of St. Croix to protest economic conditions. Much of the town of Frederiksted and the surrounding countryside was set afire. When the smoke vanished, the African laborers found new freedoms and new opportunities in the Virgin Islands.

REVOLTS IN THE COLONIES

Africans in the North American colonies asserted their right to freedom from the moment they arrived. Sometimes, they conspired, or plotted as a group, to resist their enslavement. More often, their resistance was individual because they were not allowed to form groups or communicate with each other. The Africans' determination to be free from enslavement and oppression inspired them to fight their oppressors at all cost.

COLONISTS FEAR AFRICAN RESISTANCE

The laws after 1660 expose the colonists' fear of African insurrection. The laws also show the extent of African resistance to enslavement because they were usually enacted as a response to acts of African rebellion.

Virginia passed an "Act for Preventing Negroes' Insurrections" in 1680, which "*prohibits Negroes from carrying clubs, staffs [sticks] or arms of any type. Lifting up a hand in opposition to any Christian is punishable by thirty lashes. A Negro runaway refusing*

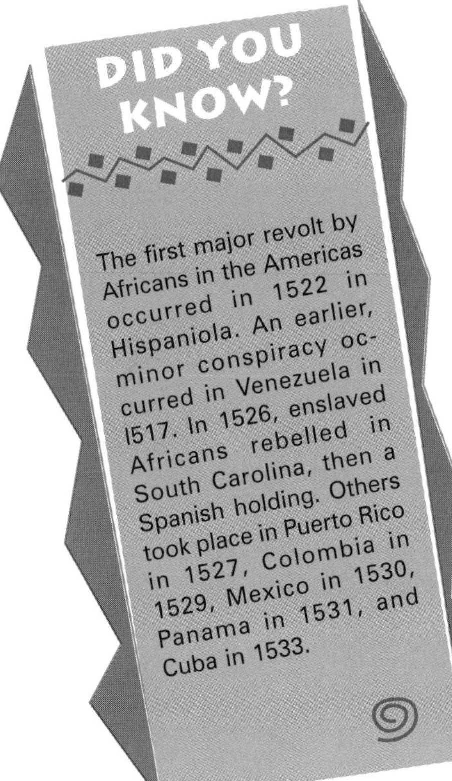

apprehension [capture] is punishable by death. Negro slaves must have a pass to leave the grounds of their owner."

In 1723 Virginia strengthened the law with a "Law for the Better Governing of Negroes, Mulattos, and Indians" which stated, *"Inasmuch as the present laws are found insufficient to restrain their tumultuous and unlawful meetings, or to punish the secret plots and conspiracies carried on amongst them . . . be it enacted . . . Conspiracy of five slaves or more is deemed a felony punishable by death. The punishment for minor crimes not deemed a felony is stated as follows: to have one ear nailed to the pillory, and there to stand for the space of one hour, and then the other ear nailed in like manner, and cut off."*

In Mississippi, an enslaved person could not beat drums or blow horns because of fear of African insurrections.

Africans were not allowed to gather without a white man being present. Only a white preacher or an African preacher who was monitored by a white man could conduct religious services.

Alarm swept through Europeans in the enslaving South in 1803 when the Haitians finally defeated the French army in the first

▲ Enslaved Africans led this revolt against the French army in Haiti in 1791.

complete overthrow of the enslavers in the Americas. All Africans looked with pride on the Haitian Revolution and saw in it their own redemption.

The Haitian Revolution began in 1791 when two religious leaders met with other enslaved Africans to plot their revolt against the French enslavers on the island. Their commitment to freedom was preached to others until there was a mass revolt led by the great general, Toussaint L'Ouverture.

Map of African Resistance

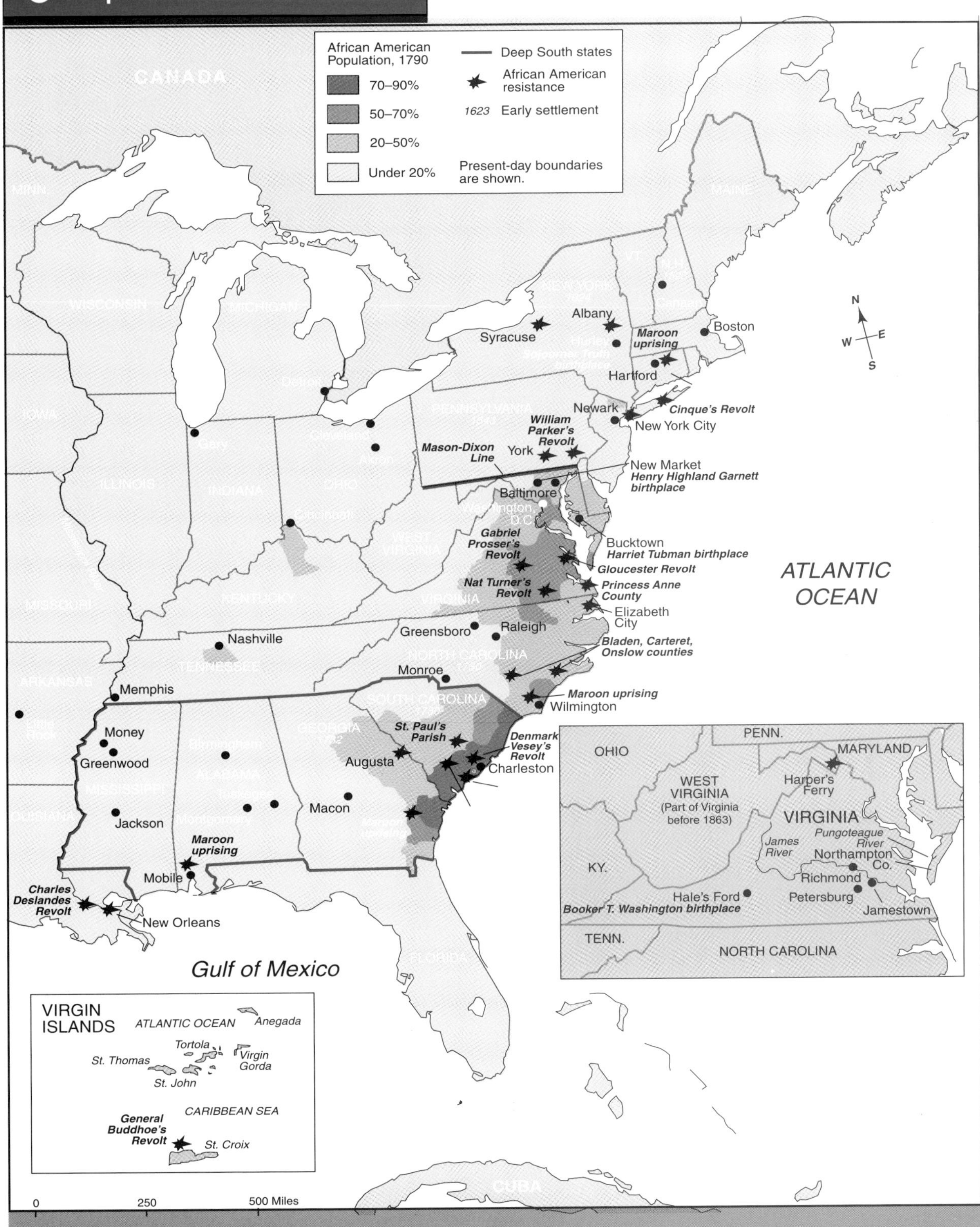

Map Skill:

Make a separate list of the areas of African American resistance from the map. Now group them according to the percentage of African Americans in the population. What pattern emerges? Are more located in the North or the South? Do you think that African Americans were strong resistors of enslavement in the Americas? Why?

African Resistance

1642	First recorded maroon community established in Virginia
1658	Africans and Native Americans rebel in Hartford, Connecticut
1663	Conspiracy between Africans and white indentured servants in Gloucester, Virginia
1672	African maroons in Virginia stage several revolts
1687	Conspiracy of Africans recorded in Virginia
1708	Africans revolt in New York
1712	Africans plot to kill whites in New York: 9 whites killed; 21 Africans executed, 6 Africans commit suicide
1720	Africans revolt in South Carolina
1722	Africans rebel in Virginia
1732	Africans mutiny in Louisiana
1739	Africans rise up in Charleston, South Carolina, and kill several whites in Stono River, South Carolina; Insurrection, led by Cato: 30 whites killed;
	African uprising in St. Johns Parish, South Carolina
1740	Uprisings in South Carolina; Conspiracy in New York City: African woman executed for committing arson
1741	Africans conspire to burn New York City: 13 Africans burned at the stake, 18 Africans hanged, 70 sold in the Caribbean
1744	Maroon uprising in South Carolina
1754	Two African females executed for arson in Charleston, South Carolina
1768	Maroons battle whites in South Carolina
1772	Maroons plunder areas of Georgia
1774	Africans revolt in Saint Andrews Parish, Georgia
1775	Five enslaved Africans conspire to poison whites in Maryland
	Two enslaved Africans conspire to poison whites in Virginia
1776	African woman executed for arson
1777	Africans petition Massachusetts legislature for end to enslavement of Africans
1779	Africans petition New Hampshire legislature for end to enslavement of Africans

◆ CENTER YOUR THINKING

1. Who were the *Cimarrones*?
2. What were some of the tactics used to prevent African rebellions?
3. How did Africans respond to the victory of Haitian Africans over the French army?
4. Why was African resistance more often individual rather than organized?
5. HOLISTIC ACTIVITY **Students as Writers of Historical Fiction** With a partner or small group, write a short story about a fictitious African leader who resists enslavement in Africa, on the Middle Passage, and then in America. Include as many historically accurate facts as possible, even though the people and events are ones you have made up. Share your story with the class.

SUGGESTED READINGS

Aptheker, Herbert, *American Negro Slave Revolts.* New York: International Publishers, 1943.

Bennett, Lerone. *Pioneers in Protest.* Baltimore, MD: Penguin Books, 1968.

Berry, Mary. *Black Resistance/White Law: A History of Constitutional Racism in America.* New York: Appleton-Century-Crofts, 1971.

Blassingame, John. *The Slave Community: Plantation Life in the Antebellum South.* New York: Oxford University Press, 1972.

Clinton, Catherine. *The Plantation Mistress.* New York: Pantheon, 1982.

Davis, Charles T., and Henry Louis Gates, Jr. *The Slave's Narrative.* New York: Oxford University Press, 1985.

Foner, Phillip. *History of Black Americans*. Westport, CT: Greenwood, 1975.

Herskovits, Melville. *The Myth of the Negro Past.* Boston: Beacon Press, 1958.

Higginson, Thomas. *Black Rebellion.* New York: Arno Press, 1889.

Winch, Julie. *Philadelphia's Black Elite.* Philadelphia: Temple University Press, 1988.

SUMMARY

Africans fought against the European Slave Trade. Many African leaders resisted the European slave traders and their African allies. Africans enslaved in the colonies also engaged in numerous rebellions against their condition. Africans in Haiti were successful in defeating the French army. *(Chapters 13, 14, and 15)*

Enslaved Africans used any available means to resist enslavement. Because European enslavement was so cruel, resistance took extreme forms, even suicide and infanticide. Many Africans who were being transported on slave ships jumped overboard to their deaths. *(Chapter 14)*

The large number of rebellions of African slaves increased the fears of the enslavers and resulted in numerous laws designed to minimize opportunities for African resistance. *(Chapter 15)*

99 Personal Witnessing

REFLECTION

Although this unit is about inhumaneness and cruelty, it is more importantly about resistance, survival, and leadership. Reflect on some of the following questions, and write about them in your journal.

- How do you exhibit leadership?
- Are you humane? Are you ever inhumane? How can you improve?
- How do you define *survival*?
- What are your personal goals for self-development?
- How does reading about the strength of character of enslaved Africans inspire you? What did you learn from their lives?

TESTIMONY

Your group has called in to a talk radio show to give your views on the topic: EVIDENCE IN MY CITY OF DEHUMANIZATION AND HOW WE CAN WIPE IT OUT. Everyone in the group should participate.

99 UNIT 5 RITE OF PASSAGE

One intent of Umfundalai is to learn as much about your family's ancestors as far back as possible. There are several different ways to learn. One way is to talk with your relatives and tape-record or write down their family stories and recollections. Another way is to do research through public records. Or, if you would have difficulty finding information about your ancestors, you may decide to research the ancestry of a historical figure who is a role model for you. Record the stories you find in your Rites of Passage portfolio.

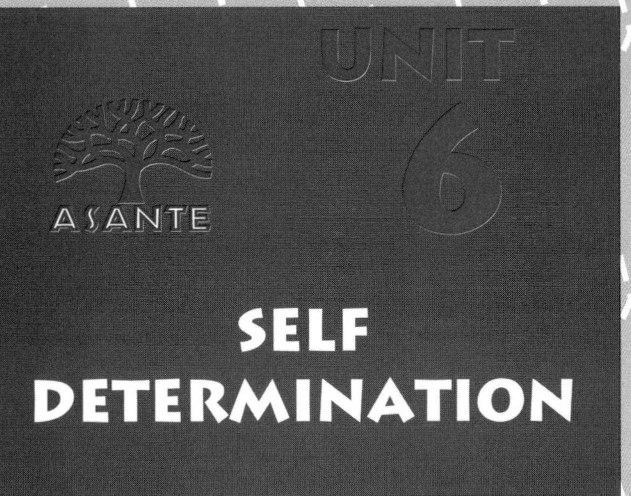

UNIT 6

SELF DETERMINATION

1750
Crispus Attucks escapes

C.E.

In small groups, write the word *freedom* on a piece of paper. Give your group two minutes in which to make a list of terms that come to mind when you see the word. Now, on another piece of paper, make three columns: *Enslaved Africans, Colonists,* and *Both*. Discuss your freedom list, and sort the terms from it into which of the three columns in which your group feels it should appear. Justify your choices and explain them to the class. Reevaluate your list after you have read this unit.

As you read Unit 6, remember that the colonists were living a great contradiction. They believed in freedom, but not for enslaved Africans. Have you ever witnessed similar discrimination? How can you guard against being guilty of this type of discrimination against others? against being discriminated against by others?

1770-1779
Africans petition their state legislatures for their freedom

1775
Africans fight at the Battle of Bunker Hill
Lord Dunmore promises freedom to enslaved African men who join the British Army.

Washington recruits free Africans as a result of Dunmore's offer

1787
Prince Hall founds African Lodge of Freemasons

1770
Crispus Attucks is killed in the Boston Massacre

1774
Africans in Boston conspire to free themselves with the help of the British

1783
Thousands of African loyalists are relocated to British colonies and Sierra Leone.

"We hold these truth to be self-evident, that ALL men are created equal, that they are endowed by their creator with certain unalienable RIGHTS, that among these are Life, Liberty and the pursuit of Happiness."

DECLARATION OF INDEPENDENCE

CHAPTER

16

ASANTE

REVOLUTION

CENTER YOUR VOCABULARY

- contest
- ideals
- assumption
- expatriate
- citizen
- abolitionist

AS YOU READ

In what ways did the Revolutionary War affect the enslavement of Africans?

Growing displeasure with British rule in the colonies led to a series of conflicts between the colonists and the British representatives who were sent to the American colonies to enforce British rule. When the colonists resisted, Great Britain responded with a show of force in 1775, setting the stage for the American Revolution. Africans found the Revolutionary War full of contradictions. America, at war with Britain to free itself, continued to enslave African people.

Africans were more concerned with the principles of freedom expressed in the Declaration of Independence than they were in freeing the colonists from British rule. Firmly committed to their own liberation, African men and women were moved by the new spirit of freedom that surrounded the colonies. They distinguished themselves on whatever front they thought offered them the best chance at liberation.

The efforts of African men and women helped the colonists win the war and achieve victory for the principles in the Declaration of Independence. Africans contested the narrow interpretation of the ideals that the American Revolution represented. They sought to expand the meaning of freedom and liberty to include people of all races. Had they been successful, the American nation would not have experienced the social revolutions that have troubled the making of our multi-cultural society and that continue even today.

THOMAS JEFFERSON

Some of the best-known American leaders enslaved Africans. Thomas Jefferson, a leading thinker and strong supporter of the war, was one of them. As a law student and a passionate supporter of human rights, Jefferson found it difficult to accept many of the assumptions, or underlying thoughts promoted as fact, that whites used to justify enslavement. Even though he was uncomfortable with the concept of enslavement, Jefferson didn't do anything to change it. To Africans, Jefferson's thinking represented the state of mind of 18th-century whites.

In the summer of 1774, Jefferson sat down to write about the hard work the colonists had put in to develop the land. America, he wrote, had been transformed by the colonists and now that progress was being made, Britain wanted to take complete control over the colonies. In actuality, Britain owned the colonies and as such had every right to assert its control. Nevertheless, the colonists disagreed and developed their own arguments in support of freedom from British rule.

Could not the Africans have said the same things about the colonists that Jefferson said about the British? After all, it was African labor that had cleared the land, planted the crops, constructed the houses, and built the factories that produced the profits that the colonists and Britain were fighting to control. Jefferson, however, was more concerned that the British had a plan to reduce the white colonists to "slavery" than he was with the colonists' enslavement of Africans. When he finally addressed the issue, it was easily resolved by blaming Britain's King George III for the enslavement of Africans. Jefferson was a very popular writer, and his works were read in all 13 colonies. In 1776, as the Virginia representative to the Continental Congress, he was given the job of writing the Declaration of Independence. Benjamin Franklin (Pennsylvania), Robert Livingston

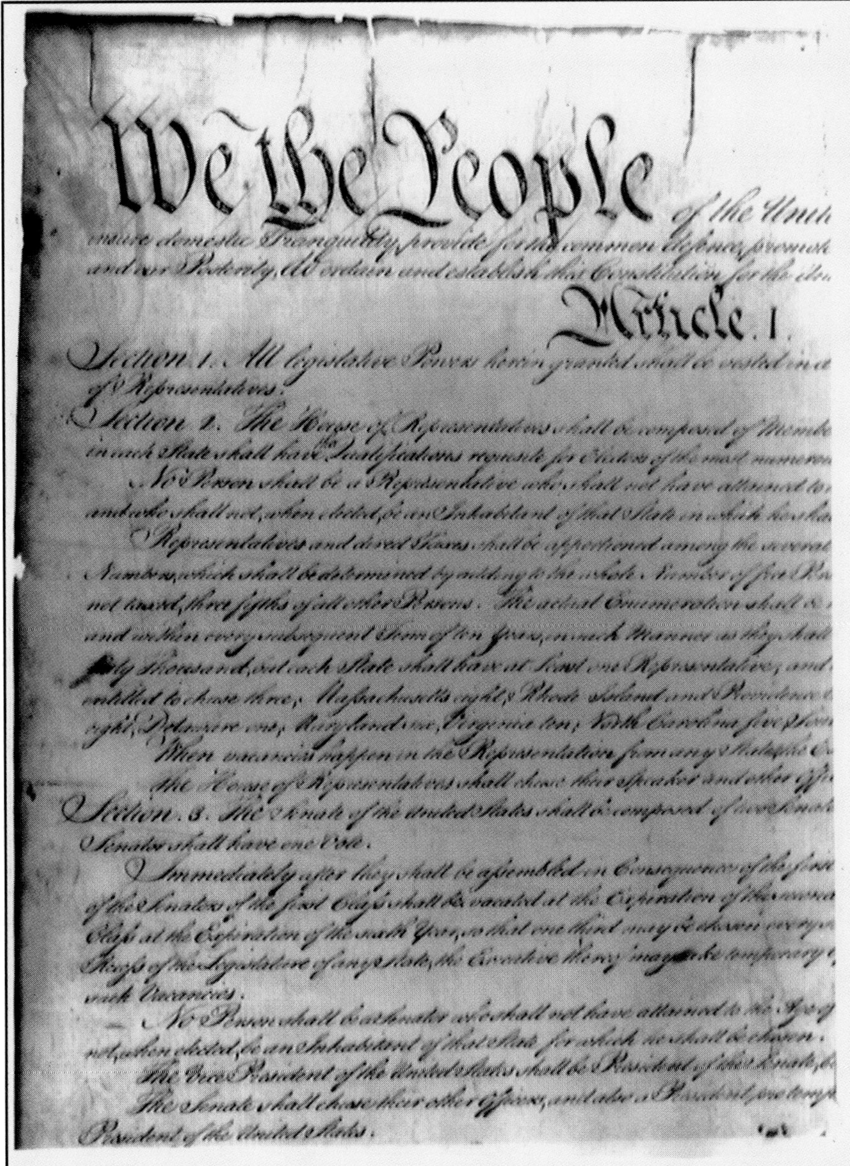
We the People

Article. 1.

Section. 1.

Section. 2.

Section. 3.

▲ The Declaration of Independence

(New York), John Adams (Massachusetts), and Roger Sherman (Connecticut) were assigned to work with him. But in the end, the document was principally Jefferson's.

The Declaration of Independence asserts that *all* men are created equal with certain unquestionable human rights. One of these rights is liberty; yet Africans were not free. Africans contested the American Revolution and all it stood for because it excluded them.

Jefferson was painfully aware of the omission of any reference to African enslavement in the Declaration of Independence. He wrote, "I tremble for my country when I reflect that God is just; that his justice cannot sleep forever." Jefferson's solution to the African presence in the United States was to expatriate, or banish, them to other countries. He reflected on the problem of race in this fashion: "Deep-rooted prejudices entertained by the whites; ten thousand recollections, by the blacks, of the injuries they have sustained; new provocations; the real distinctions which nature has made; and many other circumstances, will divide us into parties and produce convulsions, which will probably never end but in the extermination of the one or the other race."

In his autobiography, Thomas Jefferson wrote that King George III ". . . has waged cruel war against human nature itself. Violating its most sacred rights of life and liberty in the persons of a distant people, who never offended him, captivating and carrying them into slavery in another hemisphere. . . ." Without this passage or any other comparable passage against the enslavement, the Declaration of Independence succeeded in ignoring the evils of enslavement.

Even today, the United States is still struggling with the problems of race as defined by Thomas Jefferson, who was not persuaded by his own logic to free the Africans who were enslaved on his plantation.

A WAR OF CONTRADICTIONS

Africans served in the Continental Army against British troops, even though they were not acknowledged as citizens or equals in a land that enslaved some and oppressed all of them. Because they were not yet American citizens, entitled from birth to the same rights as whites, enslaved Africans found it difficult, if not impossible, to identify with the concerns of their oppressors.

To understand how Africans must have felt at that time, imagine that you are suffering from a life-threatening disease and have been told by your doctor you could die at any time. If war broke out tomorrow, what thoughts would be uppermost in your mind? Your responses to this question will be as varied as those of the enslaved Africans.

Some Africans saw an opportunity for their own personal freedom. They assumed that the colonists would make the same slogans about the freedom they wanted for themselves come true for Africans, so they gave service to the revolutionary cause. They fought with the Patriots, the colonists in the Continental Army who fought against the British. Others in the enslaved African community did not believe that the colonists would ever grant them their freedom. These Africans joined the Loyalists, people who were fighting on Britain's behalf. The Lcyalists promised at the outset to free the "slaves" of Patriots who fought on their side.

The Patriots were at a disadvantage against the Loyalists who were more experienced soldiers with better training and more equipment. Many of the Patriots had never fought in battle. They grew discouraged as the war dragged on. In some areas, Patriot generals could not find enough colonists to enlist in the Continental Army. The Patriots, particularly those in the Deep South, reluctantly turned to enslaved Africans to help fill this gap.

AFRICANS AND THE PATRIOTS

At first, General George Washington, the commander-in-chief of the Continental Army, would not let Africans enlist on the Patriot side. A huge shortage of white soldiers forced him to change his mind. The Rhode Island Regiment of Black Soldiers, which was made up of 400 enslaved Africans, was formed in 1778 because the colony did not have enough white soldiers to meet the Continental Army's request. The colony's leaders decided that any African who volunteered to serve would be declared free and would be entitled to the same wages as a white soldier. Several other colonies followed Rhode Island's lead.

Instead of an avalanche of jubilant Africans rushing to take advantage of the promised freedom, the call for African Patriots produced only a trickle of interest among the enslaved in other colonies. At the start of the American Revolution, there were 2.5 million people in the colonies. Africans, most of whom were enslaved, represented 20 percent of the population. Yet only an estimated 1 percent, or 5,000 Africans, served on the Patriot side for the entire seven years of the war. The majority of enslaved Africans did not enlist on the Patriot side because they knew they were not welcome.

The Southern colonies were even more reluctant than the Northern colonies to allow Africans to serve. Well into the war, Georgia continued to refuse to arm Africans. Service on the Patriot side was no guarantee of freedom for Africans. Many remained in bondage or were reenslaved after the war.

There were three African units in the Continental Army: the Rhode Island Regiment, the Massachusetts regiment, and a third unit sent by the French from Haiti. All three units suffered with the white soldiers at Valley Forge in the winter of 1777-1778 during the worst months of the war. The Loyalists forced Washington's army to pull back to the small Pennsylvania town of Valley Forge. Food and supplies were limited. Severe snow and ice storms added to their hardship. Nevertheless, the Continental Army, including 400 African soldiers, went on to defeat the British and the Hessians (German soldiers for hire) at the Battle of Rhode Island in 1778. The Rhode Island Regiment of Black Soldiers distinguished itself in five other battles, including Yorktown, which led to Britain's surrender.

The Haitian volunteers included many who would later lead their own country's revolution in 1791. Among the most famous were Martial Besse, Jean-Baptiste Belley, and Henri Christophe, Haiti's future king. General Besse, who had been wounded in a battle in Savannah, Georgia, during the American Revolution, returned to the United States in 1797 as a representative of the Haitian government on official business. Ironically, when he arrived in Charleston, South Carolina, in full military dress, he was stopped by U.S. authorities. They forced him to post a bond, a requirement to enter the state. South Carolina required that all "blacks" coming into the state post a bond, usually cash, to discourage free Africans from visiting. Evidently, Americans in South Carolina had very short memories and even less gratitude for the brave efforts of the Haitians.

FREE AFRICANS

At the start of the war, there were sizable populations of Africans who had escaped from bondage, were born free, had received their freedom in the wills of their enslavers, or arrived in the colonies as free people, usually as shipmen, from Europe, Africa, or the Caribbean. Fully convinced that the War of Independence was a turning point for a better future, these Africans gave their support to the organizations and activities that they felt would liberate their fellow Africans.

The War of Independence gave these Africans an opportunity to lead discussions about African liberty. Almost no records remain of the discussions that Africans must have had over these issues. The degree of African participation in the war demonstrates that Africans were passionate about their freedom.

How did Africans try to get America to live up to its ideals? Africans made it a point of duty to serve with exceptional dedication and courage. Several free Africans fought with distinction on the Patriot side. Prince Easterbrook was the first to enlist. He was wounded in the battle of Lexington and Concord in Massachusetts. Salem Poor fought with distinction at Bunker Hill. Peter Salem, another freeman, killed British Major Pitcairn at Bunker Hill. His accomplishments in battle became well known, and popular poems were written about them.

An African freeman from Virginia, William Flora, served heroically, holding back the British at the bridge over Elizabeth River in Norfolk. After the war, Flora prospered as a property owner and businessperson. He later purchased the freedom of his wife and son. Again, the irony of a new, free nation that kept enslavement as a system was evident. In spite of African bravery in the Revolutionary War, the great majority of Africans were still enslaved.

James Forten, who was to become one of the wealthiest African Americans in the country and a foremost abolitionist, a person in favor of ending enslavement, was another freeman who served the Patriot cause. During the war, he worked as a powder boy loading large cannons on a battleship. The ship was captured by the British, and Forten was imprisoned for seven months before being released.

AFRICANS AND THE BRITISH CAUSE

When Dunsmore, a British Lord, promised to free the "slaves" of Patriots if they would fight on the British side, thousands of Africans fled their Patriot enslavers and joined the British. The promise of freedom did not extend to those Africans enslaved by the British Loyalists, only those enslaved by the Patriots. Dunsmore formed an "Ethiopian Regiment" of African soldiers who wore the insignia "Liberty to Slaves" across their breasts. They were a brave company of Loyalist troops who were motivated by their desire to be free.

They often left their wives and children to join the British in fighting against the Patriots, whom they saw as defenders of enslavers.

The *Virginia Gazette*, a newspaper, appealed to enslaved Africans not to join the British. Patrick Henry, famous for his speech, "Give me liberty or give me death," called Dunsmore's move "fatal to the public safety." Patrols were stepped up to prevent Africans from joining the British. Virginians issued a proclamation giving pardons to runaway Africans who returned to their enslavers. It also warned Africans that the penalty for rebellion was death. The Virginia Proclamation was not successful. Many Africans believed that their enslavement was worse than death.

The prospect of freedom drove thousands of Africans over to the British side, especially from South Carolina and Georgia. At the end of the war, they were evacuated to the British colonies of Florida, Jamaica, and Nova Scotia, Canada, as well as to the British territories in Africa. Instead of finding the freedom they had been promised, many Africans were reenslaved in the new territories.

CRISPUS ATTUCKS: A TRAGIC HERO

The first person to fall in the 1770 Boston Massacre which started the American War of Independence was an African. His name was Crispus Attucks. He worked on the docks of the Boston harbor.

Crispus Attucks had fled bondage in 1750, he escaped from William Brown of Framingham, Massachusetts, and was never recaptured. John Adams, a Bostonian agitator who wrote articles in the Boston newspapers against the British and was later to become the second president of the United States in 1797, said that Crispus Attucks was one of a strange group of African and Irish dockworkers dressed in outlandish clothes. Adams focused his attacks on Attucks. He said, "Attucks' very looks were enough to terrify any person." Perhaps Adams was not used to seeing working-class people, particularly Africans, defying the orders of anyone, especially the British authorities.

> *"Ran away from his Master William Brown of Framingham . . . a Molatto Fellow, about 27 years of age, named Crispas 6 feet 2 inches high, short curled hair, his knees nearer together than common; had on a light coloured bearskin coat, plain brown fustian jacket, or brown all-wool one, new buckskin breeches, blue yarn stockings, and a checked woollen shirt. Whosoever shall take up said runaway, and convey him to his abovesaid master, shall have ten pounds . . . and all necessary charges paid. And all masters of vessels [ships] and others, are hereby cautioned against concealing or carrying off said servant on penalty of the law."*
>
> **Boston Gazette**

Despite Adams's biting remarks, this former enslaved African later became a symbol of the revolutionary spirit of the colonists because he was the first person to die in the War of Independence. However, to African Americans, Attucks is a tragic figure because he died fighting for a cause that did not include his freedom or the freedom of his people. This would be an agonizing pattern that would repeat itself in almost every U. S. war. Africans could fight as soldiers to protect the rights of whites, but they could not fight to defend their own rights. Indeed, Africans with thoughts of self-defense, liberation, and freedom would be branded as troublemakers and social outcasts. Yet, always burning deeply in the bosom of African Americans has been the idea of self-determination. It is a dream that has never died.

▲ On March 5, 1770, Crispus Attucks became the first man to die in the fight for freedom.

▲ The Boston Massacre was one of the events that led to the Revolutionary War.

◆ CENTER YOUR THINKING

1. Why did Africans play a role in the Revolutionary War?
2. How did Africans support the British side? How did they support the colonists' side?
3. What was Thomas Jefferson's solution to the African presence in the United States?
4. What was the contradiction between the ideals expressed by the colonists in the American Revolution and their treatment of Africans?
5. HOLISTIC ACTIVITY Students as Playwrights

   In this chapter, you read about the contradictory behavior of the colonists. They demanded their own freedom but denied freedom to Africans. In small groups, write a brief play about human contradictions. Present characters in situations that illustrate contradictions between what they say and what they do. Perform your play for the class or school.

CHAPTER 17

ASANTE

"WE EXPECT GREAT THINGS"

CENTER YOUR VOCABULARY

- petition
- sarcastic
- amendment
- redress
- civil rights
- activism

AS YOU READ

What were the ideals that colonists fought for during the Revolutionary War? How were these ideals linked to the enslavement of Africans?

The Declaration of Independence and the colonists' break with Great Britain increased Africans' demands for rights and freedom in the colonies. Between 1770 and 1779, Africans sent thousands of petitions, or formal requests, for freedom to colonial governors and legislators. Petitions and cases were most often brought on behalf of Africans by sympathetic whites who recognized the contributions that Africans had made to the war effort and were willing to demonstrate their belief in the equality of Africans by supporting African freedom. The majority of whites, however, feared that Africans, if given the opportunity to realize their full potential, would compete with them for jobs and economic advancement. To prevent this, whites made a deliberate effort to tighten the social, political, and economic chains on the African community.

Enslaved Africans made sure that their petitions were made public in an effort to increase public support for African freedom. The petitioners tried to appeal to the consciences of whites. Most petitions were unsuccessful, however, because the colonial governors and legislatures refused to consider the petitions of people they did not regard as citizens. Africans pressed their case because they believed that the time was ripe to sow the fertile seeds of African freedom in the minds of whites who were consumed with discussions of white liberty.

In January 1773, a petition for freedom went to the governor of Massachusetts from a group of enslaved Africans asking for freedom. This petition made it obvious that the enslaved did not accept their enslavement. According to the petition, the enslaved were a people who were legally prevented from enjoying "*LIFE ITSELF*." They wrote: "We have no property! We have no wives! No children! We have no city! No country!"

Three months later, another petition took the white colonists to task for enslaving Africans: "We expect great things from men who have made such a noble stand against the designs of their fellow-men to enslave them." The Africans asked for permission to work one day a week for themselves so that they could save money and purchase their freedom. They wanted to leave Massachusetts to settle in Africa. This was nearly 15 years before the Sierra Leone colony was set up by the British in 1787 and 49 years before Liberia was established by the American Colonization Society to settle free Africans in Africa. Yet already it was clear that some Africans felt they did not have a future in America.

In June of the same year, a similar petition was sent to the governor of Massachusetts. Interestingly, the tone of this petition is more sarcastic than most:

"On behalf of all those who by divine permission are held in a state of slavery, within the bowels of a free country. . . . Your petitioners apprehend they have in common with other men a natural right to be free and without molestation to enjoy such property as they may acquire by their industry, or by any other means not detrimental to their fellow men . . ."

In 1774, yet another petition, sounding very much like the Declaration of Independence, was sent to the governor of Massachusetts. The petittion was a bold reminder to the state legislature that the petitioners were a "freeborn" people who were entitled to the same rights as whites. This petition was sent again,

▲ Prince Hall

“ *[Following] the laudable example of the good people of these states your petitioners have long and patiently waited the event of petition after petition. . . . They cannot but express their astonishment that it have never been considered that every principle from which America has acted in the course of their unhappy difficulties with Great Britain pleads stronger than a thousand arguments that they may be restored to the enjoyments of that which is the natural right of all men.*”

Prince Hall
Petition to the Massachusetts Legislature

one month later, with an addition asking for a portion of the unimproved land in the province of Massachusetts. The petitioners wanted to settle on this land and start their own community. The state legislature ignored their request.

Prince Hall, who founded the African Lodge of Freemasons in 1787, signed a petition that was sent to the Massachusetts legislature six months after the Declaration of Independence. The petitioners expressed their surprise that the new Americans, of all people, would delay their request for freedom.

A group of 19 free Africans, who lost their freedom in New Hampshire, demanded in 1779 that the state restore their freedom. The group included Prince Whipple, who had crossed the Delaware in 1776 in the same boat with George Washington. Whipple and the others called themselves “natives of Africa” who had been “born free.” They demanded their freedom “for the sake of justice, humanity, and the rights of mankind” because “the God of nature gave them life and freedom, upon the terms of the most perfect equality with other men; That freedom is an inherent right of the human species, not to be surrendered but by consent . . .; That private or public tyranny and slavery are alike detestable to minds conscious of the equal dignity of human nature. . . . ”

Prince Whipple was born free in Africa and sent by his parents during the 18th century to study in America. The captain of the ship that brought him and his cousin to Baltimore seized them and sold them into enslavement. General Whipple, a white New Hampshire colonist who served as an aide to George Washington, bought Prince as his servant. The famous painting by Emanuel Leutze of Washington crossing the Delaware in a rowboat shows Prince Whipple at the oars.

SOME PETITIONS ARE APPROVED

By the early 1780s, enslaved Africans saw some progress in the legal system. In 1783, Belinda, a 70-year old African woman who had been captured in Africa when she was 12, successfully petitioned

“ Your petitioners apprehend we have in common with all other men a natural right to our freedoms without being deprived of them by our fellow men as we are a freeborn people and have never forfeited this blessing by any compact or agreement whatever. But we are unjustly dragged by the cruel hand of power from our dearest friends and some of us stolen from the bosoms of our tender parents and from a populous pleasant and plentiful country and brought hither to be made slaves for life in a Christian land. Thus we are deprived of everything that hath a tendency to make life even tolerable, the endearing ties of husband and wife we are strangers to. . . . Our children are also taken from us by force and sent many miles from us. . . . Thus our lives are imbittered. ”

Petition to the Massachusetts Legislature, 1774

the Massachusetts legislature for money. She wanted an allowance because she was too old to work and her owner had abandoned her to starve. The legislature voted to award her a small allowance for living.

Another woman, Elizabeth Freeman, also known as Mum Bett, won a lawsuit against her enslaver, Colonel John Ashley, in 1781. In her suit, Freeman stated that the Bill of Rights applied to her. The Bill of Rights is made up of ten amendments, or additions, to the Constitution that spell out in detail the freedoms of all Americans. Although her husband had been killed fighting in the Revolutionary War, the enslaver for whom she had worked all her life did not see fit to free her. She was very aware of the slogans of liberty being voiced by white colonists and the work of free Africans who were using the same language of freedom and equality to secure equal rights for Africans. Mum Bett was awarded her freedom because she had made her case that her husband was a Revolutionary War hero. What if she had been unable to make her case because of illiteracy or fear? Mum Bett was certainly not the only African woman whose husband had died in the war. The war made widows of many African women who did not have the knowledge of the methods of redress, or compensation, that Mum Bett had.

Enslaved Africans sought redress through the legal system, even though it excluded them, because they felt they were entitled to basic civil rights, or the rights of personal liberty. When these attempts failed, Africans resorted to other means of resistance such as conspiracy, flight, and revolt.

Most of the petitions were unsuccessful because Africans, as noncitizens, were appealing to a system in which they had no power. Still, enslaved Africans pressed on. In the process, they established a tradition of African American civil-rights activism, where they played an active role in fighting for freedom.

◆ CENTER YOUR THINKING

1. Who was Prince Hall?
2. What was the result of most of the petitions brought by enslaved Africans?
3. Describe one petition that was successful.
4. How did the American Revolution bring about a new movement for the freedom of enslaved Africans?
5. HOLISTIC ACTIVITY Students as Political Activists

   After the signing of the Declaration of Independence, African Americans increased their demands for freedom and sent thousands of petitions to colonial governors and legislators. In small groups, choose one example of a petition that was sent. Rewrite it in today's language, and change it to address a modern situation that your group wishes to see changed. Share your message with the class, making sure that it is impassioned and convincing.

SUGGESTED READINGS

Bibb, Henry. *Narrative of the Life and Adventures of Henry Bibb, an American Slave.* New York: Publilshed by Author, 1849.

Blassingame, John, ed. *Slave Testimony.* Baton Rouge: Louisiana State University Press, 1977.

Blockson, Charles. *The Underground Railroad.* New York: Prentice Hall, 1987.

Grimes, William. *Narrative of Events in the Life of William Grimes.* New Haven: Published privately, 1855.

Hayden, William. *Narrative of William Hayden.* Cincinnati: Published by the Author, 1846.

Mars, James. *Life of James Mars, a Slave.* Hartford, Connecticut: Lockwood Press, 1864.

Mellon, James, ed. *Bullwhip Days: The Slaves Remember.* New York: Weidenfield & Nicholson Press, 1988.

Olmstead, Frederick. *Journey in the Seaboard Slave States.* New York: Mason, 1859.

Quarles, Benjamin. *The Negro in the American Revolution.* Chapel Hill, NC: University of North Carolina Press, 1961.

Quarles, Benjamin. *The Negro in the Making of America.* New York: Collier, 1964.

SUMMARY

Africans fought in the Revolutionary War on both sides—the Patriots and the Loyalists. Africans hoped that their efforts would be rewarded by an end to enslavement. Their efforts helped the colonists to win the war. *(Chapter 16)*

The ideals championed in the war—individual freedom and human rights—did not apply to enslaved Africans. Many of the foremost champions for liberty—Thomas Jefferson, Patrick Henry, and John Adams—denied the right of Africans to live as free human beings. *(Chapter 16)*

Africans were optimistic that the ideals expressed by the colonists might lead to the end of enslavement. For the first time, Africans such as Prince Hall began to use formal legal structures to advance their case. Africans made a number of petitions to governors, legislatures, and courts. Several of these petitions were successful. *(Chapter 17)*

PERSONAL WITNESSING

REFLECTION

In their petitions for freedom, some enslaved Africans pointed out the contradiction between the colonists' Christian beliefs and their enslavement of African people. Understanding that religion is a personal, private matter, explore your feelings about religious and moral values in your journal. What is important to you? How do you get strength? How was the religion of the colonists different from the Africans'?

TESTIMONY

Imagine that you are Mum Bett or Prince Hall and that you must speak to your state legislature to defend your petition for freedom. Develop an effective, emotional speech. Have one member of your group present it to the class, or perform it as a group oral presentation.

UNIT 6 RITE OF PASSAGE

Nguzo Saba is a value system based on traditional African life and created for African Americans in the 1960s by Maulana Karenga. The seven principles of Nguzo Saba are the basis for the celebration of Kwanzaa, a seven-day family and community ritual, with each day focusing on understanding and applying one principle in your life.

Review the seven principles and your weekly and monthly applications in the Nguzo Saba section of your Rites of Passage portfolio. Evaluate your own strengths and weaknesses, and make a plan to improve in the seven principle areas. Continue keeping a record of your progress.

Your class may wish to hold a Kwanzaa celebration, even though the seven days of Kwanzaa are celebrated while most schools are closed for holiday, from December 26 through January 1. Research Kwanzaa celebrations, and prepare your class celebration, focusing on the seven important principles of Nguzo Saba, that you wish to make part of your individual Rite of Passage.

UNIT 7

FREEDOM FIGHTERS

C.E.

- **1739-1841** Africans revolt
- **1800** South Carolina rules that free Africans will be reenslaved if captured in South Carolina
- **1808** Britain makes it illegal for their citizens to participate in the European Slave Trade in West Africa and attempts to suppress it across the Atlantic Ocean
- **1825** Frances Ellen Watkins Harper is born in Baltimore, Maryland
- **1827** *Freedom's Journal*, first African American newspaper, published.
- **1829** David Walker publishes his *Appeal to the Colored Citizens of the World*

In small groups, debate both sides of redemptive violence versus nonviolence as though you were 18th-century African freedom fighters. In this unit, the term *redemptive violence* describes violence used in self-defense against enslavement and racism. Some African freedom fighters used redemptive violence, while others believed that Africans could gain freedom through persuasive nonviolence and moral arguments. Time your debate, and let the class vote on the most effective argument.

As you read Unit 7, think about what liberty means to you and your life. How does liberty relate to freedom and self-determination? What do you think of people who are willing to endanger their own lives to fight for liberty?

1843
Henry Highland Garnet publishes *An Address to the Slaves of he United States of America*

1847
Frederick Douglass publishes *The North Star* newspaper

1849
Harriet Tubman escapes enslavement and settles in Philadelphia

1850
Harriet Tubman makes more than 19 trips from the South to free enslaved Africans

1851
Sojourner Truth gives her famous *Ain't I a Woman* speech in Akron, Ohio

1860
Harriet Jacobs publishes her narrative, *Incidents in the Life of a Slave Girl*

1872
William Still publishes *The Underground Railroad*

> *"Let not those who have never been placed in like circumstances [enslavement], judge me harshly. Until they have been chained and beaten—until they find themselves in the situation I was, borne away from home and family toward a land of bondage—let them refrain from saying what they would not do for liberty."*
>
> FREDERICK DOUGLASS

CHAPTER

18

ASANTE

VIOLENCE AND FORCE

CENTER YOUR VOCABULARY

▲ defiance

▲ antebellum

▲ maroon

▲ militant

AS YOU READ

What is the role of law in society? Read for ways that the law worked against Africans in America.

By the beginning of the 19th century, Africans had two examples of violent resistance to oppression from which they could draw inspiration and hope. The first was the American War of Independence, and the second was the Haitian Revolution. Both of these struggles suggested that the only way to overthrow oppression was to carry on a constant battle against dehumanization and victimization.

Frederick Douglass said in 1846:

"Men do not go into slavery naturally—they don't go into slavery at the bidding of their fellowmen—they don't bow down their necks to the yoke merely by being entreated to do so . . . NO! Something else is necessary—the whip must be there—the chain must be there—the gag must be there—the thumb screw must be there—the fear of death must be there, in order to induce the slave to go to the field and labour for another man without wages."

Individual acts of defiance were probably the most self-empowering means of resistance for Africans. This form of resistance did not require the consent or organization of others. It allowed individuals to stand up for themselves against their oppressors. The enslaved often fought the enslavers physically, using their fists and clubs as weapons, or silently by poisoning their meals. These defiant Africans who dared to defend themselves were greatly feared by the

▲ Frederick Douglass

enslavers. When they were prevented from retaliating physically, enslaved Africans bravely endured agonizing whippings and other savage forms of torture. The goal of the enslaver was to make Africans submit to control. The goal of the defiant African was to resist being controlled. In defiance, Africans cut off their own fingers and performed other acts of self-mutilation to make themselves less useful to the enslavers. Each act of resistance sent a clear message to the enslavers that the enslaved were slaves by force, not by choice.

Africans fought their enslavement where they knew it would hit the enslavers hardest: economically. The enslaved conducted work slowdowns, started fires, committed theft, destroyed equipment and livestock, and did other things to make their enslavement unprofitable.

Perhaps the most effective form of resistance was escape. By escaping, Africans hurt enslavers economically by denying them the free use of enforced labor. Imagine how much money was lost by enslavers when Harriet Tubman, a former enslaved person, helped more than 300 enslaved Africans escape.

Later, when Africans were allowed to purchase their freedom and the freedom of their families, they endured tremendous hardships to do so because they knew that an independent African was the best argument against the false notion that Africans could not control their own lives.

The growing body of documentation of the use of torture and harsh physical punishment for "disobedient" Africans tells us something important: Africans did not accept their enslavement. The image of the submissive, or obedient, African was a figment of white wishful thinking. The very tools of enslavement—the instruments of torture, the bloodhounds, maimings (crippling) and executions, slave patrols, the use of force (including federal troops) to oppress Africans and maintain enslavement as an established system—all verify African resistance. The antebellum (before the Civil War) diaries, letters and journals, especially of Southern planters and slave traders, reveal the fear most whites felt toward the Africans they enslaved. That fear was justified because African resistance was very real.

" *When slaves volunteered, as hundreds did . . . during the American Revolution and . . . gained their freedom, that was a form of resistance. When slaves broke tools, destroyed harnesses and fences, were 'unable' to learn this or that technique, cut off their fingers, took their own lives (or the lives of their children), these were forms of resistance . . . When slaves, in tens of thousands of cases, attacked overseers and masters (and at times their families) with clubs and knives and bare hands, that was resistance. When, in preparing food, they added poison to the pot . . . When the 'carelessness' of slaves with fire . . . led insurance companies to charge more for premiums in the South than in the North, that was resistance.* "

Herbert Aptheker

One group of Africans who were especially feared by whites were the maroons. Maroons were militant Africans who escaped from enslavement and formed armed camps. They were among the earliest supporters of the use of violence to achieve liberation. In fact, between 1672 and 1864, about 50 fugitive maroon communities existed in the swamps of Georgia, South Carolina, Louisiana, Florida, Mississippi, and North Carolina. So fearful were the whites of African maroon communities that they urged their leaders to create laws controlling both the free African population and the African runaways.

The most revealing reaction to African resistance was the legislative response to African revolts. Legislators created new laws and amended slave statutes, or laws, to stiffen the penalties for African resistance. As the laws were tightened, the African freedom fighters took comfort in the knowledge that their violent protests for freedom gave them a sense of pride and the hope that someday they would overcome the odds. Despite the hardship and the obstacles that prevented Africans from breaking free, enslaved Africans demonstrated that human beings can maintain their dignity and self-worth in the most oppressive conditions. Their inspiration never wavered and they never gave up.

▼ These brutal forms of punishment were not enough to end African resistance to enslavement.

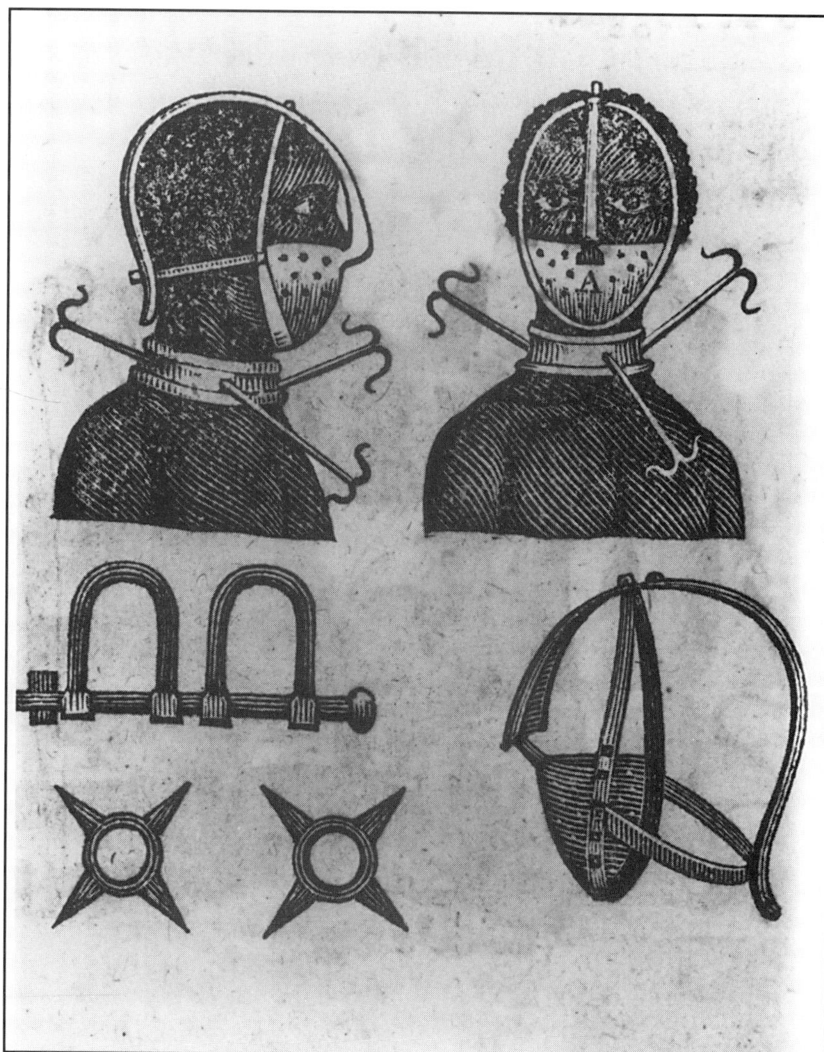

◆ CENTER YOUR THINKING

1. What were several ways that Africans resisted enslavement?
2. Who were the maroons?
3. Reread the quote by Frederick Douglass. What did he say caused a person to "go into slavery?"
4. According to the text, what was the reaction of African freedom fighters to the laws that stiffened penalties for resistance?
5. HOLISTIC ACTIVITY Students as Artists

   In small groups, create posters or stories of brave resistance by Africans. Include explanatory sentences or a story line to explain your creations.

CHAPTER 19

ASANTE

FREEDOM FIGHTERS

CENTER YOUR VOCABULARY

- ▲ redemptive violence
- ▲ freedom fighters
- ▲ resilience
- ▲ indiscriminate

AS YOU READ

What perils did Africans face in order to escape enslavement?

Often, Africans found that violence was one of the most effective ways to demonstrate their resistance to enslavement. Africans did not use violence carelessly or indiscriminately; instead, they used violence in self-defense against enslavement and racism. This might be called redemptive violence. It was the same type of violence that white Americans had used to gain their freedom from Britain and establish the foundation of democracy. Not surprisingly, most of the revolts occurred in the areas with the worst slave codes and reputations for cruelty to enslaved Africans.

The leaders of the Stono Rebellion in 1739, Gabriel Prosser in 1800 in Virginia, Charles Deslandes in 1811 in Louisiana, Denmark Vesey in 1822 in South Carolina, Nat Turner in 1831 in Virginia, Cinque aboard the *Amistad* in 1839, and Madison Washington on the *Creole* led some of the most famous revolts. Some early white historians portray these men as insane. Africans have always considered them heroes.

STONO REBELLION

The Stono Rebellion occurred in 1739 in St. Paul's Parish, South Carolina. Enslaved Africans, led by Cato, escaped from their enslavers and headed for St. Augustine, Florida. Cato and the others thought they could begin a new life as free persons among the Spaniards and Native Americans who lived there. They did not get very far. The slave-catchers, who were more organized and better armed, quickly caught up with them. Cato and his group did not give in easily. Thirty whites were killed before the runaways were captured and returned to South Carolina. In the end, 65 Africans, including the brave Cato, were shot or hung.

GABRIEL PROSSER

Gabriel Prosser was an enslaved African who led an uprising of 1100 Africans in 1800 C.E. in Richmond, Virginia. A summer rainstorm and floods interfered with the attack. Then two of the conspirators, fellow Africans who had joined in the uprising, betrayed Prosser. Prosser and 34 others were executed.

James Monroe, a veteran of the Revolutionary War who became the fifth president of the United States, was the governor of Virginia at the time. He questioned members of the Prosser rebellion. The resisters were loyal to their beliefs. None of them told any details of the uprising. On his way to be hung, Prosser, referring to Monroe's service in the American War of Independence, said:

"[I] have nothing more to offer than what General Washington would have had to offer, had he been taken by the British and put to trial by them."

> " *I have adventured my life in endeavoring to obtain the liberty of my countrymen, and am a willing sacrifice to their cause: and I beg, as a favour, that I may be immediately led to execution. I know that you have pre-determined to shed my blood, why then all this mockery of a trial?* "
>
> **Gabriel Prosser**

Africans who revolted saw themselves as freedom fighters. In his statement, Gabriel Prosser revealed himself as one of the noblest of Africans because he ventured his own life to save his fellow Africans from enslavement. In fact, his comparison of himself to George Washington was not only proper but deserved.

CHARLES DESLANDES

Four hundred enslaved Africans in St. Charles and St. John the Baptist parishes in Louisiana revolted in 1811. They were led by Charles Deslandes, a free African from Haiti, who worked on the plantation where the rebellion began. Two whites were killed, several were wounded, and several plantations were destroyed. Eighty-two Africans were beheaded, their heads strung from post to post throughout the parishes. The enslavers received $29,000 for the loss of their property from the Louisiana legislature. Africans throughout the South were saddened but not discouraged. Eleven years later, thousands of Africans would stage an even bigger attack in Charleston, South Carolina. The Deslandes uprising, though unsuccessful in liberating Africans, shows the resilience, or strength to endure and survive, that is so strongly a part of the African spirit.

DENMARK VESEY

Influenced by the Haitian Revolution of 1791, Denmark Vesey, a free African from the Virgin Islands, led thousands of Africans in an attempt to seize Charleston, South Carolina in 1822. Just like the Prosser rebellion, Vesey's plot was betrayed by one of his partners, who worked secretly for the whites.

African freedom fighters were always on the lookout for Africans who were working for whites. Africans who had developed a low self- esteem as a result of their enslavement and were fearful of being punished by whites were easily convinced to work against their own self-interest. Freedom fighters risked betrayal and certain death to organize and carry out these revolts. No risk was too great for freedom.

Vesey was captured and executed along with 46 others. His bid for freedom, though unsuccessful, inspired others who admired his courage.

Whites believed that something had to be wrong with Vesey and other Africans who tried to overthrow their enslavement. How could any African attempt to overthrow enslavement when the enslavers provided for their every need? Was it possible to own "slaves" and still be considered humane? Could you feel gratitude toward your oppressor?

Obviously, whites in Charleston had a different view of enslavement. The Charleston *Evening Star* commented that

> “ *If a slave has a bad master, he aspires to a good master*
> *And if he has a good master, he aspires to a have a better master*
> *If he has the best master, he aspires to be his own master.*”
> **Frederick Douglass**

Denmark Vesey showed such, “ingratitude to humane owners, such indiscriminate mischief to the unsuspecting, such demonical passion for blood and plunder and conflagration.” Many whites saw something wrong with Africans fighting for their freedom. This attitude continued even after Africans were freed from enslavement and had to fight against racial discrimination.

NAT TURNER

Nat Turner’s revolt in 1831 is perhaps the most famous because of Turner’s boldness and his willingness to die for his beliefs. Nat Turner was a religious man; a visionary who believed in self-actualization, or the freedom to be the best he could be. His passion for freedom made him strike out against his oppressors. Turner led 70 Africans in Southampton County, Virginia, in an uprising that left 60 white people dead. White Virginians armed with guns and other weapons put down the rebellion, but Turner escaped capture for two more months.

▲ An artist’s rendering of Nat Turner’s recapture

Copies of a pamphlet, *Appeal to the Coloured Citizens of the World*, which called upon the enslaved to overthrow enslavement, was found in the area after the revolt. The author of the pamphlet was David Walker, a free African living in Boston. Turner, who could read and write, had probably read the pamphlet. He certainly would have been aware of the Vesey revolt and was probably influenced by it.

Turner believed that God had chosen him and sent him a sign to revolt. When he was finally captured, he refused to plead guilty to the charges against him because of his "God-given right" to fight for freedom. Just before being executed, Turner said, "I am here loaded with chains and willing to suffer the fate that awaits me."

Nat Turner and about 120 other Africans were executed after this revolt. Many of them were innocent, but whites in the area went into a frenzy of retaliation. They indiscriminately killed any African they found. As a result of the revolt, many Southern states passed stricter laws against teaching enslaved people to read and write. They also placed more restrictions on what African preachers could say.

AMISTAD REBELLION

Joseph Cinque, an African prince of the Mandingo ethnic group on Africa's west coast, led 48 other Africans in a revolt on the high seas in 1839. Cinque and the others were kidnapped, probably from their home in Senegal or one of the other nearby countries in West Africa.The kidnapped Africans overpowered the slave traders on the Spanish slave ship, *L'Amistad*, which was on its way to Cuba. They sailed successfully to Long Island, New York, but when they docked there, Cinque and the others were arrested and charged with piracy and murder.

▲ Joseph Cinque led 48 Africans in an 1839 revolt aboard the Spanish slave ship *L'Amistad*.

Neither Cinque nor the others in the group spoke English. An African from the area was located who could speak Mende, their West African language. Through the interpreter, the seafaring rebels were able to plead their cause. Abolitionists, led by Lewis Tappan, also took up their cause. Cinque's defense team was led by former U.S. President John Quincy Adams.

The U.S. Supreme Court decided to set them free in 1841. A British official stationed in Cuba said that Cinque and the group had been smuggled into Cuba illegally because Britain and Spain had made a treaty outlawing the international slave trade.

The Supreme Court's judgment was a surprise, especially to whites. Anticipating a guilty verdict, President Martin Van Buren (1837-1841) had ordered the U.S. Navy to begin preparations for the resisters' return to Cuba. Instead, the group was placed aboard a ship headed for the West Coast of Africa where the British had established a colony called Sierra Leone for free Africans.

Ironically, Cinque became a business agent for European slave traders. His experiences in America and his knowledge of Western customs made him useful as a middleman in the slave trade. Cinque, like many individuals who are tempted by money and riches, became a willing agent of his own greed.

THE *CREOLE*

Two years after Cinque's fateful Long Island landing, enslaved Africans aboard the *Creole*, a slave ship on its way from Hampton, Virginia, to New Orleans, took command of the ship. The enslaved Africans, led by Madison Washington, overpowered the crew and sailed the ship to Nassau in the Bahamas, where they were granted asylum and given their freedom. They were successful because by 1841 Britain had outlawed enslavement in all its territories and the Africans could not be returned to the United States. Madison Washington is remembered for his boldness and his willingness to risk his life for his beliefs.

In anticipation of the great war between the slave-holding South and the free North, John Brown, a white man, led a revolt against enslavement at Harpers Ferry, West Virginia, in 1859.

Few people hated the enslavement of others as much as John Brown hated the enslavement of Africans by whites. Born in Torrington, Connecticut, on May 9, 1800, Brown spent his years in Ohio, Pennsylvania, Massachusetts, and New York learning all he could about the institution of enslavement and the reasons whites in the North did not do something dramatic to bring it to an end. In 1849, Brown moved to an African American community in North Elba, New York, on land donated by the antislavery philanthropist Gerrit Smith.

John Brown raised his family to believe in the same principles of freedom as he did. Working as a farmer, wool merchant, tanner, and land speculator, he managed to support his family. In 1855 Brown and five of his sons traveled to the Kansas Territory to assist antislavery forces against the supporters of enslavement in the territory. He soon became the leader of a guerilla movement in the Osawatomie region of Kansas. Brown and his followers planned an attack against the proslavery supporters who had burned the town of Lawrence, Kansas, on May 21, 1856. Three days later, John Brown and his men raided the proslavery forces at Pottawatomie Creek, killing five of the proslavers. The battle was referred to as the Pottawatomie Massacre.

Fully convinced that the proslavery forces were the enemies of freedom and justice, Brown summoned a group of whites and Africans to Chatham, Ontario, for a meeting in the spring of 1858. At the meeting, he announced his intention of setting up a stronghold in the Maryland and Virginia mountains for Africans escaping enslavement.

The group appointed John Brown commander-in-chief of the provisional government. They received financial backing from Gerrit Smith and other abolitionists in New England. By summer of 1859, Brown had set up headquarters outside Harpers Ferry, near a federal armory, to begin the process of taking over the area and establishing a stronghold. There were 16 whites and five Africans in Brown's militia, all of whom were highly disciplined and well trained.

As night fell on October 16, 1859, Brown and his men struck like lightning and overtook the guards, took control of the armory, and held about 60 people hostage. They held the armory for two days while the local militia attacked with their weapons. However, they were forced to surrender when the authorities brought in the U. S. Marines. Brown was wounded in the attack. Ten of his men were killed, including two of his own sons. Brown was charged with insurrection, murder, and treason against the state. He was tried and later hanged December 2, 1859. His body was buried in North Elba, New York. John Brown won a moral victory against enslavement. Union soldiers immortalized him in a song, "John Brown, his soul goes marching on" as they launched their campaign against the South two years later.

Striking For Liberty

1782	Several maroon attacks in Louisiana
1783	Maroon attacks continue in Louisiana
1784	Maroon attacks continue in Louisiana
1786	Maroons resist in Georgia
1788	Africans, led by Prince Hall, protest kidnapping of free Blacks
1793	Three enslaved Africans executed in Albany, New York for antislavery activities
1795	Maroon uprising in Wilmington, North Carolina
1800	Gabriel Prosser leads insurrection in Virginia
1802	Maroons and enslaved Africans form plot in Elizabeth City, North Carolina
1803	Africans mutiny in York, Pennsylvania
	Africans revolt and burn part of New York City
1804	Uprisings in Georgia, Virginia, and South Carolina
1811	Maroon uprising in North Carolina
	Revolt in St. Charles and St. John the Baptist parishes in Louisiana, led by Charles Deslandes
1812	Africans and Native Americans attack a military train in Georgia
1815	1,000 Africans take control of a fort in Georgia
1816	Maroons occupy a fort in Florida: 270 Africans killed
1817	First of the Seminole Wars in which Africans and
	Native Americans fought the United States
1818	Maroons revolt in Princess Anne County, Virginia
1821	Plot by Africans in Bladen, Carteret, and Onslow counties, North Carolina, uncovered
1822	Insurrection, led by Denmark Vesey, uncovered in Charleston, South Carolina
1826	Maroon attack in South Carolina
1829	A group of enslaved Africans kill a slave trader in a bid for freedom
	African women executed for arson in Augusta, Georgia
1830	Africans plot insurrection in North Carolina
1831	Nat Turner's revolt in Virginia: 60 whites killed
1837	Maroon attack in Mobile, Alabama
1839	Revolt aboard the slave ship *Amistad*, led by Cinque
1841	Africans take control of the vessel *Creole*, and sail to freedom in Nassau
	Armed Africans repulse an attack near Wilmington, North Carolina
1846	Dred Scott sues for his freedom
1851	Shadrach, a fugitive in Boston, is rescued from slave-catchers
	Parker's resistance, Christiana, Pennsylvania
	Jerry, a fugitive in Syracuse, New York, is rescued from slave-catchers
1854	Revolt in New Orleans
1859	John Brown's raid on Harper's Ferry

◆ CENTER YOUR THINKING

1. Why did the U.S. Supreme Court set Cinque and the other Africans aboard the *L'Amistad* free?
2. Describe one African rebellion.
3. Why did some whites think that something was wrong with Africans who fought for their freedom?
4. Think of at least two reasons that an enslaved African would betray another African.
5. HOLISTIC ACTIVITY Students as Chart Makers

   Start your own list or a group list of people from history who survived difficult times and triumphed. With each name, write a brief description of the person's accomplishments and a statement telling why you admire that person. You may also wish to start your own private list of role models.

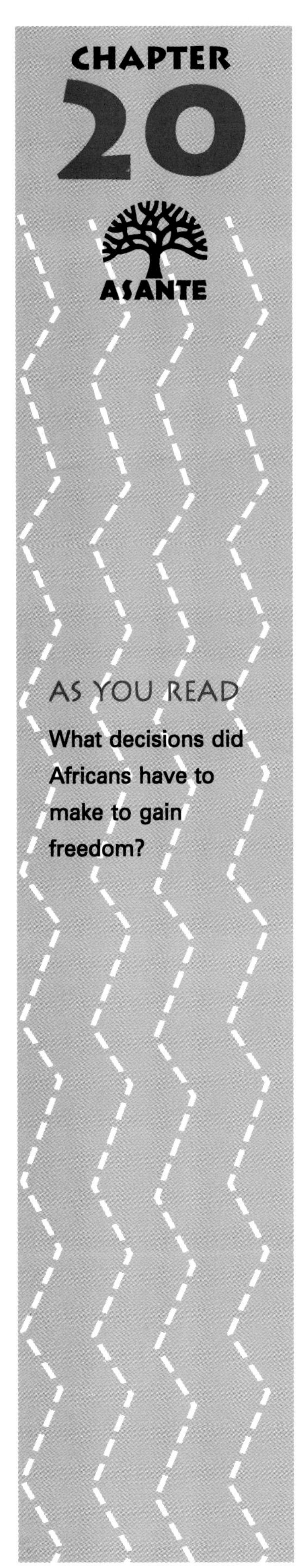

THE "UNDERGROUND RAILROAD": A COLORFUL MYTH

CENTER YOUR VOCABULARY

- ▲ Underground Railroad
- ▲ slave-hunter
- ▲ Mason and Dixon Line
- ▲ superficial

Africans who traveled the dangerous and often lonely path of the "Underground Railroad" are heroes and freedom fighters in their own right. These courageous men and women were driven by a passionate desire for freedom. By attempting to escape, they demonstrated their resistance to enslavement, but more important, they served as a shining example to others that escape was possible and worthwhile.

William Still, a 19th-century author, popularized the term *Underground Railroad* to refer to the network of people, taverns, and churches that offered help to runaway Africans escaping enslavement in the South. In his book, *The Underground Railroad*, published in 1872, Still described the routes that were taken most often by runaway Africans. These routes followed the Mason and Dixon Line, an imaginary boundary created in 1763 to divide Pennsylvania and Maryland. The Mason and Dixon Line came to represent the division between the slaveholding states and the free states. The line cut through Quaker territories in Ohio and Pennsylvania. The Quakers were a religious society that showed an early moral interest in freeing Africans from enslavement.

The Underground Railroad was a colorful way to characterize the men and women, Africans and whites who risked their lives to

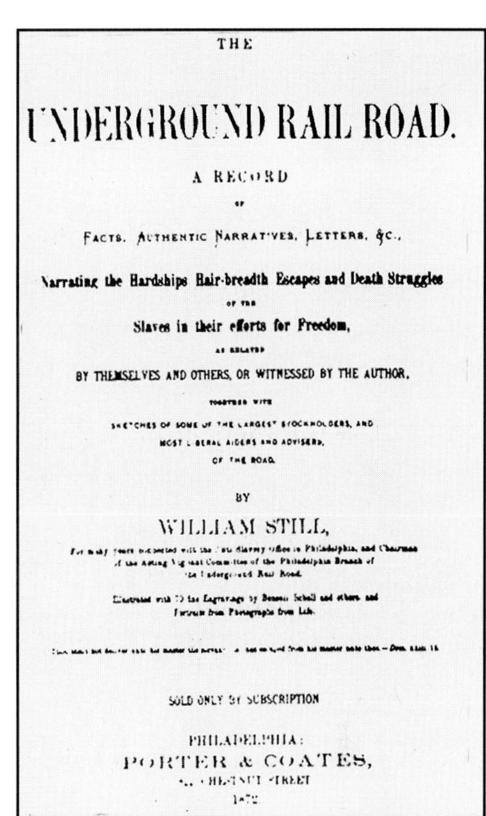

THE

UNDERGROUND RAIL ROAD.

A RECORD

OF

FACTS, AUTHENTIC NARRATIVES, LETTERS, &C.,

Narrating the Hardships Hair-breadth Escapes and Death Struggles

OF THE

Slaves in their efforts for Freedom,

AS RELATED

BY THEMSELVES AND OTHERS, OR WITNESSED BY THE AUTHOR.

TOGETHER WITH

SKETCHES OF SOME OF THE LARGEST STOCKHOLDERS, AND MOST LIBERAL AIDERS AND ADVISERS, OF THE ROAD.

BY

WILLIAM STILL,

[illegible]

SOLD ONLY BY SUBSCRIPTION

PHILADELPHIA:

PORTER & COATES,

[illegible] CHESTNUT STREET

1872

▲ William Still included real stories and letters about many men and women who escaped enslavement in his book, *The Underground Railroad,* published in 1872.

help Africans escape to the North. But in reality, the Underground Railroad was not very effective. Most of the Africans who escaped from enslavement did so on their own and by their own bravery and intelligence. Courageous Africans—men, women and children who were fortunate in escaping enslavers—had to rely largely on their own resources and skills to find their way to safety. They had no maps, food, or clothing. Their only guide was the lone North Star on the distant horizon. They were often tired, lonely, and scared as they tried desperately to cover their tracks from the keen scent of the bloodhounds and the more dangerous pursuit of the slave-hunters.

Free Africans and some whites in the North provided safe houses along the way for the runaways. But many Africans could not take advantage of these houses because they did not know where they were located. Only in the cases where there had been routine trips, as was the case with Harriet Tubman who made 19 trips to Maryland and Delaware to escort enslaved Africans to freedom, could there be a series of safe houses usable by the escaping Africans. Other Africans seeking to escape to Canada or to Mexico, had to find their own way.

▲ Escaping Africans are assisted by a Quaker family in Ohio.

Many people—some well known, others nameless—provided food, clothing, and anything else they could to speed the runaways on to safety. Levi Coffin, a Quaker, opened his home to more than 100 fleeing Africans per year. Thomas Garrett, an abolitionist famous for his support of Africans, is said to have assisted 2,700 Africans in their search for freedom.

Africans running toward freedom had to always be careful of the dreaded slave-hunters. These were individuals hired by enslavers to travel around the country looking for escaped Africans, much like bounty hunters in the wild West, who were hired to find outlaws. Bounty hunters became legends because of their tireless pursuit of outlaws. The slave-hunters, however, were often poor, landless whites who loved the thrill of the hunt and the huge rewards that enslavers were willing to pay for the enslaved's return. Slave-hunting, however, was a dangerous business for Africans, and even more dangerous for whites. Runaway Africans and their supporters often defended themselves with guns and other weapons to avoid being re-enslaved.

Much of the distrust between whites and African Americans today

▼ Escaping Africans always had to be careful of slave-hunters.

can be traced to these incidents of slave-hunting. African people were reluctant to place their complete trust in any white person because an error in judgment could mean life or death for the African. Even though enslavement officially ended more than 150 years ago, many of the attitudes formed during enslavement are still alive today. Many African Americans still hide their true feelings and identities from whites until they are convinced that they are not racist. Many whites, on the other hand, have often sensed distrust and uneasiness from African Americans, but they don't know how to break through the barriers created by the old system of enslavement. So complex was the relationship between African Americans and whites in the United States during the 19th and early 20th centuries, that social relationships were often superficial, or shallow.

Escape Routes

Map Skill: In what directions did African Americans run to escape enslavement? Where did they find some relief?

◆ CENTER YOUR THINKING

1. What is the Mason and Dixon Line?
2. How did the Underground Railroad get its name?
3. The author states that much of the distrust between whites and African Americans today can be traced to slave-hunting. Give reasons why you agree or disagree.
4. Research one of the women who made history in this chapter. Write a one-page description of her contributions.
5. HOLISTIC ACTIVITY Students as Performers

   Develop a performance to show the trust and strength needed to escape enslavement. Your performance may be a group dance, rap, or individual work.

CHAPTER 21

ASANTE

"OUR MOTTO IS FREEDOM!"

CENTER YOUR VOCABULARY

- ▲ hypocrisy
- ▲ orator
- ▲ integrated
- ▲ moral suasion

AS YOU READ

As a parent, how would you explain to your child that the land of liberty could also enslave an entire race of people?

"All men fight for their freedom." These were the fighting words spoken by Reverend Jermain Loguen in 1844. He was a faithful Christian and a strong supporter of African rights. African orators (speakers) like Loguen, who supported violence for liberation, publicized it in their speeches and writings. They believed that violence was necessary to end enslavement and oppression.

"If our rights are withheld any longer, then come war—let blood flow without measure—until our rights are acknowledged or we perish from the earth. White men fight—all men fight for their freedom, and we are men and will fight for ours. Nothing can stop the current of blood but justice to our people."

Reverend Jarmain Loguen

FREEDOM'S CHAMPIONS

David Walker, a Boston shopkeeper, published a pamphlet titled, *Appeal to the Coloured Citizens of the World,* in 1829. It urged enslaved Africans to arm themselves for resistance. "Kill, or be killed," he told them.

He exposed Americans' hypocrisy for continuing to refer to the nation as a "Land of Liberty" while ignoring the enslavement of

▲ Rev. Jarmain W. Loguen

Africans. Hypocrisy is the pretense of being more sincere than you really are. Walker characterized whites as "unjust, jealous, unmerciful, avaricious and blood-thirsty . . . always seeking after power and authority."

Born in 1785, David Walker was the son of an enslaved African man and a free African woman in Wilmington, North Carolina. Because the status of the mother determined the child's freedom, Walker was free. He left the South in 1815 because he hated the conditions in which enslaved Africans lived. He wrote, "If I remain in this bloody land, I will be avenged for the sorrows which my people have suffered." He settled in Boston and became a leader in the city's African community.

> *" The man who would not fight . . . in the glorious and heavenly cause of freedom . . . to be delivered from the most wretched, abject and servile slavery . . . ought to be kept with all his children or family, in slavery, or in chains, to be butchered by his cruel enemies. "*
>
> **David Walker**

Walker's *Appeal* was widely distributed throughout the South. The pamphlet may have influenced Nat Turner in 1831. White reaction to the pamphlet was as negative and as brutal as could be expected, given the fear whites had of African revolts. Southern enslavers pressured the mayor of Boston to stop Walker. Punitive laws, sometimes with severe punishments, were passed in several Southern states for even simple possession of the pamphlet. Georgia offered a $10,000 reward for Walker's capture alive and $1,000 dead.

Walker was aware of the dangerous stand he was taking. He died under mysterious circumstances in 1830. We must wonder if he was murdered, but we will never know.

Henry Highland Garnet was among the foremost militant orators and activists in African American history. He was born the grandson of an African king on December 23, 1815, in New Market, Kent County, Maryland. At age 10, he and his entire family escaped North on foot, without stopping for food or shelter until they reached New York City.

The Garnet family settled in New York City. Young Garnet attended the New York Free African School, one of the first public schools for Africans in the United States. At 19, Garnet attended Noyes Academy in Canaan, New Hampshire. He was joined there by two other African students, Thomas S. Sidney and Alexander Crummell, both of whom became famous for their efforts to liberate Africans. Trouble soon followed. Whites in the area felt threatened by the presence of Africans in the school. A mob of whites opened fire on Garnet and the others on the college campus. Garnet and the others returned the gunfire, holding the mob at bay. Overwhelmed by the increasing number of whites who were armed and gathering on the campus grounds, Garnet Sidney and Crumwell fled for their lives. The mob burned the school down.

▲ Henry Highland Garnet

Henry Highland Garnet continued his college education at the Oneida Institute in Whitesboro, New York. He was a natural born orator, fond of poetry, and gifted with a strong imagination. In 1840, at the age of 25, he graduated from the school and became an ordained Presbyterian minister of an integrated church for Africans and whites in Troy, New York. Garnet also worked as a schoolteacher and edited a weekly newspaper called the *Clarion*.

Three years later, at the age of 28, Henry Highland Garnet delivered his most famous address. He called his speech "An Address to the Slaves of the United States of America." His delivery stirred the leading African opinion makers in attendance at the National Negro Convention in Buffalo, New York, in 1843. Garnet spoke from the heart with a militancy and boldness that had not been seen during the Convention movement, a movement that had started 30 years earlier to bring together prominent African activists. He told them, "Let your motto be resistance," knowing full well that his words would be broadcast across the land, even into the South. Henry Highland Garnet became the key militant spokesperson for the use of violence to end enslavement. However, he was unsuccessful in his bid to have the National Negro Convention adopt his address as part of their policy.

Instead, some members favored white abolitionist William Lloyd Garrison's moral suasion position. Moral suasion favored a nonviolent approach to persuade whites to end enslavement. Interestingly, Garnet's opposition was led by Frederick Douglass. Douglass later changed his mind and supported the use of violence.

"If hereditary bondsmen would be free, they must strike the first blow . . . To such degradation [as enslavement] it is sinful in the extreme for you to make voluntary submission. . . . It is your solemn and imperative duty to use every means, both moral, intellectual, and physical, that promise success. . . . You had better all die—die immediately, than live slaves, and entail your wretchedness upon your posterity . . . Let your motto be resistance! resistance! resistance!"

Henry Highland Garnett

Frederick Douglass had no equal as a spokesperson for Africans during his lifetime. He was an activist for justice. He devoted his life and work to ending the enslavement of Africans by working with practically every leading African freedom fighter in the nation, as well as many white abolitionists. His opinions were sought on every issue pertaining to Africans.

Initially, Frederick Douglass supported nonviolence. He was a member of William Lloyd Garrison's group, which encouraged moral suasion. However, Douglass changed his position as he became more active in the antislavery movement. In the first issue of his newspaper, *The North Star*, published in 1847, Douglass says: ". . . the man who has suffered the wrong is the man to demand redress . . . we must be our own representatives and advocates . . ." *The North Star* was a fitting name for Douglass's paper because he too had fled bondage. Enslaved Africans fleeing bondage followed the North Star to guide them out of the South to the North and freedom.

Douglass explained the position most Africans took toward resistance: "Every slavehunter who meets a bloody death in his infernal business, is an argument in favor of the manhood of our race. Resistance is, therefore, wise as well as just."

A June 2, 1854, article titled, "Is It Right and Wise To Kill a Kidnapper?" published in *The North Star*, reflected as militant an attitude as Henry Highland Garnet's.

"It may be said . . . for the fugitive slave or his friends that submission . . . is far wiser than resistance. To this it is sufficient answer to show that submission is valuable only so long as it has some chance of being recognized as a virtue. . . . That submission on the part of the slave, has ceased to be a virtue, is very evident. . . . Such submission . . . only creates contempt for them in the public mind, and becomes an argument in the mouths of the community, that Negroes are, by nature, only fit for slavery; that slavery is their normal condition. . . . This reproach must be wiped out, and nothing short of resistance on the part of colored men, can wipe it out."

Frederick Douglass

Douglass believed that Africans could not depend on others for their freedom. If Africans were to be free, they would have to use force to gain their freedom from whites. "Our elevation as a race is almost wholly dependent upon our own exertions [efforts]."

◆ CENTER YOUR THINKING

1. Who was Henry Highland Garnet?
2. In your opinion, why did Frederick Douglass stop supporting nonviolence?
3. David Walker said that "all men fight for their freedom." Explain why you agree or disagree.
4. Is the debate over violence or nonviolence still going on today?
5. HOLISTIC ACTIVITY Students as Orators

   In your small group, choose a famous 19th-century antislavery activist, and develop at least one speech for him or her to give.

PASSIVE RESISTANCE: THE HIGH ROAD TO FREEDOM

CENTER YOUR VOCABULARY

- ▲ passive resistance
- ▲ patronizing
- ▲ advocate
- ▲ autonomy

Not all Africans thought it necessary to use violence. Some Africans preferred to appeal to the sense of values and morals of whites to persuade them to end enslavement. These Africans pressed for equal rights for Africans and an end to enslavement. One of them was William Whipper, a wealthy African lumber merchant whose house in Columbia, Pennsylvania, was built on the bank of the Susquehanna River. It was sometimes the first stop on free soil for Africans escaping enslavement. Escaping Africans knew to look for his house. Whipper gave them food, supplies, and money to travel further north, even to Canada, to escape being caught. He also edited a newspaper and contributed much of his time and money to the antislavery movement.

WILLIAM WHIPPER: "SUMMON OUR NOBLEST POWERS"

Whipper was one of the first Africans to support passive resistance, or nonviolent resistance, to achieve equal rights for African Americans. In 1837, he said, "when the greatest difficulties surround us, we should summon our noblest powers."

"The practice of non-resistance to physical aggression is not only consistent with reason, but the surest method of obtaining a speedy triumph of the principles of universal peace. . . . When the greatest difficulties surround us, we should summon our noblest powers . . . and for acts of wickedness committed against us let us reciprocate in the spirit of kindness . . . [for] THEIR reasoning powers are defective. . . ."

William Whipper

Whipper and other advocates, or supporters, of passive resistance believed that goodness and other moral virtues would triumph over the evil practice of enslavement. Some Africans were not easily persuaded by Whipper's reasoning. Reverend Samuel Cornish, the editor of the *Colored American,* responded to Whipper with, "We honestly confess that we have yet to learn what virtue there would be in using moral weapons in defense of kidnappers or a midnight incendiary with a torch in his hand."

The question of passive resistance versus self-defense would be argued repeatedly in the African American community. Martin Luther King, Jr., and Malcolm X argued both sides of this issue in the 1960s.

ANTISLAVERY CAMPAIGNERS

Africans in antislavery organizations complained bitterly about the patronizing, or insultingly condescending, nature of these societies. Antislavery organizations were run by whites who wanted to end African enslavement. However, most white antislavery workers did not consider Africans their equals. They adopted an attitude of superiority that made many Africans reluctant to participate in these organizations. Samuel Ringgold Ward, a preacher, charged that whites "assume the right to dictate to us about all matters. . . . They dislike to see us assume or maintain manly and independent positions; they prefer that we should be a second-rate set of folks, in intellectual matters."

While white antislavery workers were anxious to end enslavement, they were not interested in social or political equality for Africans. They refused to admit Africans to their schools and often refused to hire Africans for any job except the most menial. African antislavery workers wanted autonomy, or self-leadership. White antislavery workers believed that Africans should serve in organizations led by whites because their goals were the same. These differences contributed to the split between Frederick Douglass, one of the most outspoken leaders in the African community, and William Lloyd Garrison, the leading white abolitionist. In a speech about African freedom in the Caribbean in 1857, Douglass asserted that white abolitionists "don't like any demonstrations whatever in which colored men take a leading part. . . . [I] have been branded as an ingrate, because [I] have ventured to stand up on [my] own right, and to plead our common cause as a colored man, rather than as a Garrisonian. I hold it to be no part of gratitude to allow our white friends to do all the work, while we merely hold their coats."

Members of the Religious Society of Friends, or Quakers, most often led the antislavery societies. Quakers condemned violence, war, and other uses of force. They preferred to use passive resistance and persuasion instead. Because the predominantly white societies supported nonviolent means to end enslavement, they could not approve or encourage violent acts of resistance on the part of Africans. Most Africans, however, believed in the necessity of using violence for self-defense. Many African leaders privately supported redemptive violence, but they were publicly quiet about it because they did not want to offend their white, nonviolent supporters. This conflict would continue to produce mixed reactions from African American leaders throughout history. When violence flared up against African Americans, there were always some American leaders who urged their followers to suppress their natural urge to defend themselves and adopt a nonviolent approach. Nonviolence was not always in the best interest of the African American community, but some leaders who needed the support of whites had little choice but to give in to the demands of their white supporters.

ANTISLAVERY ACTIVISTS

- **David Walker**, a Bostonian pamphleteer, electrifies the African population and frightens the white population with the publication of his militant pamphlet, *An Appeal to the Colored Citizens of the World,* in 1829.

- **Henry McNeal Turner**, an African Methodist Episcopal bishop, promotes the overthrow of the system of enslavement in 1854 to 1858.

- **Henry Highland Garnet**, a preacher, calls for an armed revolt against enslavement in a speech at a Buffalo, New York, convention in 1843.

- **Sojourner Truth**, an orator, takes to the antislavery platform in 1828, and begins an illustrious career as an eloquent opponent of enslavement.

- **William Still**, a Philadelphian, records many of the Underground Railroad stories and heads a self-help organization, the Vigilance Committee. He also organizes a protest against segregated streetcars in Philadelphia in 1862.

- **Robert Morris**, a Bostonian lawyer and antislavery campaigner, argues in 1849 in court that segregated schools harm Africans and whites.

◆ CENTER YOUR THINKING

1. Name one famous African American antislavery activist and explain what he or she did.
2. What complaints did some Africans make about whites who were involved in antislavery organizations?
3. Give as many reasons as you can think of that Africans might have supported passive resistance. Explain your own opinion of each reason.
4. Can you predict the position Martin Luther King, Jr., and Malcolm X would take in a 20th century debate over violence or passive resistance? Are there leaders you know about today who claim to take a similar position? Who? Explain.
5. HOLISTIC ACTIVITY Students as Letter Writers

   In your small group, imagine that you are one of the highly skilled, proud, confident African abolitionists. Write a letter to one of your fellow abolitionists describing your thoughts and feelings when you think of your own children not being able to enjoy equal rights in the country of their birth.

CHAPTER 23

ASANTE

FIGHTING WOMEN

CENTER YOUR VOCABULARY

- ▲ exploited
- ▲ submission
- ▲ pseudonym
- ▲ legend

AS YOU READ

What is true courage? What gave Harriet Tubman the courage to risk her own life and freedom?

Women suffered terribly during the enslavement. While men may have been physically beaten or punished more than women, they were rarely sexually exploited as violently or as frequently as women. To exploit someone means to take unfair advantage of that person. Thousands of women suffered physical and psychological abuse in the slaveholding South. So violent was the exploitation that some women wished death upon themselves or the enslavers. In some cases, they killed their abusers. Others escaped to the North, seeking the freedom they had never experienced under enslavement.

HARRIET JACOBS

In one of the most famous narratives by a woman, Harriet Jacobs writes about her own struggle against enslavement, the struggles of other Africans, and the dehumanizing effect enslavement had on everyone. Jacobs's narrative, *Incidents in the Life of a Slave Girl,* was published in 1860 under the pseudonym (or pen name) Linda Brent to protect her identity and the identity of friends and family who helped her win her freedom. Jacobs's narrative, like so many of the enslaved's narratives, is a moving recount of shattered innocence, a mother's love, sacrifice, pain, hope, and triumph. Jacobs describes the rape of African women by whites, many of whom did not

> “ *The more my mind had become enlighted, the more difficult it was for me to consider myself an article of property; and to pay money to those who had so grievously oppressed me seemed like taking from my sufferings the glory of triumph.* ”
>
> **Harriet Jacobs**

acknowledge their children from these pairs. Men, women, children, the enslaved and the enslavers were all harmed by the brutality of enslavement.

Bruised and battered into near submission and unhealthy obedience, the Africans in her narrative refused to accept enslavement. In one gripping instance, she tells the story of how her 12-year-old brother, William, refused to be whipped. “Master Nicholas said he should be flogged, and he would do it. Whereupon he went to work; but William fought bravely, and the young master, finding he was getting the better of him, undertook to tie his hands behind him. He failed in that likewise. By dint of kicking and fisting, William came out of the skirmish none the worse for a few scratches.”

She said of herself, “though one of God’s most powerless creatures, I resolved never to be conquered.” Jacobs never allowed her spirit to be broken, even in enslavement. At age 15, she used all her wits to evade the unwelcomed attention of her enslaver, Mr. Flint. She wrote, “he told me I was his property; that I must be subject to his will in all things. My soul revolted against the mean tyranny. But where could I turn for protection?” Jacobs hid in a small attic for several years waiting for a chance to escape. She wrote: “It seemed horrible to sit or lie in a cramped position day after day without one gleam of light. Yet I would have chosen this, rather than my lot as a slave.”

Finally, Jacobs had the the moment for which she had waited so long. She seized the opportunity and fled North to freedom.

> “ *So I was sold at last! A human being sold in the free city of New York! The bill of sale is on record, and future generations will learn from it that women were articles of traffic in New York, late in the nineteenth centry of the Christian religion. It may hereafter prove a useful document to antiquaries, who are seeking to measure the progress of civilization in the United States.* ”
>
> **Harriet Jacobs**

After her escape to New York, a white friend offered to buy Jacobs from her Southern enslaver. She said she felt “grateful,” but she hated the idea of being treated like merchandise. Jacobs, like so many of the other narrative writers, was extremely critical of American hypocrisy. The nation called itself a Christian democracy, preaching justice and equality for all, while denying freedom to Africans.

Jacobs did not stop her friend from eventually purchasing her freedom. But she resented the idea that her sale had become a matter of public record. From this document, future generations would learn how slowly the wheels of progress turned.

▲ Harriet Tubman

HARRIET TUBMAN

Harriet Tubman was one of the most famous supporters of runaway Africans. A legend in her own right, her name is forever linked with the Underground Railroad. Tubman was born into enslavement in Bucktown, Maryland, around 1820 C.E. Her name was originally Araminta Ross, but she was called Harriet, her mother's name. She married a free African, John Tubman, in 1844. Tubman escaped enslavement in 1849 and settled in Philadelphia, where she associated with antislavery activists.

Tubman made her first trip back to Maryland in 1850, shortly after the passage of the Fugitive Slave Law. She personally rescued more than 300 Africans from enslavement. Tubman made 19 trips to the South, each time risking her own life and freedom to bring Africans to the North. The outspoken Tubman once pointed a gun at an African who was afraid to follow her to freedom and said, "Before I'd see you a slave, I'll see you dead and buried in your grave." The man followed her. Enslavers offered a $40,000 reward for her, dead or alive!

Tubman also served as a nurse and spy for the Union army during the Civil War. She helped approximately 750 Africans escape to Union lines during one battle alone. After the Civil War, she helped raise money for African American schools, established a home for elderly and needy African Americans, and worked for women's rights.

▲ Sojourner Truth

SOJOURNER TRUTH

Isabella Baumfree was born to enslavement in Ulster County, New York, in 1797. She changed her name to Sojourner Truth after she decided to travel (sojourn) and tell the truth about the condition of enslavement. After being emancipated in the New York State Emancipation Act of 1827, Sojourner Truth had an opportunity to do what she had always wanted to do all of her life. She became a preacher, abolitionist, and campaigner for women's rights. Having mastered both Dutch, her first language, and English, she was able to electrify her audiences in either language.

Large crowds gathered to hear her speak in Ohio, Indiana, Pennsylvania, New York, and Michigan. The story is told that on one occasion the famous African American orator Frederick Douglass was speaking to a large audience in Ohio. Douglass was discouraged because the whites did not appear ready to see the justice of the African's cause. Sojourner, who was seated in the audience, noticed his discouragement. Sojourner Truth stood up, the eyes of the 700 people in the audience fixed on her six-foot frame, and said: "Frederick! Frederick! Is God dead?" To Sojourner Truth's understanding, if God was alive and present then it was not necessary to despair. The audience, after a stunned silence, gave her a standing ovation.

Sojourner Truth participated in many antislavery events and seemed to know just about everyone in the antislavery movement. She was a friend to Harriet Beecher Stowe, Lucretia Mott, and James Mott. The white abolitionists appreciated the dignity and power of her eloquence and felt pleased that a woman had joined the African men on the platform against enslavement, even though she was often harassed for her strong speeches.

She made her famous speech, "Ain't I a Woman?" in Akron, Ohio, in 1851. She was interrupted many times by men who were against women's rights and African enslavement. Truth knew she had to do something dramatic to regain her audience's attention. In a daring move Truth bared her breasts and then asked in her now famous speech:

"That man over there says that women needs to be lifted over ditches . . . Nobody ever helped me into carriages or over mud puddles . . . and ain't I a woman? Look at me! Look at my arm! I have plowed and planted and gathered into barns. . . . Ain't I a woman? I could work as much . . . as a man . . . and bear the lash as well—and ain't I a woman? I have born thirteen children and seen most all sold off into slavery, and when I cried out with a mother's grief, none but Jesus heard—and ain't I a woman?"

When the Civil War began, she raised money to buy gifts for the soldiers, and she went into the camps to distribute the gifts herself. She aided many people during and after the war. The publication of her *Narratives* recounted the stories of her exploits in the war and her meeting with Abraham Lincoln. When she could no longer travel great distances, she lectured at the Battle Creek, Michigan, Sanatorium, and died in Battle Creek on November 29, 1883.

FRANCES ELLEN WATKINS HARPER

▲ Frances Ellen Watkins Harper

Frances Ellen Watkins Harper was another well-known anti-slavery activist. She was known as the "Bronze Muse" because of her poetry, writings, and gift for oratory. Born in Baltimore in 1825, she was the only child of free African parents. She devoted her life to ending the enslavement and oppression of her fellow Africans. Harper joined the antislavery movement and traveled extensively, lecturing about the evils of enslavement. After the Civil War, she dedicated herself to getting the right to vote for women.

"A government which has power to tax a man in peace, draft him in war, should have power to defend his life in the hour of peril. A government which can protect and defend its citizens from wrong and outrage and does not is vicious. A government which would do it and cannot is weak; and where human life is insecure through either weakness or viciousness in the administration of law, there must be a lack of justice and where this is wanting, nothing can make up the deficiency."

Frances Ellen Watkins Harper

FAMOUS AFRICAN AMERICAN ANTISLAVERY WOMEN ACTIVISTS

- ***Maria Stewart***, a writer and lecturer
- ***Mary Shadd Cary***, a journalist and an advocate of African American expatriation to Canada
- ***Ellen Craft***, who escaped from enslavement with her husband by posing as an enslaver with his loyal servant
- ***Sarah M. Douglass***, an educator and officer in the Philadelphia Female Anti-Slavery Society
- ***Sarah Parker Remond***, civil rights activist who eventually expatriated to Italy, where she became a medical doctor

NOTABLE WOMEN OF HISTORY

Sarah Allen, *Missionary*	1764-1849
Caroline Anderson, *Doctor*	1849-1919
Janie Barrett, *Teacher*	1870-1949
Matilda Beasley, *Teacher*	1834-1903
Ann Becraft, *Teacher*	1805-1833
Rosa Bowser, *Teacher*	1885-1931
Sue Brown, *Organizer*	1877-1941
Mary S. Cary, *Abolitionist*	1823-1893
Anna J. Cooper, *Teacher*	1858-1964
Anna Douglas, *Abolitionist*	?-1882
Susan Frazier, *Organizer*	1866-1901
Charlotte Grimke, *Scholar*	1834-1914
Ernma Hackley, *Artist*	1877-1922
Alice D. Nelson, *Author*	1875-1935
Mary Patterson, *Teacher*	1840-1894
Mary Peake, *Teacher*	1823-1862
Frances Preston, *Orator*	1844-1929
Charlotta Pyles, *Abolitionist*	1806-1880
Susie Shorter, *Writer*	1859-1912
Georgia Simpson, *Scholar*	1866-1944
Arnanda Smith, *Missionary*	1836-1915
May Talbert, *Reformer*	1866-1912
Susan Vashon, *Nurse*	1838-1912
Josie Washington, *Organizer*	1861-1949
Lulu Williams, *Reformer*	1874-1945

◆ CENTER YOUR THINKING

1. What is a narrative?
2. Name two famous African American women who were antislavery activists, and tell what they did.
3. Do you agree with the statement that women were exploited in ways that men were not? Explain why.
4. Explain what Sojourner Truth meant when she said, "Ain't I a Woman?"
5. HOLISTIC ACTIVITY Students as Journalists

   Your group will interview the 19th-century antislavery activists in this chapter. Write a list of questions to ask them. Now write a script of the interview, and present it for the class.

SUGGESTED READINGS

Aptheker, Herbert. *American Negro Slave Revolts.* New York: Columbia University Press, 1943.

Bennett, Lerone. *Pioneers in Protest.* Chicago: Johnson Publishing Co., 1968.

Brent, Linda. *Incidents in the Life of a Slave Girl.* New York: Harcourt, Brace, Jovanovich, 1861, 1973.

Douglass, Frederick. *My Bondage and My Freedom.* New York: Johnson Publishing Co., 1970.

Garnet, Henry Highland. *Address to the Slaves of the United States.* New York: Arno, 1968.

Giddings, Paula. *When and Where I Enter: The Impact of Black Women on Race and Sex in America.* New York: Morrow, 1984.

Northup, Solomon. *Twelve Years a Slave.* New York: Miller, Orton & Mulligan, 1855.

Price, Richard. *Maroon Communities.*

Quarles, Benjamin. *Black Abolitionists.* New York: Oxford University Press, 1969.

Walker, David. *Appeal to the Coloured Citizens of the World.* New York: Hill and Wang, 1965.

SUMMARY

Africans resisted enslavement through individual and group acts of defiance. Whites responded to the Africans' resistance of enslavement by enacting new laws and statutes that stiffened the penalties against Africans who were "disobedient." *(Chapter 18)*

Group defiance often took the form of armed rebellion. African freedom fighters including Charles Deslandes, Denmark Vesey, Nat Turner, and Joseph Cinque led heroic revolts against enslavement. Africans who resisted enslavement risked danger not only at the hands of whites, but also as a result of betrayal by other Africans who were fearful of whites. *(Chapter 19)*

While some Africans and whites risked their lives to help Africans escape from enslavement, most of the men, women, and children who were fortunate to escape to the North, Canada, or Mexico had to rely on their own resources. *(Chapter 20)*

Africans spoke out against the hypocrisy of a nation that championed the value of liberty while at the same time practicing enslavement. Many Africans argued that violence was necessary in order to end the enslavement of Africans, while others took the position that nonviolence was an important strategy in the antislavery movement. *(Chapters 21 and 22)*

Most often, white abolitionists did not view Africans as equals or accept the right of Africans to lead antislavery organizations. *(Chapter 22)*

African women often suffered the worst forms of exploitation during the enslavement. Their narratives offer firsthand accounts of violent sexual and physical abuse as well as their resistance. Harriet Tubman risked her life and freedom on 19 occasions to bring Africans to the North. *(Chapter 23)*

Personal Witnessing

REFLECTION

Reflect on the great number of Africans who risked and lost their lives so that their fellow Africans could gain freedom. Describe in your journal the beliefs and causes about which you feel strongly and passionately.

TESTIMONY

Reexamine the arguments for and against the use of violence to gain freedom. Give group testimony about nonviolent actions your class can take today to enhance your freedom. Give credit to the freedom fighters who paved the way for you to achieve these freedoms.

UNIT 7 RITE OF PASSAGE

In small groups, brainstorm, outline, and crate some "manuals" to use with young children to teach them the principles and values of Umfundalai that build character. Include descriptions of the qualities as well as activities to teach those values. If possible, arrange for your group to teach at least one of your "manuals" to an elementary school class. Include your manual in your Rites of Passage portfolio.

THE POLITICS OF OPPRESSION: FREE AFRICAN AMERICANS

C.E.

1838
Pennsylvania strips free Africans of the right to vote

1845-1856
A growing number of free Africans achieve financial success

In small groups, brainstorm a list of words that come to mind when you think of the term *oppression*. Then categorize the list into two columns: *Enslaved Africans* and *Free Africans*. Discuss and defend your choices.

As you read Unit 8, you will learn about the oppression under which most free African Americans lived and the mental and physical distress that oppression causes. When you finish the unit, reevaluate your list and discuss whether your group would move, delete, or add any terms. Explain your final lists to the class.

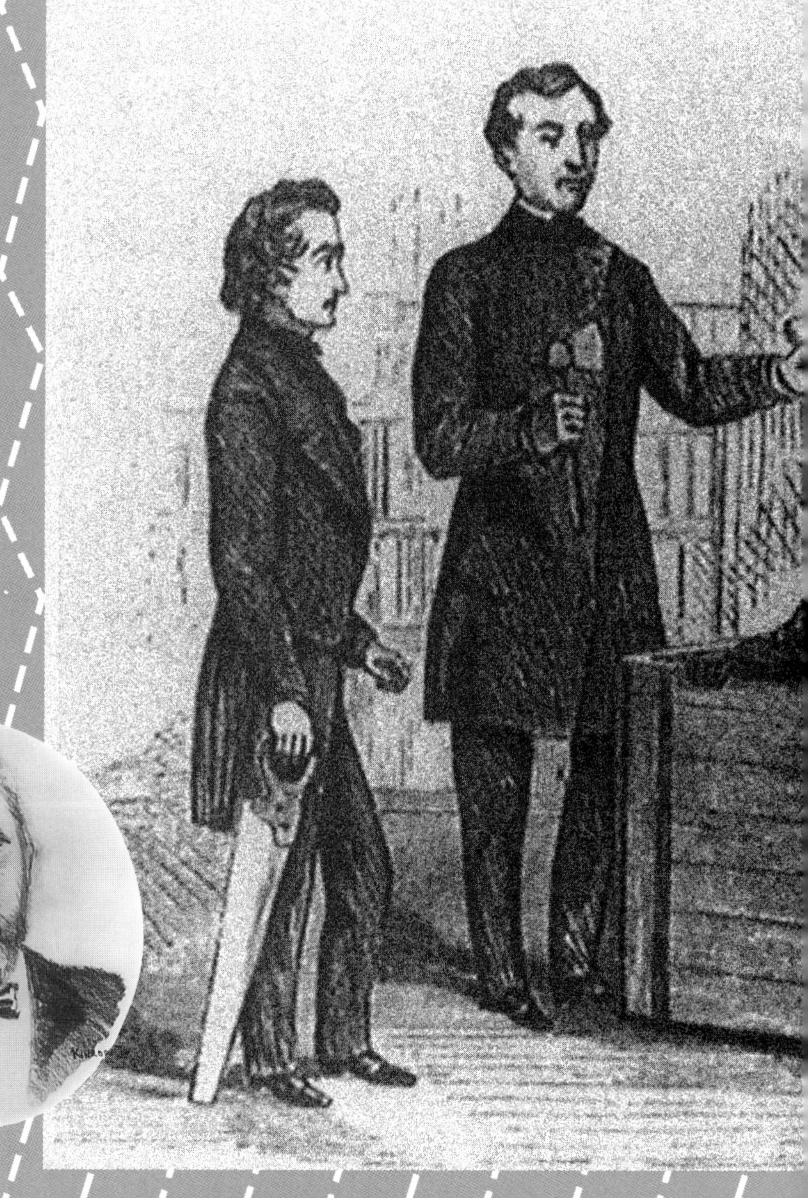

1860
30 percent of African heads-of-household own property

1846
Norbert Rillieux revolutionizes the sugar industry

"By reason of long bondage and hard slavery we have been deprived of enjoying the profits of our labour or the advantage of inheriting estates from our parents as white people do. . .and yet. . .we have been and now are taxed both in our polls and that small pittance of estate which through much hard labour and industry we have got together to sustain our selves. . . ."

PETITION TO THE MASSACHUSETTS LEGISLATURE, 1780

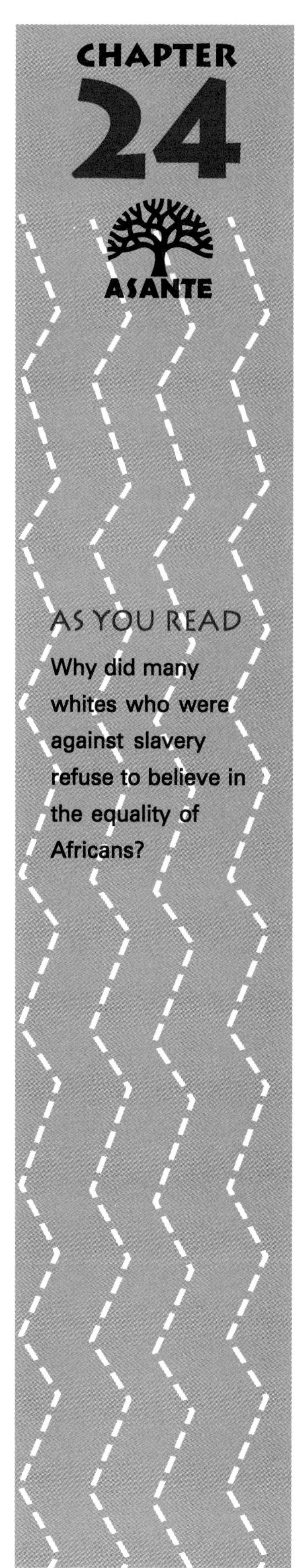

CHAPTER 24

ASANTE

AS YOU READ

Why did many whites who were against slavery refuse to believe in the equality of Africans?

A CONTRADICTION OF IDEALS

CENTER YOUR VOCABULARY

- ▲ apartheid
- ▲ double standard

From the swamplands of Florida to the narrow streets of new England, free Africans blazed a trail across the American landscape. The conditions under which they lived were as varied as the conditions under which they earned their freedom.

In 1790, there were 60,000 free Africans living in America. But by 1860 that number had leaped to nearly 500,000. The country was expanding at a rapid pace in terms of both population and the seizure of the land from Native Americans. In 1803, for example, President Thomas Jefferson concluded a deal with French General Napolean Bonaparte that sold the Louisiana territories to the United States for $15 million. The state of Texas, which was originally a part of Mexico, was annexed to the United States in 1845. Along with Texas came parts of New Mexico, Colorado, Wyoming, Kansas, and Oklahoma. These territories were all a part of Mexico. Oregon became a part of the United States in 1859.

The question of freedom or enslavement was always at the doorstep of the African in America in the 19th century. Those free Africans whose numbers had increased to nearly 500,000 by 1861 were a little better off than their fellows, but not much. Though technically free, they were threatened every day with the possibility of the loss of freedom. They were watched, harassed, beaten, cheated, and thrown in jails for little or no reason.

▲ Austin Steward was born into enslavement in 1793. At age 22, he "took" his freedom, worked hard, and became a successful business person and abolitionist.

In colonial America, the vast majority of free Africans were freed by enslavers for faithful service or because some enslavers could no longer live with the guilt of enslaving human beings. The details of how these Africans were freed are insignificant compared to the indomitable spirit of enslaved Africans who refused to be defeated and who purchased their own freedom in the harsh climate of enslavement.

Whether they lived among the abolitionists of the North or the enslavers of the South, free Africans lived with daily contradictions to their freedom. Free Africans could not attend school or vote. They were presumed enslaved until proven free. Movement from county to county or state to state was prohibited, except by permission, and this was seldom granted. The so-called "free" states in the North were hostile to Africans who moved North. Massachusetts was among the first free states to pass a law in 1788 prohibiting Africans who escaped enslavement from entering the state. By the 1830s, most Southern and some Northern states refused entry to free Africans. All of the Southern states required that free Africans carry certificates or passes at all times to prove they were free. Failure to do so meant that they would be sold by the local authorities. Many free Africans were kidnapped and sold into enslavement. They lived with the constant fear that their freedom could be challenged at any time.

Imagine what it must have been like for free Africans. Consider some examples of oppression in recent history. Consider what it was like for Jews during the reign of Hitler in Germany. Jews could not teach in schools, could not own property, could not work in hospitals, and could not marry non-Jews. Consider what it was like for the Africans in South Africa prior to the end of apartheid, the system of racial separation that served to oppress the Native population there. Native South Africans saw their property taken from them and given to whites, they could not vote, they could not own businesses in the major cities, they could not live in the better neighborhoods, and their children received inferior education. Free Africans in the 18th and 19th centuries lived in a similarly oppressive atmosphere.

Free States and Slave States (1780-1860)

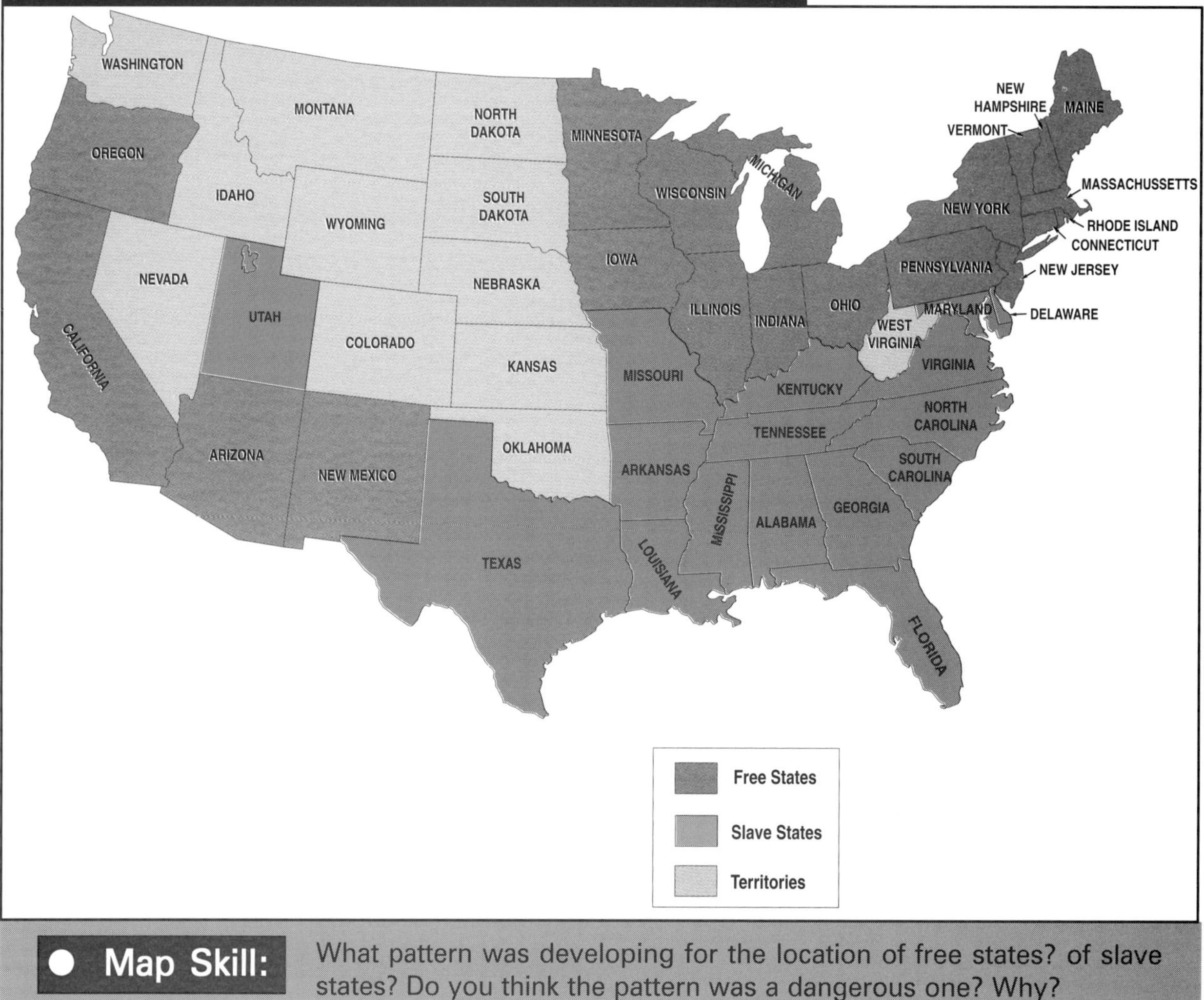

Map Skill: What pattern was developing for the location of free states? of slave states? Do you think the pattern was a dangerous one? Why?

Even the laws were against Africans. The Black Codes, a series of 19th-century laws and practices used to control the activities of free Africans in the North and the South, was like a noose around the neck of every African. Under the Black Codes, the constitutional right of assembly was sometimes denied to free Africans and was absolutely denied to enslaved Africans. For example, a 1723 Virginia law said, "All meetings by Negroes or slaves banned on any pretense whatsoever." The same Virginia law denied voting rights to Africans by declaring, "Free Negroes are not permitted to vote." Approved by the federal and local governments, the laws restricting the movement, professions, education, and social life of free Africans were unbearable. The laws made a mockery of freedom and made no attempt to extend justice to free Africans.

If the laws discriminated against Africans, local customs were even harsher. When free Africans left the safety of their homes in the morning, they had no guarantee they would return in the evening. Free Africans knew they could be accused by whites without cause. For example, someone might declare that they had walked on a sidewalk for whites, looked too arrogantly, spent too much money, or talked too loudly and have them arrested. Their only crime was being African.

WHITE FEAR OF FREE AFRICANS

Because whites feared that free Africans would encourage the enslaved to rebel and escape, many states passed laws that limited contact between free and enslaved Africans. By 1800, South Carolina had ruled that free Africans would be enslaved if they were caught helping enslaved Africans to escape. That same year, on the suspicion that free Africans were encouraging enslaved Africans to revolt, the names of 240 Africans and Native Americans were published in Massachusetts newspapers with a warning that they had better leave the state or suffer the consequences. Native Americans were often subjected to discrimination and were treated as unfairly as Africans in the 19th century. Of course, the consequences for both groups were enslavement or death.

Fear also prompted whites to prohibit Africans from carrying weapons. The fact that whites could carry weapons—and often used them against Africans—shows the double standard allowed under the law. Obviously, there was one set of rules for whites and another set of rules for Africans.

◆ CENTER YOUR THINKING

1. Name three states that were formerly part of Mexico.
2. Give two reasons that Napoleon sold the Louisiana Territory.
3. What precautions might you take to protect yourself and your family if you were a free African living in the South?
4. Describe how legislation was used to threaten the freedom of free Africans.
5. HOLISTIC ACTIVITY Students as Chart Makers

   In small groups, design a chart called THE BLACK CODES AND OTHER LAWS AGAINST FREE AFRICANS. Fold a piece of paper in half lengthwise. In the first column, list laws that were described in this chaper. In the second column, next to each law, write your group's opinion about why white people made that particular law.

CHAPTER

25

ASANTE

FREE AFRICANS IN THE SOUTH

CENTER YOUR VOCABULARY

- ▲ harass
- ▲ vagrancy
- ▲ bonds
- ▲ enterprising

AS YOU READ

How were free Africans able to achieve personal and professional success, even in the shadow of enslavement?

The danger for free Africans in the South was double that in the North. Imagine what it was like for the free African woman who lived in fear of leaving her home because she could be kidnapped by some white stranger, taken to another city or state, and enslaved against her will. Imagine the life of the African American man who, trying to make a living for his family, finds himself in debt to his employers for more money than he can earn and having little recourse to the law. In the South, unlike the North, there were no schools provided for free African children. In a few cases, white plantation enslavers who had fathered children by African women freed them and then sent the children to Europe for education. But this was extremely rare. The vast majority of Africans in the South, free and enslaved, had a difficult life.

Louisiana, Alabama, Virginia, and Kansas had very harsh laws that limited or abolished free Africans' right to speak out against enslavement. In Virginia the law said,

"If a free person by speaking or writing maintains that owners have not right of property in their slaves, he shall be confined in jail not more than one year and fined not exceeding five hundred dollars. He may be arrested and carried before a justice by any white person."

Of course, if a person could not pay the fine, he or she was enslaved. In Florida, a free African who was convicted of a crime could be enslaved.

Free Africans who lived in the South stood a good chance of being harassed or reenslaved if they remained in that region. Enslaved persons who were freed by their enslavers in Virginia, for example, had to leave the state within a year or be resold into bondage.

In North Carolina, a newly freed African who did not leave the state was reenslaved, and the payment for his or her sale went to the white person who informed the authorities.

Virginia, Tennessee, Georgia, and Mississippi required all Africans to register with the local authorities. Other states insisted that free Africans post bonds (money) guaranteeing their "good" behavior. Florida and Georgia required free Africans to have white guardians who would guarantee their good behavior. *To be good* meant to be mild mannered, respectful of white domination, and nonpolitical. In the minds of Southern whites, a free African was good if he or she accepted second-class citizenship and obeyed these oppressive laws.

Free Africans who did not accept oppression in any form were labeled *militant* and *dangerous,* when all they were seeking was the same rights as whites. Extending equal rights to free Africans opened up the possibility of equal rights for the enslaved. Faced with these possibilities, whites strengthened the laws to maintain enslavement and the institution of oppression.

To ensure that Africans did not compete with whites for jobs in the South, authorities prohibited free Africans from working in particular occupations such as teaching school, bookkeeping, or supervising whites without a license. Of course, the licenses were easily denied. Most Southern states, however, required that free Africans have a job or they could be charged with vagrancy, a crime that meant that they could be fined and enslaved for not working.

OVERCOMING THE ODDS

Despite the hardships and limitations, many free Africans prospered in the South. Their financial and personal successes are a testament to the invincible spirt and ingenuity of African people. Often shut out of the professions, Africans set out to work in the mills and factories of the rural South using the special trades and skills they had developed under enslavement. They helped to build railroads and canals that linked people together long before cellular phones, airplanes, and high-speed monorails. These skilled artisans created wealth and material goods with their labor. In the Southern cities of Charleston and New Orleans, among others, free Africans dominated the mechanical trades. In Charleston in the 1850s, for example, there were 122 African carpenters, 87 tailors, and 30 shoemakers. Free Africans also owned taverns and hotels. One of them, Jehu Jones, owned property valued at $40,000. Of course, Jones's wealth was the exception rather than the rule. However, there were a few other wealthy Africans in the South. Aaron Ashworth, a free African who ran one of the largest cattle-raising businesses in the country, owned 18.5 square kilometers (7.2 square miles) of farmland in 1846 and 2,470 head of cattle in 1850. William Goings, another free African in the East Texas town of Nacogdoches, became wealthy from land speculation and real-estate deals. The richest free African in the antebellum South was Thomy Lafon. Lafon, who lived in New Orleans, had property valued at $500,000.

Though not as wealthy, the majority of free Africans were equally enterprising. In 1860, for example, more than 30 percent of African heads of households had become landowners or leasors. In the Southern cities, 157 free Africans owned real estate, prompting Benjamin Quarles, author of *The Negro in the Making of America*, to write, "Almost without exception, these owners acquired their holdings by purchase, not by gift." By 1890, the number of free Africans owning real estate had swelled to 693.

Free Africans banded together against the oppressive conditions of the times. They gave each other moral and financial support by forming clubs and other organizations where they could meet and speak freely. In Petersberg, Virginia, for example, free Africans formed the Beneficial Society of Free Men of Color, in which each member pledged to support the others in sickness and in death. In Baltimore, which had the largest population of free Africans in 1935, there were 35 benevolent societies in operation.

▲ Norbert Rillieux

Baltimore may have had the largest population of free Africans, but the free Africans of New Orleans were among the most advanced in the South. Their record of achievement in science, literature, and the armed forces during this brutal moment in history makes them worthy of being called heroes for providing a positive example for others to follow. In 1846, New Orleans-born Norbert Rillieux created a vacuum cup that revolutionized sugar-refining methods that is still recognized today. Seventeen free African writers, poets, and playwrights banded together in 1845 to produce a 215-page anthology, *Les Cenelles.* One of the contributors, Victor Séjour went on to produce 21 plays for the Paris stage.

◆ CENTER YOUR THINKING

1. What were two states that required all Africans to register with the local authorities?
2. What are bonds? How were bonds used to control the behavior of free Africans?
3. Free Africans lived under constant threat of reenslavement. Why would free Africans risk their security by becoming involved in the antislavery movement?
4. Describe the living conditions of free Africans in the South.
5. HOLISTIC ACTIVITY Students as Authors

   Your small group is a committee of authors preparing a magazine article for African American teenagers on the spirit, ingenuity, and resilience of African people. Write and illustrate the article.

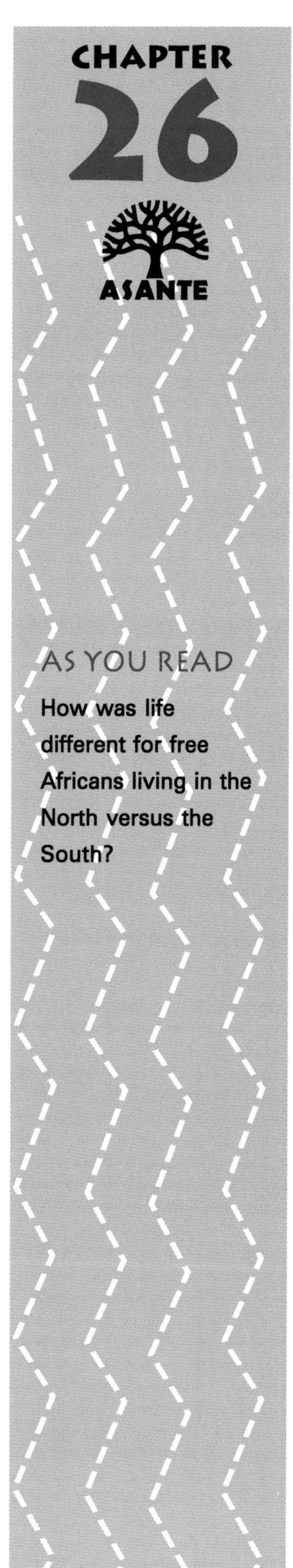

CHALLENGES IN THE NORTH

CENTER YOUR VOCABULARY

- ▲ menial
- ▲ discriminatory
- ▲ enlightened
- ▲ franchise

When Ellen and William Craft got permission from their enslavers to marry in 1846, they had no faith in the American South as a place to raise their future family. Both were skilled African workers in Macon, Georgia, and both feared that any children they had would have to live in bondage if they remained in Georgia. Neither liked or enjoyed their enslavement because, however sensitive white enslavers seemed to the enslaved people, in the end the enslaver held the key to their lives. The Crafts planned their escape. The plot was brilliantly conceived and executed.

Ellen, the daughter of a white planter and an enslaved African mother, dressed up as William's white male slaveholder and led them out of the South. She treated William as her servant so that the whites would not be suspicious of them. This daring escape required more money than an enslaved person could easily earn. William was one of the fortunate few. The slaveholder he worked for gave him permission to work as a waiter at a local hotel in his spare time. William worked hard and saved his money. He was able to save enough to buy men's clothes for Ellen to wear as a disguise. They left Georgia in December 1848, and Ellen, who could neither read nor write, put her right arm in a sling so that no one could ask her to sign her name.

A white male, wealthy enough to travel with an enslaved African but not educated enough to sign his own name, would have aroused immediate suspicion. Ellen bandaged her mouth so that she did not have to speak. Her broken English and accent would have given her away. Ellen gave the performance of a lifetime as the invalid planter headed North for medical treatment with his servant. They booked first class passage on boats and trains and stayed in the best hotels. In January 1849, they arrived in Philadelphia and met William Wells Brown, a former enslaved African who assisted them in getting to Boston and out of harm's reach.

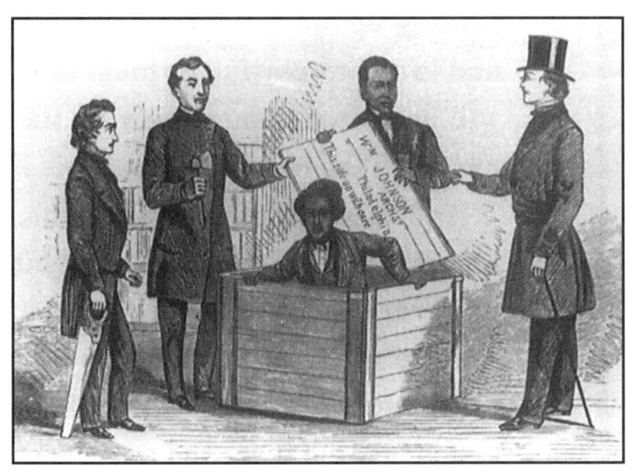

▲ Henry Brown steps out of the box he had made to ship himself to freedom.

William and Ellen Craft's passage to freedom was not unusual in its cleverness. Henry Brown, another African enslaved in Richmond, Virginia, in 1848 stepped into a box he had specially made for his escape and had a friend nail it shut. It was then shipped by the friend to the office of an antislavery committee in Philadelphia. Nearly 30 hours later, four antislavery workers pried it open and out stepped Henry "Box" Brown who said, "How do you do, gentlemen?"

Most of the travels of the free Africans were less spectacular than the enslaved Africans' escape. They did not have to show anything but their manumission papers. But they, too, wanted to get to the North because of the opportunities for jobs and less harassment.

There were three major differences between the lives of free Africans in the North and free Africans in the South. The restrictions against free Africans in the North were less severe; free Africans had greater opportunity for self-expression and thus were able to protest their unequal treatment; and some Africans had the right to vote.

After the American Revolution and the Constitutional Convention of 1787, free Africans in Pennsylvania, Massachusetts, Maine, New Hampshire, Vermont, and New York had the right to vote. In New York, for example, free Africans could vote if they had $250 worth of real estate. This requirement did not apply to whites. The right to vote was also short-lived. By the start of Civil War in 1861, free Africans in these states had lost the freedom to vote.

FREE AFRICANS IN THE NORTH

Free Africans in the North were restricted to the lowest paying jobs: domestic service and common labor. Like their counterparts in the South, many of the free Africans in the North had learned various trades during their enslavement. But as free people, they could not put their training to full use because white workers were fearful of losing their jobs to Africans who were more skilled or who would work for lower pay. These discouraged but determined Africans went to work as waiters, cooks, maids, and porters. They worked behind the scenes in the unskilled jobs that whites found objectionable.

This situation did not last long. Between 1830 and 1860, European immigrants, lured by the promise of gold and great wealth, flocked to the United States in droves. As the job market shrank, the new immigrants, who knew little about the history of the nation except that Africans were enslaved, began to compete directly with free Africans for these menial jobs.

Like their counterparts in the South, free Africans in the North rose to the challenge. They worked long hours and saved their pay. Soon, free Africans were buying their own homes and operating their own businesses. In New York in 1856, free Africans had $200,000 in bank deposits. In Cincinnati, free Africans owned property in excess of $500,000. Free Africans dominated the food-service industry, working as cooks, waiters, and owners of restaurants. Some Africans opened up barber shops and beauty salons.

In St. Louis, free Africans were very visible in the fur trade. They worked as hunters, guides, interpreters, and traders. James Beckwourth is perhaps the most famous. Beckwourth, while employed as a trader by the American Fur Company, discovered the lowest point across the northern Sierra Nevadas. Today, this point is called Beckwourth Pass.

Independent business operators such as James Forten, Stephen Smith, and William Whipper employed other free Africans and some whites. Forten hired Africans to work in his Philadelphia factory. Smith and Whipper were very successful lumber merchants in Columbia, Pennsylvania.

PENNSYLVANIA: AN EXAMPLE OF OPPRESSION

Pennsylvania had the largest population of free Africans in the North during the 19th century. Free Africans in the state were subjected to the same discriminatory laws that free Africans faced in other Northern states.

Pennsylvania's laws, from the granting of its charter to William Penn, in 1681, were designed to keep free Africans in an inferior position. A law passed as early as 1693 directed the police to punish any African traveling around the state without permission from a slaveholder. Now, more than 100 years later, free Africans could not gather or speak freely without the permission or presence of a white person. An entire century had passed without a change in the way Pennsylvanians saw Africans.

Nevertheless, Pennsylvania became one of the major destination points for Africans fleeing enslavement in the South between 1835 and 1860. The state attempted to have a law passed in 1813 that would require all free Africans within the state to register and carry passes. This law would have prevented any more runaway Africans from entering the state.

▲ James Forten hired other Africans to work in his factory.

James Forten, a wealthy free African and abolitionist, argued that the proposed law violated the Constitution. Fortunately, because of the vocal objections of Forten and other Africans, and the enlightened understanding of Quaker abolitionists, the law was never passed. Forten had led a successful campaign.

All of Forten's family were involved in the antislavery cause. His son, Robert, carried on his work in the 1830s. His daughter, Harriet, married Robert Purvis, another wealthy African American. The Purvises contributed a great deal of money and time to the antislavery movement. Margaretta, another of his daughters, was an officer of the Female Anti-Slavery Society in Philadelphia in 1845.

"We hold these truths to be self-evident, that God created all men equal, is one of the most prominent features in the Declaration of Independence, and in that glorious fabric of collected wisdom, our noble Constitution. This idea embraces the Indian and the European, the savage and the saint, the Peruvian and the Laplander, the white man and the African, and whatever measures are adopted subversive of this inestimable privilege, are in."

James Forten

His granddaughter, Charlotte, went to South Carolina in 1862 to teach newly freed Africans. She later married activist Archibald Grimke.

Pennsylvania, in 1838, stripped free Africans of the right to vote. This right was not regained until the passage of the 15th Amendment in 1870. Robert Purvis, one of Forten's sons-in-law, was among the many Africans who repeatedly protested their disenfranchisement, or loss of rights. The franchise usually refers to the right to vote. It has been broadened to include the civil rights that all U.S. citizens are entitled to under U.S. law.

Purvis wrote "Appeal Of Forty Thousand Citizens Threatened With Disfranchisement To The People Of Pennsylvania," which asked:

"Was it made the business of the [Pennsylvania State Constitutional] Convention to deny 'that all men are born equally free,' by making political rights depend upon the skin in which a man is born, or to divide what our fathers bled to unite, to wit TAXATION and REPRESENTATION?"

He reminded Pennsylvania whites that:

"Our fathers fought by the side of yours in the struggle which made us an independent republic. . . . We do not believe our disfranchisement would have been proposed, but for the desire which is felt by political aspirants to gain the favor of the slaveholding states . . . to gratify those who disgrace the very name of American liberty, by holding our brethren as goods and chattel. . . . We freely acknowledge our brotherhood to the slave, and our interest in his welfare. . . . [We] lay our claim before you, with the warning that no amendments of the present Constitution can compensate for the . . . conversion into enemies of 40,000 friends."

Purvis was referring to the 40,000 Africans in Pennsylvania who considered the government of Pennsylvania their enemy for taking away their right to vote. Africans still lost their right to vote in Pennsylvania.

TAXATION WITHOUT REPRESENTATION

Free Africans had to pay the same taxes as white Americans but often had no access to the public services, education, and political institutions for which they were paying.

In 1780, four years after the Declaration of Independence, Paul Cuffe, a wealthy free African sailmaker, along with six other free Africans petitioned the Massachusetts legislature for representation because they were taxed. "No taxation without representation" was, of course, the rallying cry for white colonists during the American Revolution. Cuffe and his group, by using the same slogan as the colonists, sought redress for Africans who did not enjoy the rights of citizenship. As wealthy Africans, Cuffe and others paid more taxes than whites who were less wealthy, but they were denied the rights that taxes provided.

This pattern of activism demonstrated by Forten, Purvis, and Cuffe would become increasingly important as time progressed. The signs of discontent were evident everywhere. Africans began to escape their enslavement in increasing numbers, joining with Native Americans in the South and in the West to form alliances against whites, whom both groups saw as a threat to their freedom.

Both the immigration from Europe and the expansion in the West produced even more conflicts in a society that was already experiencing social and political turmoil.

◆ CENTER YOUR THINKING

1. Name three states in which free Africans were able to vote.
2. How did Ellen and William Craft escape to the North?
3. Why did Pennsylvania become one of the major destination points for Africans fleeing enslavement?
4. Take a survey of ten or more adults in your community to find out if they voted in the last election. Share and discuss the results with your class and family.
5. HOLISTIC ACTIVITY Students as Playwrights & Teachers
   Work with a partner or a small group to write a brief play about Ellen and William Craft's escape from enslavement. Include a conversation between them in which they plan the trip and talk of their fears, their feelings, and the precautions they plan to take. Then include a conversation held after they reach freedom in Philadelphia in which they recount and analyze their plans and the actual journey. Perform your plays for young children to teach them about enslavement and resistance to it.

SUGGESTED READINGS

Bennett, Lerone. *The Challenge of Blackness*. Chicago: Johnson Publishing Company, 1972.

Brotz, Howard, ed. *African American Social and Political Thought, 1850-1920*. New Brunswick: Transaction, 1992.

David, Jay, ed. *Black Defiance: Black Profiles in Courage*. New York: Willliam Morrow, 1971.

Harding, Vincent. *There is a River*. New York: Random House, 1981.

Litwack, Leon. *North of Slavery: The Negro in the Free States*. Chicago: University of Chicago Press, 1961.

UNIT REVIEW 8

ASANTE

SUMMARY

Between 1790 and 1860, the size and population of the country underwent tremendous growth. Whites seized land from the Native Americans, Texas and other parts of Mexico were annexed to the United States. *(Chapter 24)*

Free Africans who lived in the South faced daily threats and the chance of being enslaved again. Despite these conditions, there are many examples of the prosperity and success that they were able to achieve. They formed clubs and organizations to provide a system of support. *(Chapter 25)*

Even the so-called free states of the North were hostile to Africans. Many of the Northern states passed laws limiting the movement of Africans and permitting many Africans to be kidnapped and sold into enslavement. Still, the restrictions against free Africans in the North were less severe. However, while they paid the same taxes as whites, they often had no access to the services and institutions for which they were paying. *(Chapters 25 and 26)*

REFLECTION

Write your reactions, thoughts, and feelings about this unit in your journal.

TESTIMONY

Prepare your personal or small-group testimony on the strength of the Africans you have studied in this unit. Your testimony may take any form you select—a speech, a dance, music.

UNIT 8 RITE OF PASSAGE

In Unit 7, you created a set of manuals to teach children character-building values and qualities. Now, create a manual(s) to teach children why and how to show respect and obedience to their parents, and why and how to show respect to their elders. Be sure to include discipline in speech and action in the manual, and the African origins of valuing what one's elders say. Include descriptions of the qualities as well as activities. If possible, arrange for your group to teach at least one of your "manuals" to an elementary school class. Include your manual in your portfolio.

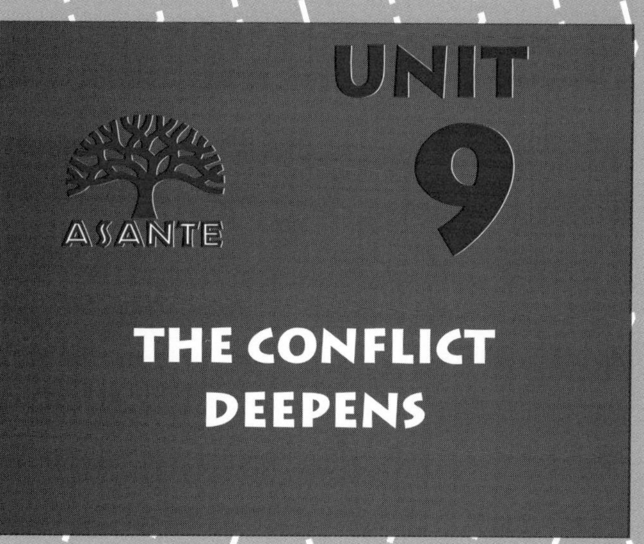

1828
John Calhoun writes
The South Carolina Exposition

In small groups, discuss and formulate at least one law which, if passed, would be favorable to your group but unfavorable and unfair to some other group. Select an existing or potential law about which your group is concerned and discuss the fairness of it. For example, you might select a law that is being challenged before the Supreme Court. If a law is favorable for the majority of people but unfair to a minority of people, is it a good law? Why or why not? Debate and explain your group's position.

As you read Unit 9, think about the need for laws to keep societies in order and to protect individuals. Think about how we determine the fairness of a law. What happens when a law is discriminatory? What process occurs to change it? In this unit, you will learn about deliberately discriminatory laws that were passed to deny rights and citizenship to African Americans.

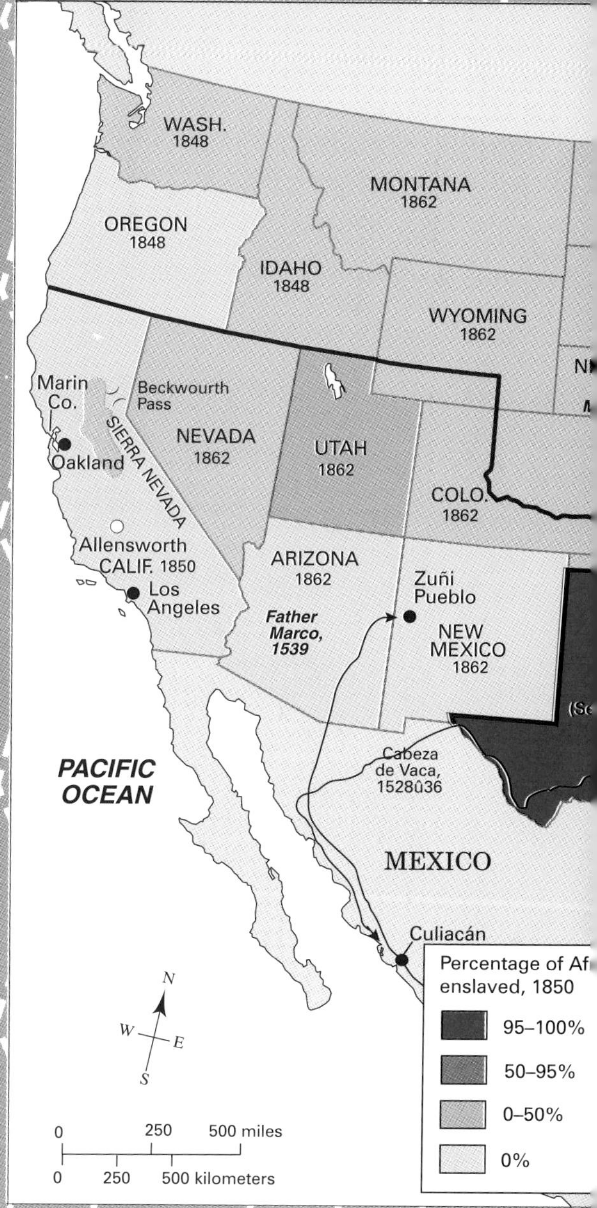

1831
70,000 Native Americans (Cherokee, Muskogee, Chickasaw, Choctaw, and Seminoles) are uprooted from Florida and Georgia and marched west to Oklahoma on what became known as the Trail of Tears

1851
William Parker's Resistance occurs on September 11 in Christiana, Pennsylvania.

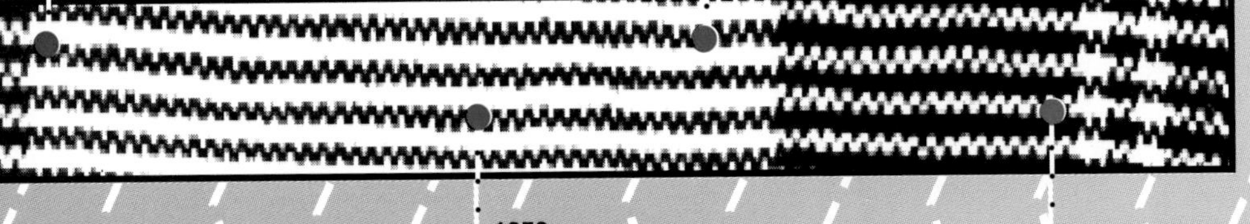

1850
James Beckwourth discovers pass in the Sierra Nevadas that becomes a major route to California

1861
Abraham Lincoln takes the office of president.

> *"I had no rod wherwith to smite the stream, and thereby divide the waters. I had no Moses to go before me and lead the way from bondage to the promised land. Yet I was in a far worse state than Egyptian bondage; for they had houses and land, I had none; they had oxen and sheep, I had none; they had wise counsel to tell them what to do, and where to go, and even to go with them, I had none."*
>
> HENRY BIBB, AN ENSLAVED AFRICAN FROM KENTUCKY.

Historical Map 1780-1865

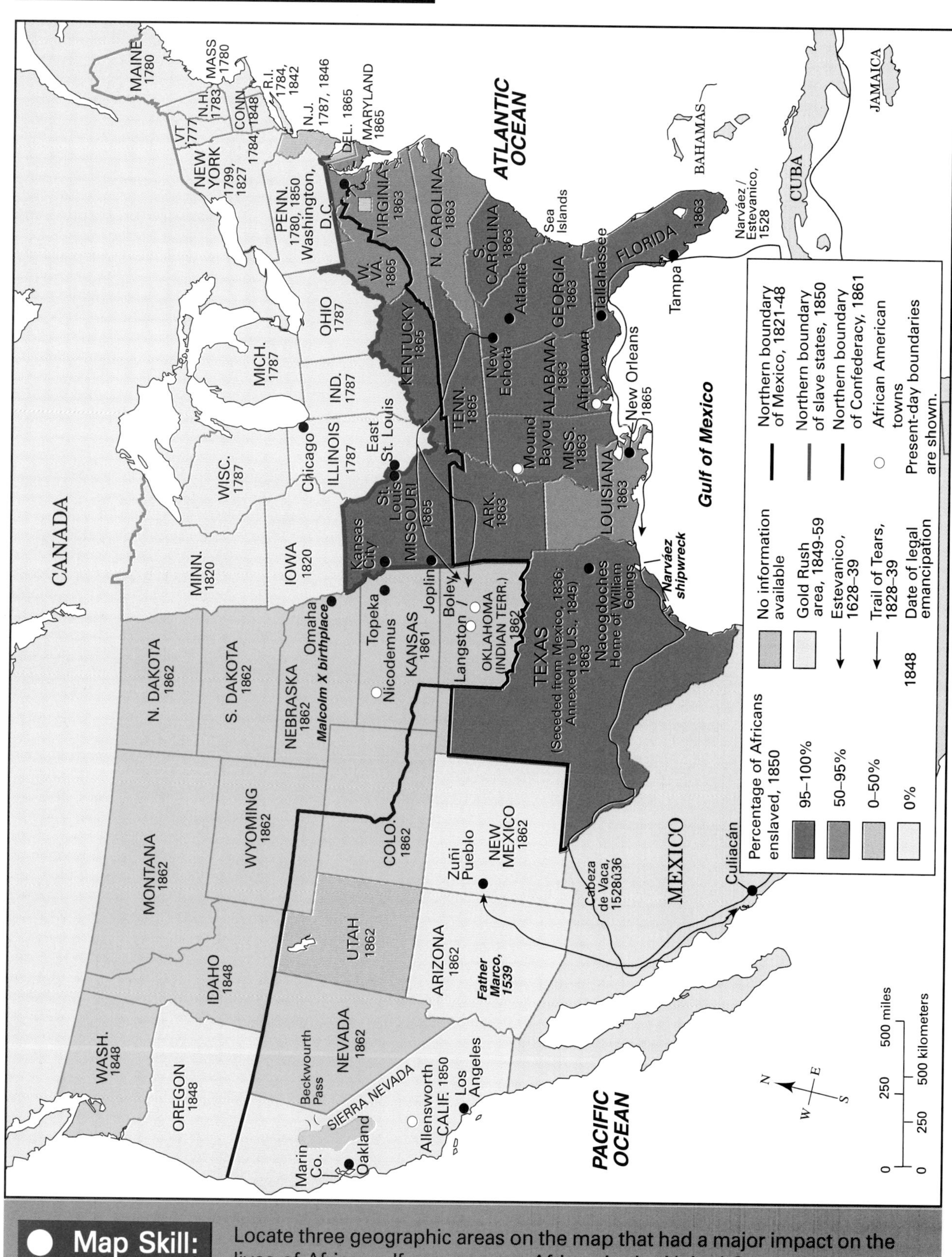

Map Skill:

Locate three geographic areas on the map that had a major impact on the lives of Africans. If you were an African in the United States during this period, where would it be better to live? What conflicts would you face?

CHAPTER

27

ASANTE

RACE AND CLASS DIVIDE THE NATION

CENTER YOUR VOCABULARY

▲ Manifest Destiny
▲ depression
▲ zeal
▲ Americans

AS YOU READ

What were some of the pressures Africans faced as they worked with whites to expand the West?

Africans in the 19th century were beginning to define their own unique struggle for liberty. Their experience was not the same as that of white immigrants. Whites who moved to America during the 19th century happily saw the country as the answer to the overwhelming economic, religious, and social problems they had experienced in Europe. They still believed that the streets in America were paved with gold, and they joined a great migration that had begun a century before. Confident, hopeful, and inspired by the promise of freedom, independence, individualism, and Manifest Destiny, they came to the new land.

MANIFEST DESTINY

Perhaps more than anything else, it was this sense of mission, the idea of taming a continent and taking possession of a vast land for themselves, that motivated the Europeans who came to America. Despite the fact that the land was occupied by people who were born on the land and had lived there for thousands of years, the Europeans felt an almost religious zeal, or intense enthusiasm, to conquer it from sea to sea. The idea of Manifest Destiny was born.

Manifest Destiny included the deliberate policy of fighting the Native Americans in the West so that the mission of reaching the Pacific Coast could be accomplished by Europeans. This policy was first used in the early 1600s to justify forcing the Native Americans of the region off their land. Some 200 years later, whites were using the same policy to push Native Americans in the Southeast as far west as they could.

In the 1830s and 1840s, both sides battled for control of the land during the Seminole Wars. Hundreds of Africans fought on the side of the Seminoles and became fugitives with them in the swamps of Georgia and Florida. In 1831, more than 50,000 Cherokee, Muskogee, Chickasaw, and Choctaw people were uprooted from their land and forced to march westward to Oklahoma. More than 4,000 of them died from cold, hunger, and sickness on what became known as the *Trail of Tears.*

EXPANSION

Between 1826 and 1860, the country underwent tremendous changes. The population nearly tripled from 12.9 million in 1830 to 31.4 million in 1860. The number of Africans in the nation in the same period jumped from 2.3 million to 4.4 million. There were close to 14,000 immigrants from Europe arriving in the Americas in 1826. By 1851, this number had skyrocketed to more than 474,000. Lured by offers of cheap land, good jobs, servants, and great wealth, whites left the poverty-ridden communities of Europe and made the long and dangerous journey to the Americas in great numbers.

When gold was found in California in 1848 and 1849, the mad rush to enter the United States intensified. People came from every region of Europe as well as China and Japan. Meanwhile, the majority of Africans were still officially enslaved, and because the enslavement did not end until 1865, few Africans were able to participate in the Gold Rush.

ECONOMIC DEPRESSION

In 1837, an economic depression plunged the country into a financial panic. Many banks and businesses failed. Many people lost their jobs and life savings. This depression, or economic downturn, came on the heels of an earlier depression in 1834. In Pennsylvania, for example, the coal mines and factories that had employed thousands of uneducated immigrants closed down.

Undoubtedly, this contributed to the racial tensions of the time, as rich and poor whites came into conflict and the North and the slaveholding South fought bitterly with each other. Poor white immigrants felt that they were in competition with Africans for jobs. Africans, many of them more highly skilled than the white immigrants, resented the fact that the only thing the whites had going for them was the color of their skin. Africans were angry but not surprised. They had more than 200 years of evidence that in a racist society, color counts for more than skill or intelligence.

DISTANCE BETWEEN THE RACES

By 1860, eight new states joined the Union and the land mass of the country had almost doubled as Americans forced their way west. The new transcontinental railway system linked the eastern territories with the far West, making the country seem smaller, physically. Socially, however, the distance between the races and classes of people who now called themselves *Americans* was still huge. As the nation grew, so did its problems.

CHALLENGES IN THE WEST

Ever since the exploration of the Zuni pueblo in New Mexico by Estevanico in 1539, the western part of the North American continent held an attraction for Africans. Estevanico, an African, had been on the Spaniard Panfilo de Narvaez's ill-fated expedition to Florida in 1528, had been held prisoner by the Native Americans for seven years, and then escaped to New Spain. From there, he made his way across the continent looking for the Seven Cities of Gold. He is credited with opening up the Spanish world with his exploration of New Mexico and Arizona. But that was more than 300 years earlier than the challenges Africans would face in the 19th century as oppressed people fighting against another oppressed people, the Native Americans.

▲ Estevanico

Many of the Africans who moved westward in the 1800s did so in the service of the army. The Congress created six African regiments in the regular army. This was reduced to two infantry and two cavalry regiments immediately after the Civil War. One historian writes, "In a number of battles during the Indian Wars the four black regiments, especially the cavalry units, showed that in most situations they were equal to the white soldiers." The historian's surprise at the African soldiers' outstanding horsemanship is ironic because of the strong, historic presence of cavalry in the West African armies of the Sudan region. Even today in northern Ghana, Nigeria, Senegal, and other countries of West Africa, one finds this tremendous horsemanship.

Service in the army provided African soldiers with opportunities for new experiences. However, these units were often used to fight Native Americans and to fill outposts in the western territories. In the 1870s, for example, African soldiers made up more than 50 percent of the fighting men stationed in New Mexico.

African soldiers faced enormous pressures in the West. Not only was there severe discrimination from the white officers but ridicule from the Native Americans as well. The Native Americans nicknamed them the "Buffalo Soldiers" because most of the African American soldiers wore their hair in locks. Galloping across the plains on horseback with their hair streaming behind them in the wind, one could mistake them for buffaloes.

Although the Native Americans respected the fighting prowess and courage of the Africans, they found it difficult to accept the fact that Africans were fighting on the side of the whites. Given this conflict, the number of African soldiers who deserted and crossed the border into Mexico during the 1800s is estimated to have been in the hundreds.

As the West grew, the African population increased. Africans began to travel west as advance scouts for wagon trains, cowhands, and laborers. There were others who went on their own to find their own place in the great expanse of the West. They were eager for

▲ A generation of African settlers make their home on the Great Plains in the West.

liberty and just as eager to demonstrate their capacity to survive. They settled the African American towns of Langston and Boley, Oklahoma, and later Allensworth, California, and other African American towns.

Many Africans got out of the army and became cowhands, driving large herds across the plains and prairies. Many of the small towns of the West, particularly in Texas, Kansas, Nebraska, and Colorado, have old African American populations that grew up during the period when the Ninth and Tenth Cavalries rode the plains.

◆ CENTER YOUR THINKING

1. Name at least three factors that motivated Europeans to come to America.
2. Why did Europeans feel they had a right to the land even though it had been occupied for thousands of years by other people?
3. Explain why the Africans who settled in the West are compared with the cavalry in the West African armies.
4. How did the economic depression of 1837 contribute to the racial tension between Africans and whites?
5. HOLISTIC ACTIVITY Students as Graphic Artists

   Trace a large outline map of the United States on paper. Then, in small groups, make a list of the important events you wish to mark and illustrate on the map. Some examples might be the 1831 Trail of Tears, the Gold Rush, enslaved Africans working in the fields of the South, and immigrants arriving in the United States.

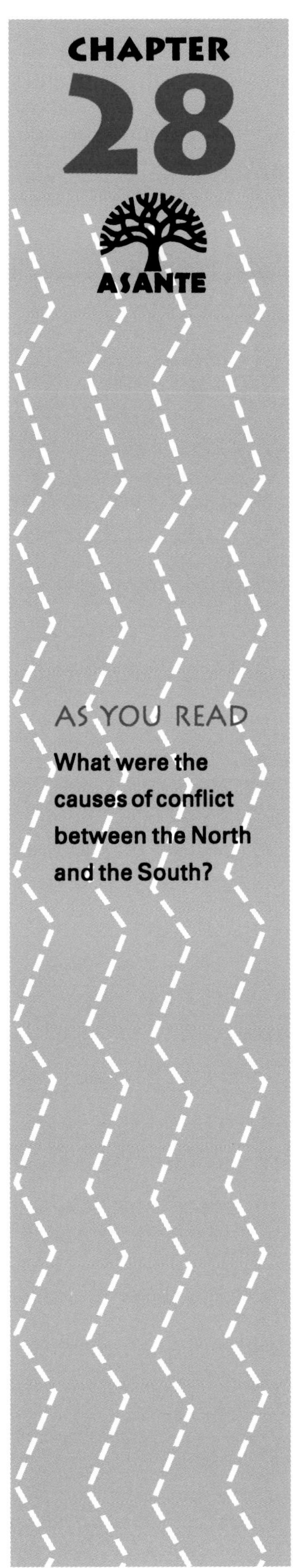

SOURCES OF CONFLICT

CENTER YOUR VOCABULARY

- ▲ tariff
- ▲ unconstitutional
- ▲ revoke
- ▲ secede
- ▲ states' rights
- ▲ Africans' rights

AS YOU READ

What were the causes of conflict between the North and the South?

By the mid 1830s, the entire nation was focused on the issue of African enslavement. State legislatures spent most of their time debating enslavement, as did the federal government. It was like turning on the evening news and seeing a discussion on African enslavement on every channel every day! Imagine what a television news program of the time would have been like. Your eyes would have been glued to the screen. You would have watched Africans burning sugar-cane or cotton fields to protest their enslavement. Perhaps there would have been special reports on Africans being lynched, Africans petitioning the legislature, and congressional debates. You might have felt frightened or angry, or both.

Discussion of the issue was so frequent that in 1836, the Congress passed the Gag Rule which banned discussing "slavery" in Congress. The Gag Rule reaffirmed an earlier congressional decision that Congress had no right to decide issues of "slavery" for individual states. Each state wanted to be able to decide its own future over the "slavery" issue. Actually, had there not been a civil war, the United States could possibly still have a couple of states that would be "slave" states. Some Africans might even have revolted and formed a state of their own.

By making each state responsible for its own laws on enslavement, the federal government did not have to enforce laws that the South would dislike. In the end, however, as President Abraham Lincoln would argue, you could not have a country where half had enslavement and the other half did not.

As you might expect, the presidential campaign of 1848 turned on the issue of enslavement. Abolitionists formed the Liberty Party in 1840 to stop enslavement. Some Africans were nominated for state and national offices on the Liberty Party ticket, and many Africans were in support of the Liberty Party.

By 1848, the Liberty Party had merged with other groups that wanted to stop the spread of enslavement to new territories. The new group was called the Free Soil Party. It was passionately opposed to the extension of "slavery" into the new territories. Although it lasted for no more than four years, the Free Soil Party, comprised of many abolitionists and supported financially and morally by Africans in the North, sought to limit "slavery." Because the party was not supported by a large majority of whites, all of whom had the power to vote, the party never really had a chance of winning the election. However, the party did succeed in raising the question of the future of enslavement in the United States to a national level.

The rise of enslavement as a part of the national consciousness caused the Republican party to place enslavement at the top of its political agenda. The party offered Abraham Lincoln as a presidential candidate in the election of 1860, and in 1861, on the brink of civil war, Abraham Lincoln and the Republicans took office. The nation now had 18 free states in the North and 15 "slave" states in the South. The North's goal was to stop enslavement from spreading into the West. The South's goal was to have more slaveholding states.

The northern states were largely industrial while the southern states were largely agricultural. African labor was used in both the North and the South; however, the North paid Africans for their labor, while the South benefited from the free labor they exploited from the enslaved. Slaveholders made huge profits from African labor but did not give Africans their fair share of the profit.

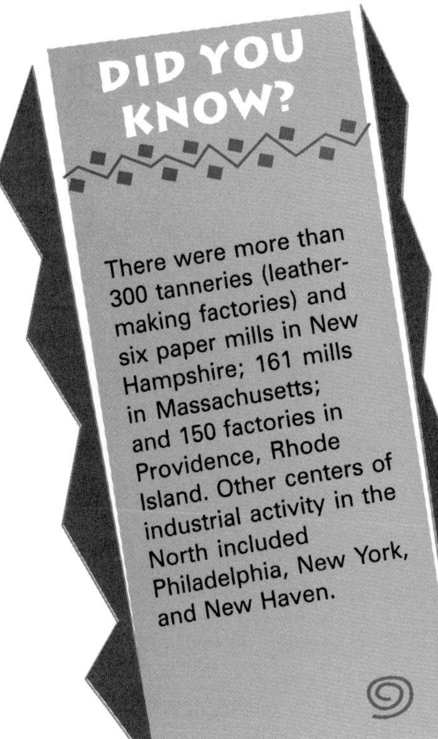

The use of paid labor in the North and "slave" labor in the South was a major source of conflict. The North felt that the South had an unfair advantage in the unending source of "slave" labor, while Northern workers had to be paid. In reality, less than 10 percent of Southerners enslaved Africans; 50 percent of the 385,885 slaveholders enslaved fewer than five Africans each. Fewer than 3,000 Southern white families formed an aristocracy, or elite class, with each family enslaving more than 100 Africans! The rich dictated the economic situation and made it possible for poor whites to feel assured of white domination. Yet, all whites did not enslave Africans, and all whites did not approve of enslavement.

Both North and South insisted uncompromisingly on special laws to serve themselves. The conflict deepened.

The South supplied raw materials, especially cotton, for northern factories and to France and Great Britain. More than 60 percent of the cotton grown in the South was exported to France

▲ The cotton gin revolutionized the production of cotton in the South.

and England. The North did not think it was fair for them to have to compete with cotton goods from England and France. In 1828, the North managed to get Congress to pass a high protective tariff, or tax, on goods, especially cotton goods, that were imported into the country. The South was opposed to the tariff because they feared that their European customers might stop buying U.S. cotton with the tax increase on their materials.

The southern states said the tariff was unconstitutional. They said that the industrial North did not have to contend with foreign competition, while the agricultural South did. *The South Carolina Exposition,* written in 1828 by Vice President John C. Calhoun, expounded the concept that no state should have to obey a federal law that was in violation of the Constitution.

In 1832, South Carolina cited Calhoun's *Exposition* as grounds for revoking, or canceling, a new tariff. Southerners threatened to secede from the union. The stage was set for actual separation.

The South strongly supported the doctrine of states' rights. This is the right of states to pass laws that override unconstitutional federal laws. The South would use the states' rights idea over the years to deny Africans' rights in certain states, despite the guarantees for all in the Constitution.

◆ CENTER YOUR THINKING

1. What raw materials were produced by the South?
2. Explain the Gag Rule.
3. Why was the North concerned about the free "slave" labor in the South?
4. What were some of the issues that separated the Liberty, the Free Soil, and the Republican parties?
5. HOLISTIC ACTIVITY Students as Television Writers

   If television had existed in the 19th century, what would the coverage of African enslavement have been like? What debates would have occurred on the news programs? Write a script for a 19th-century television program. If time permits, perform it for the class.

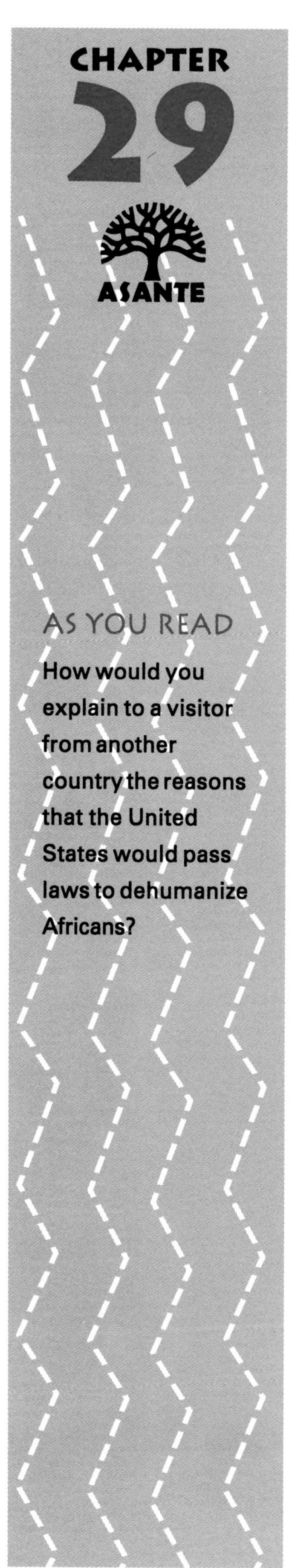

AS YOU READ

How would you explain to a visitor from another country the reasons that the United States would pass laws to dehumanize Africans?

OUTLAWED

CENTER YOUR VOCABULARY

▲ Fugitive Slave Law
▲ exodus
▲ civil disobedience
▲ compromise

The passage of the Fugitive Slave Law was perhaps the most significant event to happen in the antebellum period, the period just before the Civil War. It became a test of the nation's ability to live together with two opposing and radically different viewpoints. It also prompted the Reverend Jarmain W. Loguen, one of the leading voices for change to say, "I don't respect this law—I don't fear it—I won't obey it! It outlaws me, and I outlaw it, and the men who attempt to enforce it on me."

The Fugitive Slave Law of 1850 gave full power to the federal government to deny rights to Africans forcefully. The law denied the testimony of alleged runaways. This meant that runaway Africans could be placed in custody without a warrant or a hearing. The law assumed that Africans were guilty rather than innocent. Runaway Africans were not guaranteed an investigation of their case. If their case went to trial, they could not testify on their own behalf. A federal commission was set up to decide who owned the escapees. Any federal marshal who failed to carry out the harsh measures dictated by the Fugitive Slave Law could be fined $1,000. Federal marshals were also liable for the full value of any fugitive escaping from their custody. Persons who knowingly blocked a fugitive's arrest, assisted a fugitive's escape, or harbored or concealed

“You of the old Bay State [Massachusetts] . . . have a Daniel who has deserted the cause of freedom. . . . Honorable Senators may record their names in its [Fugitive Slave Law] behalf, and it may have the sanction of the House of Representatives; but we, the people . . . are superior to both Houses and the Executive . . . [C]ompromises . . . make right yield to wrong.”

Samuel Ringgold Ward

“I place the governmental officials on the ground that they place me. I will not live a slave, and if force is employed to re-enslave me, I shall make preparations to meet the crisis as becomes a man.”

Rev. Jarmain W. Loguen

“Fellow-Countrymen: I cannot begin by saying ‘Fellow-citizens,’ for that would be an unwarrantable assumption, under the circumstances. . . . [T]he courage and patriotism of the colored man is of a higher character than that of the white man. There is not a man of fair complexion before me who has not something in this country to protect which the colored man does not possess; and [yet] . . . in the moment of danger [they are] willing to discharge their duty to the country. . . . They are the friends, and not the enemies of the country. . . . If they were white, the people would say, without hesitation, ‘Let this Union be dissolved.’”

Charles Remond

a fugitive faced a fine of up to $1,000 and imprisonment for up to six months. Anyone found guilty of breaking this law was also required to pay $1,000 for each escaping fugitive.

The law also made it a federal crime for any citizen to refuse to aid in the recapture of a fugitive. At the very least, anyone who did not actively uphold the Fugitive Slave Law could be charged with civil disobedience—refusal to obey governmental demands.

Attempts by enslavers to recapture runaway Africans increased. Because there were no safeguards, many free Africans were kidnapped and sold into enslavement. Now, the capture and enslavement of Africans was financially rewarding for whites who wanted to make extra money.

“Now, this bill strips us of all manner of protection. But while it does this, it throws us back upon the natural and inalienable right of self-defense—self-protection. It solemnly refers to each of us . . . the question . . . whether we will protect ourselves, even if, in so doing, we have to peril our lives, and more than peril the useless and devilish carcasses of Negro-catchers. Let the men who would execute this bill beware. Let them know that to enlist in that warfare is present, certain, inevitable death and damnation. Let us teach them, that none should engage in this business, but those who are ready to be offered up on the polluted altar of accursed slavery . . . and so let all the black men of America say, and we shall teach Southern slavocrats (whites who believed in slavery) and Northern doughfaces [Northerners who are Southern sympathizers], that to perpetuate the Union, they must beware how they expose us to slavery, and themselves to death and destruction.”

The Impartial Citizen

African leaders vehemently denounced the Fugitive Slave Law, and Africans reacted violently to its enforcement. A mass exodus, or departure, of Africans from the United States into Canada and the Caribbean began. Africans now had to flee the “free” states because they could be captured and enslaved again. Approximately

20,000 Africans fled to Canada from 1850 to 1860. Harriet Tubman took runaway Africans "all the way to Canada after the passage of the [law], explaining that she could not trust Uncle Sam with her people any longer."

Samuel Ringgold Ward condemned the law and its supporters, especially Senator Daniel Webster of Massachusetts, who was considered by many Africans to be a traitor to the antislavery movement.

Reverend Jarmain W. Loguen, a fugitive in Syracuse, spoke about his determination to disobey the law. Loguen left no doubt that he was prepared to defend himself if challenged.

Frederick Douglass, in his famous speech "The Meaning of July Fourth for the Negro" denounced the law as the nation's ultimate hypocrisy.

Charles Remond spoke before the New England Anti-Slavery Convention to deny what many people wanted to believe—that the Fugitive Slave Law was a necessary compromise to keep the Union together.

The Impartial Citizen, an African newspaper, editorialized that many Africans would resist by using any means necessary.

◆ CENTER YOUR THINKING

1. Name a country outside the United States to which Africans fled following the passage of the Fugitive Slave Law.
2. Explain two reasons that Africans reacted strongly to the passage of the Fugitive Slave Law.
3. Discuss at least three provisions of the Fugitive Slave Law and how these provisions affected Africans, free and enslaved.
4. What is *civil disobedience?* What impact did it have on Africans and whites who did not support enslavement?
5. HOLISTIC ACTIVITY Students as Newspaper Editors

   The Fugitive Slave Law was a setback for Africans. Once again, they had to use their strength and determination to overcome hardships imposed by white Americans. After reading the excerpt from *The Impartial Citizen* newspaper, work in your small group to design and produce a four-page newspaper for Africans in 1850.

CHAPTER 30

ASANTE

DRED SCOTT

CENTER YOUR VOCABULARY

▲ sanctuary ▲ *Dred Scott* decision

AS YOU READ

Why did the Supreme Court rule that Africans "had no rights which the white man was bound to respect?"

Africans who had moved to the Kansas-Nebraska territories to escape enslavement found themselves now at risk. Many joined with the white revolutionary John Brown to fight against the enslavers and their supporters. The possibility of enslavement taking hold in Missouri, Kansas, and Nebraska meant that Africans had lost one more sanctuary, or place of protection, where they could be free from enslavement.

In 1854, Congress passed the Kansas-Nebraska Act, which widened the gap between abolitionists and the slaveholding South. The Kansas-Nebraska Act repealed the long-standing Missouri Compromise of 1820, which banned enslavement in Kansas and Nebraska. The Africans in these territories were gripped with fear at the prospect of losing their freedom. Their fear soon gave way to a firm resolve to resist enslavement at all cost. Some of these Africans rode with the brave John Brown on various raids against the enslavers in northern Virginia. Brown later led an attack on October 16, 1859, in Harpers Ferry, Virginia. He was sentenced to death and hanged for leading this uprising.

DRED SCOTT

Barely three years had passed since the devastating effect of the Fugitive Slave Law when Africans were slapped with yet another

▲ John Brown

disastrous ruling. By the time the Supreme Court handed down the *Dred Scott* decision, Africans harbored deep resentment toward the white legislators.

Dred Scott was an enslaved African whose owner, a surgeon in the U.S. Army, took him on several trips. Two of those trips included Illinois and Wisconsin, free territories. A suit was filed in 1846 on Scott's behalf in Missouri, where he resided, asserting that he was a free man in Illinois and Wisconsin because those areas did not allow enslavement.

The Missouri courts ruled against Scott, and the case was taken to the federal courts. In 1857, the U.S. Supreme Court handed down the landmark decision effectively denying citizenship to African Americans by rejecting Dred Scott's claim to freedom. The *Dred Scott* ruling decided the position of all enslaved Africans in the nation. It made Africans, free and enslaved, even more insecure because it gave federal legal authorization for the complete stripping of rights from them. The 1857 ruling said, in effect, Africans were not and could not be citizens in the land of their birth because the majority of white people did not want them to be.

▲ Dred Scott brought suit to obtain his freedom.

Roger B. Taney, the chief Supreme Court justice, said about Africans in the course of stating the Court's decision:

"They had more than a century before [the signing of the Declaration of Independence] been regarded as beings of an inferior order, and altogether unfit to be associated with the white race, either in social or political relations; and so far inferior, that they had no rights which the white man was bound to respect; and the Negro might justly and lawfully be reduced to slavery for his benefit. He was bought and sold, and treated as an ordinary article of merchandise and traffic, whenever a profit could be made by it. This opinion was at that time fixed and universal in the civilized portion of the white race. It was regarded as an axiom [principle] in morals as well as in politics."

This would be considered one of the most unfortunate opinions in the history of the American nation because it enshrined the second-class status of Africans.

The *Dred Scott* decision simply reinforced the attitude long held by most white Americans that Africans were not citizens of the United States. James W. Bryan, a white delegate from North Carolina, remarked at the 1835 North Carolina Constitutional Convention which disenfranchised North Carolina free Africans:

"I do not acknowledge any equality between the white man and the free negro, in the enjoyment of political rights—the free negro is a citizen of necessity, and must, as long as he abides among us, submit to the laws which necessity and the peculiarity of his situation compel us to adopt."

Stephen Douglas, a white senator from Illinois, said in 1858, during a debate with Abraham Lincoln as they were running for president of the United States:

"I am opposed to negro citizenship in any and every form. I believe this government was made on the white basis. I believe it was made by white men, for the benefit of white men and their posterity forever. I do not regard the negro as my equal. He belongs to an inferior race, and must always occupy an inferior position."

This state of affairs was to last, legally, until Reconstruction when the 14th Amendment gave citizenship rights to African Americans. The attitudes that allowed the *Dred Scott* decision to be implemented did not change, as evidenced by the states' laws enacted after Reconstruction in the late 1860s. These laws continued to deny civil rights to African Americans until they were struck down by the passage of the Civil Rights Act of 1964.

A PUBLIC MEETING

WILL BE HELD ON

THURSDAY EVENING, 2D INSTANT,

at 7½ o'clock, in ISRAEL CHURCH, to consider the atrocious decision of the Supreme Court in the

DRED SCOTT CASE,

and other outrages to which the colored people are subject under the Constitution of the United States.

C. L. REMOND,

ROBERT PURVIS,

and others will be speakers on the occasion. Mrs. MOTT, Mr. M'KIM and B. S. JONES of Ohio, have also accepted invitations to be present.

All persons are invited to attend. Admittance free.

▲ African Americans met frequently to discuss and denounce the *Dred Scott* decision.

The legacy of the *Dred Scott* decision persists today as African Americans continue to struggle with the problems of racial discrimination. African Americans still fear the power of the white majority to make and enforce laws that deny rights to some of the nation's citizens. Do you understand why the African American population has produced numerous civil rights and human rights leaders?

◆ CENTER YOUR THINKING

1. Who was Dred Scott?
2. What is meant by the term *second-class citizen*? To whom does it refer?
3. What reasons were given by white political leaders for their opposition to the granting of citizenship rights to Africans?
4. Explain why "African Americans still fear the power of the white majority to make and enforce laws." Do you agree or disagree? Explain your opinion.
5. HOLISTIC ACTIVITY Students as Graphic Artists

   In small groups, research the *Dred Scott* case, and make a poster or other presentation of the case that explains the implications and outcomes of the decision. Be sure you include the significance of the case for Africans seeking liberty and freedom in the United States.

CHAPTER 31

ASANTE

WILLIAM PARKER'S RESISTANCE

AS YOU READ

Were Africans, freed and enslaved, considered citizens of the United States? Why?

CENTER YOUR VOCABULARY

▲ treason ▲ tenets

William Parker's Resistance in Christiana, Pennsylvania, was the first major action against the Fugitive Slave Law of 1850. The incident is an example of Africans' commitment to freedom and to resisting the Fugitive Slave Law. Whites, however, had a different view of Africans who practiced self-defense. William Parker's Resistance was a public example of the different responses of Africans and white Americans. It magnified the contrast between the reality of Africans' lives and the false view whites had of Africans. Fighting back had become a regular habit for Africans.

On September 11, 1851, Edward Gorsuch, a Maryland enslaver, tried to recapture four escaped Africans. He and five other white men went to Philadelphia to have Fugitive Slave Commissioner Edward Ingraham swear out four fugitive-slave warrants.

The four escaped African men had fled to live close to William Parker, the leader of a local African self-defense organization. Gorsuch knew where the escapees were because William Padgett, a local fugitive catcher living near Christiana, had told him.

As Gorsuch and his friends arrived in Philadelphia, Samuel Williams, a member of an African abolitionist watch group, was watching their every move. Williams and the abolitionists warned Parker about the danger he was in.

The slave-catchers rode up to William Parker's home just before dawn. Edward Gorsuch and Marshal Kline broke into the house. They were forced to retreat when Parker and his family aimed their guns at the intruders. Eliza Parker, William's wife, blew a horn in a prearranged signal to call the members of the self-defense organization. The slave-catchers shot at her, but she continued blowing the horn. About 25 African neighbors arrived with whatever weapons they could find, to protect Parker and the others from the intruders.

Gorsuch and his men fought on, but the Africans stood their ground and defended themselves. When it was all over, Edward Gorsuch was dead, his son was seriously wounded, and the rest, including the deputies, had run away in fear.

Parker and other members of the organization escaped to Canada. Many people helped them, including Frederick Douglass. Parker gave Douglass the gun he had used in the resistance. Later, Eliza Parker stole away to Canada and joined her husband.

With the Parker resistance, Africans in the Christiana area, many of whom had nothing to do with the incident, were arrested without cause. Thirty-six Africans were charged with treason (betrayal of one's country) against the United States, including William Parker and the others who had fled. White prosecutors argued that by disobeying the Fugitive Slave Law, the Africans were "levying war" against the United States. The major defense counsel was antislavery activist and opponent of the Fugitive Slave Law Thaddeus Stevens.

President Fillmore mentioned William Parker's Resistance in his second annual message to the nation in December, 1851. As expected, his remarks were critical of the resisters, whom he saw as a "lawless" and "violent" mob.

Most whites condemned the resisters, while Africans raised money and gave moral support to them. Africans expressed solid support for the rebels. The Colored Freemen of Ohio issued a resolution at their convention on January 14, 1852, supporting the resistance.

" It is deeply to be regretted that in several instances officers of the Government, in attempting to execute the law for the return of fugitives from labor, have been openly resisted and their efforts frustrated and defeated by lawless and violent mobs; that in one case such resistance resulted in the death of an estimable citizen. I have regarded it as my duty to give all aid legally in my power to the enforcement of the laws. "

President Fillmore's 1851 Message to the Union

" We sympathize deeply with . . . the men at Christiana who so honored a Christian name, by protecting their homes, and refusing to be made slaves; and have learned from their example that liberty is dearer than life, and eternal vigilance its only guarantee. "

Colored Freemen of Ohio

▲ Ellen Craft disguised herself as a man to escape enslavement.

William and Ellen Craft, who had escaped to England, praised the rebellion in a November 29, 1851, letter: "We think a few more such cases as the Christiana affair will put a damper upon slave-catchers."

Frederick Douglass saw the resisters as "heroic defenders of the just rights of man against manstealers and murderers."

The Impartial Citizen, an African newspaper in New York, supported the resistance, as did most other newspapers in the African community: "On our first page will be found extracts from several papers, in different sections of the country, in regard to the resistance recently offered to the kidnapping miscreants from Maryland, at Christiana, Pa."

The September 25, 1851, *National Anti-Slavery Standard* described the resistance as a reasonable response to the "midnight incursions of man-hunters, with their treacheries, stratagem, their ruffian outrages, and bloody violence . . . menacing the defenseless people of colour with a 'reign of terrour.'" The paper asserts the humanity of the Christiana resisters when it goes on to say:

"That Gorsuch should have been shot down like a dog seems to us the most natural thing in the world. The example . . . set at Christiana we have no doubt will be followed, and perhaps improved upon hereafter, for coloured flesh and blood . . . is very like that of a lighter shade, and shrinks from stripes and chains, and will be prompt to try a measure which even in its worse result is better than Slavery."

William Parker's Resistance was a severe test of the tenets or truths of American democracy and law. It exposed the contradiction between the theory of the American creed—which asserts that all men are created equal and have unalienable rights including life, liberty, and the pursuit of happiness—and the reality of the practice of the enslavement and oppression of Africans.

Ironically, the participants in William Parker's Resistance were charged with treason against a country that denied Africans citizenship. To be charged with treason against one's country, the accused must be considered a citizen of that country. Clearly, whites used the legal system for their own advantage while denying Africans equal access to the system.

William Parker explained the alienation from American society that Africans felt when he said that if Africans and whites were equal under the law, then he would obey the law instead of resisting. “But . . . the laws for personal protection are not made for us, and we are not bound to obey them. If a fight occurs I want the whites to keep away. They have a country and may obey the laws. But we have no country.” Parker and the other resisters did not feel bound to obey a law that stripped them of basic human rights and protection of those rights. Since the federal government offered them no protection, Africans felt it was up to them to use any means necessary to secure and protect themselves.

◆ CENTER YOUR THINKING

1. What was Willlliam Parker's Resistance, or the Christiana Resistance?
2. What was President Fillmore's reaction to William Parker's Resistance?
3. How did Africans support Parker's resisters?
4. Compare the meanings of the terms *treason* and *civil disobedience.*
5. HOLISTIC ACTIVITY Students as Strategic Planners Parker's Resistance did not change laws nationwide. African Americans continued to work for lasting legislative changes. Imagine that you and your small group have met in secret after the Parker Resistance to develop a strategic plan to change laws nationwide. You want to stay nonviolent. What will you do to stay nonviolent? Where will you argue for change?

SUGGESTED READINGS

Katz, Jonathan. *Resistance at Christiana*.

Still, William. *The Underground Railroad*.

SUMMARY

Europeans who came to North America were motivated by desire and a sense that it was their manifest destiny to take possession of the vast continent. Conflicts between poor white immigrants and Africans sometimes arose because the whites felt they were in competition with more highly skilled Africans for jobs. *(Chapter 27)*

Africans were among the early settlers in the West. They established African American towns in Oklahoma and California. Many Africans arrived initially as explorers and scouts. *(Chapter 27)*

Throughout the early 19th century, Africans continued to press for the abolition of enslavement. The agitation of Africans and white abolitionists against enslavement prompted the banning of any discussion of "slavery" in Congress and the reaffirmation by Congress that each state was responsible for determining the future of enslavement within its territory. However, the use of paid labor in the North and enslaved African labor in the South created economic conflicts that both North and South sought to resolve through special laws. *(Chapter 28)*

In the mid-19th century, Congress passed two acts—the Fugitive Slave Law and the Kansas-Nebraska Act—to make it more difficult for enslaved Africans to escape to freedom. The legislation also contained provisions that threatened free Africans with enslavement. Many Africans departed to Canada and the Caribbean. The legislation affirmed that the United States did not consider the rights of Africans, both free and enslaved, worth protecting. *(Chapters 29 and 30)*

Africans reacted violently against the enforcement of the laws. Ironically, though Africans were not granted the rights of citizenship, Africans who defied the laws were charged with treason against the United States. *(Chapter 31)*

REFLECTION

Reflect on the issues building up to conflict between Africans and whites. Was conflict to be inevitable? Write your reflections in your journal.

TESTIMONY

In a small group, using any format you choose, give your opinion of those who worked to free Africans during this era.

UNIT 9 RITE OF PASSAGE

What are some changes that you feel need to be made in your school or community? Discuss this in your group. Then, take a group leadership role. Create an action plan for a campaign for change. How will you inform people of the change you advocate and your ideas for action? How will you make your action effective? Include a copy of your action plan in your Portfolio.

ASANTE

UNIT 10

STRIKING FOR LIBERTY AGAIN!

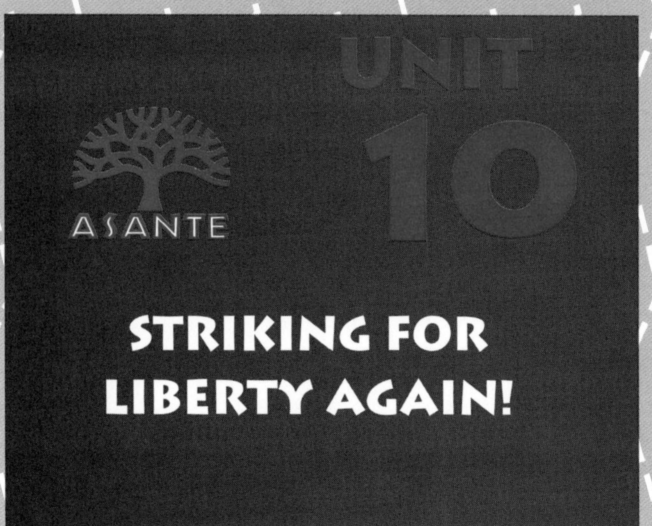

1830
The name Jim Crow emerges from a Southern folk song; it would later come to symbolize the segregated system of the United States

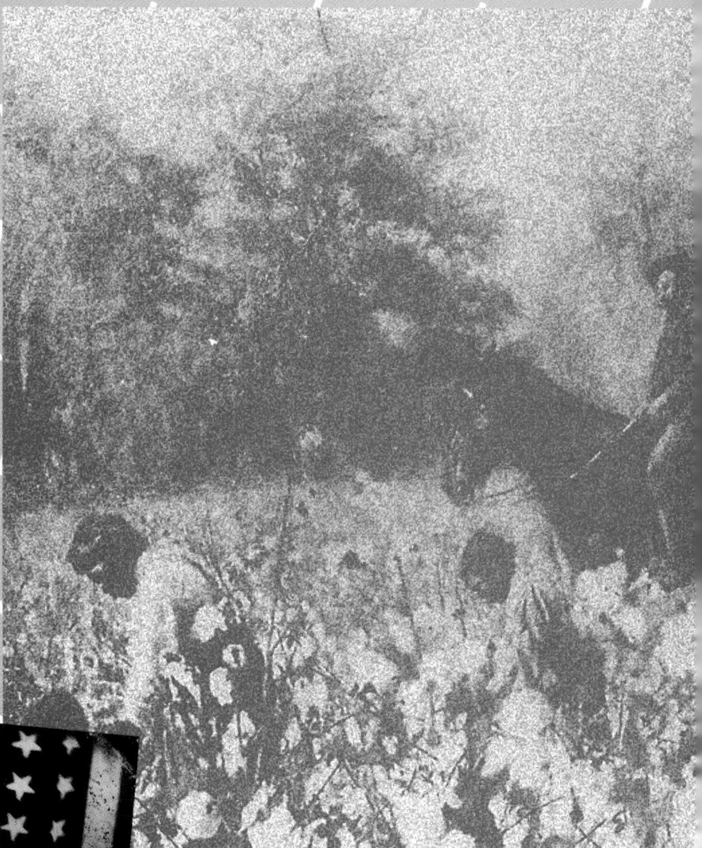

In small groups, list the reasons you have already learned over the years for the Civil War. How many of those reasons would turn out favorably for African Americans? Were there any unfavorable results for African Americans? any disappointments? List all you know. Now write a list of questions you have about the role of and impact on African Americans.

As you read Unit 10, meet with your group and discuss the answers to your questions. At the end of the unit, share your questions and answers with other groups. What new information did you learn about the Civil War?

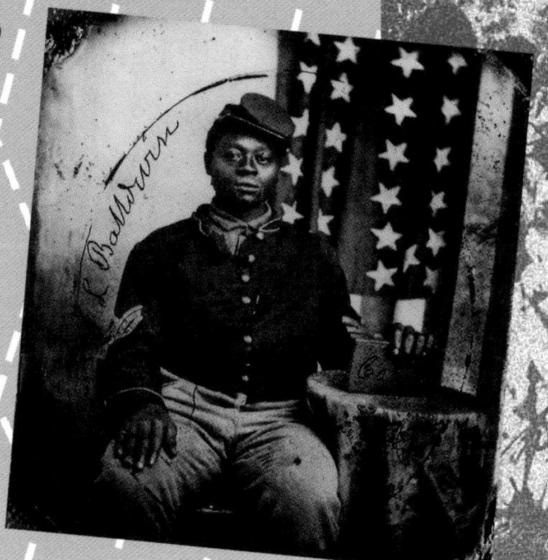

1861
Civil War begins April 12 when Fort Sumter is attacked

1863
Virginia, Arkansas, North Carolina, and Tennessee join the Confederacy

1864
Sergeant William Walker leads his company in a protest against unfair practices in the Union Army; he was tried by Army officials and executed

1860
South Carolina becomes the first state to secede from the Union. Mississippi, Florida, Alabama, Georgia, Louisiana, and Texas follow; these states become known as the Confederate States of America

1862
Robert Smalls captures a Confederate gunboat

"Let not those who have never been placed in like circumstance [enslavement] judge me harsly. Until they have been chained and beaten—until they find themselves in the situation I was, borne away from home and family towards a land of bondage—let them refrain from saying what they would not do for liberty."

FREDERICK DOUGLASS

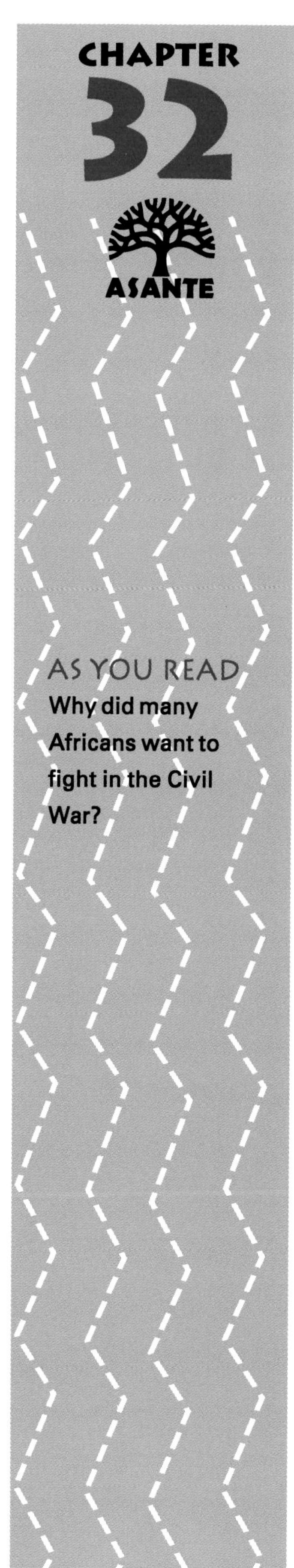

SECESSION BEGINS

CENTER YOUR VOCABULARY

- ▲ Civil War
- ▲ enlist
- ▲ deserted
- ▲ Confederacy
- ▲ contrabands
- ▲ regiment

On the brink of civil war, the Union had only 18 free states, mostly in the North, and the South had 15 slave states. Most Africans in the United States lived in enslavement in the South. Northerners did not want African enslavement in the new territories opening up in the West. Southerners wanted the new territories to become slaveholding states. Africans throughout the Union wanted their freedom.

You will remember that the northern and southern regions of the country had become very different. The North was industrial; the South agricultural. Africans were free in all of the northern states by 1855, but enslavement was still practiced in the South. Enslaved Africans constantly challenged the right of white planters to keep them in bondage. Southerners believed that the federal government should stay out of the affairs and rights of individual states. They argued for the preeminence of states' rights over federal rights. The argument became so hot and emotional that Africans began to sense an end to enslavement. Everyone seemed poised for battle in 1859 and 1860.

Southern whites had been threatening to break away from the Union for years before the Civil War. In a civil war, the people in one country or group take opposite sides and fight against each other.

Secession 1860-1861

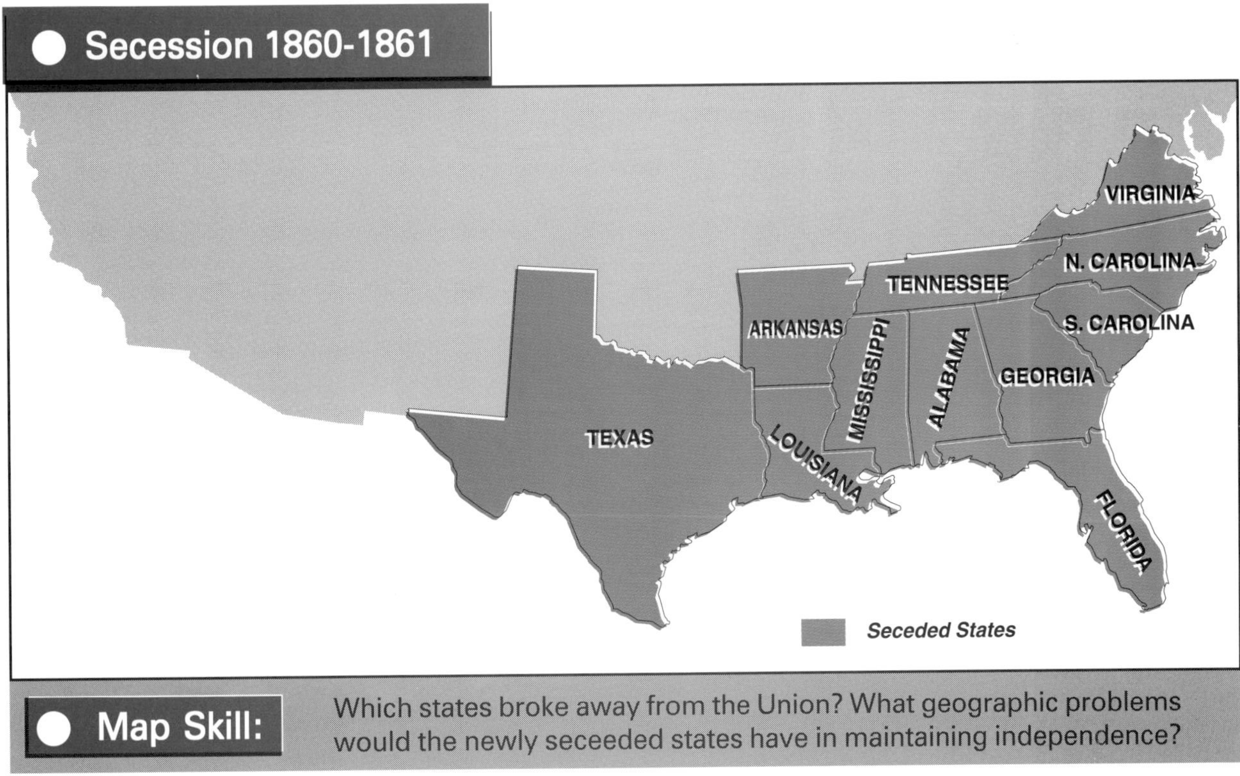

Map Skill: Which states broke away from the Union? What geographic problems would the newly seceeded states have in maintaining independence?

Abraham Lincoln's election as president in November 1860 caused more calls for secession.

In December 1860, South Carolina became the first state to secede, or break away, from the Union. Mississippi, Florida, Alabama, Georgia, Louisiana, and Texas followed. By the time Lincoln was sworn into office in March 1861, South Carolina and the others had formed their own country, which they called the Confederate States of America, or the Confederacy.

The leaders of the Confederacy believed that President Lincoln would give in to Northern abolitionists and end African enslavement. Without the enslaved's free labor, the Confederate states were fearful that their economy would collapse. African people saw the conflict as an opportunity to end enslavement.

The Civil War began on April 12, 1861, when the Confederacy fired on Fort Sumter in the Charleston, South Carolina, harbor. President Lincoln had sent supplies to the fort to show that it was still under his control even though it was inside the Confederacy. Confederate leaders regarded the fort and all of President Lincoln's representatives as an intrusive foreign power.

MEN OF COLOR, TO ARMS! NOW OR NEVER!

This is our Golden Moment. The Government of the United States calls for every Able-Bodied Colored Man to enter the Army for the THREE YEARS' SERVICE, and join in fighting the Battles of Liberty and the Union. A new era is open to us. For generations we have suffered under the horrors of slavery, outrage and wrong; our manhood has been denied, our citizenship blotted out, our souls seared and burned, our spirits cowed and crushed, and the hopes of the future of our race involved in doubts and darkness. But now the whole aspect of our relations to the white race is changed. Now therefore is our most precious moment. Let us Rush to Arms! **Fail Now and Our Race is Doomed** on this the soil of our birth. We must now awake, arise, or be forever fallen. If we value Liberty, if we wish to be free in this land, if we love our country, if we love our families, our children, our homes, we must strike NOW while the Country calls: must rise up in the dignity of our manhood, and show by our own right arms that we are worthy to be freemen. Our enemies have made the country believe that we are craven cowards, without soul, without manhood, without the spirit of soldiers. Shall we die with this stigma resting on our graves? Shall we leave this inheritance of shame to our children? No! A thousand times No! **We WILL Rise!** The alternative is upon us; let us rather die freemen than live to be slaves. What is life without liberty? We say that we have manhood—now is the time to prove it. A nation or a people that cannot fight may be pitied, but cannot be respected. If we would be regarded *Men*, if we would forever **SILENCE THE TONGUE OF CALUMNY,** of prejudice and hate; let us rise NOW and fly to arms! We have seen what **Valor and Heroism** our brothers displayed at **PORT HUDSON and at MILLIKEN'S BEND;** though they are just from the galling, poisoning grasp of slavery, they have startled the world by the most exalted heroism. If they have proved themselves heroes, can not we prove ourselves men? **ARE FREEMEN LESS BRAVE THAN SLAVES?** More than a Million White Men have left Comfortable Homes and joined the Armies of the Union to save their Country; cannot we leave ours, and swell the hosts of the Union, to save our liberties, vindicate our manhood, and deserve well of our Country?

MEN OF COLOR! All Races of Men—the Englishman, the Irishman, the Frenchman, the German, the American, have been called to assert their claim to freedom and a manly character, by an appeal to the sword. The day that has seen an enslaved race in arms, has, in all history, seen their last trial. We can now see that **OUR LAST OPPORTUNITY HAS COME!** If we are not lower in the scale of humanity than Englishmen, Irishmen, white Americans and other races, we can show it now.

MEN OF COLOR! BROTHERS and FATHERS! WE APPEAL TO YOU! By all your concern for yourselves and your liberties, by all your regard for God and Humanity, by all your desire for Citizenship and Equality before the law, by all your love for the Country, to stop at no subterfuges, listen to nothing that shall deter you from rallying for the Army. Come forward, and at once Enroll your Names for the **Three Years' Service. STRIKE NOW,** and you are henceforth and forever **FREEMEN!**

African Americans saw the Civil War as an opportunity to end African enslavement. ▶

Confederate soldiers fired on the fort. A war between the North and the South could no longer be prevented. Virginia, Arkansas, North Carolina, and Tennessee then joined the Confederacy. Virginians in the western part of the state did not secede. They formed the state of West Virginia in 1863. The Southern border states of Missouri, Delaware, Kentucky, and Maryland remained in the Union.

THE AFRICAN VIEW OF THE CIVIL WAR

At the start of the war, free Africans immediately tried to enlist (sign up) in the Union Army. In African eyes, the Civil War was the revolutionary war they would have led if they could have, to gain their personal freedom and civil rights from white enslavers who valued property rights over human rights. But only a handful of Africans were free. Only a few were not physically owned by whites. Free Africans were still enslaved by racial prejudices that would take more than the Civil War to correct. Enslaved Africans, of course, were still bound by the physical, psychological, financial, legal, and social chains of enslavement.

▲ This early photograph shows an unknown Civil War soldier.

Like so many other Africans in America, Frederick Douglass, a free African in the North, saw the Civil War and African participation in it as a way to end enslavement for all Africans. In an editorial titled "Men of Color, To Arms!" published by Douglass in 1865 in his newspaper, *The Douglass Monthly*, Douglass wrote, "This is our golden opportunity. Let us accept it. Let us win for ourselves the gratitude of our country, and the best blessings of our posterity through all time."

Douglass believed that if Africans distinguished themselves in the Civil War, they would win their freedom. He asked President Lincoln to allow Africans to enlist in the Union Army:

"Once let the black man get upon his person the brass letters, U.S., let him get an eagle on his button, and a musket on his shoulder, and there is no power on earth which can deny that he has earned the right to citizenship in the United States."

Despite their small numbers, free Africans volunteered for the Union army. They were refused. President Lincoln was afraid that the slaveholding Southern border states of Missouri, Maryland, Delaware, and Kentucky would join the Confederacy if Africans were allowed to enlist. Africans formed drill companies and boot camps while they waited for the policy preventing them from fighting to change.

Although they were prevented initially from enlisting in the Union Army as soldiers, African Americans were never prevented from serving in the Union Navy, where they had jobs such as cooks, dishwashers, and launderers. These jobs were part of the necessary support services that the navy needed to function in the war. However, Africans distinguished themselves on numerous occasions. As civilians on board the battleships, Africans defended the ships with such skill and courage that they would eventually break down the barriers preventing them from fighting.

▲ Robert Smalls

African's service in the navy convinced many whites that Africans made good soldiers. But there were still some whites who did not believe that Africans could think or learn modern warfare. Robert Smalls, an enslaved African, proved them wrong. Smalls and his African troop captured a Confederate gunboat, *The Planter*, in Charleston and sailed it to Union lines in 1862. He later served as a representative in the South Carolina state legislature.

Large numbers of enslaved Africans, eager to fight for their freedom, fled to Union lines to enlist. Unfortunately, many of them were returned to the enslavers. However, General Benjamin Butler, a Union commander, considered runaway Africans as confiscated contraband, or illegal property, and refused to return them to the enslavers.

Even though the escapees were no longer enslaved, they were still treated badly. Runaway African fugitives in the Union Army were forced to work as cooks, grave diggers, laborers, nurses, scouts, and spies before they were allowed to enlist as soldiers.

▲ The Emancipation Proclamation allowed Africans to enlist officially in the Union Army in 1863.

The Emancipation Proclamation, issued by President Lincoln, gave Africans in the states that were in revolt against the Union their freedom. The proclamation finally allowed the enlistment of Africans in the Union Army in 1863. A decline of white enlistments, several defeats of Union armies, and the South's continuing refusal to return to the Union forced Abraham Lincoln to reconsider allowing Africans to fight in the war. Many white Union soldiers deserted (left the army) to avoid serving with Africans. Two Illinois white regiments (battle groups) were disbanded because of so many desertions.

Many whites were willing to fight for the Union but did not want to fight for or with Africans. Nevertheless, Africans felt obligated to fight for their own freedom.

Frederick Douglass set up enlistment centers in many large cities in the North. Two of his own sons enlisted. Many other African leaders participated in the recruitment of African soldiers. To these recruiters, Africans had to show their willingness to fight for an end to enslavement.

But even though Africans fought and died valiantly in the Civil War, there were many whites, including Abraham Lincoln, who would never consider Africans citizens of the United States. The irony of the situation remained: Africans willing to die for their freedom too often found whites unwilling to accept them on equal terms.

◆ CENTER YOUR THINKING

1. How did African enslavement contribute to the outbreak of war? How did the Emancipation Proclamation impact the war?
2. How did the Southern argument for state's rights over federal rights hurt Africans?
3 What forms of mistreatment were experienced by Africans who served in the Union army?
4. In your opinion, were Africans justified to fight in the war? Explain.
5. HOLISTIC ACTIVITY Students as Writers
   In small groups, reread the account of the 1863 anti-African riot in New York City. Imagine that your group represents African families who were attacked but have recovered. Write a story to be published in a newspaper. Include your plans for the future, your feelings, and your dreams.

▲ There were many outbreaks of violence against Africans leading up to the Civil War.

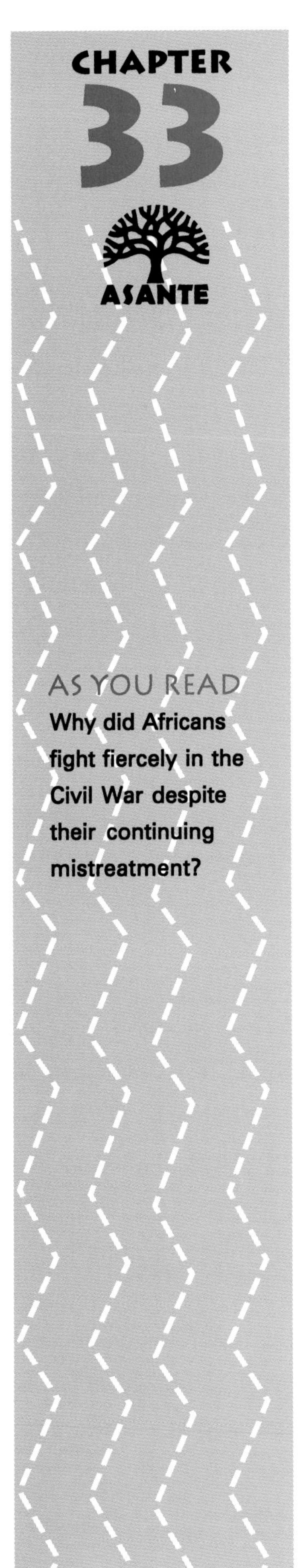

AS YOU READ
Why did Africans fight fiercely in the Civil War despite their continuing mistreatment?

AFRICANS IN THE CIVIL WAR

CENTER YOUR VOCABULARY

- ▲ emancipated
- ▲ economics
- ▲ mob violence
- ▲ draft riots

African enslavement played a major role in the Civil War. In the Revolutionary War, the colonists united to fight for their freedom from Great Britain. In the Civil War, Americans were divided on the issue of African freedom. Africans, on the other hand, were united in their desire to be free. Many northern whites referred to the Civil War as "the war to free Africans." They believed the war was being fought to decide the question of paid versus "slave" labor. The North complained bitterly that they had to pay Africans to work while the South benefited from the enslaved's free labor. Northern whites believed that if Africans were emancipated, they would compete with them for jobs.

Economics, or the production of wealth, is often the underlying cause of many human conflicts. German and Irish immigrants who had recently come to the United States to escape poverty in Europe were anxious about competing with Africans for jobs. They were fearful that Africans, if freed, would flock to northern cities and work for lower wages than whites. This fear caused several white mob attacks on Africans before the Civil War. One such attack led to a riot at Clinton Hall in New York in 1833. In 1834, serious destruction of property by white rioters sent alarm through the abolitionist communities. Repeated incidents of mob violence

continued after the Civil War. The reason for these riots seemed to be prompted by more than the prospect of African freedom. By the time the Civil War began, some whites outrightly refused to fight Southern whites because they did not feel it was their duty to protect African rights.

In 1863, a more serious outbreak of violence occurred after the first draft law in the nation was passed. It was called the Conscription Act of March 3, 1863. In trying to make the law easy to digest for the rich community, the legislators provided the opportunity for a draftee to hire a substitute or purchase his release from military service for $300. Only the wealthy could take advantage of this opportunity. Those who did not have enough money were drafted to fight in the war. Some hired substitutes and others could not do it because they did not have the money. When the names of the first draftees were published, a fierce outbreak of violence occurred. The draftees did not want to go to war over the issue of enslavement. They did not want to fight for African's rights.

In New York City, the names of the draftees were circulated in published newspapers. The riots took nearly 1,200 lives and caused considerable property damage. This was the most vicious anti-African riot in the history of New York City. The streets were littered with the dead and dying. Several hundred Africans were killed. Their mutilated bodies were hung from lampposts in the streets. The riots prompted more Africans to move to friendlier territory in Canada, particularly to the provinces of Ontario and Nova Scotia, for safety.

DID YOU KNOW?

In addition to the Union Army, another 30,000 African Americans served in the Union Navy, making up 25 percent of Union sailors.

UNION ARMY TREATMENT OF AFRICANS

The treatment of African soldiers in the Union Army reflected widespread racist attitudes toward African people. Once again, Africans were considered laborers, not soldiers. They were allowed to do only the most backbreaking, low-level work, such as digging ditches and cleaning up dead bodies.

▲ Sergeant-Major Christian Fleetwood received theCongressional Medal of Honor for bravery in the Civil War.

▲ Sergeant William Carney received the Congressional Medal of Honor for bravery in the Union attack on Fort Wagner, South Carolina, July 18, 1863.

CONGRESSIONAL MEDALS OF HONOR TO AFRICAN AMERICAN SOLDIERS

Recipients	Birthplace
Private William Barnes	Maryland
First Sergeant Powhatan Beaty	Virginia
First Sergeant James Bronson	Pennsylvania
Sergeant William Carney	Massachusetts
Sergeant Decatur Dorsey	Maryland
Sergeant-Major Christian Fleetwood	Maryland
Private James Gardiner	Virginia
Sergeant James Harris	Maryland
Sergeant-Major Thomas Hawkins	Ohio
Sergeant Alfred Hilton	Maryland
Sergeant Major Milton Holland	Texas
Corporal Miles James	Virginia
First Sergeant Alexander Kelly	Pennsylvania
First Sergeant Robert Pinn	Ohio
First Sergeant Edward Radcliff	Virginia

Finally, when Africans were allowed to fight, they received inferior equipment and guns. Until late in 1864, African soldiers were paid $7 a month compared to the $16 per month white soldiers received in the Union Army. In addition, African soldiers had to buy their army uniforms. White soldiers were given extra money to cover the cost of their uniforms.

Africans protested their unequal treatment in the armed services. In 1864, Sergeant William Walker, an African in the Third South Carolina Volunteers stationed in Jacksonville, Florida, led his company in a protest against the unfair practices in the Union Army. He was tried by army officials and executed. Other African soldiers who protested their treatment were shot or jailed.

James Gooding, a member of the Massachusetts 54th Regiment of U.S. Colored Troops, wrote to Lincoln in a plea for equal treatment: "Mr. President . . . the patient, trusting descendants of Africa's clime have dyed the ground with blood in defense of the Union and democracy."

Abraham Lincoln's reply was cold and unsympathetic. Lincoln wrote: "Negroes have larger motives for being soldiers than white men. They ought to be willing to enter the service upon any condition."

▲ Major Martin R. Delany was a veteran of the Civil War and a medical doctor.

But Africans did not enter the war "upon any condition;" they entered it to fight for their liberty, and fight they did. More than 38,000 soldiers lost their lives during the Civil War. This was a mortality rate nearly 40 percent higher than that of white soldiers. In fact, the largest single loss of any outfit in the Union Army was in the Fifth United States Colored Heavy Artillery unit. In that unit, 829 soldiers lost their lives. President Lincoln's idea that Africans had "larger motives" for being soldiers than whites gives some indication that Lincoln himself believed that the war was truly not necessary and should not have been fought over the question of African American freedom.

REMEMBER FT. PILLOW!

Despite the abuses and mistreatment they received in the Union Army, African soldiers fought fiercely because they knew that they would be tortured and killed if they were captured by the Confederacy. The South declared that it would execute African soldiers in the Union Army, as well as their white Union officers, if they were captured. Confederate soldiers under the command

of General Nathan Bedford Forrest brutally murdered many of the African soldiers who had surrendered after a battle at Fort Pillow, Tennessee, in 1864. "Remember Fort Pillow" became a rallying cry for African soldiers as they fought against the Confederacy.

The Confederacy passed laws that allowed the capture of enslaved Africans if they were to be used for menial jobs in the Confederate Army. A few captured Africans were forced to do the lowest of tasks, but, generally, the law was not effective. The Confederacy was losing ground quickly in the contest. Valiant African soldiers were showing their bravery on the side of the Union Army. Supplies were being depleted as the production of food on the plantations stopped. The Confederate Army was being beaten badly. In desperation, the Confederate States offered freedom in March 1865 to any enslaved African who would fight in the Confederate Army. The Civil War ended before this could be put into effect.

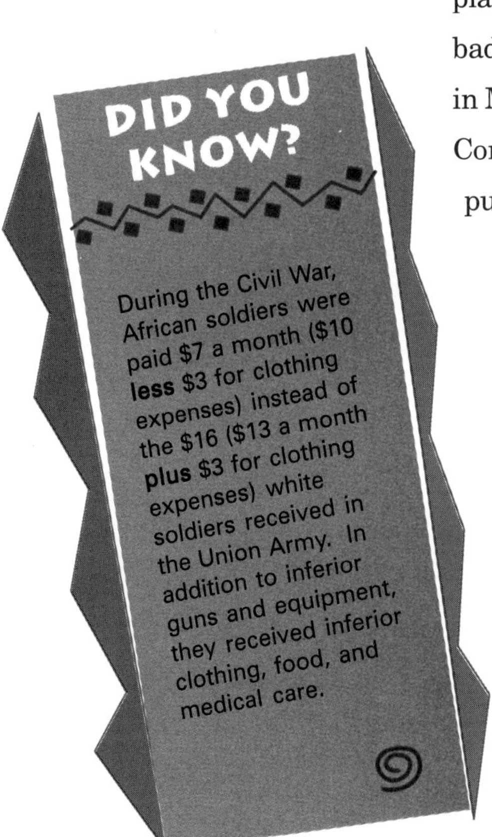

◆ CENTER YOUR THINKING

1. What is a civil war? Which was the first state to break away from the Union? Name the other states that followed. What did these states name their country?
2. Why were the leaders of the Confederacy concerned about Lincoln being sworn into office?
3. African fugitives were eager to fight for the Union. Many were considered contraband. Define the word *contraband* and tell what this meant to the Union Army. What kinds of jobs were given to African fugitives in the Union Army?
4. Analyze the reasons that the many heroic contributions made by Africans were still not enough for whites to want them to receive full citizenship. Support your reasons with facts from this and earlier chapters.
5. HOLISTIC ACTIVITY Students as Historians
   In small groups, make two columns on poster paper. Label one column AFRICANS WERE OPPRESSED IN THE CIVIL WAR, and the other column AFRICANS DISTINGUISHED THEMSELVES IN THE CIVIL WAR. Use quotes, biographical information, descriptions, illustrations, and factual accounts to present your views.

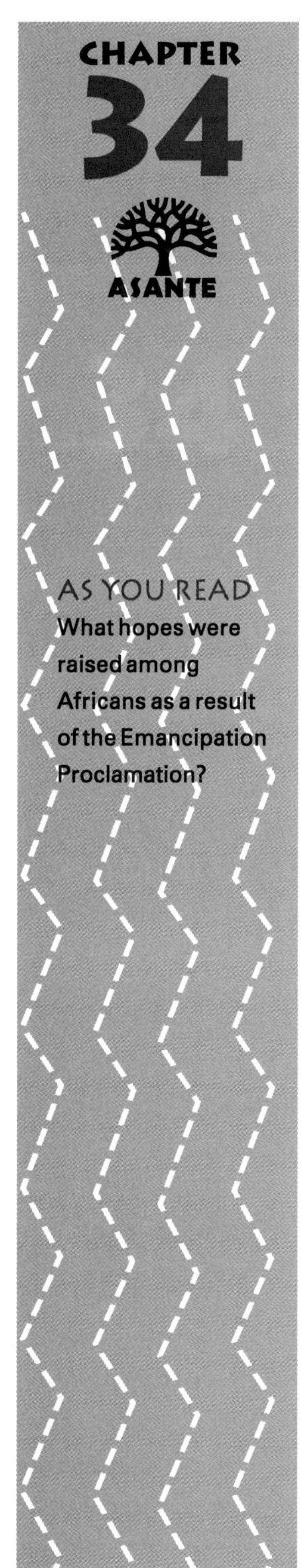

EMANCIPATION—A LAST RESORT!

CENTER YOUR VOCABULARY

- ▲ agitate
- ▲ postscript
- ▲ African Americans
- ▲ expedient

"A house divided against itself cannot stand. I believe this government cannot endure permanently half slave and half free. I do not expect the Union to be dissolved—I do not expect the house to fall—but I do expect it will cease to be divided. It will become all one thing, or all the other," said Abraham Lincoln in 1858. Yet, when he began his presidency in 1861, Lincoln made it clear that he wanted to stay out of any issue concerning African enslavement. Continued agitation and the outbreak of the Civil War forced President Lincoln to deal with it.

ABRAHAM LINCOLN

During his first year in office, President Lincoln proposed an emancipation plan to purchase enslaved Africans gradually from their enslavers. He proposed to pay enslavers with federal funds for the loss of their "property." Lincoln believed his plan, if approved, would maintain the Union, end enslavement, and compensate enslavers. As for Africans, Lincoln planned to send them to colonies in Haiti, Liberia, or Central America. Lincoln never had a chance to put this plan into effect. When the Civil War broke out in 1861, he turned his attention to the war effort.

In 1862, during the Civil War but before Africans could serve, President Lincoln said: "If I could save the Union without freeing any slave, I would do it; and if I could save it by freeing some and leaving others alone, I would also do that." He left no doubt as to what his objective was: the saving of the Union.

In an 1862 meeting with African American leaders, Lincoln said:

"You and we are different races. I think your race suffers very greatly by being among us, while ours suffers from your presence. There is a great unwillingness on the part of our people for you free, colored people to remain with us. But for your race among us there would be no war."

He went on to say: "This place I am thinking about having as a colony . . . is a very excellent one for any people and with great material resources . . . and especially because of the similarity of the climate to your native land."

However, he was speaking to a generation of Africans who were born in America. They believed they had as much right as whites to consider themselves Americans. They were African Americans, American citizens of African descent who wanted to stay in their country. In Lincoln's mind, America was a white land, though stolen from Native Americans, and Africans were unwelcome guests.

Lincoln, like most whites, did not consider Africans to be citizens of the United States. Furthermore, he blamed Africans for causing the Civil War. Lincoln was not alone in these thoughts. Many whites believed as he did.

Africans responded to these widespread beliefs by continuing to expose white hypocrisy. Some whites were comfortable enslaving Africans for profit, but they were quick to deny responsibility for the social problems caused by the system of enslavement they had set up.

George Vashon, a 19th-century African American educator, lawyer and writer, responded: "The Negro may be the bone of contention in our present civil war, but he has not been its cause. That cause must be sought in the wrongs inflicted upon him by the white man. The Negro may be the scab indicative of the disease but his removal, even if possible, will not effect a cure."

Frederick Douglass argued that:

"It is not the innocent horse that makes the horse thief, not the traveler's purse that makes the highway robber, and it is not the presence of the Negro that causes this foul and brutal stupidity of those who wish to possess horses, money and Negroes by means of theft, robbery and rebellion."

The free African American community in Queens, New York, asked, "Why not declare slavery abolished, and favor our peaceful colonization in the Rebel states, or some portion of them?" There was never a formal response to this proposal.

As a postscript to the Civil War, the treatment of African Americans after Lincoln's assassination deteriorated. When Lincoln was killed by John Wilkes Booth while attending a play at the Ford Theater in Washington, the African American community was saddened. Many African Americans, while recognizing Lincoln's faults, realized that he had made emancipation happen. No president before Lincoln had entertained publicly the idea of African freedom. African Americans wished to participate in his funeral, but their request was denied initially by federal officials in Washington, D.C. A few African Americans were allowed to march, but only at the end of the procession. In New York City, no African Americans were allowed to walk in the procession. The African American community would remember the sadness of that day. White officials, resentful of Africans since the 1861 draft riots, decided that the presence of African Americans would anger some whites.

EMANCIPATION PROCLAMATION

For most enslaved Africans, Lincoln's Emancipation Proclamation did not really make much difference. Although its announcement meant that Lincoln had heard the arguments of African and white abolitionists, he was only doing what was expedient (advantageous). The Emancipation Proclamation was primarily a political measure designed to make the Confederacy give up its rebellion. Lincoln issued a warning to the seceded states in September 1862 that the enslaved Africans in those territores would

be set free if those states did not rejoin the Union. Lincoln called it the Union's "last card." The proclamation went into effect in January 1863.

The border states of Delaware, Maryland, Kentucky, and Missouri did not secede, so the Proclamation did not free enslaved Africans in those states. They remained enslaved until the end of the Civil War in April 1865.

The proclamation also had implications for European interests. It prevented France and Great Britain from taking action against the North for blockading Southern ports. The South provided much of the cotton that these European countries needed. On the other hand, the Russians allied themselves with the Union and sent ships to New York in case France or England tried to break the North's blockade. International public opinion was swayed by the Emancipation Proclamation in favor of the North.

At home, opinion was mixed. Some whites felt that Lincoln had betrayed them. White abolitionists and the African American community rejoiced that a major victory had been won over racial oppression. They knew, of course, that other battles remained.

I'SE FREE!

▼ Many Africans got word of freedom as they worked in the cotton fields.

An enslaved African was hard at work in the cotton fields of Virginia when a friend came running through the fields shouting

Although President Abraham Lincoln issued the Emancipation Proclamation, freeing enslaved Africans, he would have been willing to sacrifice their freedom to preserve the Union. ▶

"I'se free! I'se free!" "Is dat so?" she exclaimed. Dropping her hoe, she ran about 11 kilometers (7 miles) to her old place, found her mistress, looked at her real hard, and then shouted "I'se free! Yes, I'se free! Ain't got to work fo' yo' no mo'. You can't put me in yo' pocket now!"

There were numerous stories and legends that grew out of emancipation that will forever hold a special place in the hearts of African Americans. On that fateful day, April 9, 1865, when the Civil War finally ended and all Africans were free, it was impossible to hold back the emotions that were released after 246 years of bondage in the United States. No event would stand out with greater clarity than the day Africans heard of their freedom. As the times changed and generations passed, these stories were told time and again. When the descendants of the enslaved moved North, they took these stories with them. That was how Kathryn L. Morgan came to learn of her great-grandmother Caddy, a strong-willed, defiant African who had been sold many times in her life but never ceased to torment her enslavers. Of all the stories of this remarkable woman's life, the one that became the favorite among her children, grandchildren, and great-grandchildren was about the day she learned of her freedom.

As the euphoria wore off, Africans began to take a closer look at what freedom really meant. The newly freed Africans owned nothing, not even the clothes on their backs. Emancipation meant that African Americans were finally free of their enslavers. It did not provide them with a means to support themselves. Furthermore, emancipation could not, and did not, end the prejudice and racism that had existed for so long.

Few individuals have expressed the true meaning of freedom in all its complexities as Jourdon Anderson, a former enslaved African. Jourdon put his former enslaver's request for him and his family to return to the South to the ultimate test. He asked his old "master" pay his wages for the 32 years of service that were taken by force during the enslavement (see p. 260). We must wonder if Anderson and the millions of other Africans who were defrauded of their labor ever saw payday.

> ...we have concluded to test your sincerity by asking you to send us our wages for the time we served you. This will make us forget and forgive old scores, and rely on your justice and friendship in the future.

> If you fail to pay us for faithful labors in the past we can have little faith in your promises in the future.

> We trust the good Maker has opened your eyes to the wrongs which you and your fathers have done to me and my fathers, in making us toil for you for generations without recompense.

Dayton, Ohio, August 7, 1965

To: My Old Master, Colonel P.H. Anderson,

Big Spring, Tennessee

Sir: I got your letter and was glad to find you had not forgotten Jourdon, and that you wanted me to come back and live with you again, promising to do better for me than anybody else can. I have often felt...

I want to know particularly what the good chance is you propose to give me. I am doing tolerable well here: I get $25 a month, with victuals and clothing; have a comfortable home for Mandy (the folks here call her Mrs. Anderson), and the children, Milly, Jane and Grundy, go to school and are learning well; the teacher says Grundy has a head for a preacher. They go to Sunday-School, and Mandy and me attend church regularly. We are kindly treated; sometimes we overhear others saying, "Them colored people were slaves" down in Tennessee. The children feel hurt when they hear such remarks, but I tell them it was no disgrace in Tennessee to belong to Col. Anderson. Many darkies would have been proud, as I used to was, to call you master. Now, if you will write and say what wages you will give me, I will be better able to decide whether it would be to my advantage to move back again.

As to my freedom, which you say I can have, there is nothing to be gained on that score, as I got my free-papers in 1864 from the provost-Marshal-General of the Department at Nashville. Mandy says she would be afraid to go back without some proof that you are sincerely disposed to treat us justly and kindly—and **we have concluded to test your sincerity by asking you to send us our wages for the time we served you. This will make us forget and forgive old scores, and rely on your justice and friendship in the future.** I served you faithfully for thirty-two years and Mandy twenty years. At $25 a month for me, and a $2 a week for Mandy, our earnings would amount to $11,680. Add to this the interest for the time our wages has been kept back and deduct what you paid for our clothing and three doctor's visits to me, and pulling a tooth for Mandy, and the balance will show what we are in justice entitled to. Please send the money by Adams Express, in care of V. Winters, esq., Dayton, Ohio. If you fail to pay us for faithful labors in the past we can have little faith in your promises in the future. We trust the good Maker has opened your eyes to the wrongs which you and your fathers have done to me and my fathers, in making us toil for you for generations without recompense. Here I draw my wages every Saturday night, but in Tennessee there was never any pay day for the negroes any more than for the horses and cows. Surely there will be a day of reckoning for those who defraud the laborer of his hire.

In answering this letter please state if there would be any safety for my Milly and Jane, who are now grown up and both good-looking girls. You know how it was with poor Matilda and Catherine. I would rather stay here and starve and die if it comes to that than have my girls brought to shame by the violence and wickedness of their young masters. You will also please state if there has been any schools opened for the colored children in your neighborhood, the great desire of my life now is to give my children an education, and have them form virtuous habits.

P.S.—Say howdy to George Carter, and thank him for taking the pistol from you when you were shooting at me.

From your old servant,

Jourdon Anderson

◆ CENTER YOUR THINKING

1. Name two countries to which President Lincoln planned to send Africans.
2. How did Africans respond to the debate over emancipation?
3. Describe President Lincoln's position on the issue of enslavement.
4. The Emancipation Proclamation has been called a last-ditch effort to force the Confederacy to give up its rebellion. Explain.
5. HOLISTIC ACTIVITY Students as Political Leaders
   Imagine that all Africans in America have been relocated to a separate colony in a southern state just after the Civil War. Working with your group, develop a plan of leadership to organize the new colony. Write the plan down in broad strokes. Everyone in your leadership cabinet must agree.

SUGGESTED READINGS

Bennett, Lerone. *Pioneers in Protest.* Baltimore: Penguin Books, 1968.

Bracey, John H., Ed. *American Slavery: The Question of Resistance.* Belmont, California: Wadsworth Publishing, 1971.

Chester, Morris. *Thomas Morris Chester: Black War Correspondent.* Baton Rouge: Louisiana State University Press, 1989.

Cornish, Dudley. *The Sable Arm: Negro Troops in the Civil War.* New York: Norton, 1966.

McPherson, James. *The Battle Cry of Freedom.* New York: Oxford University Press, 1988.

McPherson, James. *The Negro's Civil War.* New York: Vintage, 1965.

Quarles, Benjamin. *Black Abolitionists.* New York: Oxford University Press, 1969.

Rawick, George. *From Sundown to Sunup.* Westport, Ct.: Greenwood Publishing, 1972.

SUMMARY

The northern states did not want African enslavement to spread to the new territories opening up in the West. Many southern states decided to withdraw from the United States to form their own country. Their secession resulted in the Civil War. Africans were eager to serve in a war that they thought would end enslavement. At first, the government was reluctant to allow them to enlist, but Africans eventually distinguished themselves through service in the army and navy. *(Chapter 32)*

The Emancipation Proclamation granted freedom to Africans in the Confederate states and allowed Africans to enlist in the Union Army. Many whites refused to fight side by side with Africans. Others reacted violently to draft laws that, in their view, required them to fight a war that would benefit Africans. *(Chapter 32)*

Economic competition was a major factor in the conflict between whites and Africans. Many whites felt that the Civil War was about the question of paid versus slave labor. Northern whites thought the freed Southern Africans would compete with them for jobs. *(Chapter 33)*

Africans who enlisted in the Union Army were given inferior equipment and paid less than their white counterparts. Because wounded Africans received substandard medical care, more died. Still, Africans were willing to risk death in battle or as a result of capture by the Confederacy because they believed that their sacrifice would result in the end of enslavement. *(Chapter 33)*

President Lincoln's main motive for ending the enslavement of Africans was the preservation of the Union. Lincoln made it clear that he was not interested in the rights of Africans. In fact, he advanced several plans to send Africans to colonies in Africa, Central America, or the Caribbean. *(Chapter 34)*

Personal Witnessing

REFLECTION

Reflect on the continuing fight for freedom of African Americans and the continued difficulties in ensuring that the rights of African Americans is a political priority. Are there parallels today? Write your reflections in your journal.

TESTIMONY

As your group testimony, develop your own creative expression of the conflicts African Americans faced in deciding whether to support the Civil War or not and, if so, which side they would support.

UNIT 10 RITE OF PASSAGE

Choose a poem, song, or story to present in the oral tradition of Africa. Practice your presentation. You may give individual presentations, or group presentations. If possible, perform your oral presentations for a class of young children. Include your presentation in your Portfolio.

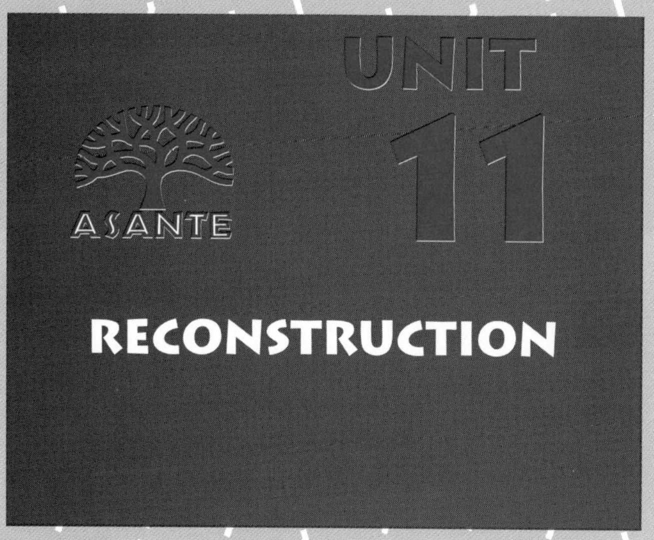

1865
- Abraham Lincoln is assassinated at Ford Theater in Washington
- Civil War ends April 9. Enslaved Africans in the United States are emancipated
- Congress passes 13th Amendment, January 31
- Ku Klux Klan is formed
- Black Codes are established in the South

1865-1877
- African American votes help elect officials in every Southern state except Virginia, Texas, and Georgia

Three concepts . . . *Jim Crow, pseudoslavery, and "40 acres and a mule,"* were disappointments for African Americans. Before your group discusses these, assign a concept to each person, and do brief research so that you understand each term. Then, as a group, make a list of your questions about each term. Predict how your group thinks that each concept disappointed African Americans. At the end of the unit, evaluate your predictions, and consider whether these concepts still relate to African Americans today.

As you read Unit 11, think about power. Can power be both good and bad? When have you used power over others? When have others used power over you? How did you feel? As you read, consider the results of shifting power from one people to include others in freedom.

1866
President Johnson extends the life of the Freedmen's Bureau

1867
Grandfather Clause is instituted in Louisiana to prevent the newly freed Africans from voting

1868
Congress passes 14th Amendment, July 21

1870
Congress passes 15th Amendment, March 30
African Americans campaign for free public education

1881
African Americans leave the South for Kansas and Oklahoma

1882-1902
More than 3,000 African Americas are lynched

1883
U.S. Supreme Court rules that the public accommodation section of the 1875 Civil Rights Act is unconstitutional

1890-1910
Mississippi leads states in adoption of literacy tests as a voting requirement for African Americans

1896
A U.S. Supreme Court ruling makes segregation legal and constitutional

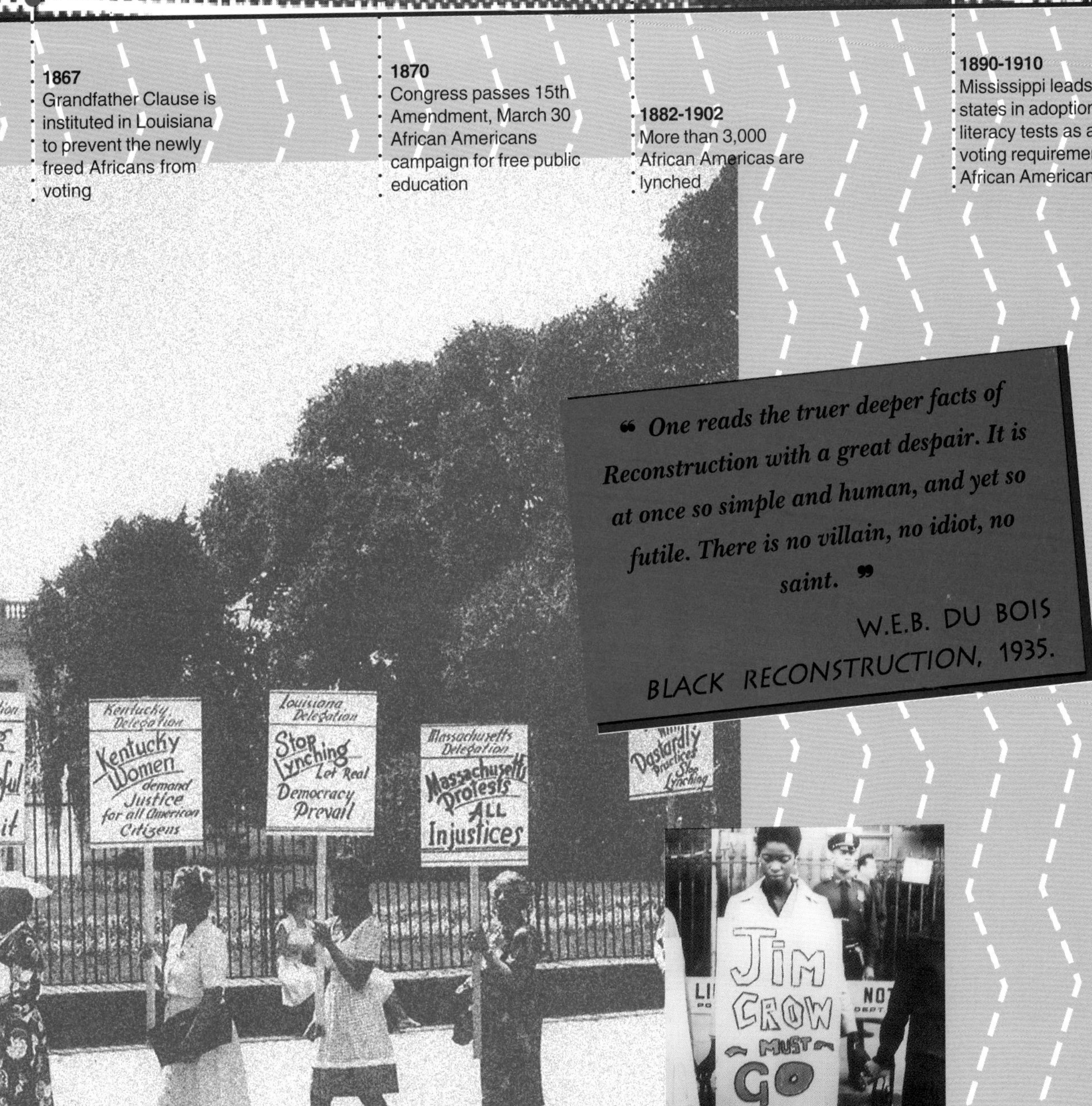

“One reads the truer deeper facts of Reconstruction with a great despair. It is at once so simple and human, and yet so futile. There is no villain, no idiot, no saint.”

W.E.B. DU BOIS
BLACK RECONSTRUCTION, 1935.

RECONSTRUCTION

CENTER YOUR VOCABULARY

- ▲ enfranchisement
- ▲ reconstruction
- ▲ suffrage
- ▲ amnesty
- ▲ undermine
- ▲ equitable

The enfranchisement of African Americans by the 15th Amendment of the United States Constitution in 1870 was one of the greatest steps ever taken toward democracy. But it was the reconstruction of freedom, a period when the enfranchisement of political privileges of African Americans made a world of difference, that brought the country to a new level of biracial participation in government. The right to vote also meant the right to run for office. Africans became senators, members of Congress, and political leaders to a greater degree than ever before in history.

What did these new politicians do to change the American society? They brought new attitudes toward property and people. Before the Reconstruction, property was mainly controlled by enslavers who exercised complete authority in the Southern states. After the Civil War and with the enfranchisement and election of African Americans, the South was transformed. African American politicians sought to open public schools, public highways, and hospitals, and to provide for the poor and the homeless. Their progressive ideas were introduced throughout the South and became the symbols of Reconstruction.

DEAL WITH US JUSTLY

In 1865, the *Colored Tennessean*, an African American newspaper, expressed what African Americans expected from emancipation: "Deal with us justly. Tell us not that we will not work, when it was our toil that enriched the South. Talk not to us of a war of races, for that is to say you intend commencing to butcher us whenever you can do so with impunity. All we want is the rights of men. . . . We do not intend leaving this country. . . . We were born here. . . . We are Americans. Deal with us justly . . . . That's all we want. That we mean to have, come what may!"

13TH AMENDMENT

Neither slavery nor involuntary servitude, except as a punishment for crime whereof the party shall have been duly convicted, shall exist within the United States, or any place subject to their jurisdiction.

The Civil War ended on April 9, 1865, when Confederate General Robert E. Lee surrendered to Union General Ulysses Grant at the Appomattox Court House in Virginia. The nation began the business of reconstructing, or putting back together, the Union. This period was called *Reconstruction*.

14TH AMENDMENT

All persons born or naturalized in the United States, and subject to the jurisdiction thereof, are citizens of the United States and of the state wherein they reside. No state shall make or enforce any law which shall abridge the privileges or immunities of citizens of the United States; nor shall any state deprive any person of life, liberty, or property, without due process of law; nor deny to any person within its jurisdiction the equal protection of the laws.

During the Reconstruction years from 1865 to 1877, some rights were given to African Americans, especially in the South. The U.S. Constitution was amended between 1865 and 1870, changing it to address the rights of African Americans. The 13th Amendment outlawed enslavement in 1865. The 14th guaranteed rights and equal protection under the law to African Americans in 1868. It also established federal jurisdiction over states' right. The 15th Amendment gave African Americans suffrage, or the right to vote, in 1870.

LINCOLN'S RECONSTRUCTION PLAN

15TH AMENDMENT

The right of citizens of the United States to vote shall not be denied or abridged by the United States or by any state on account of race, color, or previous condition of servitude.

Abraham Lincoln issued a plan of amnesty (pardon) and reconstruction for the South in December 1863, more than 16 months before the Civil War ended. Under his plan, Confederates could reorganize their states' governments if they took an oath of allegiance to the Union. All property, except enslaved Africans, was to be returned to them.

African Americans were not going to be allowed to vote. They were outraged at this cowardly act. African Americans questioned how Lincoln could begin a war that destroyed so many lives only to turn around and give white Southerners the power to control the people they had so brutally enslaved.

Lincoln's plan was defeated. Instead, Congress passed the Wade-Davis Bill in 1864. It restricted the rights of ex-Confederate Southerners to vote or hold office. It also banned enslavement and established temporary military governors in the ex-rebel states to ensure that the states obeyed the Reconstruction laws.

Still, there was no mention of voting rights for African Americans. Lincoln vetoed the Wade-Davis Bill. President Lincoln was assassinated on April 14, 1865, and Vice President Andrew Johnson became the 17th president of the United States.

Like Lincoln, the new president believed in uniting the Union; however, he absolutely did not believe that Africans should have equal rights with whites. At first, President Johnson supported the plan Lincoln had started. However, as he grew more supportive of the rights of the rebellious states, he found himself in conflict with Congress. Soon, President Johnson was vetoing bills meant to support the newly freed Africans.

▼ The Brooks forces evacuating the state house at Little Rock

Despite the political maneuvers between President Johnson and Congress, African Americans were able to make some progress. Between 1865 and 1877, Africans voted and elected officers in every Southern state except Virginia, Texas, and Georgia, which were the only states to voluntarily reenter the Union. Congress had made it clear that in order for a state to reenter the Union, it had to give Africans the right to vote. Virginia, Texas, and Georgia agreed reluctantly.

Without the protection of Union military governors and troops, African Americans were intimidated and whites continued to dominate the state legislature. Military governors in the rebellious states reorganized the governments to allow African

John R. Lynch

▲ John R. Lynch represented Mississippi in the U.S. House of Representatives.

AFRICAN AMERICANS IN THE U.S. HOUSE OF REPRESENTATIVES 1869-1901

▶ Seven of the 20 African American Congressman served during Reconstruction.

(Top Row) Robert C. DeLarge, Jefferson H. Long (Front Row) Hiram R. Revels, Benjamin S. Turner, Josiah T. Walls, Joseph H. Rainy, R. Brown Elliott.

Richard Cain	South Carolina
Henry Cheatham	North Carolina
Robert DeLarge	South Carolina
Robert Brown Elliottt	South Carolina
Jeremiah Horalson	Alabama
John Hyman	North Carolina
John Mercer Langston	Virginia
Jefferson Long	Georgia
John Lynch	Mississippi
Thomas Miller	South Carolina
George Washington Murray	South Carolina
Charles Nash	Louisiana
James O'Hara	North Carolina
Joseph Rainey	South Carolina
Alonzo Ransier	South Carolina
James Rapier	Alabama
Robert Smalls	South Carolina
Benjamin Turner	Alabama
Josiah Walls	Florida
George Henry White	North Carolina

▲ The South Carolina legislature of 1873 passing an appropriations bill

Americans to vote. In some states, African Americans were able to elect many representatives; in others, they were still struggling to achieve political representation.

RECONSTRUCTION

What did Reconstruction mean in terms of education? Because of the intense desire on the part of African Americans for education, numerous schools and colleges were established. In the state of Mississippi, for example, the numbers of African Americans enrolled in educational institutions in 1876 outnumbered the number of whites in such institutions. There were 89,813 African Americans enrolled in school compared to 78,404 whites. The average daily attendance was 60,514 for African Americans, and only 40,381 for whites. The average monthly salary for African American first-grade teachers was $65.50, and for whites $68.40.

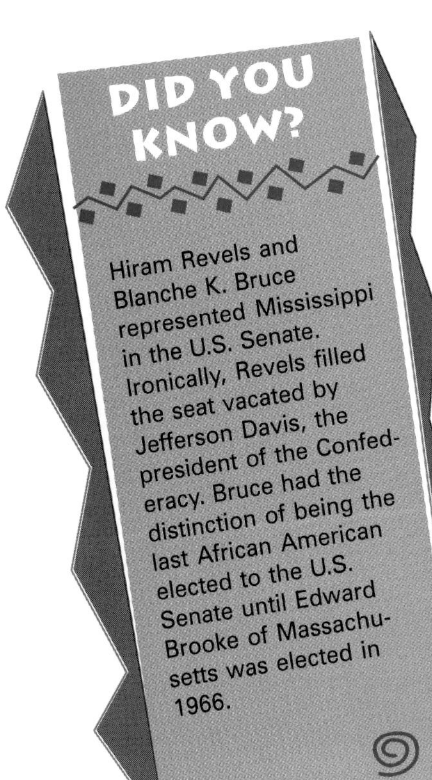

There was great tragedy in the response of whites to African American power. It became impossible to prevent whites in the South from making pervasive assaults on African Americans. Some plantation owners refused to allow Africans who had been enslaved to leave their lands. Others sent out armed groups of whites to prey on African Americans who were looking for work. Dead bodies of African Americans were often found alongside the roads. The only protection for the ordinary African American was the Freedmen's Bureau and the Union military still stationed in the South. This was so, even though African Americans had the vote.

African Americans in the state legislatures put democratic reforms, free public school, and new social legislation into effect. The South Carolina Constitution of 1868, written with the participation of a majority of African American delegates, was a model of modern

RECONSTRUCTION ACHIEVEMENTS

- Hospitals
- Homes for the Aged
- Homes for the Deaf
- Homes for the Blind
- Public Schools
- New Roads
- Public Buildings
- Banks
- Bridges

democracy. It started with the broad statement "We, the People," and continued to declare that all navigable rivers were free public highways and not private, that representation should be based on population rather than property, and the establishment of universal manhood suffrage without distinction of race or color. It also made a provision for separate property for married women. The constitution lasted for 27 years without essential changes.

In a similar vein, the constitution of 1868 in Mississippi abolished property qualifications for jury service and educational qualifications for suffrage. In addition, this constitution prohibited private corporations from using privileges to finance their operations. This abuse had existed since 1830. It was the only state constitution ever submitted to popular approval at the polls. It remained in effect for some 22 years.

In an ironic twist of fate, Africans Americans in the majority of the South had the vote, as defined by Congress in the 15th Amendment, while Southern whites who had rebelled against the Union did not.

African Americans did not use their voting powers to retaliate against Southern whites. Instead, they tried to work within the system. They attended constitutional conventions and made alliances with legislators who served their interests. African American public officials, whose ancestors two centuries earlier were considered by whites to be suitable only for brute labor, were impressive in their carriage and conduct. This spirit of cooperation with whites, many of whom still hated African Americans, was to be repaid in a few years. Unfortunately, repayment would come as a whirlwind of white violence and terror.

FREEDMEN'S BUREAU

Congress established the Bureau of Refugees, Freedmen, and Abandoned Lands (Freedmen's Bureau) in 1865 to deal with the problems of reconstructing the South. It was headed by General Oliver Otis Howard, for whom Howard University was later named.

▲ Job training grew out of the many programs put in place by the Freedmen's Bureau.

The bureau was made up of civil servants, African American social and religious workers, Northern moralists, and missionaries. While there may have been competing interests, they all worked for social change.

Many of the Southern whites worked hard to undermine or discredit the bureau's efforts. Because they made up the majority, they were able to push through plans that were not in the best interests of African Americans. Nevertheless, the bureau under Howard's leadership opened up new opportunities for thousands of African Americans.

Howard attempted with limited success to initiate what he thought was equitable or fair treatment for freed African Americans. He tried to redistribute plantation lands to the formerly enslaved. One of the first acts the bureau performed was the creation of 4,000 day, night, and industrial public schools for freed African Americans. Some 250,000 African Americans rushed to take advantage of the offer of education during the first year. By 1870, African Americans had campaigned for free public education for African American and white children throughout the South. It was the Freedmen's Bureau's plan that captured the imagination of the African American community, as well as the imagination of those whites who sought an expanded democracy. Elements in the plan included:

- Overseeing the creation and enforcement of wage contracts.
- Appearing in courts as the best friend of the freedman.
- Furnishing the freedmen with a minimum of capital and land.
- Establishing schools.
- Creating hospitals and outdoor toilets.

The temporary nature of the Freedmen's Bureau meant that Southern whites felt that they simply had to outwait the Freedmen's Bureau's tenure. By 1870 the bureau had dwindled. During the next ten years, whites would recapture control of the political and social mechanisms of power in the South and overturn much of what the bureau and the African American legislators had accomplished.

FORTY ACRES AND A MULE

Thaddeus Stevens, a radical white abolitionist and U.S. representative from Pennsylvania, first used the phrase "40 acres and a mule." He was promoting his plan for economic independence for African Americans. Stevens wanted to treat the seceded Southern states like conquered territory. He suggested in 1865 that President Johnson divide the Southern plantations into 40-acre farms and give them along with a mule to African Americans. The newly freed African Americans welcomed this plan. So many of them were jobless and homeless now that the enslavement had ended. Stevens's plan ran into immediate opposition from President Johnson and white Southerners and was soon abandoned.

Many African American leaders brought other plans to Congress. Sojourner Truth, an outstanding orator and African American activist, campaigned for African Americans to get their fair share of land grants in the West. She said in 1871: "I am urging the people to sign petitions to Congress to have a grant of land set apart for the freed people to earn their living on. Instead of sending these people to Liberia, why can't they have a colony in the West?" Truth was referring to colonization plans put forward by many white leaders to send African Americans back to Africa or to various colonies in South America and the Caribbean. She believed that Africans were U.S. citizens and, therefore, had the same right as whites to live in the United States. She felt that African Americans were entitled to the federal land grants in the West that were reserved for the railroads and white Americans.

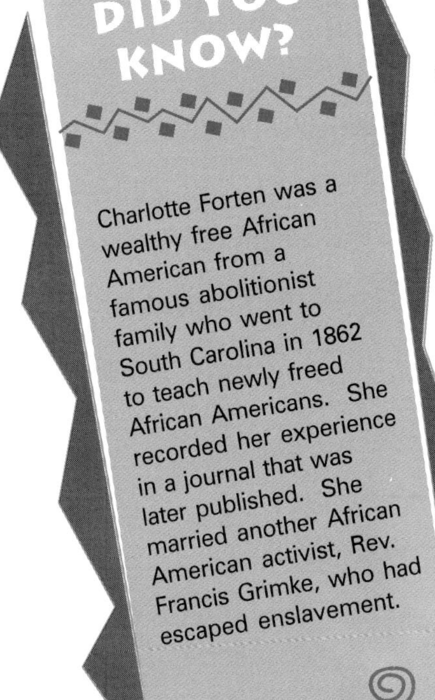

AFRICAN AMERICAN RECONSTRUCTION POLITICIANS

Alonzo Ransier and Richard Gleaves of South Carolina, A. K. Davis in Mississippi, and Oscar Dunn, P. B. S. Pinchback, and C. C. Antoine of Louisiana all served as lieutenant-governors. Pinchback acted as governor of Louisiana in 1873 for six weeks after the white governor was removed. African Americans were serving as state supreme court judges, justices of the peace, and superintendents of education.

▲ Alonzo Ransier served as lieutenant-governor of South Carolina.

Despite the rapid gains made by African American legislators and other elected officials, racism hovered like a storm cloud over every part of their lives. In 1868, the Georgia House of Representatives refused to seat state senators and 25 state representatives who had been elected because they were African American. One of the men was Bishop Henry McNeal Turner, who had served as a chaplain to U.S. Colored Troops during the Civil War. There were many other daily insults that showed that whites did not intend to share their full power and influence with African Americans.

African Americans who served in the U.S. House of Representatives between 1869 and 1901 worked hard to overcome the racist policies that were being put in place under the Johnson presidency. Many of them were well educated. Many had served in the Union Army or

Navy. A few had been enslaved. They were used to severe discrimination, and they were committed to ending Johnson's presidency. The hopes that the period of Reconstruction generated, however, were to be dashed once again as whites stubbornly refused to acknowledge the citizenship of Africans.

▲ This struggle over the Speaker's chair in the Louisiana state house, January 4, 1875, shows whites' resistance to sharing their full power with African Americans.

Reconstruction ended in 1877 with the rights of African Americans still unprotected. Fighting against white attempts to suppress their right to vote, African Americans engaged in efforts to prevent the turning back of the clock. Time was running out. The whites, whose population was far greater than that of African Americans in most states, were at an advantage. Only Mississippi and South Carolina had almost as many African Americans as whites. Southern whites who had experienced the agony of losing the Civil War, the participation of Africans in political offices, and the destruction of the "slave" economy began to use illegal measures to suppress African Americans' right to vote. There were threats, fraud, and murders. However, most of the Southerners were convinced that the most effective way of eliminating African Americans' right to vote would be through the legal system. Reconstruction ended with the election of Rutherford B. Hayes in 1876. Fourteen years later, Judge Calhoon, according to the *Clarion Ledger*, September 11, 1890, told the Constitutional Convention of Mississippi, "Let's tell the truth if it bursts the bottom out of the Universe. We came here to exclude the Negro. Nothing short of this will answer." But despite the best efforts of those who hated them, the African American population in the South grew. However, the dark clouds of oppression were gathering once again as the white population, now invested with power by the federal and state governments, made their presence felt once again.

◆ CENTER YOUR THINKING

1. What was the Reconstruction? When did it begin?
2. Describe one amendment to the Constitution that was intended to benefit African Americans.
3. Discuss President Lincoln's plan for amnesty and reconstruction for the South.
4. What steps did the government take to restrict the rights of African Americans?
5. HOLISTIC ACTIVITY Students as Playwrights
   Write, design, and produce a play for your class that is set at the end of the Civil War. Three groups of people live in a small Southern town—whites who do not like new laws giving African Americans citizenship rights, white abolitionists, and newly freed African Americans.

CHAPTER 36

ASANTE

AS YOU READ

What new systems of enslavement, or pseudoslavery, hurt African Americans during Reconstruction?

OBSTACLES TO RECONSTRUCTION

CENTER YOUR VOCABULARY

- ▲ sharecropping system
- ▲ convict labor system
- ▲ pseudoslavery
- ▲ Exodusters
- ▲ impeach
- ▲ vagrancy

Thousands of Africans trailed behind the Union soldiers in General Sherman's triumphant march from Atlanta to Savannah, Georgia. When the festivities died down, what remained was a people without land or capital, without schools or hospitals, without farming tools or carpentry tools, without churches or clubs. Sherman granted Africans who were under his authority a piece of land "not more than 40 acres of tillable ground . . . of which land the military authorities will afford them protection until such time as they can protect themselves or until Congress shall regulate their title."

On March 3, 1865, Congress incorporated a Freedmen's Bank and passed a law setting up a Freedmen's Bureau. The bureau anticipated opposition from the white South. Southern whites believed that the movement from "slavery" to free labor would mean catastrophe for the South's economy. Whites in the North were concerned about the impact of the war debts on the national economy and sensitive to the additional cost of financing programs that would take Africans from "slavery" to freedom. The Freedmen's Bureau under the leadership of General Howard became a government for the South. It made and interpreted laws, collected taxes, punished crime, and used military force as necessary. Because it had to enforce laws to protect African Americans, the bureau often incurred the anger of whites. Some of the bureau's rules also caused irritation to African Americans. When the bureau found wage-earning jobs, it expected that African Americans would accept the jobs, a practice called *forced labor*. It was soon abused by those contracting with the bureau for the labor of Africans.

PSEUDOSLAVERY

Employers exploited African American labor by creating new systems to reenslave African Americans. These systems were called *pseudoslavery*.

The sharecropping system went into effect as African Americans signed contracts with white farms owners to rent land and equipment in exchange for a portion of the crop or a share of the profits whenever the goods were sold. The farm owners overcharged and cheated African Americans so badly that at the end of the year, they were still in debt to the farm owners, with only their labor to offer as payment.

The convict labor system allowed white farm owners to rent convict labor from the state. The convicts were not paid. Of course, because African Americans were charged with vagrancy and jailed if they did not accept the job offered by the Freedmen's Bureau, the white planters had a ready source of cheap labor. Moreover, sharecroppers who protested their treatment by white landowners were charged with contract violations and jailed. Now the landowner could rent the same labor through the convict labor system for free.

An example of how the system worked to the obvious disadvantage of the African American worker is shown in this letter from a white planter in Alabama to the county sheriff: "I am in need of a Negro farm hand and I am depending on one from you. . . . I would like to get a Negro named G----- W------." The sheriff would search for the African American's name, George Walters in this example, on his list of prisoners and turn that person over to the white planter. George Walters would be obligated to work for the white planter, for free, until his sentence was fulfilled.

EXODUSTERS

African Americans responded to the unfair sharecropping and convict labor systems by protesting to authorities. When that did not work, they decided to leave. Because they would be charged with vagrancy or contract violations and jailed, they often left in secrecy. Like the enslaved who escaped during the enslavement period, they, too, had to run away. The white planters tried to stop them with threats and acts of violence, but they left on boats, wagons, and foot.

One of the major migrations away from the pseudoslavery in the South occurred between 1879 to 1881. Some 60,000 African Americans bought land in Kansas. They called themselves *Exodusters* because they considered themselves to be making an exodus out of bondage. The Exodusters were led by Benjamin "Pap" Singleton. He was a formerly enslaved African who had fled to Canada before the Civil War. Exodusters established several African American towns in the West, including Boley and Langston, Oklahoma, and Nicodemus, Kansas.

"NO FRIEND OF OUR RACE"

The principal foe of African American rights was President Andrew Johnson. Frederick Douglass had said when Johnson became vice president, "Whatever Andrew Johnson may be, he certainly is no friend of our race." Douglass was absolutely correct. Under Johnson's presidency, African American rights were taken away. The warning signs that the rights of African Americans would be contested came early when Johnson granted pardons to many of the former Confederates. In the Georgia Sea Islands, land that had been given or sold to free Africans was taken away from them and returned to former enslavers.

Johnson was not in favor of giving African Americans the right to vote. Douglass and other leaders felt the vote was absolutely necessary for full citizenship. Johnson's reply was that giving the African Americans the vote would cause a race war in the South.

He suggested that African Americans hold to Lincoln's original plan that African Americans colonize outside the United States.

Douglass responded to the president in an open letter in 1866 saying: "We admit the existence of this hostility and hold that it is entirely reciprocal. But you obviously commit an error by drawing an argument from an incident of slavery and making it a basis for a policy adapted to a state of freedom. The cause of this antagonism is removed and you must see that it is altogether illogical . . . to legislate from slaveholding and slave-driving premises."

The president was also opposed by radical Republicans in Congress. They were led by the abolitionist Thaddeus Stevens, who supported harsh, punitive measures against the ex-Confederates. Johnson vetoed a law extending the life and powers of the Freedmen's Bureau and the Civil Rights Act of 1866. Congress overrode the president's veto. Johnson's final break with Congress came when Johnson opposed the 14th Amendment. Republicans and other moderates rallied against him by electing anti-Johnson people to Congress in 1866. Congress, led by Thaddeus Stevens, unsuccessfully attempted to impeach, or bring charges against, Johnson in 1868.

By the end of Johnson's administration, Southern whites had regained their stronghold over African Americans. The wheels of progress came to a screeching halt. Johnson's strong anti-African policies created a white backlash, taking away African Americans' new-found voting rights. Africans Americans who tried to vote were intimidated, physically threatened, or killed. President Rutherford B. Hayes, Johnson's successor, was no better. In a show of support for white Southerners who helped elect him, Hayes withdrew Union troops from the South. African Americans in the South were left alone, totally unprotected.

Southern white politicians on the floor of the U.S. Congress proudly voiced their racist beliefs. White supremacists James Vardaman of Mississippi, Carter Glass of Virginia, and Cole Blease and Ben Tillman of South Carolina, were some of the most vocally racist members of Congress. Vardaman said in 1908 that the idea that

▲ The first vote

Africans were human was "the most damnable and dangerous doctrine . . . in America." Glass proclaimed, "The people of the original thirteen southern states curse and spit upon the Fifteenth Amendment—and have no intention of letting the Negro vote. White supremacy is too precious a thing to surrender for the sake of a theoretical justice that would let a brutish African deem himself the equal of white men and women in Dixie." Blease said, "In all Bible history and all profane history, you will find that the superior race has ruled and controlled: and the white people of this country are going to rule it, and control it, if it be necessary, to wipe the black race off the face of the earth."

These were among some of the most racist leaders of the country whose sole aim was to strip African Americans of all rights. Their words and attitudes are similar to contemporary racists like David Duke, the former Grand Dragon of the Ku Klux Klan from Louisiana. Duke ran unsuccessfully for a seat in the U.S. Congress in 1990. Duke promotes the same ideas today. It is easy to see how white racism was translated into public policy by passing discriminatory laws and *de facto* practices.

> "About last April, two freedmen were hung in Clark county. On the night of May 11, a freedman was taken from his bed by his master and others and was hung, and his body still hangs to the limb."

SOURCE REPORT OF THE JOINT COMMITTEE ON RECONSTRUCTION, 39TH CONGRESS, 1866

Freedmen's Bureau
Mobile, Alabama

July 29, 1865

Sir,

I have the honor to report some testimony I have received of murders and barbarities committed on the Freedmen of Clark, Choctaw, Washington and Marengo Counties. About last April, two freedmen were hung in Clark county. On the night of May 11, a freedman was taken from his bed by his master and others and was hung, and his body still hangs to the limb. About the middle of June, two colored soldiers showed their papers and were permitted to remain all night at a plantation. In the morning, the planter called them out and shot one dead, wounded the other, and then with the assistance of his brother they pursued the one who had escaped with dogs. At Bladen Springs, a freedman was chained to a pine tree and burned to death. About two weeks later, another was burned to death also at Bladen Springs. In late May, a freedman was shot outside a planter's home and the body dragged into the stable, to make it appear he had shot him in the act of stealing. A preacher states from the pulpit that the roads in Choctaw County stunk with the dead bodies of servants that had fled their masters. The people around Bladen declare that no negro shall live in the county unless he remains with his master and is obedient as heretofore.

In Clark County, a freedman was shot through the heart; his body lies unburied. About last May, a planter hung his negro woman servant in the presence of the entire neighborhood. Said planter had killed the woman's husband three weeks before. About last April, two women were caught near a plantation in Clark County and hung. Their bodies are still suspended.

This is only a few of the murders that are committed on the helpless and unprotected freedmen of these counties. I have been careful in authenticity, and very much that has been related to me, I have declined accepting as testimony, although I believe its truth. The history of these cases, besides others, I have in full, with all their horrible particulars.

W.A. Poillon
Assistant Superintendant
Freedmen's Bureau

> "At Bladen Springs, a freedman was chained to a pine tree and burned to death. About two weeks later, another was burned to death also at Bladen Springs. In late May, a freedman was shot outside a planter's home and the body dragged into the stable, to make it appear he had shot him in the act of stealing."

> "This is only a few of the murders that are committed on the helpless and unprotected freedmen of these counties. I have been careful in authenticity, and very much that has been related to me, I have declined accepting as testimony, although I believe its truth."

◆ CENTER YOUR THINKING

1. What is pseudoslavery? How were sharecropping and convict labor used as pseudoslavery?
2. How did African Americans combat pseudoslavery?
3. Why did Frederick Douglass state that President Andrew Johnson was "no friend of our race"?
4. What was the Freedmen's Bureau, and what were some criticisms that were made of the bureau?
5. HOLISTIC ACTIVITY Students as Pioneers
   In small groups, imagine that you are part of the 60,000 African Americans who joined the Exodusters in their move from the South. Write a speech for Benjamin "Pap" Singleton to give your group as you head West.

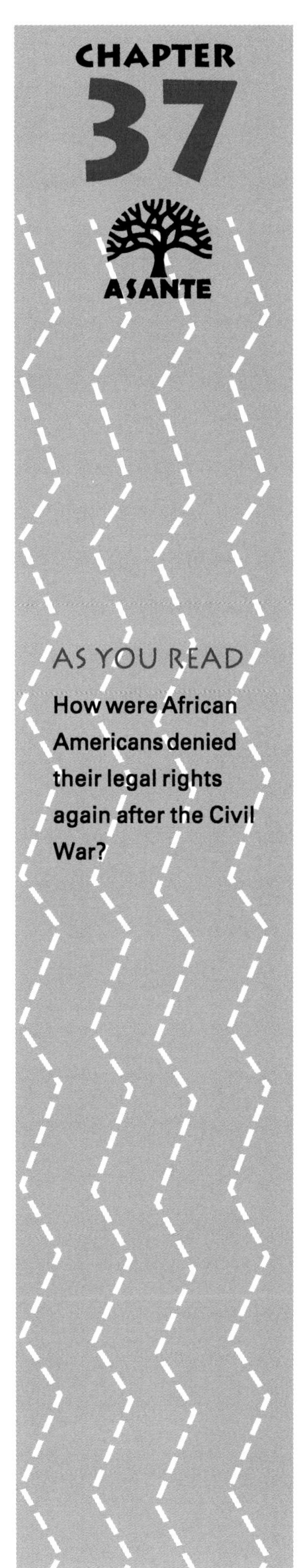

LEGAL BARRIERS TO EQUALITY

CENTER YOUR VOCABULARY

- Jim Crow
- abridgement
- Grandfather Clause
- stringent
- mixed heritage
- *Plessy v. Ferguson*

T.J. Rice, a white actor who painted his face black to ridicule African Americans in his comic performances, referred to Jim Crow, apparently an African American man, in his song: "Wheel about and turn about and do just so. Every time I wheel about I jump Jim Crow." The origin of the term, *Jim Crow*, is unknown, but it was in use early in the 1830s. Some say the term comes from an enslaver named Crow, and some say it refers to the phrase *black as a crow*. Jim Crow came, however, to be associated solely with segregation and discrimination.

Southern whites, secure in the knowledge that the federal government would not step in on behalf of African Americans, began a systematic abridgement (reduction) of African American rights. The laws that whites passed legislating segregation and other discriminatory practices were called Jim Crow laws. They were enacted on the basis of states' rights, which gave the local governments in each state the right to enact and enforce their own laws.

LOSS OF SUFFRAGE

The Grandfather Clause was an example of a Jim Crow law. Instituted in Louisiana, the law excused anyone from meeting the

▲ A woman protests the Jim Crow laws.

stringent (harsh) voting requirements if his grandfather had voted before 1867. Of course, African American men did not have suffrage, or the right to vote, before 1870. This meant that practically all African Americans had to meet Louisiana's strict voting requirements. White Louisianans did not.

EXAMPLES OF VOTING REQUIREMENTS

Poll taxes were one of several new voting requirements instituted in many Southern states. This meant that a man had to pay to vote. Women did not have the vote yet. Many African Americans could not afford the poll tax.

In 1890, Mississippi adopted literacy tests as a requirement to vote. This meant that a man had to prove that he could read before he could vote. During the enslavement, most Africans were not allowed to learn to read. Now that they were free, many had not yet learned. Those who could read were given very difficult or foreign language passages to read. A white man scored the results.

By 1910, seven other Southern states followed Mississippi's lead because of its success in depriving African Americans of the vote. Africans who could read risked their lives to register their vote and participate in democracy.

Property requirements were also initiated for voting. Many African Americans, just free of enslavement, did not own property.

White primary elections were established. Primaries determine who will run for office from each political party. However, because primaries are not covered by the 15th Amendment, African Americans could not vote in the primaries. The creation of primaries meant that African Americans did not have a choice in selecting which candidate would get to run.

The South Carolina Democratic party issued a plan in 1876. Article 12 said, "Every Democrat must feel honor-bound to control the vote of at least one Negro, by intimidation, purchase, keeping him away or as each individual may determine, how he may best accomplish it." This racist document went on to say in Article 16, "Never

Here, you see the outside, then the inside of the U.S. Supreme Court building in Washington, D.C. The Supreme Court is the highest court in the nation. Nine justices, or judges, sit on the court.

threaten a man individually. If he deserves to be threatened, the necessities of the times require that he should die."

Following South Carolina's lead, Southern whites often blocked the entrances to polling places. They did not let African Americans enter. They stole ballot boxes. They changed polling places to secret locations. They threatened to fire African American workers if they didn't sign work contracts that said they had to vote for the dominant Democratic ticket. The newspapers published the names of African Americans who registered to vote so that whites could retaliate against them.

These blatantly illegal and criminal policies could not have succeeded without the cooperation of white authorities. Many African Americans lost their lives defending their political rights. They are the true unsung heroes of liberty.

LAWS ALLOWING SOCIAL DISCRIMINATION

The U.S. Supreme Court ruled in 1883 that the public accommodation section of the 1875 Civil Rights Act was unconstitutional. It had guaranteed nondiscrimination in public facilities. This ruling reversed an earlier one that banned segregation. Southern states rushed to set up "legal" segregation. They no longer had to let Africans into any public facility reserved for whites.

PLESSY V. FERGUSON

In 1896, segregation was the law of the land, even in the nation's capital. The U.S. Supreme Court decided, eight to one, that the state of Louisiana was within its rights to arrest Homer Plessy, an African American, for violating its Jim Crow laws. Plessy broke the law by sitting in a railroad car reserved for whites. Plessy had his own problem with color and racial identity. He defended his actions by claiming that his mixed heritage (from black and white parents) did not make him African American. Plessy felt that because he looked more white than African American, he should be treated like whites.

The Supreme Court disagreed. The Court ruled that if he had even one drop of African blood, he was an African and would be treated like other Africans. The *Plessy v. Ferguson* decision established the separate -but-equal doctrine. This meant that African Americans and whites could have separate public facilities as long as they were equal. The facilities were seldom if ever equal.

PEONAGE

South Carolina and most other states forced African Americans to work on farms as hired hands or domestic servants for whites. Otherwise, African Americans were charged with vagrancy or loitering. If they were charged with vagrancy, they were forced to work in the same jobs as hired hands or domestic servants, but for no pay. James Orr, the Reconstruction governor of South Carolina from 1865 to 1868, wrote President Andrew Johnson in 1865 explaining, "The vagrant Laws are stringent but necessary. . . . Many

[African Americans] will not work without the compulsion of law." Of course, the newly emancipated Africans had been compelled to work for the past 250 years.

African Americans could not testify against whites in courts. They could be witnesses only if another African American was involved in the case.

None of these laws applied to whites. African Americans were once again trapped in a type of enslavement, or pseudoslavery. Another term for this is *peonage*.

◆ CENTER YOUR THINKING

1. What were the Jim Crow laws?
2. Give an example of what is meant by the Grandfather Clause.
3. What were the major issues addressed by the *Plessy v. Ferguson* case?
4. Discuss the strategies used by whites to strip African Americans of their right to vote.
5. HOLISTIC ACTIVITY Students as Historians
   Analyze the different laws and legislation designed by individual states to keep African Americans from exercising full citizenship rights. Write a critique of these laws, giving special attention to their historical implications for today.

CHAPTER

38

ASANTE

SOCIAL BARRIERS TO EQUALITY

CENTER YOUR VOCABULARY

- ▲ lynching
- ▲ prejudice
- ▲ massacre
- ▲ misdemeanor

AS YOU READ

What is lynching? How was it used to control African American resistance? Was it effective?

Whites used every means at their disposal to maintain the social barriers between themselves and African Americans. Charles Darwin's theory of evolution and Herbert Spencer's elaboration of it as social evolution gave whites another reason to argue that they were superior.

Whites resorted to violence and outrageous acts to strip African Americans of their rights. They formed racist and terrorist hate groups such as the Ku Klux Klan, Knights of the White Camellia, Knights of the White Rose, Pale Faces, Red Jacks, Knights of the Black Cross, White Brotherhood, and Constitutional Guards. Thousands of African Americans were killed during and after Reconstruction. Lynching, the murder of individuals by mob action without lawful trial, became the means to control African American resistance to oppression in the post-Reconstruction years.

The Ku Klux Klan was formed in 1866 by six former Confederate officers. They reorganized that same year to form the Knights of the Invisible Empire. Their campaign of terror and intimidation was designed to restore white supremacy in the United States. It often resulted in lynching and other acts of murder. In two of the most serious acts in Memphis and New Orleans, the police took part in the massacre, or large-scale slaughter, of African Americans.

▲ Members of the Ku Klux Klan wrapped themselves in sheets to hide their identities as they persecuted African Americans.

Mob violence came to symbolize the deep hatred some white Americans had for African Americans. Racism, the persecution of others because of their race, was deeply imbedded in the legal and political system. It was established primarily in the Southern states. This period of unyielding prejudice (unreasonable bias) resulted in various forms of violence against African Americans. African Americans' rights were violated repeatedly. They were prevented from walking on sidewalks. They could not eat in restaurants, they could not stay in hotels, and they could not vote in elections.

African American men were often accused of sexually assaulting white women or of killing their employers. Both of these charges, whether true or not, often meant that the African American person would be subjected to mob rule and mob violence rather than a fair trial in a court of law.

LYNCHING

Between 1882 and 1920, more than 3,000 African Americans were documented as having been lynched. Of course, many cases went undocumented. Most of the lynchings took place in the South, althtough a fairly sizable number of lynching were also carried out in the North. In 1911, Zachariah Walker was taken from a hospital and burned alive in Coatesville, Pennsylvania, for allegedly shooting a policeman.

Lynching exposed the ugliest side of human nature. It became a festive occasion for the entire family. Whites took pleasure in the

> *Not all or nearly all of the murders done by white men, during the past thirty years in the South, have come to light, but the statistics as gathered and preserved by white men, and which have not been questioned, show that during these years more than ten thousand Negroes have been killed in cold blood, without the formality of judicial trial and legal execution. And yet, as evidence of the absolute impunity with which the white man dares to kill a Negro, the same record shows that during all these years, and for all these murders only three white men have been tried, convicted, and executed. As no white man has been lynched for the murder of colored people, these three executions are the only instances of the death penalty being visited upon white men for murdering Negroes.*
>
> Ida B. Wells, ***A Red Record***

barbarity. Pictures were taken, and people picnicked while African Americans were being murdered. Newspapers announced the date and location of the lynchings, and even printed articles and pictures of the event.

White leaders and organizations refused to come out against the lynching of African Americans. They were told and believed that the African Americans who were lynched were all rapists.

The courageous African American journalist Ida B. Wells was the leading antilynching crusader. A militant activist, she said in 1892 that a Winchester rifle should have a place of honor in every African American home. She also said that African Americans should hold their lives as dear as those of the white lynchers. "When the white man . . . knows that he runs as great a risk of biting the dust every time his Afro-American victim does, he will have greater respect for Afro-American life."

Wells knew firsthand that alleged rape was rarely the reason for lynching. In 1892, three of her friends were lynched in Memphis, Tennessee: Thomas Moss, Henry Stewart, and Calvin McDowell. The three were successful grocers who were viewed with jealousy by white storeowners in the area. A group of whites, armed with guns, came to their store to destroy it. The men fought back, shooting three whites. Moss, McDowell, and Stewart were arrested and jailed. Their case never went to trial. A white mob took them from the jail and tortured and murdered them.

▲ The courageous Ida B. Wells led the fight against lynching.

Wells worked to expose the real reasons for lynching. She conducted extensive research. She showed conclusively that suspected rape was not the reason for most of the lynchings, as whites alleged. During her research she wrote "that five women have been lynched, put to death with unspeakable savagery during the past five years. They were certainly not under the ban of the outlawing crime. It shows that men, not a few, but hundreds, have been lynched for misdemeanors, while others have suffered death for no offense known to the law, causes assigned being 'mistaken identity,' 'insult,' 'bad reputation,' 'unpopularity,' 'violating contract,' 'running quarantine,' 'giving evidence,' 'frightening children by shooting at rabbits,' etc." Wells's research proved that the majority of African Americans were being lynched for misdemeanors (minor offenses) and not for the crime of rape for which they were commonly accused.

▲ Between 1882 and 1920, more than 3,000 African Americans were lynched.

The horrors of lynching prompted Mary Church Terrell, a leading activitist and antilynching crusader to write: "Lynching is the aftermath of slavery. The white men who shoot negroes to death and flay them alive, and the white women who apply flaming torches to their oil-soaked bodies today, are the sons and daughters of women who had but little, if any, compassion on the race when it was enslaved."

Terrell also argued an important point that was often overlooked in the discussions on lynching and rape. She wrote, "In the South, the negroe's home is not considered sacred. . . . White men are neither punished for invading it, nor lynched for violating colored women and girls. . . ."

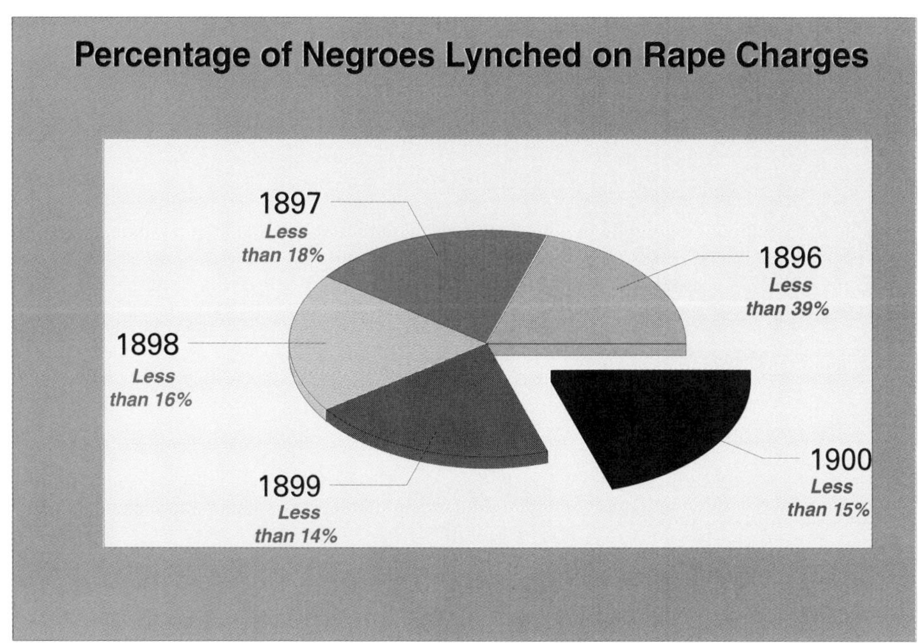

▲ Marchers protest lynching.

W. E. B. Du Bois called upon African Americans to resist lynching militantly: "We have crawled and pleaded for justice and we have been cheerfully spit upon and murdered and burned. If we are to die, in God's name let us perish like men and not like bales of hay. . . . I believe in peace. I shudder at revolution. But when in 1906 the Atlanta mob began killing Negroes wholesale, I went and bought a repeating shotgun and loaded it with buckshot. I have got it yet."

African Americans resisted lynchings by fighting back. They defended themselves with guns and other weapons when they could. They were often outnumbered. Nevertheless, African American newspapers praised the efforts of those who died fighting and encouraged others not give in to fear.

In 1917, 10,000 people marched down Fifth Avenue in New York City in a silent protest sponsored by the National Association for the Advancement of Colored People (NAACP). It was a courageous act in an era of danger and terror.

▲ A mob of whites chases their victim in 1919.

African American protests against racism did not go unchallenged. Segregationists were often able to continue their absurd practices because they used mobs of angry whites to frighten African Americans. They threatened those who resisted insults or those who attempted to vote or defend themselves. These mobs were responsible for some of the worst violence against African Americans in the United States.

In the North, segregation was not as severe. But it was a fact of life. Northern whites attacked African Americans in mobs as viciously as whites in the South did. Outbreaks of mob violence in the North seemed to occur more often in poor communities. African Americans in urban areas suffered the most. They were in direct competition with recent immigrants from Europe. African Americans and poor whites struggled for jobs, housing, and other social services.

The conflicts between both groups deepened. In 1908, whites in Springfield, Illinois, destroyed the African American community there and killed eight African Americans. In 1917, 40 African Americans were murdered during a riot in East St. Louis, Illinois. Three African Americans were killed in riots in Chester, Pennsylvania. White policemen often did little or nothing to protect African Americans and sometimes engaged in the rioting themselves.

RED SUMMER

The summer of 1919 was called *Red Summer* because there was so much blood shed in violent acts. There were 25 race riots in 1919 alone. The most violent occurred in Chicago, which lasted 13 days. Twenty-three African Americans and 15 whites were killed. More than 300 African Americans and 178 whites were injured. Red Summer was the opening act for the turbulence that was coming in the 1950s and 1960s.

◆ CENTER YOUR THINKING

1. Who was Ida B. Wells? How did she fight lynching?
2. Explain how the Ku Klux Klan and other secret racist organizations worked.
3. What did Mary Church Terrell mean when she wrote, "Lynching is the aftermath of slavery."
4. Why is mob action without legal control dangerous? How did African Americans make legal and real progress despite prejudice and mob violence.
5. HOLISTIC ACTIVITY Students as Negotiators
   You must give a speech to talk an angry mob out of violence during Red Summer. What will you say? Write and give your speech.

SUGGESTED READINGS

Botkin, B.A. *Lay My Burden Down.* Chicago: University of Chicago Press, 1945.

Cox, Oliver C. *Caste, Class, and Race.* New York: Doubleday, 1948.

DuBois, W.E.B., *Black Reconstruction in America.* New York: Harcourt, Brace, and World, 1953.

Franklin, John Hope. *From Slavery to Freedom.* New York: Alfred Knopf, 1956.

Painter, Nell Irvin. *Exodusters: Black Migration to Kansas After Reconstruction.* New York: Alfred Knopf, 1977.

Raper, Arthure E. *The Tragedy of Lynching.* Chapel Hill: University of North Carolina Press, 1933.

SUMMARY

When the enslaved Africans were finally emancipated following nearly 250 years in bondage, they owned nothing. They faced even more prejudice and racism. The country was led by a president who believed in the inferiority of Africans. Still, African Americans were able to vote and participate in the political life of the nation as elected officials. *(Chapter 35)*

The Freedmen's Bureau initially opened up new opportunities for thousands of African Americans. *(Chapter 35)*

The Freedmen's Bureau soon became the means to develop the sharecropping and convict labor systems to replace "slave" labor. The harsh conditions that emerged from the post Civil War era caused many African Americans to migrate away from the South. Whites used public policies, intimidation, and violence to take away many of the newly won gains of African Americans. *(Chapter 36)*

The Jim Crow laws were enacted by the legislatures of Southern states to institute segregation and other discriminatory practices. These laws were created as requirements for voting—conditions that African Americans could not meet. The federal government did not intervene to protect the rights of African Americans. The Supreme Court, in the landmark ruling, *Plessy v. Ferguson,* bolstered the cause of segregationists. *(Chapter 37)*

Although many whites used every means possible, including secret organizations such as the KKK, to discourage and even murder African Americans, courageous Africans Americans such as Ida B. Wells fought back rationally and successfully. *(Chapter 38)*

Personal Witnessing

REFLECTION

Write in your journal your thoughts about Thaddeus Stevens's plan to support economic independence for newly freed African Americans by giving them "40 acres and a mule." What do you think might have happened if Steven's plan had been approved.

TESTIMONY

Your small group has decided to write an editor at the *Colored Tennessean*, an African American newspaper, to give your opinions of the laws that have just been enacted at this point in history. Draft your letter, conveying your emotions as well as persuasive logic. Share it with the class.

UNIT 11 RITE OF PASSAGE

You have shared manuals with young children to teach Umfundalai qualities in earlier units. In your small group, develop manuals with activities that you can do with young children to assist those who are less fortunate than you. Be sure that you teach children not to pity others, but to respect them equally with themselves. Children should learn that everyone needs a helping hand sometimes. If possible, arrange for your group to teach some of the Umfundalai qualities from one of your "manuals" to an elementary school class. Include your manual in your Portfolio.

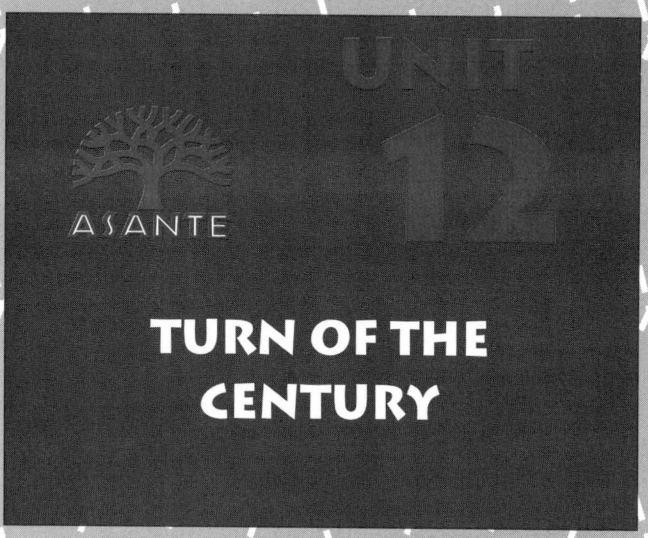

TURN OF THE CENTURY

In small groups, preview the chapter titles in this unit. Brainstorm lists of your reactions to the chapter titles. Make a list of predictions about the unit. Next, make a group list of questions that you would like to have answered as you read the unit.

As you read Unit 12, you will learn how African Americans had to fight for their freedom over and over again. What kinds of character strengths, skills, and personalities do you think African Americans needed to endure the ongoing struggle for freedom? Are these same traits valuable today? How?

1856
Booker T. Washington is born in Hale's Ford, Virginia

1877
Federal troops are withdrawn from the South, signaling the fall of Reconstruction

1881
Booker T. Washington founds Tuskegee Institute

1890
The Mississippi Constitutional Convention begins the systematic exclusion of African Americans from the political life of the South

1895
Booker T. Washington makes his famous Atlanta Exposition speech
Robert Smalls presents a proposal at the South Carolina Constitutional Convention to guarantee the right of every citizen to register to vote

1896
The National Association of Colored Women is founded in Washington, D.C.

1898
Race riots take place in Wilmington, North Carolina

" *The right and most effective way to look at the Negro's relationship to American culture is to consider it not as an isolated race matter and minority group concern, but rather in the context of the whole American culture* "

MARGARET JUST BUTCHER, THE NEGRO IN AMERICA

1901
Booker T. Washington dines at the White House with President Theodore "Teddy" Roosevelt

100 African Americans are lynched
Booker T. Washington's autobiography, *Up From Slavery*, is published

1908
W.E.B. Du Bois publishes *Souls of Black Folk*

1917
NAACP rallies 10,000 in a silent protest march against lynching
Race riots occur in East St. Louis, Illinois, and Chester, Pennsylvania

1919
The summer of 1919 is known as "Red Summer" because of the 25 race riots that occur

CHAPTER 39

ASANTE

TIDES OF CHANGE

CENTER YOUR VOCABULARY

- ▲ Oklahoma Grandfather Clause
- ▲ liberation
- ▲ majority
- ▲ token

AS YOU READ

Reconstruction raised the hopes of African Americans for equality. How do you think African Americans felt in the period following Reconstruction?

Like a shattered chandelier, the dream of full participation in American society broke into many pieces with the collapse of Reconstruction. The fall of Reconstruction had a tremendous impact on the 20th century. Between 1895 and 1915, every Southern state passed laws permitting the Democratic party to declare that only whites could vote in its primary elections. Accomplishments that had seemed assured and rights that had seemed protected during Reconstruction were swept away.

Throughout the South, African American leaders attempted to stop the whirlwind of racism expressed as disenfranchisement. At the 1895 South Carolina Constitutional Convention, Congressman Robert Smalls, an African American hero of the Civil War, presented the convention with proposals guaranteeing the right of every citizen to register and vote. The proposals were rejected strictly along racial lines by 130 to 6. The six African American delegates to the constitutional convention who voted in favor of the proposal were disillusioned and discouraged.

Even the Supreme Court of the United States refused to intervene on behalf of the African American population in disputes with states over voting. It wasn't until 1915 that the Supreme Court finally declared the Oklahoma Grandfather Clause unconstitutional. The clause said that only those people whose grandfathers had voted in previous elections could vote. The vast majority of African Americans were immediately excluded. Who among them had grandfathers who could vote when the vote was clearly denied to enslaved Africans prior to Emancipation?

Riots broke out in Wilmington, North Carolina, in 1898 and in Atlanta, Georgia, in 1906 over the campaign to disenfranchise African voters. Whites attacked African Americans at the polls as they attempted to exercise their legal right to vote. Throughout the 20th century, resistance to white animosity would be constant and strong. The African American community was coming to the eventual realization that physical emancipation did not mean complete liberation.

African American authors Langston Hughes and Milton Meltzer agreed with C. Eric Lincoln's view that "by the turn of the century white supremacy had won its political battle. The high hopes of the blacks which had been born during the Reconstruction era were dashed. The blacks of the South were no better off than slaves again, insofar as their right to the ballot was concerned."

The signs of the times all pointed to continuing the struggle. There was no way to avoid racial conflict resulting from economic deprivation, disfranchisement in the Southern states, and lynchings. Resistance was certain to increase to a whole new level as African Americans were pushed to the outer edge of society by segregation.

▲ Booker T. Washington

Among the momentous events that would shape this era was Booker T. Washington's meeting with President Theodore Roosevelt at the White House one month after Roosevelt's election in 1901. Although Roosevelt had been accused of trying to discredit the role of African American soldiers in the Spanish American War (1891), he had satisfied the majority of African Americans with his token gestures, inviting Washington to the White House and stating publicly that he believed in the equality of all people. Needless to say, the president was roundly attacked by the white press and many of the leading white opinion makers for dining with Washington.

During the 1920s, there were many more protests and marches against lynching. The NAACP tried to convince Congress to pass a bill to stop lynching. The bill passed in the House of Representatives. Southern senators caused the bill to fail in the Senate. ▶

The problems of the African American community did not improve any. With the coming of motion pictures, the popular stereotypical images of African Americans were indelibly imprinted in the minds of whites. Negative images of Africans were reenforced in the motion pictures of the early 20th century.

There were many problems that came with migration to the urban North. People eager to work could not support themselves or their families on their low wages. Very often, they had to share cramped living quarters with several family members. Overcrowed tenements mushroomed in the urban communities of the North. African American children, those who were not working in the factories, often with their parents, were idle and had few recreational or educational opportunities. Because segregated parks were off-limits to African Americans, the children learned to play stickball and other street games.

Even John Hope Franklin, the optimist historian, would write, "The century, which had opened with such a note of optimism, very early revealed overtones of despair that equaled, if they did not surpass, any which the Negro had experienced." African Americans knew that the patterns of discrimination, brutality, exclusion, and violence were as severe as they had been since the end of the enslavement. In fact, 100 Africans were lynched in 1901, the first year of the 20th century.

The century would include the First Major European War, the emergence of major civil rights organizations, the political and intellectual maturity of W.E.B Du Bois, the Harlem Renaissance, Marcus Garvey and the Universal Negro Improvement Association, the Second Major European War in Europe and the Pacific, the Vietnam War, Martin Luther King, Jr., and the Freedom Movement, the rise of African American female authors to star status, and the Afrocentric movement in art, fashion, literature, history, education, and economics.

In many ways, the title of John Hope Franklin's book *From Slavery to Freedom* tells us only part of the story. Africans came from enslavement to *some* freedom, understanding all too well that freedom in America had to be won again and again. Perhaps because of this understanding, few people truly grasp the full meaning of freedom in the United States as do African Americans.

The outlook on the future of African Americans of the time is typified by the young African American girl in St. Louis who, when asked, "What do you want to be when you grow up?" responded, "Everything that I can be." At the dawn of the 21st century, African Americans are well-represented in every sector of society, in every occupation and profession, and in every science. Freedom and opportunity, however, are to be found inconsistently. But the determination to add full equality to freedom finds African Americans becoming everything that they can be.

◆ CENTER YOUR THINKING

1. Which political party declared that only whites could vote in its primary elections?
2. What was one strategy used by whites to disenfranchise African Americans?
3. Describe the conditions that African Americans faced as a result of their migration to the urban North.
4. Discuss how the fall of Reconstruction impacted on the 20th century.
5. HOLISTIC ACTIVITY Students as Magazine Reporters You and your group are magazine reporters at the turn of the century. You want to interview African Americans in the South for an article on how the collapse of Reconstruction has impacted them. You are thinking of calling the article "Shattered Dreams," but you want to present a hopeful side, too. Make a list of questions you will ask. Discuss what you think the responses will be. Write your article.

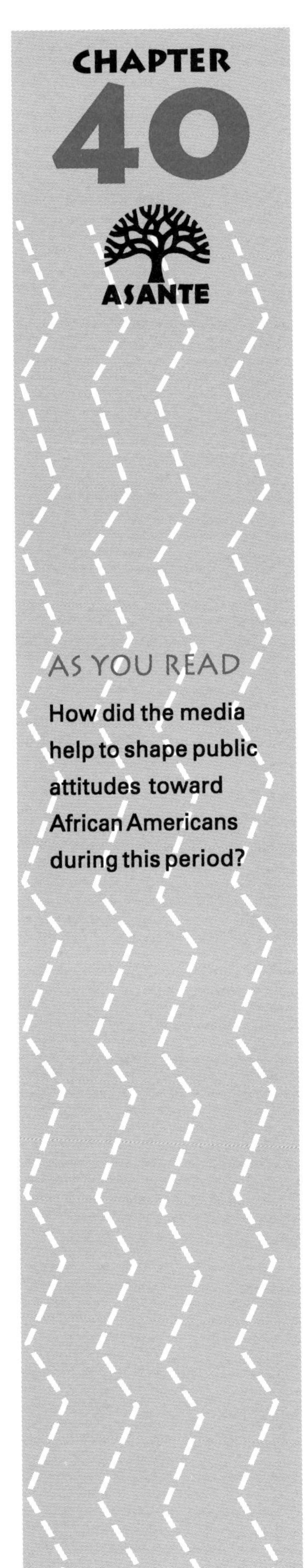

COUNTERING RACISM AND SEGREGATION

CENTER YOUR VOCABULARY

- ▲ marauder
- ▲ condemn
- ▲ humanity
- ▲ innuendo

In July 1917, a white tavern owner shot and critically wounded an African American worker in East St. Louis, Illinois. Ironically, rumors spread among whites that an African American had killed a white man. Mobs of angry whites attacked any African American they found on the streets. Rumors spread in the African American community that an African American man had been shot dead. The riot began. It was all senseless. W.E.B Du Bois would later write:

> *"So hell flamed in East St. Louis! The white men drove even black union men out of their unions and when the black men, beaten by night and assaulted, flew to arms and shot back at the marauders, five thousand rioters arose and surged like a crested storm-wave, from noonday until midnight; they killed and beat and murdered; they dashed out the brains of children and stripped off the clothes of women."*

In New York, the National Association for the Advancement of Colored People (NAACP) led 10,000 marchers down fabled Fifth Avenue. The mood was somber and quiet except for young boys and girls in front beating muffled drums as in a funeral procession. The marchers carried signs that called upon President Woodrow Wilson to condemn lynching and mob action. Later, President Wilson, seeming to agonize over the decision, issued a statement in support of law and order, but failed to condemn lynching outright.

HARD TIMES AHEAD

At the top of the 20th century, the entire nation seemed eager to prove that African Americans were not human and therefore did not deserve to be treated with dignity. Negative images of African Americans were found in newspapers, magazines, and scholarly books. White scientists were still trying to prove that African Americans were inferior to Europeans. Indeed, even restaurants used spoons and forks with distorted images of African Americans. Some churches preached against whites associating with African Americans. Others denied African Americans membership.

The first full-length American film, *Birth of a Nation*, made in 1915 by W. D. Griffith, who is credited with numerous advances in filmmaking, magnified the tensions between African Americans and whites for all the world to see. Although Griffith's film is responsible for indelibly stamping negative images of Africans on the celluloid screen, the W. D. Griffith Award is still given out today as a mark of excellence in cinematography, an irony not lost on many African Americans.

On the surface, the movie seemed innocent enough. The film begins in a pre-Civil War setting with two white families, one in the North and one in the South. The families are brought together when their children fall in love with each other. The son is from the North and the daughter is from the South. The audience already knows the problems the young couple will face.

As the story unfolds on the screen, the real theme of the movie emerges. The movie attacks the humanity of Africans with blunt racism, innuendos (hints), and subtle references to white superiority. The Africans in the film are afraid of their own shadows and terrified of the Ku Klux Klan, a white supremacist group. African women are shown beating African men with brooms, and Africans who had been portrayed earlier in the film as "faithful servants" turn out to be thieves, spies, and rapists.

When the Civil War breaks out, Africans who support the Union Army are portrayed as traitors. No attempt is made to explain why

Africans such as the ones shown here gave their full support to the Union Army. They were portrayed falsely as traitors in the film *Birth of a Nation*. ▶

Africans in the South would become spies or risk their lives for the Union cause. Given the negative images many whites already had of Africans, this distortion of the facts only served to fuel more distrust and hatred of African Americans.

When the war is won by the North, African Americans are elected to high government offices and are shown to be tough on the white Confederate soldiers. Once again, this was a deliberate attempt to stir up hatred between the races, especially since African American Reconstruction legislators in the South were doing their best to foster a spirit of cooperation between African Americans and whites.

President Woodrow Wilson, a Southerner from Virginia who had been president of Princeton University, promoted the movie at the White House. Despite the demonstrations against the movie by leading African American activists of the time, President Wilson ignored the racist content of the movie and promoted it as a great achievement in filmmaking, but in the minds of African Americans, this was an issue of content versus technology. When one makes a bomb, the issue is not simply how well the bomb is made but how it will be used and what impact it will have on people. The impact of *Birth of a Nation* was worse than an exploding bomb for the African American community.

By supporting the movie, President Wilson showed that he did not support the cause of African Americans. From 1913 to 1921, the period of his presidency, the African American population experienced the highest number of lynchings in the history of the nation. Taking their direction from the president, white Southerners felt it was open season on killing Africans. Wilson introduced segregated facilities in both the nation's capital and national federal offices. Quite easily, given this atmosphere, popular white magazines like *Scribner's* and *Harper's* called African Americans "niggers" and "darkies." The nation had one of its cruelest moments. It was only through the courage and determination of the African American communities with their strong men and women organizers that this period was survived.

SEGREGATION

The negative images of African Americans that were popularized at the turn of the century helped to maintain a system of legal separation. This was called *segregation*. Many new laws were written by lawmakers in the South to separate the races and deny African Americans the same opportunities and treatment as whites.

Segregation was responsible for many racist and ridiculously absurd practices. For example, African American women were often called *aunty*; African American men were often called *uncle*. It was a deliberate way to avoid calling an older African American *Mr.*, which many whites saw as a title reserved for white men. Some whites even used the disrespectful *boy* to address men twice their age.

▲ Mary McLeod Bethune

Mary McLeod Bethune, one of the greatest African American educators of the century, told a story about her first visit to the White House. She was invited by President Franklin Roosevelt in honor of her outstanding achievements as an educator. One by one, the dignitaries and invited guests entered the White House and were greeted by the doorman: "Good evening, ma'am. Good evening, sir." When it was Bethune's turn, the doorman said, "Good evening, aunty." Bethune, stopped, looked at the man closely and asked in all seriousness, "Which of my brother's children are you?"

Throughout the South, one could find all kinds of absurdities that were allowed by law. In Oklahoma and Texas, for example, there were separate phone booths for black and white people as they were called. In Florida and Georgia, textbooks were kept in separate warehouses so that white and black students would not have to handle the same books. The absurdities of racism were simply astounding: white and black cemeteries, white and black Bibles to swear on at the court house, white and black sections of trains and buses, white and black water fountains, and the separation of white and black blood at the blood banks. African Americans were often not permitted to try on clothes at department stores and could not get rooms in major hotels.

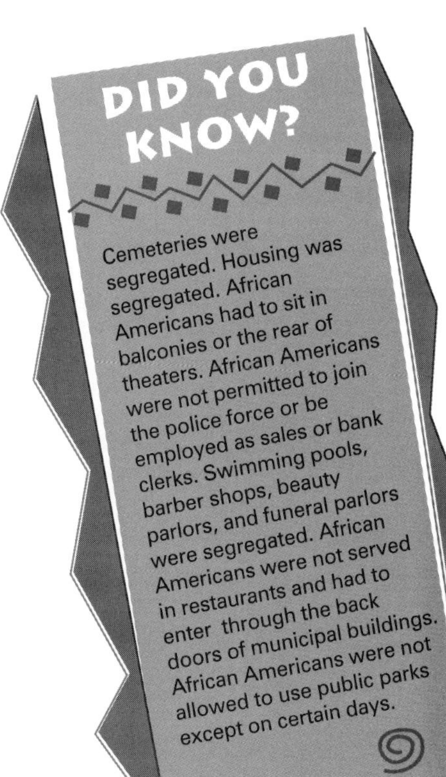

Segregation was not based on any fact. It was based entirely on the whims, fears, and prejudices of whites. Responding to these whims required restraint, judgment, and courage because African Americans realized that they were often dealing with individuals who believed their absurd prejudices. Each day, thousands of African American men, women, and children had to make their own decisions about responding to thinly veiled insults and overt prejudicial attacks. This was simply survival. African Americans who carelessly protested these insults were punished and sometimes killed.

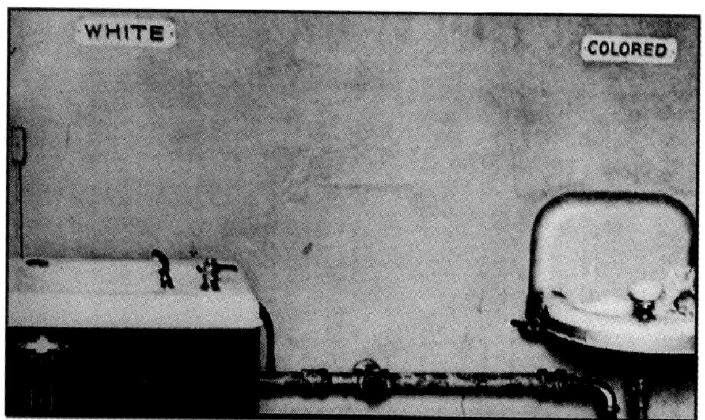

▲ Segregation allowed separate sinks for whites and African Americans.

PROTEST MARCHES

One of the first serious responses by African Americans in the 20th century was organized protest marches, which were led mainly by preachers of independent Baptist and Methodist churches because they could organize immediate demonstrations by their members. Increasingly, as the NAACP became stronger, it took the lead in protesting the offenses against African Americans. African American protests against segregation rarely went unchallenged. Mobs of whites, often led by the Ku Klux Klan, threatened those who protested, sought equal opportunity with whites, and campaigned for political equality.

In the face of constant attacks, abuses, and hostility, many African American men and women sought their freedom in the North, heading for the cities of New York, Philadelphia, Chicago, Detroit, Boston, and Cleveland. However, the vast masses of African Americans remained tied to the land in the South. There were memories, relatives, and obligations that kept many older people in the South. Those who had no relatives in the North or knew no one there felt that at least in the South they had a home and perhaps some land. Instead of traveling to the North to live among people they did not know, they chose to live with the evil they knew.

A young African American boy leads a protest against segregation. ▶

◆ CENTER YOUR THINKING

1. Define *segregation*.
2. What was President Woodrow Wilson's response to the NAACP march down Fifth Avenue?
3. How did W. D. Griffith's film magnify tensions between African Americans and whites?
4. In your opinion, what does the statement, "Segregation was responsible for many racist and absurd practices" mean? Give at least three examples to support your answer.
5. HOLISTIC ACTIVITY Students as Filmmakers
   Think about the kind of film you would have made on the same subject as *Birth of a Nation*. Plan your film. In small groups, write an outline for a script for your film. Explain to the class how yours is different from W. D. Griffith's film.

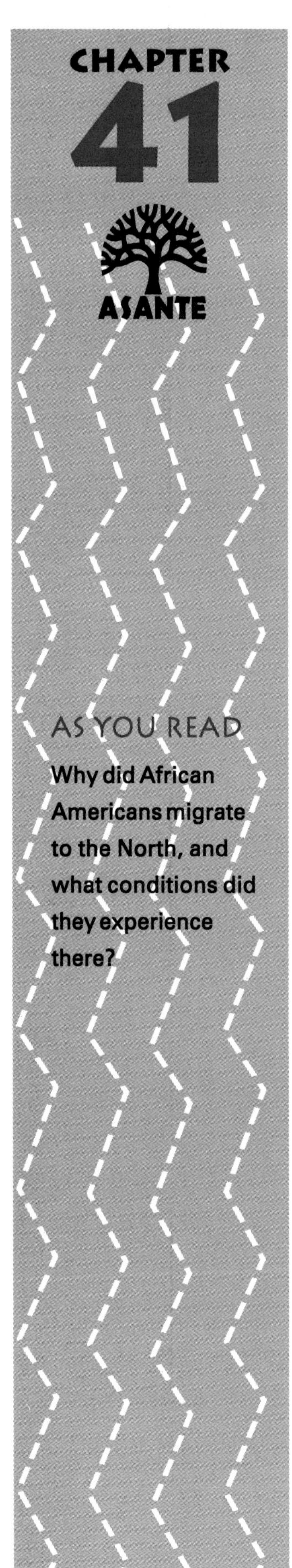

LONG GONE ON SHIPS OF STEEL

CENTER YOUR VOCABULARY

- ▲ condescending
- ▲ internalized
- ▲ Great Migration
- ▲ mental enslavement

Imagine what the scene must have been like during the early 1900s in Chicago, Philadelphia, New York, and Detroit. Trains were filled with African Americans moving North. The Georgia Southern Lines, the Ohio and Chesapeake, and many other train lines transported the masses, huddled in "ships of steel," across the vast reaches of the American landscape. Waiting relatives made their way through the crowds looking for "Cousin John" and "Nephew Dimp" or "Aunt Bessie." High-pitched voices of recognition and joy shrieked through the terminals, "Hey girl, how you been? Ain't seen you in a long time!"

Sitting on segregated trains, suffering the indignity of not being able to eat in the all-white dining cars, remembering loved ones left behind, and suffering insults from condescending Southern conductors did not dampen the spirit and the excitement these African Americans felt on their way North. African Americans were hopeful that the North would offer more opportunities for a better life.

By 1920, nearly 2 million African Americans had deserted the wide, open spaces of the South for the dense, overcrowded city life in the North. This mass movement to the North was called the *Great*

▲ This painting by Jacob Lawrence captures the spirit of the Great Migration.

Migration. The south side of Chicago, the Black Bottom of Detroit, south Philadelphia, and Harlem in New York were the major destination points for migrating African Americans. Here they were able to see the Southern culture transplanted. They had Georgia sugarcane syrup, Louisiana red hot sauce, and neckbones in the grocery stores. They had color, music, and dance. These communities promised the migrants jobs and security.

In these cities, they met no promised land and no heaven on earth, but they did find communities relatively free of the brutal segregation and harsh discrimination they had left in the South. African Americans felt a sense of protection in the Northern cities because the laws were more liberal and progressive. Access to the political process was easier. African Americans voted to elect political candidates who supported their causes. They formed organizations that agitated for further political privileges.

The NAACP defended the legal rights of many African Americans in the North and South. Through its network of lawyers, African Americans had a champion in the courts to challenge the prejudice

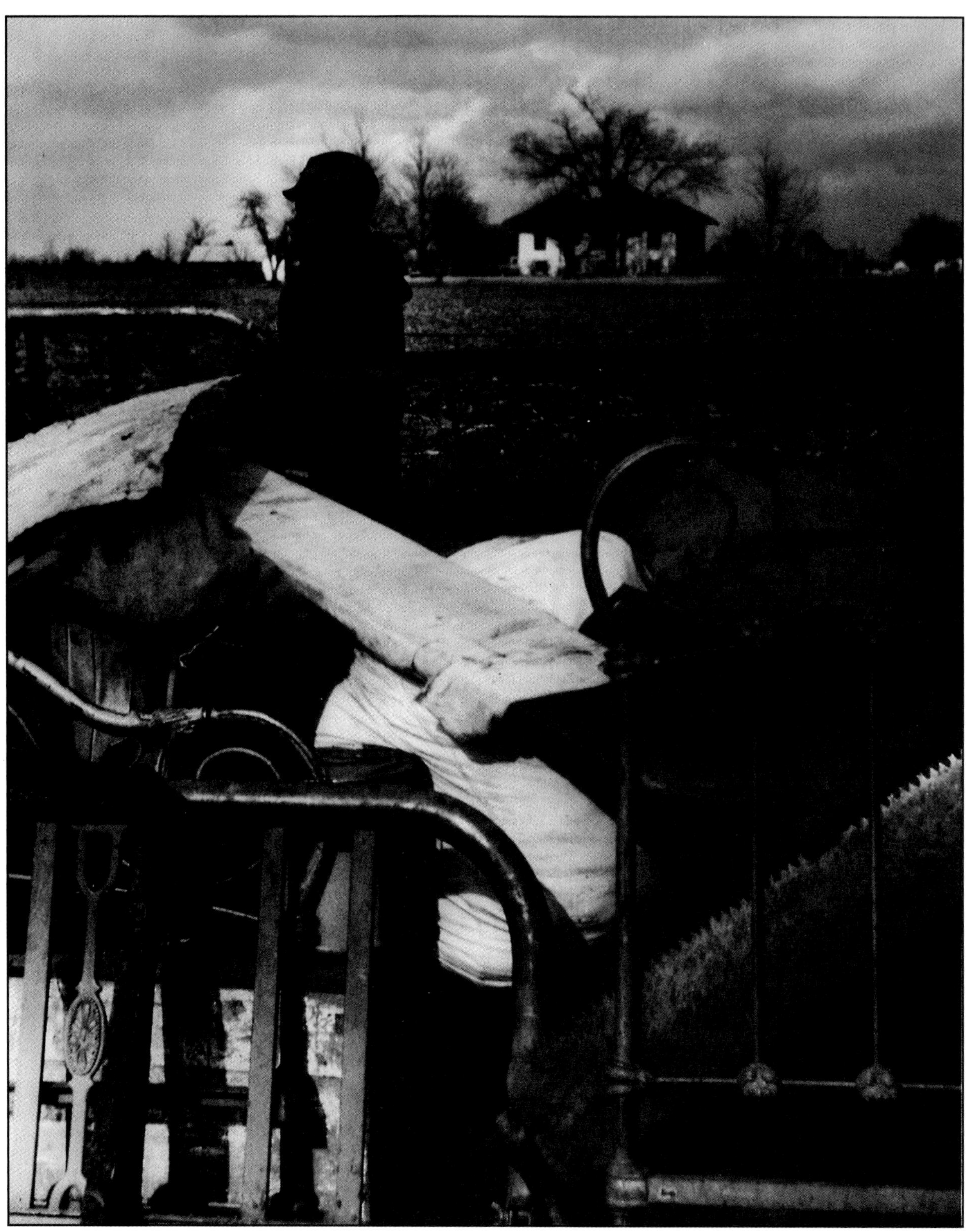

▲ African Americans packed their humble possessions and headed North looking for a better life.

they found in employment, housing, education, and many other aspects of their daily lives in ways they could not have done before.

Nevertheless, there were many other struggles to overcome. African American workers in the North had to face the growing

▲ An injured man sits on a curb after a mob attack.

problem of obtaining membership in the labor unions, which dominated the workforce in the industrialized North. Prejudice against African Americans and whites' refusal to work with them were among the many challenges African Americans faced.

Prejudice in the workforce spilled over into the communities in which both groups lived. The steady rise in the African American population in the North was a constant source of tension between whites and African Americans. As African Americans moved into the neighboring white communities, whites tried to keep them out by firebombing their homes. The tensions between the races were encouraged by the Ku Klux Klan and other racist groups who wanted to keep the races divided. By the summer of 1919, Red Summer, race relations were at an all-time low. From June to the end of the year, there were approximately 25 race riots of varying sizes and intensity. Many people lost their lives, scores more were injured, but it was the African American community that was hit the hardest. Faced with the daunting task of rebuilding, African Americans had to come to terms with the growing realization that physical emancipation did not mean final liberation.

After 246 years of enslavement, many African Americans had internalized the negative images and ideas advanced by white preachers, writers, and scientists. The sum total of their experience was the substitution of physical enslavement with a new system of mental enslavement. Embedded in the new system was the idea of white superiority and "black" inferiority. Two leaders, Booker T. Washington and W.E.B. Du Bois, major interpreters of the African American experience during the early part of the 20th century, understood the necessity of overcoming white supremacy and "black" inferiority in the minds of Africans. Their tactics would be economic and political empowerment of the African American community.

◆ CENTER YOUR THINKING

1. What term is used to describe the mass movement of African Americans to the North?
2. Give three examples of ways in which African Americans brought Southern culture with them to the North.
3. Compare and contrast mental enslavement and physical enslavement.
4. What were the underlying reasons for the frequent incidents of mob violence in the North?
5. HOLISTIC ACTIVITY Students as Lawyers
   Your group is a team of NAACP attorneys in the 1920s who fight for the legal rights of African Americans. First, create a case you wish to defend (or research a real case). Now, prepare a summary of your defense. Share it with the class, and have them vote as a jury would on the effectiveness of your argument.

CHAPTER 42

ASANTE

NEW IDEAS FOR A NEW CENTURY

CENTER YOUR VOCABULARY

- autobiography
- agitation
- accommodation
- progressive
- color line
- advance man

AS YOU READ

How did African American leaders differ on their approaches to advancing the African American community?

The Kenyans have a proverb that says, "when elephants rumble, the grass is crushed." In the case of African Americans' leading spokespersons, Booker T. Washington, William Monroe Trotter, Ida B. Wells, and W.E.B Du Bois, the issues of the masses were often forgotten in the struggle with each other. However, they were all sincere in their desire to see the advancement of the African American community.

Booker T. Washington: Up from Slavery was the name he gave to his autobiography, because Booker Taliaferro Washington had pulled himself "up from slavery" to found and operate a great industrial arts school for African Americans in Tuskegee, Alabama. Born in Hale's Ford, a community in Franklin County, Virginia, in 1856, he was nine years old when enslavement was abolished in Virginia. As a young boy, Washington worked in the coal mines in West Virginia. At age 16, he attended Hampton Institute. He graduated four years later, in 1876. By the time he was 25, Washington had founded his own college. Tuskegee Institute opened its doors to African Americans in 1881 with Washington as its president.

At Tuskegee, Washington offered courses in agriculture, dairy farming, and science for African American farmers. Within a few years, he had built a thriving school and had attracted some of the

▲ A math class in progress at Tuskegee Institute

greatest African American minds, including the genius, George Washington Carver. Carver devoted his life to research projects that would greatly improve the production of agriculture in the South. Carver created more than 300 products from the peanut. The products he created from the peanut, and later from the soybean, revolutionized the economy of the South by liberating it from an excessive dependence on cotton. He also made discoveries in fungi that improved agriculture. Carver's work made Tuskegee a center for agricultural science that is still highly respected today.

In 1895, Booker T. Washington, largely because of his fame for Tuskegee's success, was asked to speak to a group of Southerners at the Atlanta Cotton States Exposition. In this speech, he defined his views on the relationship of African Americans and whites in America. He believed that African Americans should not seek political power nor should they seek to be educated in the same way that

▲ Booker T. Washington pulled himself up from slavery.

whites were educated. He believed that African Americans should work with their hands and dismiss the idea, at least temporarily, that they could influence the politics and policies of the United States.

In an 1895 speech, now called the Atlanta Compromise Speech, Washington stated, "The wisest among my race understand that the agitation of questions of social equality is the extremest folly, and that progress in the enjoyment of all privileges that will come to us must be the result of severe and constant struggle rather than of artificial forcing." He went on to assure the white audience that they could be as sure in the future as they had been in the past "that your families will be surrounded by the most patient, faithful, law-abiding, and unresentful people the world has seen." The white community showered him with many gifts of money for his school. The white press made him the spokesperson for the entire African American community.

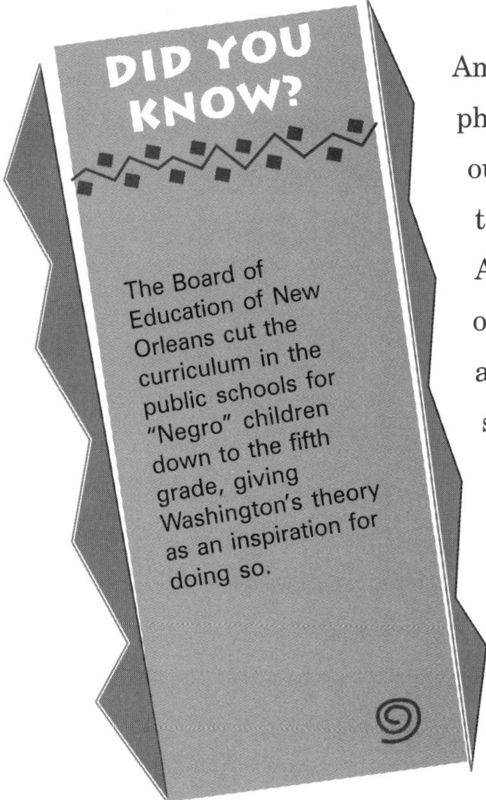

Washington's speech brought great criticism from African American leaders. Alarmed by what many called Washington's philosophy of accommodation, other African Americans set out to discredit the idea that African Americans wanted only to accommodate, or please, whites. In fact, some African American leaders even believed that Washington was soft on lynching. Lynching was one of the most sensitive issues among African Americans. Washington, in a classic statement, said, "It is unreasonable for any community to expect that it can permit Negroes to be lynched or burned in the winter, and then have reliable Negro labor to raise cotton in the summer." Washington's casual reference to lynching and the absence of any sense of outrage greatly angered some African American leaders. Washington, however, was appealing to whites on the basis of what he believed was in the best economic interest of whites. To Washington, the economic appeal to whites was stronger than the moral or social appeal that lynching was a cruel, murderous act. Washington believed that African Americans would best achieve their constitutional rights by working for economic empowerment and moral values. As a result, he tried to enlist moderate white Southerners in his movement.

Washington thought that moderate whites would be more supportive of his cause once they realized that African Americans were only trying to improve their moral and financial base. Washington believed that whites would resist African Americans who wanted political power or social equality. His philosophy blended values that everyone respected with a short-term economic gain for African Americans. The vocational education that African Americans received at Tuskegee Institute gave them basic skills with which they could proudly earn a living with their own hands, a quality respected by whites and African Americans alike.

This was an era of emphasis on education and social responsibility in the U.S., and the philanthropy of humanitarians who donated to African American education, combined with the force of Washington's

▲ Andrew Carnegie gave extensive financial support to Tuskegee Institute.

personality and abilities, produced a growth spurt for African American colleges and universities.

In 1903, Tuskegee Institute received a $600,000 donation from white industrialist Andrew Carnegie, who admired Washington's creed of hard work, education, and self-help. "To me, he seems one of the foremost of living men because his work is unique," Carnegie said of Washington. Carnegie had immigrated to the U.S. from Scotland and built his fortune from nothing with his own hard work. Carnegie represented the best of a group of socially conscious U.S. millionaires who wanted to see progress, and used a part of his fortune to ensure that African Americans were a part of that progress.

By 1915, Booker T. Washington's philosophy was under severe attack. Twenty years earlier, it seemed that this charming and eloquent educator held the American public in the palm of his hand with his idea of accommodation. While Washington had done well personally and Tuskegee had prospered through the generosity of white humanitarians like Andrew Carnegie, the condition of the African American population in the South was little improved. Washington's philosophy was replaced by the progressive ideas of African American leaders in the North.

In his later years, even Washington himself grew uncomfortable with his own philosophy. We now know that Washington secretly gave money to self-help organizations and community-oriented groups. He also personally financed several early court cases against segregation, again in secrecy. This strategy of a public and a private agenda worked to keep his white audience satisfied, but it did not end the hostile criticism from the African American community.

With Washington's death went a history of people. Many other African American leaders died that year. For example, Robert Smalls,

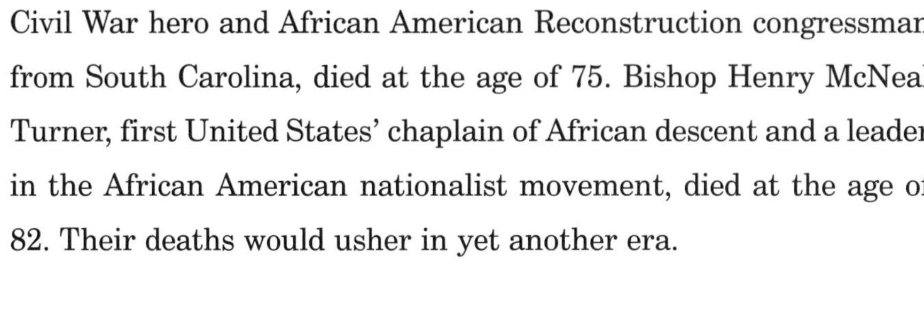

Civil War hero and African American Reconstruction congressman from South Carolina, died at the age of 75. Bishop Henry McNeal Turner, first United States' chaplain of African descent and a leader in the African American nationalist movement, died at the age of 82. Their deaths would usher in yet another era.

> *What man is a worse enemy to a race than a leader who looks with equanimity on the disfranchisement of his race in a country where other races have universal suffrages by constitutions that make one rule for his race and another for the dominant race. . . . This habit of always belittling agitation, that very thing which made him free, and by which he lives and prospers is one of [Washington's] greatest faults.*
>
> **William Monroe Trotter**

WILLIAM MONROE TROTTER: "THE ADVANCE MAN"

William Monroe Trotter, African American scholar and publisher, has been generally considered "the advance man of a new breed of black activists" for his commitment to total equality. Trotter, a Harvard graduate on fire with anger against racism and accommodation, started a newspaper in Boston called the *Guardian*. He thundered against Booker T. Washington and his accommodation philosophy. Trotter believed that constant agitation, not accommodation, was the only way to make whites treat African Americans equally. In his view, Washington had betrayed the African American community.

▼ The outspoken Ida B. Wells was one of Washington's greatest critics.

IDA B. WELLS: CRUSADER AGAINST LYNCHING

Diversity in the opinions of the African American leadership by the time of Washington's death was great and growing deeper. Ida B. Wells of Holly Springs, Mississippi, rose to prominence as the most outspoken African American female of this period. Wells was a graduate of Rust College in Mississippi. She was a teacher, a journalist, and African Americans' most devoted crusader against lynching. In a brilliant essay written in 1904, she said, "Industrial education for the Negro is Booker T. Washington's hobby. The Negro knows that now, as then, the South is strongly opposed to his learning anything else but how to work."

▲ W.E.B. Du Bois was a civil rights activist and a founding member of the NAACP.

W.E.B DU BOIS: CHAMPION OF AFRICAN AMERICAN INTEREST

Other voices would be heard, among them the reasoned and balanced voice of W.E.B. Du Bois. Considered one of the leading intellectuals of this period, Du Bois's greatest work was yet to be achieved. Du Bois, along with William Monroe Trotter and Ida B. Wells, raised his voice in support of full equality.

If Ida B. Wells and William Monroe Trotter were the frontline defenders in the struggle for equality, Du Bois was the careful marksperson. His aim, to be sure, was at Washington's accommodation philosophy, but he also saw clearly that Washington was not the chief enemy of African Americans. In 1903, more than a decade before Washington's death, Du Bois co-authored a book, *The Negro in America* with Washington. Perhaps it was the time both men spent working together or Du Bois's gift of perception that allowed him to praise Washington's achievements and yet firmly reject his philosophy of accommodation.

Author of 21 books and hundreds of articles, Du Bois was the first person to define the 20th century according to African American interests. He prophetically said that the problem of the 20th century would be "the problem of the color line." He was right. The problems of racism, represented by skin color, would continue to the turn of the 21st century.

Prior to receiving his Ph.D. from Harvard in 1895, the year Washington gave his Atlanta Compromise Speech, Du Bois attended Fisk University in Nashville, Tennessee. His knowledge and awareness of racial oppression was formed by his time in the South. He wrote, "I saw discrimination in ways of which I had never dreamed. I came in contact for the first time with a sort of violence that I had never realized in New England. A new loyalty and allegiance replaced my Americanism: henceforward I became a Negro." It was from this place and this point that he could make an objective judgment and evaluation of the course of Booker T. Washington's strategy.

> “ *I saw discrimination in ways of which I had never dreamed; the separation of passengers on the railways of the South was just beginning; the race separation in living quarters throughout the cities and towns was manifest; the public disdain and even insult in race contact on the street continually took my breath; I came in contact for the first time with a sort of violence that I had never realized in New England. A new loyalty and allegiance replaced my Americanism: henceforward I became a Negro.* ”
>
> W.E.B. Du Bois

◆ CENTER YOUR THINKING

1. Name three leading African American spokespersons, and briefly describe the contributions of each.
2. What were Booker T. Washington's views regarding accommodation, and why were these views criticized by some African American leaders?
3. Who was the African American leader who wrote that the problem of the 20th century would be "the problem of the color line"?
4. Do you agree with the leader in question 3? Explain.
5. HOLISTIC ACTIVITY Students as Speech Writers
   In small groups, choose two of the leaders you read about and write a speech for each of them to give. Practice giving the speeches to your group or class.

SUGGESTED READINGS

Cone, James. *The Spirituals and the Blues*. New York: Orbis Books, 1991.

Franklin, Vincent P. *Black Self-Determination.* New York: Lawrence Hill, 1984.

Durham, Philip, and Everett L. Jones. *The Adventures of the Negro Cowboys*. New York: Dodd, Mead, 1966.

Katz, William Loren. *The Black West*. Garden City, N.Y.: Doubleday, 1971.

Reddings, Saunders. *The Lonesome Road*. Garden City, N.Y.: Doubleday, 1958.

Stuckey, Sterling. *Going Through the Storm*. New York: Oxford University Press, 1994.

SUMMARY

After the collapse of Reconstruction, African Americans found that emancipation did not guarantee that their rights would be respected or protected. Throughout the South, laws were passed leading to the disenfranchisement of African Americans. Threatened and real violence were used regularly against African Americans to prevent them from exercising their legal rights. *(Chapter 39)*

The first full-length American film, *Birth of a Nation*, indelibly stamped negative images of African Americans on the celluloid screen. An outcome of the popular dehumanization of African Americans was the highest number of lynchings in the history of the nation and, the maintenance of legal segregation. African Americans, of course, actively resisted these conditions. *(Chapter 40)*

Conditions became so bad in the South that African Americans migrated to the North, but discrimination, violence, and rioting occurred in the Northern cities, too. African Americans formed organizations such as the NAACP to protect their enfranchisement and defend their legal rights. *(Chapter 41)*

Booker T. Washington rose to success and fame. His philosophy of accommodation gained favor in the white community, but criticism from many African Americans. In his later years, Washington secretly donated to various African American organizations. By 1915, Washington was dead and the condition of African Americans was little changed. *(Chapter 42)*

Ida B. Wells and W.E.B. Du Bois were two other great African American intellectuals of the time who crusaded against racism. Ida B. Wells was a teacher and journalist, and her articles against lynching captured the attention of many. Du Bois authored more than 21 books and hundreds of articles focusing on the problems of racism and color as the most important modern problem to be solved. *(Chapter 42)*

PERSONAL WITNESSING

REFLECTION

What makes a man or woman a leader? Reflect upon the qualities needed for leadership that the people you've learned about in this unit have exhibited. They were dependable, well-reasoned, fought timelessly for equal rights, worked intensely, resisted threats of violence, and handled pressure well. What other qualities did they have? What qualities do you admire most? What leadership qualities do you want to develop yourself?

TESTIMONY

African American women have always taken leadership roles in the fight for liberty and freedom, but you may have learned less about them in your education so far. With your group, prepare an oral presentation for young children to describe and give honor to ten African American women leaders about whom you think all children should be aware.

UNIT 12 RITE OF PASSAGE

Now is a good time for your class to meet with parents or adult mentors and elders to begin planning the Rites of Passage ceremony. Where will it be held? What group of people will be the adults who judge which of you is qualified and worthy? What will the program be? What African traditions need to be researched to ensure their authenticity? How will you display the completed Portfolios? How will the worthy be recognized? Write an action plan and schedule for planning the ceremony. Include the action plan and schedule in your Portfolio.

UNIT 13

STAND UP FOR YOUR RIGHTS

1902
Langston Hughes writes his famous poem "The Negro Speaks of Rivers"

1914
Marcus Garvey founds the Universal Negro Improvement Association and African Communities League in Kingston, Jamaica

1915
The Booker T. Washington era ends with his death
Carter G. Woodson establishes the Association for the Study of Negro Life and History
Ernest Just receives Spingarn Medal from NAACP
Second Great Migration

Many African American leaders knew that, after centuries of oppression, African Americans would have to fight not only for legal rights in the ongoing war against racism and discrimination, but also for ways to correct the psychological damage done by continued enslavement and segregation. In small groups, list your predictions of the actions that African American leaders would take to correct the psychological damage. At the end of the unit, check your predictions and correct them.

As you read Unit 13, notice that African Americans on the road to freedom had to "pass through the passion and fire of the activist." Do you think an activist must be passionate? How does belief change the way an activist progresses?

1916
Marcus Garvey enters the United States and establishes UNIA and ACL in New York City

1917
The United States enters the First Major European War, April 6
African Americans such as Charles Young agitate to become military officers

1918
African American troops are warned by Robert Moton that their status will not change after the War

1920-1940
The Harlem Renaissance

1921
"Black" Tulsa is destroyed by riots

1925
A.Phillip Randolph organizes the Brotherhood of Sleeping Car Porters
Al[illegible] coins the te[illegible] *New Negro*

1929
October 29, the Great Depression begins

1930
Nation of Islam founded in Detroit

1936
Jesse Owens wins four gold medals at the 1936 Olympics in Berlin

1937
Joe Louis wins the world heavyweight boxing title

1940
Air Force opens a segregated training center for African American pilots

1946
Jackie Robinson breaks the color barrier in professional baseball

1950
Ralph Bunche wins the Nobel Peace Prize

"We demand, in the interest of national unity, the abrogation of every law which makes a distinction in treatment between citizens based on religion, creed, color or national origin. This means an end to Jim Crow in education, in housing, in transportation and in every other social, economic and political privilege; and especially, we demand, in the capital of the nation, and end to all segregation in public places and in public institutions."

A. PHILIP RANDOLPH,
SURVEY,
NOVEMBER 1942

CHAPTER 43

ASANTE

THE FIRST MAJOR EUROPEAN WAR

AS YOU READ

In what ways were African Americans trained to feel inferior? In what ways did the war give them a fresh outlook?

CENTER YOUR VOCABULARY

- agency
- self-reliance
- African-centered curriculum
- miseducation

The period following Booker T. Washington's death saw exciting and dynamic developments. Carter G. Woodson, the Harvard-trained historian, would create the Association for the Study of Negro Life and History in Chicago. Ernest Just, the first African American biologist to be recognized for his achievements as a scientist, would contribute important research on the cell, and Marcus Garvey would enter the United States and establish the Universal Negro Improvement Association. But it would be the unrest throughout the country, the 56 African Americans lynched in 1916, and the race riots in East St. Louis, Houston, and Philadelphia and Chester, Pennsylvania, that would make the next few years remarkable for their brutality. Demands for freedom from oppression, segregation, and discrimination would be echoed repeatedly as a new round of African American leaders prepared to fight for full justice.

CARTER G. WOODSON

Carter G. Woodson was a scholar and an agent for change who was far ahead of his time. He recognized the need for agency among African Americans at a time when there was very little to affirm African history and culture. He saw that African Americans needed to take action themselves rather than being acted upon.

▲ Carter G. Woodson

Taking advantage of the opportunity given to him by the Omega Psi Phi fraternity to address their weekly meeting, Woodson, in a spectacular display of agency, seized the moment to press for the creation of an organization that would focus on African American studies. Woodson's call to action (agency) gave rise to the Association for the Study of Negro Life and History, the preservation of African American culture, and numerous other contributions. He became the founder of the *Journal of Negro History* and the father of the concept of African American History Month, which originally was called Negro History Week.

But it was in his classic book *The Miseducation of the Negro* that he recorded his most powerful opinions about education. Woodson's contention that African Americans were educated away from their own history, or miseducated, created quite a sensation when it was read in 1933. He believed that the institutions set up immediately after the Civil War and in the early 20th century to educate African Americans were guilty of psychological or mental enslavement. This was true because African Americans knew more about the literature, music, art, and culture of other races than they knew about their own race. Woodson believed that African Americans were being trained to feel inferior. From this vantage point, African Americans would have a difficult time viewing their own art, literature, music, or culture on an equal footing with that of Europeans. Woodson saw this type of education as a continuation of enslavement. He believed that this method of education would create a race of people who would accept the idea of European cultural superiority in everything as a matter of course and deny their own culture. Woodson was prophetic in his ability to predict the future. Today, many schools struggle to create an African-centered curriculum that places all students at the center of learning to help them value their own history and culture.

▲ Ernest Just

Other figures appeared in this period who were as distinguished for their intellectual and artistic contributions as Carter G. Woodson was in education. Ernest Just, the first African American trained as a research biologist, received the first Spingarn Medal from the

NAACP for his achievements as a scientist. In economics, Robert C. Weaver, Charles L. Franklin, and Abram Harris were outstanding as government advisers on matters of African American employment and housing. In history, there were pioneers such as Charles H. Wesley, W.E.B. Du Bois, Rayford Logan, and Benjamin Quarles, who introduced the study of African and African American history to the formal classroom. Other fields and interests provided the research and writings of Anna Julia Cooper, Drusilla D. Houston, J. Saunders Redding, Kenneth Clark, Margaret Walker, Sterling Brown, Ralph Bunche, George W. Carver, Percy Julian, Charles Drew, John Hope Franklin, Arthur Davis, and others.

The road to freedom, although maintained by scholars and artists, was paved with the passion and fire of the activist. Here the Universal Negro Improvement Association (UNIA), founded by Marcus Moziah Garvey in 1916, captured the imagination of Africans around the world. Self-reliance was a key point in the philosophy of this institution. Garvey said:

"The Universal Negro Improvement Association teaches our race self-help and self-reliance, not only in one essential, but in all those things that contribute to human happiness and well-being. The disposition of the many to depend upon the other races for a kindly sympathetic consideration of their needs, without making the effort to do for themselves, has been the race's standing disgrace. . . ."

IMPACT ON AFRICAN AMERICANS

The First Major European War, often called World War I, slowed European immigration to the United States but had a profound impact on the African American population. The war produced an economic boom in the country that created new opportunities for African Americans who had had difficulty finding work. Manufactured goods, food, clothing, and medical supplies, to name a few, were in high demand. Factories could not get enough white workers to manage the increase in orders brought on by the war. This shortage of labor created jobs for African Americans. Many of the barriers against African American workers came tumbling down as industry sought to increase its labor force. Skilled and unskilled African American workers were hired. Factory owners sent representatives to the South to pay African Americans to come to the North and work. African Americans who ventured to the big cities wrote their families and friends to join them in the urban areas of the North where they could all find jobs.

THE SECOND GREAT MIGRATION (1915-1920)

Beginning in 1915, approximately 2 million African Americans moved to the industrial centers of the North. Job opportunities there set off a second wave of African American migration to the North. This was called the *Second Great Migration.* This mass movement of African Americans to the North hurt the South's economy, which was based on agriculture. For Southern whites, this mass movement of African Americans to the North was a major disaster. They told African Americans that the North had harsh winters and that they would freeze to death. They said that the winds in Chicago were more cruel than racist whites in the South. They told them that Mr. Hawk, the name African Americans gave to the Chicago winter winds, was a tougher master than the old enslavers of the South. Yet, African Americans still left the South in droves on buses, trains, and in old cars. There are stories of some even walking from Memphis to Chicago, so eager were they to escape the poverty and discrimination that haunted them in the South. Some Southern states charged high licensing fees for labor scouts from the Northern companies who came to the South looking for African American workers. Those who could pay the fees often found that there were laws against inducing African Americans to leave the South.

As the war in Europe wore on, it became evident that the United States would become involved. When President Woodrow Wilson declared On April 1, 1917, that "the present German submarine warfare against commerce (trading ships) is a warfare against mankind," even the South courted African American workers. Wages in the South increased significantly. For the first time in the South, many African Americans were able to get semiskilled jobs in the trades.

▲ Cadet Henry O. Flipper, class of 1878, U.S. Military Academy

America's participation in the war, in President Woodrow Wilson's words, was to "make the world safe for democracy." President Wilson clearly believed that the German autocracy had to be eliminated, but the majority of the American people did not want the United States to enter the war. However, on April 6, 1917, the United States formally entered the war, abandoning its policy of neutrality.

A TEST OF LOYALTY

Once again, the African American community looked at the possibility of fighting in a war for rights that did not exist for them in their own country. Once again, the full measure of democracy was denied to African Americans; yet they were asked to fight for the rights of others. However, in this war, there were competing interests for African American support. German spies, sent to the United States to influence African Americans not to participate in the war, reminded the African American community that they did not have democracy in the United States. African Americans knew that President Woodrow Wilson's declaration that the United States would fight for "the things which we have always carried nearest our hearts—for democracy, for the right of those who submit to authority to have a voice in their own governments" did not apply to them. The German spies were influential enough to cause some African Americans to speak out against the war. Others boldly denounced American hypocrisy and said that the United States had to be made safe for democracy before the world could be made safe for democracy. These critics believed that there was little difference between German racism and American racism. As in previous wars, when the test of loyalty was required of them, African American soldiers, full of generosity and perhaps political

▲ March 1919, New York City: a wounded soldier talks to spectators at a parade of the 369th Colored Infantry.

▲ Cadet John H. Alexander, class of 1887, U.S. Military Academy

naiveté born of their own heartfelt desire for equality and liberty, went off to defend their American homeland. African Americans have never lost any love or loyalty for racists anywhere in the world. They knew too well the legacy of enslavement. This was not the issue for the African American soldiers. Every African American soldier who fought believed that those who judged Africans on the basis of race and color would learn eventually that all humans are created equal. They believed that their duty in the moment of national crisis was to protect the nation of their birth.

African American soldiers displayed their courage and loyalty for all the world to see. At a time when the African American population was only 10 percent of the American population, 13 percent of the soldiers were African Americans. Throughout the 20th century and many more wars, African Americans sacrificed their lives for the United States and the principles they valued.

At the same time in Europe, almost 300,000 Senegalese Africans were called upon by the French to fight the Germans on the Oureq and the Marne rivers. Some 30,000 African soldiers from the Congo and about 20,000 African soldiers from the Caribbean participated in the defense of Europe.

In many respects, the African soldiers who fought for the French were better off than the African Americans who fought for the United States. The French accepted the Senegalese and Congolese as equal members of French society and culture; the white Americans were still not sure about the role of Africans in America.

THE ENEMY WITHIN

White America's refusal to accept African Americans as their equals created many unnecessary conlicts. African American soldiers were commanded often by illiterate and prejudiced whites who subjected the soldiers to unnecessary dangers and hardships. At times, it seemed that African American soldiers faced as much hostility and danger from the United States Army as they faced from the enemy.

▲ A youthful Charles Young graduates from the U.S. Military Academy in 1890.

The United States Army made a deliberate attempt to prevent African American soldiers from becoming officers. Students from Howard University in Washington, D.C., agitated for change, marching in front of the White House and circulating posters demanding that African Americans be trained as officers. They kept the issue alive in the news. The War Department reluctantly changed its policy.

Colonel Charles Young, the highest-ranking African American graduate of West Point, was a likely candidate for promotion. He had been a hero of the Spanish American War, leading four African American units under his command. Instead of making him an officer, the army retired him, claiming that he had high blood pressure. While Young openly acknowledged that he had the disease, he did not suffer excessive attacks from it. Furthermore, it is unlikely that it would have impeded his duties as an officer. To demonstrate his strength and endurance, Young rode his horse from Texas to Washington, D.C., in a show of prowess. This had little effect on the War Department's decision to retire him from service.

When the army finally permitted African American officers to lead their troops, African Americans received more citations than

Colonel Charles Young (second from left) stands with his staff aboard the *S.S. Orduna.* ▶

▲ February 1919, New York City: African American troops from the 369th Infantry on a victory march up Fifth Avenue.

any other U.S. regiment in France. Needham Young and Henry Johnson of the 93rd Infantry's 369th Regiment became the first individual African Americans to receive the Croix de Guerre (Cross of War medal) from the French government for outstanding performance in battle. The 370th and the 8th Illinois African American regiments, both led by African American officers, were honored similarly.

The United States, reception of the returning African American soldiers was in stark contrast to the high honors they received from the French. In 1918, President Woodrow Wilson sent Robert Moton of Tuskegee to France to warn the African American troops that there would be no change in their status upon their return to the United States. Furthermore, he wanted African American soldiers to know that if they acted differently in a social or political sense when they returned, they would be punished. President Woodrow

▲ Robert Moton

Wilson wanted the African American troops who helped to make the world safe for others to know that they should not try to do the same for themselves.

African American soldiers returning from the war were greatly influenced by their interaction with other Africans from the Caribbean and Africa. The war had given them a new outlook on life. The returning soldiers were the forerunners of the Harlem Renaissance. They had fresh ideas, new opinions, and a sense of worldliness that was exciting and dazzling.

First Major European War (1914-1918)

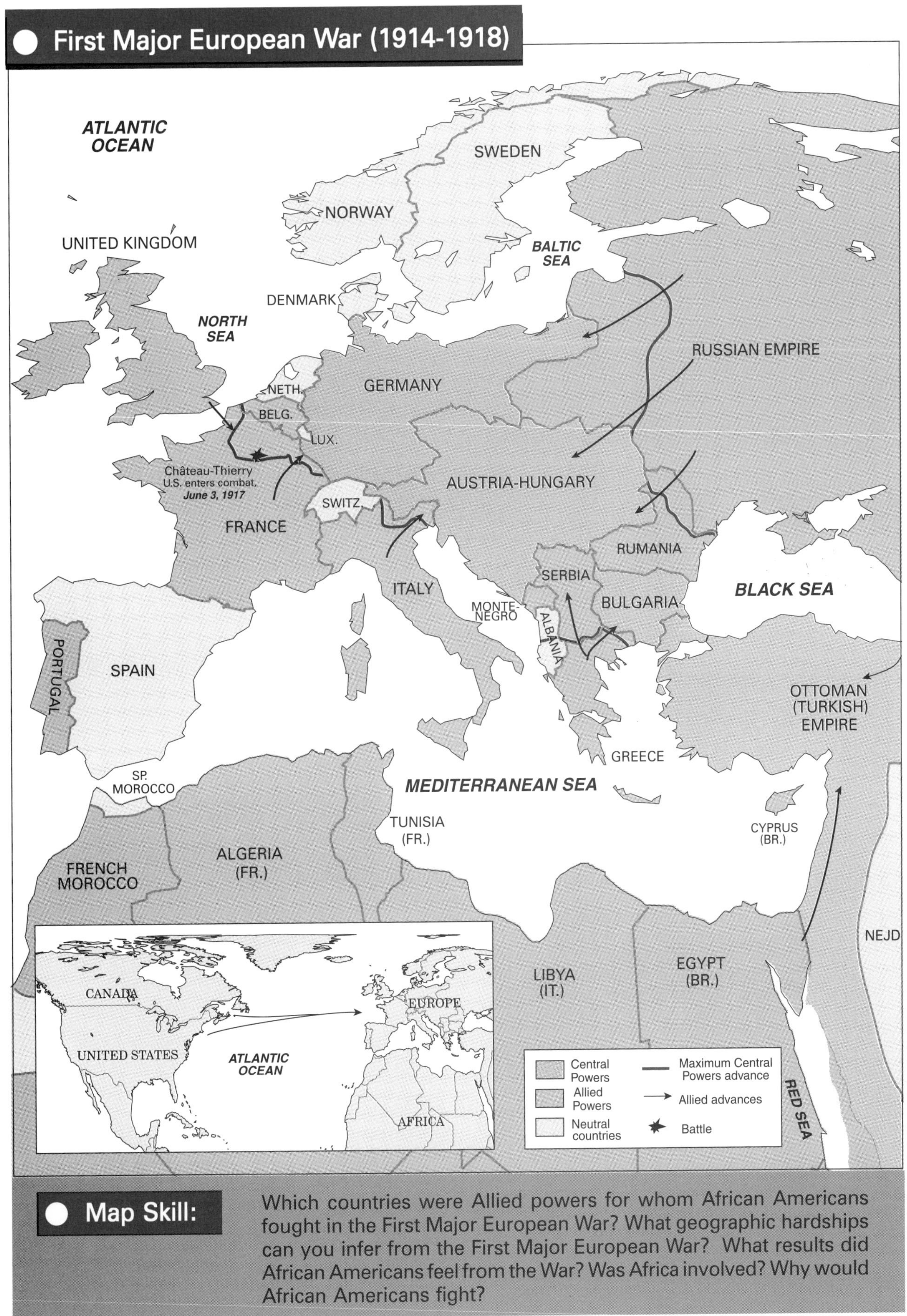

Map Skill: Which countries were Allied powers for whom African Americans fought in the First Major European War? What geographic hardships can you infer from the First Major European War? What results did African Americans feel from the War? Was Africa involved? Why would African Americans fight?

◆ CENTER YOUR THINKING

1. What was the Association for the Study of Negro Life and History? Who was its founder? Why was it established?
2. Compare African American participation in the Civil War with that in the First Major European War.
3. What were the causes of the Second Great Migration? How did it impact the South?
4. Are Carter G. Woodson's views on education still relevant today? Explain your opinion.
5. HOLISTIC ACTIVITY Students as Book Reviewers

   An editor of a professional magazine for teachers is publishing a book review of this *African American History* textbook. The editor has asked your group to write a summary of Chapter 43 to include in the review as an example of the type of textbook this is. Write your summary. Share it with the class.

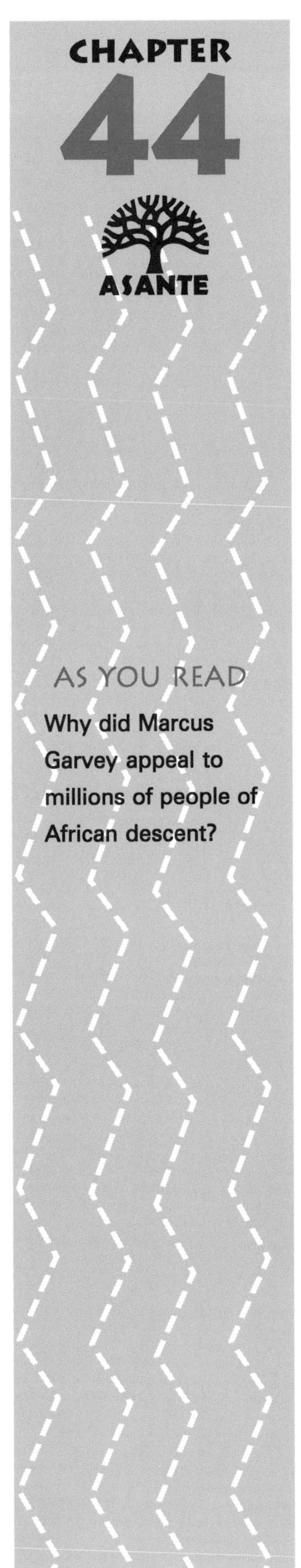

"UP YOU MIGHTY RACE"

CENTER YOUR VOCABULARY

- ▲ perspective
- ▲ Black Cross
- ▲ self-determination
- ▲ colonialism
- ▲ Garveyite
- ▲ collective economics

AS YOU READ

Why did Marcus Garvey appeal to millions of people of African descent?

Marcus Moziah Garvey arrived in New York City in 1916 from Kingston, Jamaica, one year after the death of Booker T. Washington and during the intensification of the war in Europe. Garvey had longed to meet Washington, the African American educator who had inspired him to build an organization for the uplifting of African people. Garvey combined all of the eloquence of Washington with African Americans' natural affection for Africa to develop a perspective, or point of view, that would capture millions. No mass leader in the history of the African American people was as electric as Garvey. Perhaps no one, with the exceptions of Martin Luther King, Jr., and Asa Philip Randolph, had the genius of organization and talent for mass demonstrations that Garvey did. He regularly led great pageants of elegantly dressed Africans through the streets of Harlem and organized businesses, clubs, and political study groups in an effort to raise the consciousness of African Americans about their own heritage and possibilities. Thousands of people smiled with pride as the legions of Garvey's supporters paraded the streets of Harlem. Garvey was the spark that rekindled African Americans' pride in their ancestry and heritage. He was a shining example of African Americans' glorious past on the continent and a beacon of hope for African Americans' future in the United States.

▲ Marcus Garvey dressed in uniform as the president of the Republic of Africa in a motorcade through Harlem.

Garvey's philosophy began with the simple idea of having pride in one's own heritage. His message struck a strong chord among all people of African descent who were free from bondage but not free from the colonialism that had made them feel shame and humiliation in being African. Garvey's aim was to remove this burden from the African race. "Up you mighty race," he thundered. "You can accomplish what you will." Appealing to the instinct of loving one's homeland, he said to his audiences, "Africa for the Africans at home and abroad." Garvey's vision of Africans united, under the rule of African people, stirred the African populations in the Americas and the Caribbean as nothing had ever done before. He made it possible for Africans throughout the world to visualize African armies, African navies, and African dignitaries working for African interests. It had been a long time since this was so in the history of Africans.

Using the African culture for his appeal, Garvey dramatized his aims by putting on political, cultural, social, and economic demonstrations of grand proportions. Garvey created a flag of red (for the blood), black (for the race), and green (for the land). He organized the African Orthodox Church where Africans could worship God in their own image. He set up the Black Cross, Garvey's version of the Red Cross, to aid and assist those in need. By 1921, he was able to have a formal installation of himself as the provisional president of the Republic of Africa. He was surrounded by a royal court of *Dukes of the Nile and Niger* made up of important members of his organization from all over the African world.

Marcus Garvey stated in "The Principles of the Universal Negro Improvement Association," a speech delivered at Liberty Hall, November 25, 1922:

"In view of the fact that the black man of Africa has contributed as much to the world as the white man of Europe and the brown man and yellow man of Asia, we of the Universal Negro Improvement Association demand that the white, yellow and brown races give to the black man his place in the civilization of the world."

Garvey's genius for marketing his ideas and his enthusiasm for his policies attracted people worldwide. Millions became Garveyites, members of the Universal Negro Improvement Association and African Communities League, organizations set up in 1914 by Garvey to accomplish the goals of self-determination and collective economics. In Garvey's opinion, African American people had to decide their own fate rather than wait for others to determine how they would live. He believed that collective economics meant that African Americans would pool their resources to set up their own businesses. The organization's flag became the "Flag of the Black Race." The colors remained the same, except that the green now represented the future of the race. Garvey collected $10 million during a two-year period, more money than any African had ever collected from the African world. With this money, he was able to set up restaurants, hotels, factories, and laundries, and to incorporate the steamship company, the Black Star Line. *The Negro World*, a weekly newspaper, was the instrument through which African Americans learned about Garvey's ideas.

As the organization grew in size, Garvey lost personal control of many of its facets, and soon the organization was involved in legal problems. By 1925, he was under arrest for mail fraud. Many scholars believe that the authorities were looking for a way to stop the mass appeal of Garvey's movement. Garvey was convicted and served two years in an Atlanta penitentiary. He was expelled from the United Sates and forced to return to Jamaica in December 1927. The organization still exists, but never recovered from the loss of its charismatic founder. Garvey died in London in 1940, but his ideas live on today.

Marcus Garvey, 1887-1940

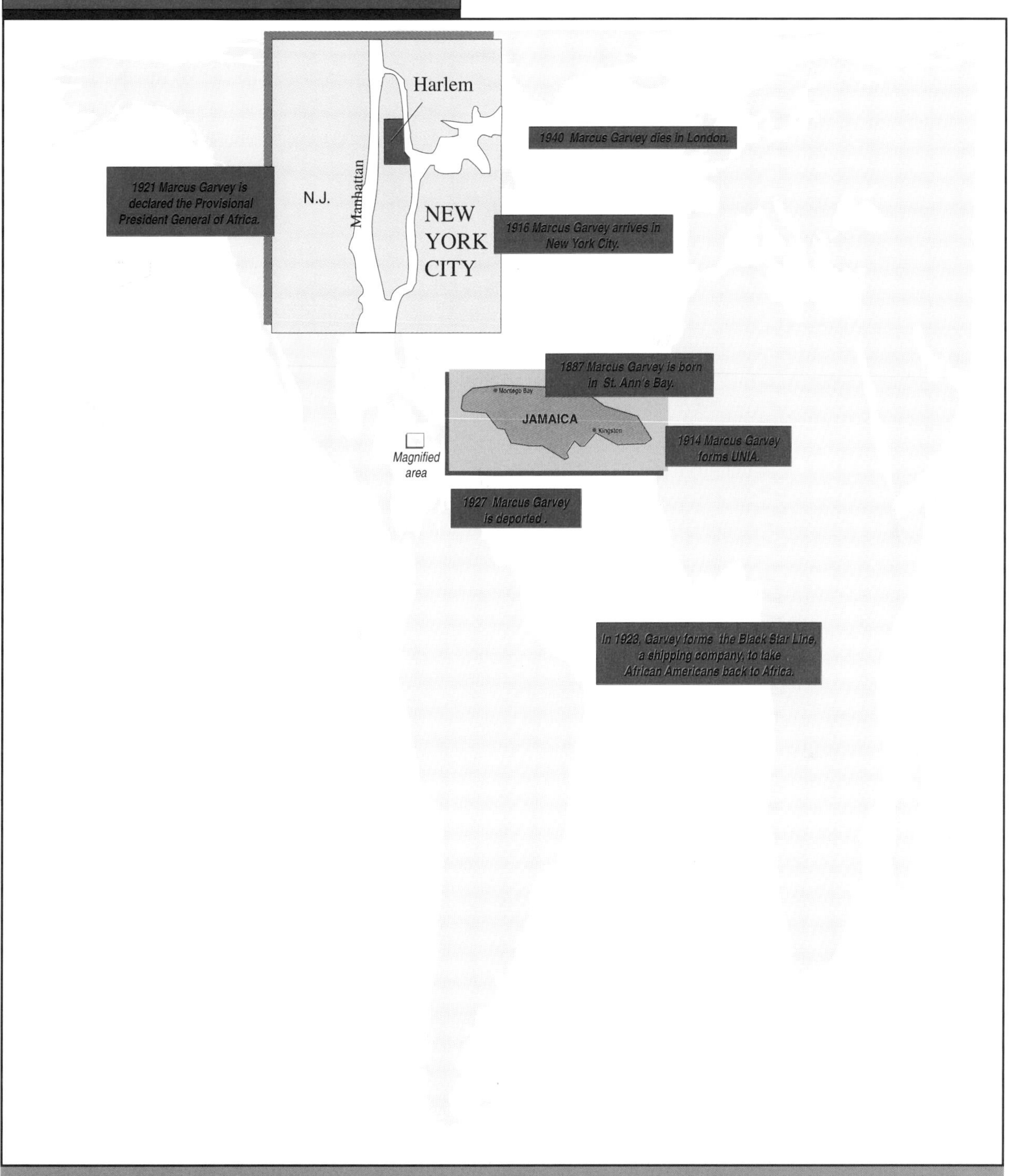

Map Skill: Where is Jamaica in relationship to Africa? to the U.S.? Why were Garvey's ideas so appealing to Africans worldwide?

◆ CENTER YOUR THINKING

1. Name the organization that was established by Marcus Garvey.
2. Explain Marcus Garvey's philosophy.
3. Define and compare *self-determination* and *collective economics.*
4. In your opinion, why was Marcus Garvey one of the most electric leaders in the history of the African American people?
5. HOLISTIC ACTIVITY Students as Artists

   Create a work or performance that expresses the ideas, lifework, and philosophy of Marcus Garvey, and your group's or your personal opinion of him. You may choose any format for your creation.

CHAPTER

45

ASANTE

THE HARLEM RENAISSANCE

CENTER YOUR VOCABULARY

- ▲ renaissance
- ▲ Philadelphia clubwoman
- ▲ New Negro
- ▲ Funga

AS YOU READ

How could African Americans make such great contributions to American society while being denied the full measure of democracy?

Armed with confidence, talent, and training, young African American men and women blazed a trail of artistic expression that began in the 1920s and lasted 20 years. Cultural expression was their aim. Harlem was the attraction. Big, bustling, and brimming with opportunity, Harlem in the early 1920s and 1930s was the "capital of the African American world." Nestled on the northern tip of the Manhattan Island between Eighth Avenue to the west and the Harlem River to the east, Harlem was a place where the best music, art, and culture of African Americans could be experienced. There were playwrights, sculptors, musicians, journalists, painters, choreographers, and political activists vying for cultural space and a place in the sun. The Harlem Renaissance was a rebirth of African culture and art.

Harlem drew the best of the African poets, jazz and blues musicians, singers, and writers from the Americas, the Caribbean, and some African lands. Langston Hughes, the poet, came from Kansas. Zora Neale Hurston, the novelist, came from Florida. Claude McKay came from Jamaica; and Alain Locke, when he could, came from Philadelphia. They came, like the thousands before them, to what seemed to be a sacred gathering of the African world. Harlem streets, filled with gaiety and laughter, paid tribute to the men and

Harlem, New York, 1900-Present

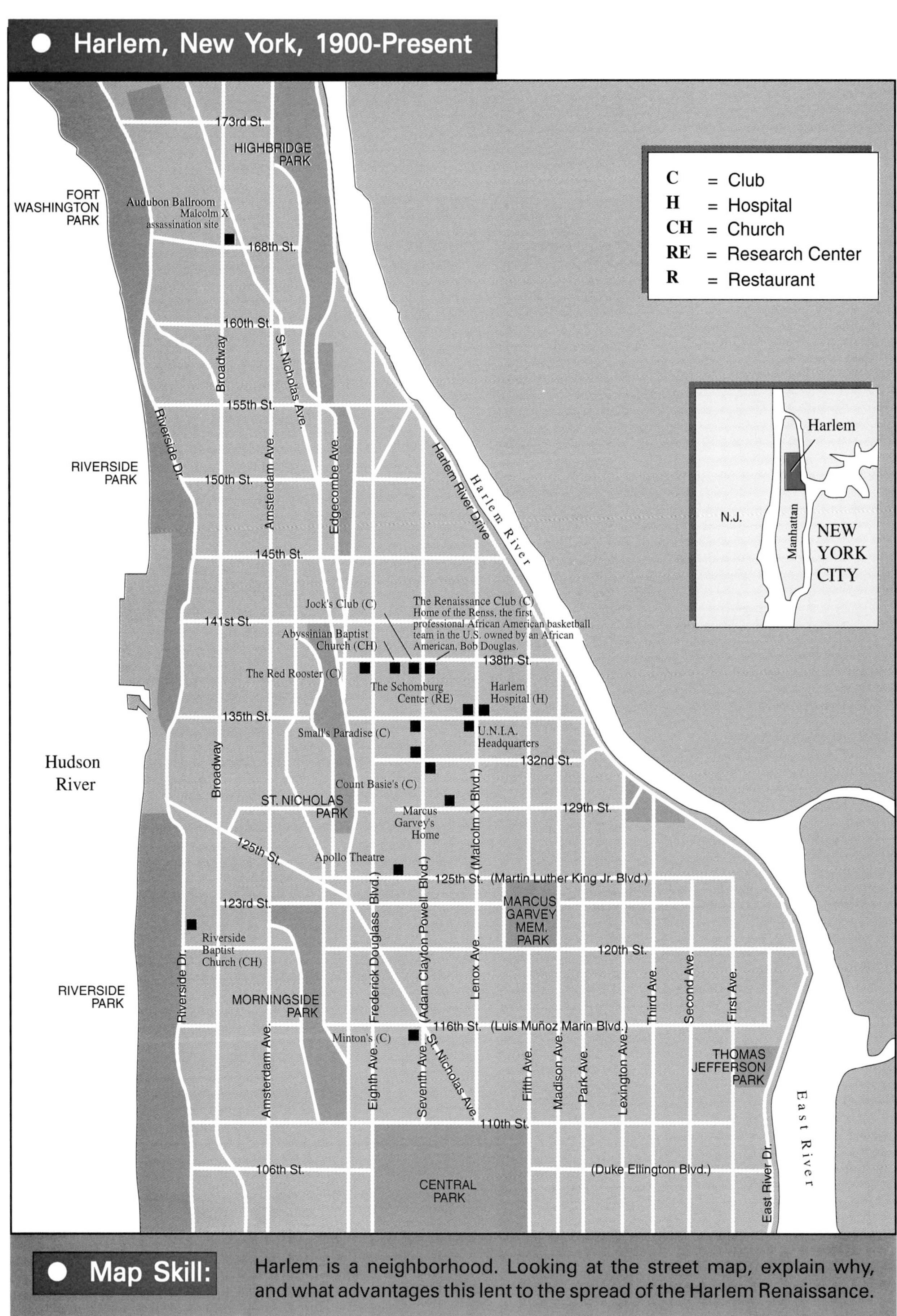

Map Skill: Harlem is a neighborhood. Looking at the street map, explain why, and what advantages this lent to the spread of the Harlem Renaissance.

▲ Harlem's best and brightest talent:
Top from left: Arna Bontemp, Melvin Tolson, Jacob Reddick, Owen Dodson, Robert Hayden
Bottom from left: Sterling Brown, Zora Neale Hurston, Margaret Walker, Langston Hughes

women who rewrote the story of African literary, musical, and choreographic traditions. They were to Harlem and the African American world what they became to the rest of the world: icons of creative genius and the dawning of a new day. The words on everyone's lips in Harlem in the 1920s were *New Negro*. The New Negro represented a new image of African Americans that would put to rest the stereotyped image of the shuffling African.

Langston Hughes became the best-known poet of the Harlem Renaissance. After graduating from high school in Cleveland, Ohio, Hughes took the train to Toluca, Mexico, to visit his father before going to college. His mother had wanted him to get a job to help her pay the bills because she did not have the support of her husband. Hughes's father, filled with bitterness against racism and prejudice in the United States, had packed his bags and moved to Mexico. With his mother's blessing, young Hughes was now on his way to see his father. In 1920, while crossing the Mississippi River on the train at dusk, the Joplin, Missouri, teenager, jotted down on an envelope his thoughts about the whole history of Africans and rivers.

▲ Claude McKay

THE NEGRO SPEAKS OF RIVERS

I've known rivers:

I've known rivers ancient as the world and older than the flow of human blood in human veins.

My soul has grown deep like the rivers

I bathed in the Euprhrates when dawns were young.

I built my hut near the Congo and it lulled me to sleep

I looked upon the Nile and raised the pyramids above it.

I heard the singing of the Mississippi when Abe Lincoln went

down to New Orleans, and I've seen its muddy bosom

turn all golden in the sunset.

I've known rivers:

Ancient, dusky rivers.

My soul has grown deep like the rivers.

Langston Hughes

Little did he know that this poem would make him famous. It would be acclaimed by literary critics and magazine editors and sung from the pulpits of Baptist churches. Hughes's poem would become one of the most quoted pieces of African American writing in American history. When he arrived in Harlem to attend Columbia University in 1921, he was only 19 years old but already an accomplished writer. He would later compose in every known genre of literature—journalism, short stories, novels, poetry, plays, essays, travel journals, and satire.

In June 1926, at 24 years of age, Hughes wrote an African American Declaration of Independence for all African American artists that was published in *The Nation*, a popular national magazine. Hughes's declaration stated boldly that the contributions of African American writers were as much a part of literature as European American writing. This declaration would serve as a cultural yardstick for future African American writers. His own success was a powerful

▲ Langston Hughes

example of what African Americans could do if they believed in themselves. Since that time, hundreds of composers, musicians, playwrights, and artists have flourished in the African American community.

Hughes's declaration struck at the heart of the psychological dislocation among some African Americans that made them resent his poetry for its emphasis on African themes and subjects. It was as if these lost Africans believed that African Americans were not worthy of poetic consideration. Hughes's declaration spoke most directly to those African Americans who were denying their own cultural heritage. To emphasize his point, he wrote a short profile of the *Philadelphia clubwoman.* This elite African American woman of the 1920s represented a class of wealthy urban African American women who were trying desperately to distance themselves from things African.

▲ Zora Neale Hurston

"The old sub-conscious 'white is best' runs through her mind. Years of study under white teachers, a lifetime of white books, pictures, and papers, and white manners, morals, and Puritan standards made her dislike the spirituals. And now she turns up her nose at jazz and all its manisfestations—likewise almost everything else distinctively racial. She does not want a true picture of herself from anybody."

Hughes's insights into the problems that African Americans would have to overcome in order to express and promote their culture were remarkable for a young man of his age.

HARLEM GREATS

▲ James Weldon Johnson

The Harlem Renaissance revived, defined, and uplifted the best of African American traditions. The works of these cultural giants are forever recorded in history. James Weldon Johnson, the author of "Lift Every Voice and Sing," was well-known for his writings and his civil rights activism. This song, called by some the Negro National Anthem, was never called that by Johnson. He wrote it in 1915 to honor the 50th anniversary of the death of Abraham Lincoln. Johnson was not alone in his recognition of whites who had worked

▲ Duke Ellington

for national unity and human rights. Both Zora Neale Hurston and Langston Hughes knew and paid tribute to Carl Van Vechten, a financier and avid supporter of African American literature in the 1930s and 1940s.

Along with the literary giants were the musical geniuses. None stood so tall at the time as Duke Ellington, whose band played to full houses in the Harlem nightclubs. Whites came from downtown Manhattan and the outlying communities of New Jersey to hear the dynamic jazz of Ellington's band. Among his famous tunes were "Mood Indigo" and "Take the A Train." It is believed that Ellington wrote more than 1,000 musical compositions—more than any other American composer.

▲ Dancers perform "Take Me to the Water" from Alvin Ailey's masterwork *Revelations*.

Like the musicians, the choreographers and dancers led the way to the renaissance. Pearl Primus, who migrated from Barbados to New York, became one of the pioneers in interpreting traditional African dance for the U.S. audience. Her rendering of *Funga*, a traditional West African welcome dance, has become the most popular traditional African dance in modern times. When Primus died in 1994, she had become one of the most celebrated dancer-choreographer-teachers in U. S. history. Katherine Dunham, another choreographer and dancer, was inspired by Haitian and Jamaican dances, and brought them to the U. S. stage.

Other professional dance companies would be started by choreographers who were influenced by the work of Primus and Dunham. In fact, the great Alvin Ailey would create a truly African American dance company, the Alvin Ailey American Dance Theatre, dedicated to many of the cultural motifs that appeared in the works of Dunham and Primus. Arthur Mitchell, on the other hand, influenced certainly by the role that dance played in the African American community and by the earlier giants in the field, found inspiration in European ballet as well. He created the Dance Theatre of Harlem.

There was an outpouring of polyrhthms on the dance stage that had never been seen before. The development of serious African American and African dance companies would mean that dance

Dance greats, choreographer Alvin Ailey *(left)*, founder of the Alvin Ailey Dance Theater, stands with American Ballet Theater's dancer Cynthia Gregory and dancer/choregrapher Arthur Mitchell of the Harlem Dance Theater. ▶

▲ James Baldwin

▲ Gwendolyn Brooks

▲ Alain Locke

would not be simply European ballet. The presence of companies, from Senegal, Zaire, and Nigeria helped to invigorate the artistic world of dance. Local communities in San Francisco, Los Angeles, Minneapolis, Buffalo, Cincinnati, Chicago, and Milwaukee developed African American dance companies and Joan Myers Brown of Philadelphia created the successful Philadanco to ensure that the African presence in dance in the United States would be felt.

This was an age of change and transformation as new ground was broken by writers such as James Baldwin, whose *The Fire Next Time* has been called one of the greatest examples of the essay in U.S. history, and Gwendolyn Brooks, poet laureate of Illinois and Pulitzer Prize winner.

ALAIN LOCKE: FATHER OF THE HARLEM RENAISSANCE

In 1925, Alain Locke, a philosopher, writer, professor at Howard University and the first African American Rhodes scholar, created the term *New Negro* to describe the renewed confidence and pride many African Americans had in themselves. There was a renewed sense of self-determination and respect for African traditions in the air, and Locke sought to document it with the book *The New Negro*. He not only championed the intellectual but also the artistic achievements of the African race during the 1920s and, according to some scholars, this made him the official father of the Harlem Renaissance. Locke became the symbol of the transformation going on in the African American community. He was well educated, self-confident, and proud of his cultural heritage. Locke interpreted the advances in art and culture as reflecting the movement from the farming lifestyle of the rural South to the more complex life of the urban North. He believed that with greater numbers of African Americans living in the North, East, and Midwest there would be more opportunity for personal growth. He believed that the liberal policies of the North would allow African Americans to develop their true potential and break away from the Southern stereotype that some whites refused to let die. This prompted Locke to write that for generations "in the mind of America, the Negro has been a formula rather than a human being—a something to be argued about, condemned or defended, to be 'kept down,' or 'in his place,' or 'helped up,' to be worried with or worried over, harassed or patronized, a social bogey or a social burden."

But in the 1920s, this view of African Americans was rapidly being replaced by a new sense of self-respect, dignity, and confidence. African Americans were demanding integrity and equal treatment. In Alain Locke's words, the New Negro was coming of age.

◆ CENTER YOUR THINKING

1. Why was Harlem called *the capital of the African American world?*
2. What was the Harlem Renaissance? Name and describe three of its most important contributors.
3. Who were the so-called *New Negroes*?
4. How did the Harlem Renaissance challenge negative stereotypes of African Americans?
5. HOLISTIC ACTIVITY Students as Rap Artists
   In small groups, create a rap about the Harlem Renaissance personalities and the energy of the era. Describe the energy and electricity of the time.

CHAPTER

46

ASANTE

THE GREAT DEPRESSION

CENTER YOUR VOCABULARY

- ▲ optimism
- ▲ stock market
- ▲ Nation of Islam
- ▲ militancy

AS YOU READ

As you read about the Great Depression, think about your own personal definition of freedom. What conditions are needed for a person to be free?

African American businesses experienced an all-time high in 1929 right before the American economy crashed. Banks closed down and thousands of people were unable to get their money out of the banks. Those who had money in the banks were now as poor as those who did not. Many people suffered from hunger. Times were hard and misery was everywhere. This was the Great Depression. Numerous cities, such as Birmingham, Tulsa, Atlanta, and Memphis, which had booming African American businesses, were hit hard by the Depression.

The Great Depression became a part of American consciousness at the same time that Louis Armstrong, Duke Ellington, Paul Robeson, Bill "Bojangles" Robinson, and other African American entertainers were becoming household names. Martin Luther King, Jr., was born on January 15, 1929, marking the year with a small bit of the optimism that was, of course, unknown at the time. By October 29, 1929, the bubble had burst. That date will live in economic history as the most damaging economic crisis the United States has ever faced. Prices on the stock market, where goods are bought and sold, frequently plumeted to zero. Rich people committed suicide. Financiers had heart attacks. The times were terrible.

▲ Paul Robeson

African American businesses were hit the hardest. African Americans in the cities suffered more than those who lived in the rural areas. Grown people stood on street corners and cried because they had no money, no job, and no way to support their families. The Great Depression lasted about 12 years, but its effect on the African American community was longlasting. By 1940, almost 30 percent of African American men and 33 percent of African American women were officially still unemployed. In some cities, the effect of the depression was devastating. In Atlanta, Georgia, 65 percent of the people on welfare were African Americans. In Norfolk, Virginia, 81 percent of African Americans were forced to take public assistance. When jobs did become available, white businesspeople gave the jobs to whites first. Africans were the last to be hired and, if someone had to be fired, were often the first to be fired. With limited capital and few opportunities to receive large loans from banks, the African American community was also limited in its ability to create jobs for its own community.

▲ Bill "Bojangles" Robinson on stage in *The Hot Mikado*

Some African American communities had never recovered from the devastation of the white riots that occurred after the First Major European War. Little Africa, a small African American community in Tulsa, Oklahoma, was among those hardest hit. On May 30, 1921, a white girl, Sarah Page, alleged that Dick Rowland, a 19-year-old African American, had attempted to assault her in an elevator in the Drexel Building in downtown Tulsa. The stories that came out about this incident were contradictory and confusing. In one account, Rowland took her by the arm as they entered the elevator. In another account, he accidentally stepped on her foot. At any rate, Sarah Page refused to press charges against Rowland. Nevertheless, on Tuesday, May 31, at 9 p.m., a crowd of 400 to 500 whites gathered outside the jail where Rowland was being held. By 10:30 p.m. more than 2,000 whites had gathered.

The aim of the mob was to seize Rowland and lynch him, but the intervention of the African American community prevented that from happening. When word of the white crowd reached Little Africa, as

Long lines of jobless men wait to get a free dinner at New York's Municipal Lodging. ▶

the African American community was called, 75 African American men went down to the jail with their guns to ensure the safety of the prisoner. The police pleaded with the armed men to return home, assuring them that the prisoner would be safe. But as the African American men were leaving, a white man rushed up to one of the armed men and attempted to disarm him. Shots rang out, and when the smoke had cleared and the din was silent, two African Americans and ten whites were dead.

The following morning, 10,000 whites, representing every class of the Tulsa community, descended upon Little Africa with weapons, machine guns, and airplanes. Numerous homes were burned, the entire business section of the community, one of the most thriving African American business districts in the United States, was destroyed. One writer said that in terms of destruction and ratio of casualties to population, the Tulsa riot was unequaled in U.S. history. An estimated 200 African Americans and 50 whites were killed on that fateful day June 1, 1921. Yet it had also been shown that the small African American population of Tulsa would come to the aid of a defenseless African American—a simple shoeshine boy without any great social or economic standing, except the greatest of all: he was a human being.

Ten years later, in the middle of the Depression, Tulsa's once-thriving African American community had not bounced back to its pre-riot prominence. The conditions in Tulsa and other cities, like East St. Louis and Atlanta, were overwhelmingly miserable.

The defeat of President Herbert Hoover and the rise to power of Democratic president Franklin Delano Roosevelt in 1932 rekindled the hopes of African Americans. His promise to bring the United States out of the Great Depression was called the New Deal. The African American community turned to the Democratic Party. Sharp tensions between the haves and the have-nots created a nation torn between assisting rich corporations and helping the masses of poor people.

Prior to Hoover, the African American community had believed the old saying about the Republican Party being the "deck and all else the sea." They had voted Republican because it was the party of Abraham Lincoln. However, President Roosevelt distinguished himself as the first Democratic president to reach out to African Americans and attempt to moderate some of the suffering. His actions restored faith in the possibility for true equality and freedom. He instilled hope in the economic recovery of the nation with his New Deal program.

Roosevelt's New Deal impacted the African American community in symbolic as well as real ways. Roosevelt made some highly publicized appointments of African Americans to the federal government. But it was in the economic area where Roosevelt's policies were actually felt by the people. For example, he created the relief and public works programs to ease the burdens of unemployment. Although more whites than African Americans received jobs through these agencies, African Americans benefited from the unemployment aid programs because a higher proportion of the African American population was unemployed. Roosevelt was the first U.S. president of the 20th century to inspire the confidence

▲ Jesse Owens captured in flight during a broad jump in 1936 at the Berlin Olympics. Owens won four medals, but Adolph Hitler refused to present him with the medals he had won.

of African American people. By 1936, the African American vote changed dramatically from Republican to Democrat. To many African Americans, Roosevelt was bringing the country back to life, and the time for optimism was here again.

BREAKING NEW GROUND

In sports, great things were happening on the world stage. In 1936, Jesse Owens astonished the Germans and many white Americans with his impressive Olympic wins in Berlin. One year later, on June 22, 1937, Joe Louis defeated James J. Braddock for the world heavyweight championship in one of the classic battles of the sport. Owens and Louis broke the barriers of what the world believed was possible for African Americans. The rise of African American athletes was predicted by these early victories of contestants now free to compete on the world stage.

In 1946, Jackie Robinson was chosen by the Brooklyn Dodgers to play baseball for their team. Like his heroes Owens and Lewis, Robinson had the mark of excellence. After several months in the

Joe Louis raises his hand in victory as the new heavyweight champion of the world. ▶

▲ Jackie Robinson and a friend pose for fans before a game.

Negro National League, he was chosen by the Dodgers to become the first African American to play in the richer, more expansive major league, which was dominated by white players.

Robinson carried himself well and handled both the sport and the spectators with grace and courage. He was an excellent player in all areas of the game. Following Robinson into the majors were the likes of Larry Doby, Roy Campanella, Willie Mays, and the great Hank Aaron. These were the pioneers and they were no less important than the giants of the international arts stage such as Marian Anderson, or diplomats such as Ralph Bunche who negotiated the first Arab-Israeli agreement after the creation of Israel in 1948. Anderson rose up from racial discrimination by the Daughters of the American Revolution, who did not want her to sing at the Constitutional Hall, and was allowed to sing at the Lincoln Memorial because of the intervention of Eleanor Roosevelt, President Franklin Delano Roosevelt's wife. Bunche was the first African American to receive the Nobel Prize for Peace.

▼ Ralph Bunche and Marion Anderson

African Americans came to the challenges of racism and discrimination with a new-found belief in their own capacity for victory over segregation and bias. This optimism found an African American population ready for anything. A cadre of leaders, both men and women, had come through the fire of the Great Depression and the war against racism and was now prepared for leadership. A. Philip Randolph, head of the Brotherhood of Sleeping Car Porters; Charles Hamilton Houston, legal counsel for the NAACP; Thurgood Marshall, Houston's protegee and colleague; and Mary McLeod Bethune mapped new strategies for securing African American rights. But they were primarily concerned with legal rights. They did not concentrate on correcting the psychological damage that had been done to African Americans by the institutions of enslavement and segregation. These were lawyers and educators, skilled in the practical politics of power, the idea of elections, and the concept of group rights based on the fact that African Americans had been enslaved and persecuted as a group. Others would come forth to try and heal the soul, the spirit, the psyches of African Americans. They would be teachers and preachers, cult leaders and psychologists, historians and sociologists.

The founding of the Nation of Islam by W.D. Fard and Elijah Poole was in keeping with the idea that African Americans should seek their own methods of liberation. One of the areas needing liberation was religion; the other was economic self-determination. Poole, the son of a Georgia preacher, became Elijah Mohammed, the spirtual leader of the Nation of Islam (NOI). He established chapters of his organization in every major city in the North. The first chapter was founded in Detroit in 1930.

Declaring themselves Muslims, members of the NOI called for a total separation of African Americans and whites. Many gave up their "slave" names and adopted the unknown *X* as a surname. The *X* symbolized their African names that were lost in the *mfecane*. This was directly related to the Nation of Islam's belief that African Americans were lost in terms of culture, religion and economics. How can you be free if you do not control your own name? How can you be free if you do not control your own image of God? How can you be free if you do not control your own economics? These were the questions Elijah Mohammed, the powerful leader of the Nation of Islam, asked his audiences. Many people responded to him because they could not deny the truth of his statement. "You are not a Negro, you're a so-called Negro. You don't know your name because you were given the name of your enemy."

There was a militancy in the air that caused African Americans to defend themselves against all attacks. Some cases, particularly those in the South with charges of rape, were bitter because they involved all of the prejudices and stereotypes that whites had build up about African American men. Perhaps the most celebrated case of the 1930s, however, was the case of the nine African American youths who were convicted, on questionable testimony, of raping two white women in Scottsboro, Alabama. The alleged rape of the two women and the arrest of the boys prompted demonstrations and protests throughout the country.

The new spirit of justice prevailed in the case of the Scottsboro boys, as they were called, and there were more situations suggesting progress. Mary McLeod Bethune, William H. Hastie, Robert C. Weaver, and Ralph Bunche established reputations as solid political analysts and strategists, and they served the Roosevelt Administration well.

◆ CENTER YOUR THINKING

1. What was the Great Depression?
2. What were some of the long-term effects of the Great Depression on the African American community?
3. Why did the election of President Franklin Delano Roosevelt rekindle the hopes of African Americans?
4. Explain the definition of *freedom* expressed by the Nation of Islam. In your opinion, is this definition relevant today? Explain.
5. HOLISTIC ACTIVITY Students as Newscasters
   You are a group of radio newscasters reporting live on the 1921 Tulsa riot. Write a script, and include a commentary on your opinions. End your broadcast with advice on how to avoid such violence in future years. Perform your broadcast.

SUGGESTED READINGS

Aptheker, Herbert, ed. *A Documentry History of the Negro People in the United States*. New York: Citadel Press, 1969

Bernard, Jacqueline. *Journey Toward Freedom*. New York: W. W. Norton, 1967.

Chace, M., William and Peter Collier. *Justice Denied: The Black Man in White America*. New York: Harcourt, Brace and World, 1970.

Curtis, James C. and Lewis Gould. *The Black Experience in America: Selected Essays*. Austin: University of Texas Press, 1970.

Franklin, John Hope, and Isidore Starr. *The Negro in 20th Century America*. New York: Vintage Press, 1967.

Pease, Jane H., and Willia Pease. *Bound with Them in Chains*. Westport, Connecticut: Greenwood Press, 1972.

Pinkney, Alphonso. *Red Black, and Green: Black Nationalism in the United States.* Cambridge: Cambridge University Press, 1978.

SUMMARY

African American activists, scholars, and scientists countered racial injustices by making valuable contributions in many areas of American life. They created organizations to build self-reliance and to preserve the culture and contributions of African Americans. *(Chapter 43)*

During the First Major European War, large numbers of African Americans migrated to the North where they played a major role in meeting the needs of the wartime economy. African Americans also supported the war effort by fighting on the battlefield. However, once again, their contributions did not result in improvement in the way they were treated by whites. *(Chapter 43)*

Marcus Garvey's ideas inspired millions of people of African descent. He focused on the need for pride in one's own heritage and on self-determination and collective economics. *(Chapter 44)*

Harlem in the early 1920s was a magnet that drew people of African descent. Some of the most creative and talented artists, writers, intellectuals, and musicians came to Harlem and created what came to be known as the Harlem Renaissance. *(Chapter 45)*

The collapse of the American economy disproportionately affected African Americans. In the period leading up to the Great Depression, many African American communities had been able to achieve a large measure of economic success. Despite the Great Depression, many African Americans developed a new sense of confidence, optimism, and a militant determination to change their status. *(Chapter 46)*

PERSONAL WITNESSING

REFLECTION

Reflect on Carter G. Woodson's belief that the schools in the U.S. in the early 1900s were guilty of psychological enslavement because of their ideas of European cultural superiority and their denial of African culture. How do you feel about Woodson's ideas? What are your thoughts about education then? about education today?

TESTIMONY

A famous Marcus Garvey quote is, "Up you mighty race. You can accomplish what you will!" As a group, write some other statements that Garvey could have made had your group just gone to hear him speak. Create a poster or other presentation of Garvey-style sayings that your group has written.

UNIT 13 RITE OF PASSAGE

Analyze the areas of creative work that you do and select one to focus on for excellence. Your area could be any expression of creativity, including the arts, writing, painting, designing games, and designing clothing. Decide on an activity that you personally will create and include in your Portfolio to show your creative energies at work.

UNIT 14

WE WILL NEVER TURN BACK

1925
A. Phillip Randolph organizes the Brotherhood of Sleeping Car Porters (BSCP)

1935
BSCP joins the American Federation of Labor (AFL)

1939-1945
Second Major European War

With all their gains, each generation of African Americans became more determined to continue progressing and fighting than ever before. Activism was now a part of the African American character. Is activism important to you? Do you consider yourself to be an activist? In small groups, make a list of people you have learned about in this book whom you consider to be positive role models of activism. Design a group tribute to the people you admire.

In this unit, you will learn about the determination of African Americans to continue their demand for equality and fair treatment in the face of constant racism and discrimination by white Americans. Their activism never wavered. Has this struggle ended? As you read, make notes of the lessons from this unit that you would like to remember to apply to your own life.

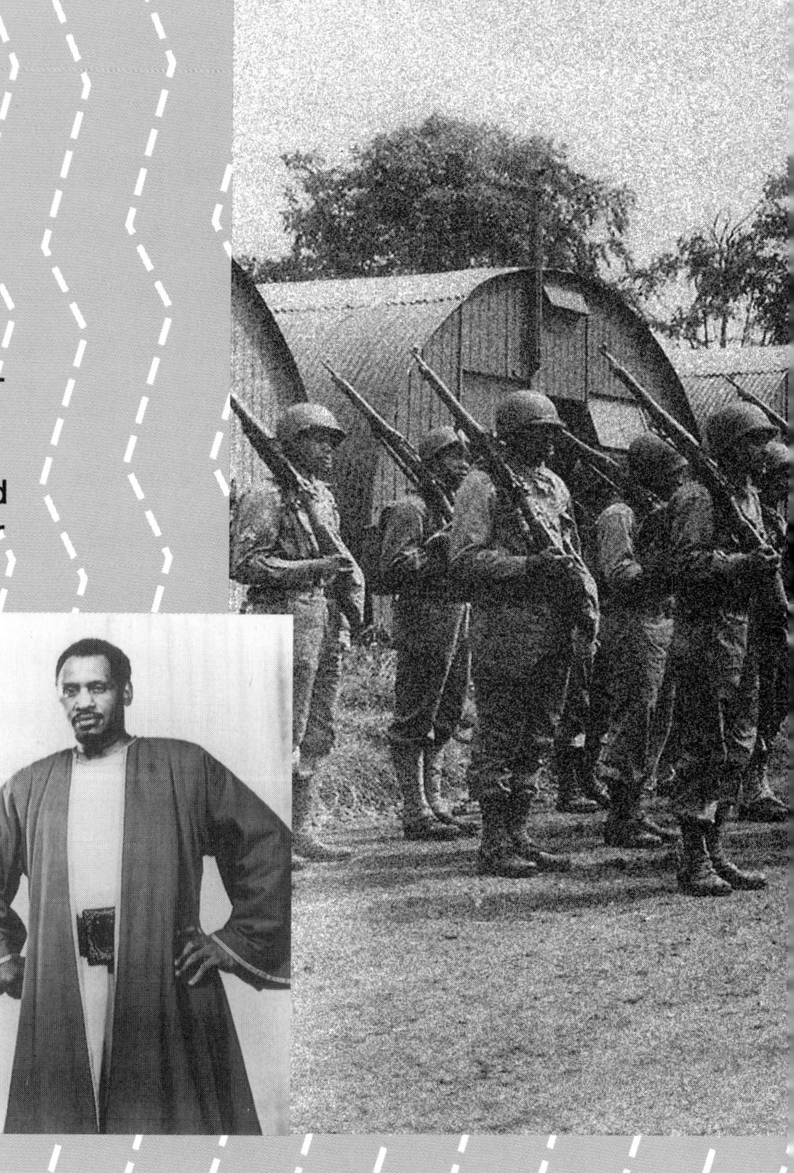

1941
A. Phillip Randolph threatens March on Washington

President Roosevelt issues an executive order prohibiting employers from discriminating against African Americans in the war industries

Dorie Miller downs four Japanese planes

Segregated air field opens at Tuskegee, Alabama

1958
Robeson's passport is returned

1946
Four African Americans lynched in Walton County, Georgia

1950
Paul Robeson's passport is seized for "un-American activities"

> *"Done made my vow to the lord*
> *And I never will turn back*
> *I will go, I shall go*
> *To see what the end shall be."*
>
> AFRICAN AMERICAN SPIRITUAL

CHAPTER

47

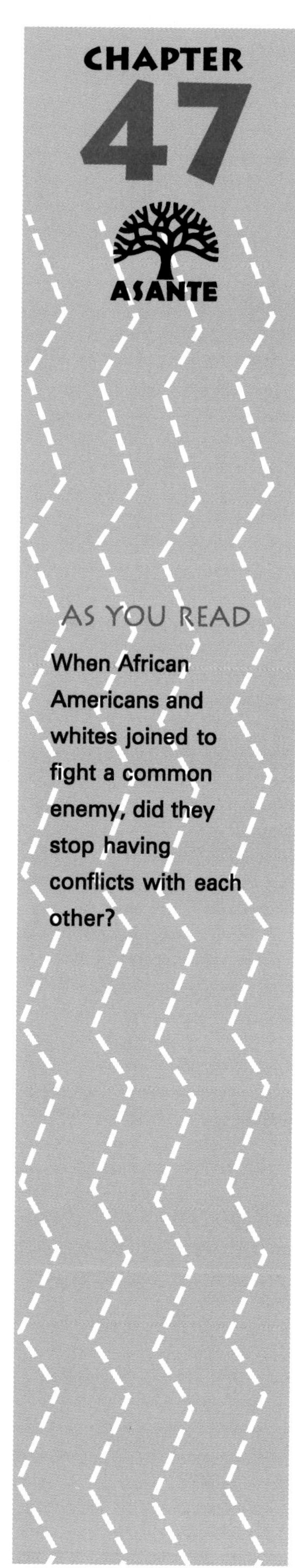

AS YOU READ

When African Americans and whites joined to fight a common enemy, did they stop having conflicts with each other?

THROUGH THE STORM

CENTER YOUR VOCABULARY

- ▲ treason
- ▲ acquitted
- ▲ imperialism
- ▲ passes

Franklin Delano Roosevelt performed admirably as president given the fact that he had inherited a nation that was nearly bankrupt. Yet, the persistent problem of discrimination would not go away. When the war in Europe began in 1939, the United States still had no more than 150 African Americans working in its defense industry. There were more than 150,000 whites, more than 1,000 times the number of African Americans who were employed in the defense industry. Of course, thousands more workers would be required when America entered the Second Major European War, which was also known as World War II. But discrimination against African American workers in favor of white workers would continue throughout the war.

The military, which geared up to join the allied effort in the Second Major European War, was still segregated. Many outbreaks of violence and discrimination were committed against African Americans in military service. The *Baltimore Afro-American* newspaper urged African Americans to leave the military rather than serve in segregated camps in the South. The government threatened the newspaper's owners with charges of treason. Treason, the betrayal of one's country, is a crime punishable by death.

In 1941, African American labor leader A. Philip Randolph organized a march of 100,000 people on Washington, D.C., to protest

▲ A. Phillip Randolph

the exclusion of African Americans from the defense industry. Walter White, the NAACP executive secretary, and Adam Clayton Powell, Jr., a New York City representative to the U.S. Congress, were among those who joined Randolph's effort. The threat of a protest march of this size was enough to move President Franklin Roosevelt to issue Executive Order 8802 prohibiting employers from discriminating against African Americans in the war industries. But the order did not address hiring practices, so it had no effect on employers who hired only whites as long as they could get away with it.

RACISM AND THE SECOND MAJOR EUROPEAN WAR, 1939 - 1945

Once again in Europe the rise of the doctrines of imperialism, the practice of trying to control the wealth of other nations, and racial supremacy in Germany would move African Americans to respond to the call-to-arms of their nation. One million African Americans served in the Second Major European War. It was commonly referred to as World War II because it eventually included Asia with the entry of Japan in the war among the Europeans. Japan attacked the United States forces at Pearl Harbor, Hawaii, and later occupied China, the Philipines, and Guam. African Americans went to war once again against segregation and discrimination in the United States armed forces and against the Germans and Japanese on the battlefields.

Pearl Harbor, a U.S. territory, was attacked on December 7, 1941, by the Japanese. Dorie Miller, an African American cook on board the ship, *USS Arizona,* shot down four Japanese planes although he had not been trained to use the guns due to discrimination. He received a medal for his action. By 1943, he was missing in action and presumed dead. A grateful African American community named many sons after Dorie Miller, and he became their leading folk hero of the war.

▲ Dorie Miller

Neither military heroics nor medals changed the conditions of discrimination in the American armed forces. Whites retained a false attitude of superiority toward African Americans in the service. Even though African Americans were eventually trained, the commanding

▲ African American troops stationed in Northern Ireland during the Second Major European War line up in front of their barracks.

officers were still white. After a lawsuit was threatened, the Air Force finally opened a segregated training facility at Tuskegee, Alabama, in 1940 to train African American pilots to fight in the war. By the end of the war in 1945, there were nearly 600 African American pilots, and the famous Tuskegee Flyers, as they were called, became legendary for their courage and skill in the air.

On the ground, several fighting units distinguished themselves. Some of the most heroic were the 761st Tank Battalion, known as the Black Panthers, the 24th Infantry, and the 92nd Division of the 183rd Combat Engineers. The 761st and the l83rd Combat Engineers were units made up entirely of Africans Americans who participated in the liberation of prisoners from the Nazi concentration camps of Dachau and Buchenwald in Germany. The 761st Tank Battalion won 391 awards for l83 days of combat, the longest period any unit ever served under constant enemy fire without relief. The 76lst knocked out 331 German machine-gun nests occupied by German soldiers and captured a German radio station. The 24th Infantry routed the

▲ An African American pilot completes his training. This African American pilot and others like him are the beneficiaries of a long struggle to end discrimination in the armed forces.

Japanese in the Pacific islands of New Georgia; the 92nd, as part of the Fifth Army, pushed into Italy from the South. The 94th Infantry lost more than 3,000 men. They won 65 Silver Stars, 65 Bronze Medals, and more than 1,200 Purple Hearts. Not even this display of heroism would save the African American soldiers from the cruelty of white American soldiers. Nevertheless, African American soldiers continued to exemplify loyalty and patriotism to their country.

TENSIONS ABROAD

In Asia, the situation was similar to that in Europe. When they were not fighting the Japanese, African Americans and white Americans were often busy fighting each other. On Christmas Eve 1944, a serious riot occurred on the island of Guam in the capital city of Agana. The island had been taken from the Japanese by African American and white units. Though these units were segregated, they often came into contact with each other in the capital city of Agana.

Christmas Eve on the African American base began on a peaceful note. A group of nine African American soldiers had received passes (special permission) to go into Agana. The soldiers left the base excited at the prospect of a fun-filled leave from their army duties. When they arrived in the city, the African Americans soldiers began talking to the Asian women there. Some of the white soldiers grew resentful and opened fire on the African American soldiers, driving them out of the town. Eight of the soldiers arrived back at the camp safely; the ninth was feared wounded or killed. Some 40 African Americans then loaded two trucks and drove into the town looking for the missing soldier. An African American soldier who had been left behind on the base telephoned the military police in Agana and warned them that the 40 soldiers were headed toward the city. The all-white U.S. military police blockaded all the roads leading to the city. When they spotted the African American soldiers, they told them that the missing soldier had not been killed or wounded, but had

▲ Members of the 93rd Division, the first African American ground troops to be used in combat in the South Pacific, struggle up a hill with an injured soldier.

hidden in a ditch until nightfall and had returned to the camp. The African Americans turned their trucks around and headed back to their camp.

Shortly after midnight on Christmas morning, a truck filled with white marines entered the segregated African American camp. The whites claimed that one of their soldiers had been hit with a piece of coral thrown by one of the African Americans. Instead of arresting the men who were shouting threats at the soldiers from the truck, the white commanding officer of the African American company pleaded with the whites to leave. They finally left.

Tensions remained high all during Christmas Day. Two drunken white marines shot and killed an African American soldier who was walking from the town of Agana back to his camp. Within hours, another African American soldier was shot by another drunken white soldier in Agana. Word about the killings reached all quarters of the four African American units at the camp. Anger boiled over on both sides. Around midnight, a jeep filled with whites fired on the African American camp. Guards in the camp returned the fire, injuring a white military-police officer. The whites in the jeep took cover and fled toward Agana. The African Americans followed in quick pursuit. They were stopped at a roadblock, arrested, and charged with unlawful assembly, rioting, theft of government property, and attempted murder.

In a quickly arranged trial, the men were brought before a military court. Fortunately, NAACP Executive Secretary Walter White was traveling in the area. Hearing of this injustice, White felt compelled to defend the African Americans soldiers, even though he was not a lawyer. The African American soldiers were convicted and sentenced to serve several years in prison, but their sentence was overturned when Walter White and the NAACP appealed to the secretary of the Navy.

ON THE HOME FRONT

Back on the home front, the war created more industrial jobs in the North and attracted a growing population of African Americans from the South. Nearly 2 million more African Americans went North to find work in the defense industries. The presence of so many African Americans in Northern cities created fear and apprehension among whites. Riots against African Americans broke out in many cities and at many plants and mills. The North was not so different from the South in some respects. In each region of the nation, the mere presence of African American soldiers and African American workers was uncomfortable for many whites. Arriving home from the battlefront, African Americans were often in more danger in their own country than they had been in Europe or Asia. On July 25, 1946, four African Americans—two soldiers who were only recently honorably discharged from the United States Army and their wives—were lynched in Walton County, Georgia. Two weeks later, another brutal lynching of an honorably discharged African American soldier occurred in Minden, Louisiana. It was revealed later that the former soldier had refused to give a white man a war souvenir that he had brought back from overseas. For this refusal, he lost his life to a mob of whites.

When the war was over, African Americans demanded better treatment and a more just society. This was particularly true in the case of education. Segregated schools had been established all across the country. African American students had inferior educational materials, inferior buildings, and less money than students at all-white schools. The time had come for the United States to make reality measure up to the country's ideals of justice and fair play.

The African American soldiers returning home from war sparked a social revolution. So explosive and contagious was the hunger for equality in the 1950s that it seemed at one time, there were as many movements for freedom as there were preachers and activists in the African American community. There had been many moral victories won by 1954, the date of the beginning of the modern Civil Rights Movement. There would be no going back. The Civil Rights Movement had begun.

◆ CENTER YOUR THINKING

1. Why were the owners of the *Baltimore Afro-American* threatened with charges of treason?
2. Name two African American fighting units that distinguished themselves during the Second Major European War.
3. Contrast African American participation in the Second Major European War with previous wars.
4. Describe your views on whether or not African Americans should have participated in the Second Major European War.
5. HOLISTIC ACTIVITY Students as Writers
   Arriving home from the battlefield, African American soldiers were often in more danger in their own country than they had been in Europe or Asia. Think of a wounded, decorated member of the 94th Infantry, for example, going home to Southern segregation and discrimination. Write a chapter in the memoirs of such a person. Use a style that fits the period.

Second Major European War

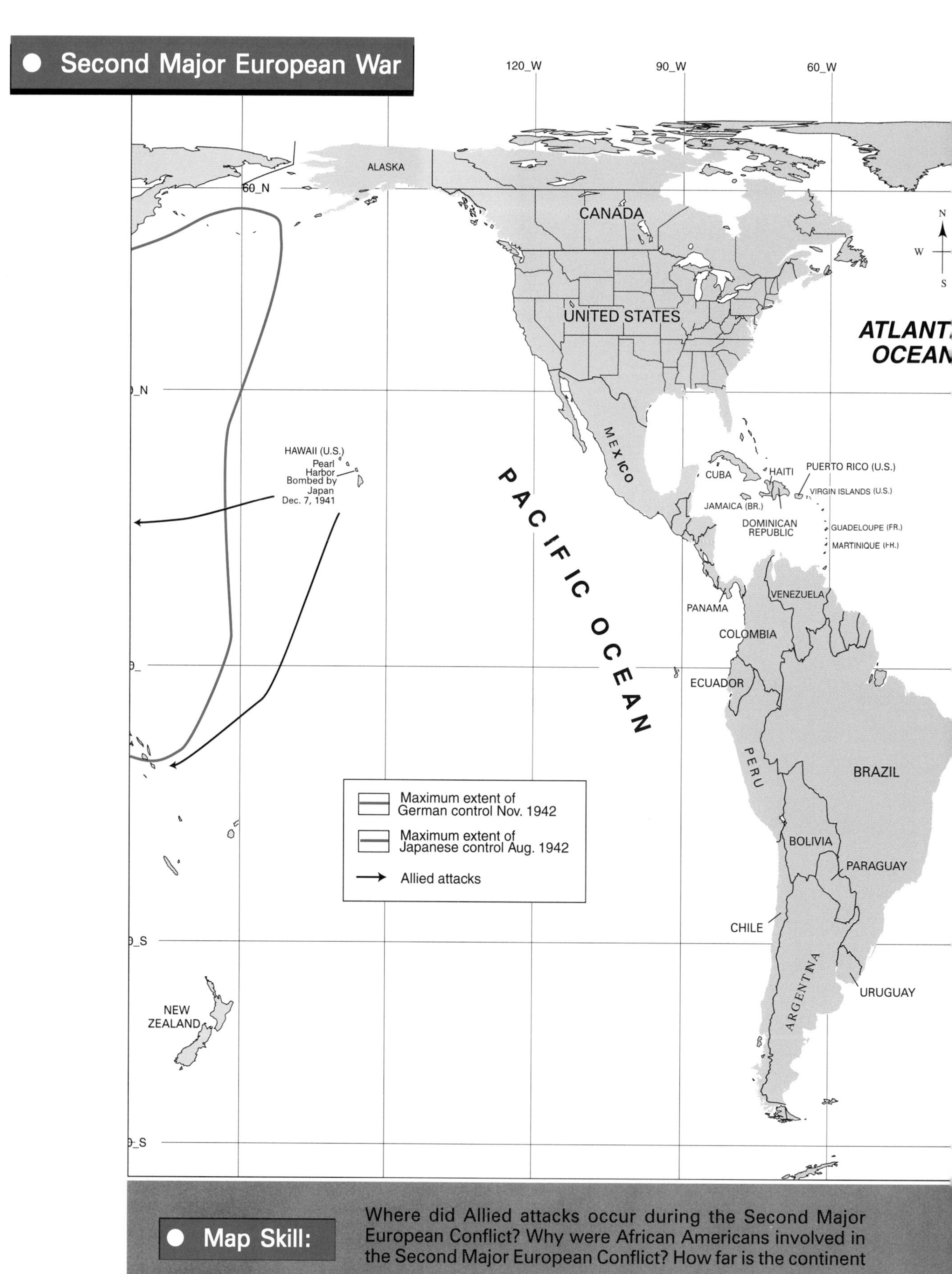

Map Skill: Where did Allied attacks occur during the Second Major European Conflict? Why were African Americans involved in the Second Major European Conflict? How far is the continent

of African from the closest conflict? Did this Conflict end racial discrimination? What results did African Americans feel from the Conflict?

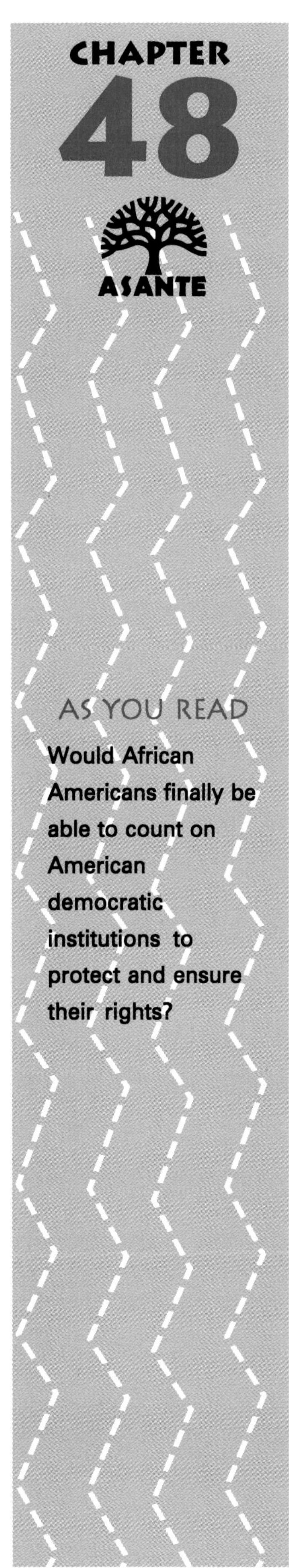

AS YOU READ

Would African Americans finally be able to count on American democratic institutions to protect and ensure their rights?

CONTESTING THE MEANING OF DEMOCRACY

CENTER YOUR VOCABULARY

- ▲ communism
- ▲ stigma
- ▲ rhetoric
- ▲ socialism
- ▲ blacklisted
- ▲ censored

"All my life I'd been sweated and stepped on and Jim Crowed. . . rode behind the 'Colored' signs of streetcars, as though there was something disgusting about me. I heard myself called 'nigger' and 'darky' and I had to say 'Yes, sir' to every white man. . . . I had always detested it, but I had never known that anything could be done about it. And here, all of a sudden, I had found organizations . . . . that weren't scared to come out for equality for the Negro people, and for the rights of workers. . . . the Communist program is the only program that the Southern workers—whites and Negroes both—can possibly accept in the long run. . . ." These words, spoken by Angelo Herndon, explained African American interest in communism and other alternative political movements in the U. S.

Some African Americans in the middle of the 20th century had tired of the rhetoric, what they saw as meaningless words about democracy and equality in the United States. Discrimination, prejudice, and brutality were so commonly expressed against African Americans that observers and students of political history as well as the common people joined with others to call for a new approach to justice. This call was answered by many different philosophies, including communism.

Communism embraced the theory that all means of producing wealth should be owned by the government. It put forward the idea that class position, or your social and economic place in society, is more important than race or the struggle for justice. This concept appealed to many African Americans who were held to the lowest social levels because of their race. African Americans and whites worked equally, side by side, in communist organizations. This was indeed a rare sight in the 20th-century U.S., and it drew several outstanding members of the African American community to communism.

W.E.B. Du Bois and Paul Robeson, political activists and civil rights campaigners, were among the most prominent African American supporters of the Communist Party. Although Du Bois became a member late in his life, he was a long-time interpreter of communist causes. He believed that the philosophy of communism condemned racism in a way that was unknown in the American democratic tradition.

▲ Singer, actor, Paul Robeson's political affiliations at times attracted more publicity than his performances.

Paul Robeson was an outstanding intellectual, actor, artist, and promoter of civil rights. During the 1930s, Robeson visited the Soviet Union several times, spoke out against the Nazis, supported aid to China, and became the chairman of the Council of Africa in the early 1950s. At the height of the Cold War in 1950, when anti–Soviet and anti communist feelings were at their highest levels in the United States, Robeson's passport was seized for supposedly un–American activities. He found it difficult to support himself in his career as a singer and actor because concert halls in the United States were afraid of government harassment if they booked him for performances. Without a U.S. passport, Robeson could not work outside the United States.

His passport was not returned to him until eight years later, in 1958. Almost as soon as he received his passport, he made preparations for a trip to the Soviet Union along with W.E.B. Du Bois. In his autobiography, he said of his persecution, "Here I stand . . . I speak as an American Negro whose life is dedicated, first and foremost, to winning full freedom for my people in America."

The majority of African Americans, however, did not see the Communist Party as a solution for ending racism and discrimination. A small number became interested in socialism, a theory that the means of producing wealth should be owned by the community as a group. Capitalism, on the other hand, allowed individuals to own the means of producing wealth. African Americans believed that socialism would allow them to participate in the wealth of the society on an equal basis and put an end to racial strife. African Americans did not trust local governments, especially in the South, to implement social reforms on their own accord. They believed that under socialism, equal participation by the entire community would wipe out many of the social injustices against African Americans.

Like communism, socialism had its flaws. In 1920, the Socialist Party issued a demand that the 13th, 14th, and 15th Amendments outlawing enslavement, guaranteeing equal protection under the law, and giving African Americans the right to vote be fully enforced. But as late as 1932, the party was refusing to endorse demands for social equality for African Americans. Underlying socialism and communism was the belief that class, not race, was the major factor in the oppression of African Americans. The African American community knew that in the United States, race still held sway, and it rarely mattered that an African American had money or class if whites sought to discriminate or persecute.

Some African American leaders believed that working-class whites would support African American freedom. One of the most famous socialists who acted on this belief was A. Philip Randolph, the eminent father of African American unionism.

A. PHILIP RANDOLPH

A. Philip Randolph was a trade union leader who organized the Brotherhood of Sleeping Car Porters (BSCP) in 1925. BSCP was an African American trade union of African American railroad porters. After a long, bitter struggle, BSCP negotiated better working conditions for African Americans employed by the Pullman company.

▲ An older A. Philip Randolph remained an activist until his death in 1979, organizing the Negro American Council in 1960 and founding the A. Randolph Institute in New York City in 1964.

BSCP joined the American Federation of Labor (AFL), the largest all–white labor union in the country, in 1935. Randolph served as a member of New York City's Commission on Race and as president of the National Negro Congress. In 1942, he was appointed to the New York Housing Authority and in 1955 he was appointed to the AFL-CIO executive council.

Like Randolph, many African American activists, intellectuals and artists found some aspects of socialism and communism attractive, but some of them were afraid to acknowledge support publicly for these views because of the fear of retaliation from anticommunist authorities. African Americans, already victims of racism and oppression, were persecuted during the McCarthy or Red Scare era for their socialist beliefs.

McCarthyism

The Red Scare or McCarthy era occurred in the early 1950s during the presidencies of Harry Truman and Dwight Eisenhower. During this time, Congress conducted investigations about suspected communist activity in the United States. Wisconsin Senator Joseph McCarthy rose to prominence as the leading anticommunist agitator. He accused hundreds of decent people of being traitors to their country. He conducted hearings and called people to Congress on the slightest accusation or suspicion. The hearings were televised, which assured that the stigma, or mark, of being accused would last. Many prominent African Americans were stigmatized by Joseph McCarthy as communists or communist sympathizers. Those who were not lived in fear of being falsely accused.

▲ Poet, novelist, and playwright Langston Hughes had to defend himself against charges of being a communist.

Actress Lena Horne was censored and placed on a list of artists who were considered anti-American because she was suspected of being a communist. People who were placed on such a blacklist could not get jobs because no one would hire them. Writer Langston Hughes had to appear before Congress's House Un-American Activities Committee to defend himself against charges that he was a communist. Actors Canada Lee and William Marshall watched their careers wither because they could not find acting jobs after being accused of being communist and anti-American. Other prominent African Americans such as Alphaeus Hunton, the secretary of the Council on African Affairs, were jailed for several months. Others were questioned and asked to collaborate with the government in building cases against the African Americans and whites they knew. Even National Executive Secretary of the Civil Rights Congress William Patterson was jailed in 1954 on suspicion of being a communist.

Other well-known African American communists and socialists received even harsher treatment. Claude Lightfoot, a Communist Party leader from Chicago, Illinois, received a five-year jail sentence and a $5,000 fine. Communist organizer Claudia Jones was imprisoned and later deported to England. Communist Henry Winston was sentenced to eight years in prison and subsequently went blind due to improper medical care.

The McCarthy era was a classic example of how fleeting freedom could be. All classes of people were hounded out of jobs and their professions by the McCarthy movement. African Americans were not the only Americans stripped of constitutional rights during this period. However, it was doubly ironic that African Americans were persecuted for having political differences with an American ideal that had rarely supported their rights.

◆ CENTER YOUR THINKING

1. Define *communism.* Define *socialism.*
2. Name three African Americans who were persecuted because of their involvement in the Communist Party.
3. Why were African Americans attracted to communism, socialism, and other alternative political movements?
4. Compare and contrast communism and socialism.
5. HOLISTIC ACTIVITY Students as Political Leaders
   You and your group are African American political leaders during the time of Paul Robeson, W.E.B. Du Bois, and A. Philip Randolph. Your group must write a proposal for an entirely new political party to answer the needs of African American people. Write or prepare an oral presentation of the principles you propose as the foundation for this new party. Describe the types of actions the party will take in its fight for freedom.

SUGGESTED READINGS

Robeson, Paul. *Here I Stand.*

Franklin, V. P. *Black Self Determination.*

White Walte. *A Man Called White*. New York: The Viking Press, 1948.

SUMMARY

Despite their contributions during the Second Major European War, African Americans still faced conditions of discrimination and an attitude of false white superiority. *(Chapter 47)*

African Americans were drawn to communism and other alternative political movements in hopes of enhancing their freedom. Many African American activists were jailed, censored, or lost their jobs as a result of their political activities. *(Chapter 48)*

PERSONAL WITNESSING

REFLECTION

What does it mean to have political systems? In early African countries, did people organize themselves around political structures and issues? Think about all the different types of political and social systems there are in the world. How are they different? What are the good or necessary qualities of an effective system? Write your thoughts in your journal.

TESTIMONY

Write and give your testimony in a speech explaining why a decision to join a political party such as the Communist Party in response to racism and injustice was understandable in this time period.

UNIT 14 RITE OF PASSAGE

Create roleplays to perform for young children to teach them respect and good manners for others and especially for the opposite sex. Show creatively in your roleplay why it is desirable to show respect for and good manners to others. Include a description of your roleplays in your Portfolio.

THE FREEDOM MOVEMENT'S MARCH ON LIBERTY

In your group, brainstorm a list of conditions in the world that you would like to change as political activists. List them. Then discuss and list some tactics that you would use to change them. Are any of your tactics the ones used by African Americans in their fight for rights?

As you read Unit 15, think of leaders whom you respect as people who can get others to move and change. Think abut the energy and spirit of a people excited by the fight for freedom and about passionate leadership and a fierce determination to achieve freedom.

1941
A.Phillip Randolph organized march on Washington

1952
Malcolm Little joins the Nation of Islam. He would become Malcom X

> "...The real revolution
> was taking place on another level.
> It was happening in the minds of Black People
> with little or no education
> and the natural poetry of themselves
> was beautiful to behold."

THE TIMES WAS
THE EARLY SIXTIES

1955
Emmett Till, a 14-year-old boy, is murdered in Mississippi

1964
Martin Luther King receives Nobel Peace Prize
Mississippi Freedom Democratic Party under Fannie Lou Hamer tries to be seated at the National Democratic Convention in Atlantic City

1967
150 race riots occur in the United States

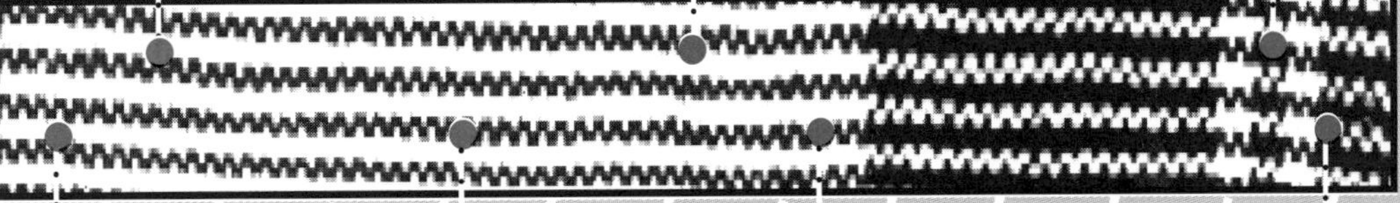

1954
Beginning of modern Civil Rights Movement
Brown vs. the Board of Education of Topeka, Kansas

1963
March on Washington

1965
Malcolm X is assassinated in Harlem

1968
Martin Luther King, Jr., is assassinated in Memphis

CHAPTER 49

ASANTE

THE CIVIL RIGHTS MOVEMENT

CENTER YOUR VOCABULARY

- ▲ boycott
- ▲ civil disobedience
- ▲ scatting
- ▲ Negro spirituals
- ▲ civil rights
- ▲ defect

AS YOU READ

How would you respond if you were forced to give up your seat on a bus because you were an African American?

The 1950s will live in African American history as a time of incredible change. In 1954, a 15-year-old girl was forced off a Montogmery, Alabama bus, handcuffed, and taken to jail simply because she refused to give up her seat to a white man. The African American community rumbled with talk of a bus boycott, or strike, but the young woman and the community were afraid.

The following year, Rosa Parks, an African American seamstress and longtime member of the local NAACP, boarded a bus and sat down in the first available seat. The law of Montgomery, Alabama, was the same as it was throughout the South: African Americans had to sit in the back of the bus. Each bus had a painted line that separating the seats at the front of the bus from the seats in the rear. Whites could sit up front, but African Americans had to sit in back of the line. Rosa Parks was arrested on December 1, 1955, for refusing to give up her seat on a public bus to a white man. Her arrest would spark public outcry and strike a legal blow to desegregation. Rosa Parks changed history by refusing to sit in the back of the bus to accommodate whites.

Parks's arrest set off sparks of rage in the African American community. The community rose up against her arrest and boycotted

▲ Rosa Parks defied custom and law by refusing to give her seat to a white man.

the bus company. Old and young people set their alarms for the crack of dawn to begin the long walk to work and school. They walked past the buses, now nearly empty except for white passengers. The boycott was televised and broadcast across the nation. African Americans throughout the country understood how Parks must have felt. Many of them had been in similar circumstances themselves.

Soon, the boycott grew into a movement across the South. Almost every city from Macon, Georgia, to Dallas, Texas was caught up in the Montgomery drama. Like Parks, African Americans had decided that they, too, would no longer sit in the back of any bus anywhere in the South to accommodate whites.

Dr. Martin Luther King, Jr., a young man of 26 and a new minister in Montgomery, Alabama, found himself in a situation that would become a turning point in African American history. When African Americans in Montgomery called upon the African American civic

Empty buses cruised the streets of Montgomery, Alabama, as African Americans staged a six-month boycott of segregated buses. ▶

▲ A church-operated station wagon is used to transport African Americans boycotting segregated city buses in Montgomery, Alabama.

and church leaders in the city to conduct a bus boycott, Dr. King rose to the occasion. He was elected president of the Montgomery Improvement Association, (MIA) which organized the boycott.

The MIA organized car pools to transport the boycotters from home to work. Dr. King presented the MIA's demands for bus desegregation to the city. The city refused to consider the demands, Dr. King took the issue to the federal courts.

Dr. King and more than 100 other African Americans involved in the bus boycott were jailed and charged under a 1921 antiboycott law. The homes of some of the leaders of the boycott, including Dr. King's, were firebombed. African American domestic workers and others employed by whites were threatened with the loss of their jobs if they continued to support the boycott. The leaders of the boycott responded with fiery sermons that roused the African American community to action. Demonstrators marched through the streets singing the wonderful old Negro spirituals, hymns of encouragement and strength. The television cameras rolled, capturing forever on film one of the greatest defects in the U.S. system of democracy. A new era of mass demonstration and public protest was born.

▲ Dr. King, Mrs. Rosa Parks, and David Boston at a freedom march rally, June 1963.

Dr. King used the new technology of television to dramatize events for maximum appeal and power. Scenes of African Americans praying in church while racist whites kicked, punched, and abused them stirred viewers as nothing had before.

With the help of Fred Gray, Dr. King's brilliant attorney, the movement was fueled and ready to travel. Gray, also 26 at the time, mastered the technique of keeping Dr. King out of jail. Whenever Dr. King or any of the other demonstrators were arrested, Gray came to their aid, always with television cameras rolling in the background. Under the watchful eye of the camera, Gray was able to negotiate the boycotters' release almost as quickly as they were arrested. The MIA's actions in the courts and in the streets brought quick results.

One year after the boycotts began, the Supreme Court ruled that segregation on public transportation violated the U.S. Constitution. The Supreme Court ruling was a boon to African American activists, like Dr. King, who used civil disobedience to challenge the laws that allowed segregation and discrimination. Civil disobedience is the challenging of particular laws by breaking them as a means of effecting change. African Americans conducted sit-ins, freedom rides, marches, and other forms of protest in attempts to force the courts to overturn unjust laws.

Events skyrocketed. Bus boycotts were successful in Tallahassee, Tampa, and Atlanta. Freedom rides and sit-ins throughout the South focused the nation's attention on the problems of racial discrimination. This period in African American history is often called the Second Reconstruction because so many forces were working to effect change in the South. White merchants often came to the support of African Americans, especially in communities where African Americans were in the majority. The forces of movement and change were pushing the country into a new day when "all of God's children would be free" as one Negro spiritual proclaimed.

VOICES FROM THE PAST

The voices of the older warriors from generations past guided the new warriors in their struggle for civil rights, the equal rights guaranteed to African Americans under the U.S. Constitution. Revolutionaries such as Paul Robeson and W.E.B. Du Bois had done their parts to overturn the social and legal injustices against African Americans while fighting their own personal battles against injustice. Their affiliation with communist organizations caused some whites in the South to say that the communists were behind the freedom movement. What the whites were really voicing was their own fear that African Americans had finally realized that their freedom would have to be won by fighting because it would never be given freely or easily.

The Civil Rights Movement of the 1950s and 1960s made the sacrifices of Du Bois, Robeson, Douglass, Truth, Walker, Whipper, and the many other forerunners to African liberation worthwhile. Inspired by the examples of the Montgomery Improvement Association, many of the other African American organizations stepped up the pace for equal rights. The Southern Christian

Leadership Conference, the Student Nonviolent Coordinating Committee, the radical NAACP lawyers, the activist Urban League, and the demonstrative Congress of Racial Equality (CORE) were among the most visible. African American students, intellectuals, and artists immersed themselves in the cause. Names of such writers as James Baldwin, John Killens, Gwendolyn Brooks, Alonzo Davis, Lorraine Hansberry, Ossie Davis, Haki Madhubuti, Sonia Sanchez, Etheridge Knight, Bing Davis, Samella Lewis, Larry Neal, Nikki Giovanni, and LeRoi Jones (Imanu Amiri Baraka) came to identify a whole new school of African American art and literature. This new form was more powerful in its message and appeal than the Harlem Renaissance had ever been.

The Black Revolution is passing you bye
negroes
Anne Frank didn't put cheese and bread away for you
Because she knew it would be different this time
The naziboots don't march this year
Won't march next year
Won't come to pick you up in a
honka honka VW bus
So don't wait for that
negroes
They already got Malcolm
They already got LeRoi
They already strapped a harness on Rap
They already pulled Stokely's teeth
They already here if you can hear properly
negroes
Didn't you hear them when 40 thousand indians died from
exposure to
honkies
Didn't you hear them when viet children died from
exposure to napalm

Nikki Giovanni

The musicians, as always, were on the forefront of change. They began to play hard jazz with a new spirit and energy. This innovative music form created a new art form called *scatting*. Scatting allows a musician to verbalize his emotions in seemingly meaningless words. This technique was the forerunner to rap in the 1980s and 1990s.

◆ CENTER YOUR THINKING

1. Why was Rosa Parks arrested?
2. What is a boycott?
3. How was television used as an effective civil rights strategy? What might have been the effect of its use?
4. Describe the MIA boycott. Could the same tactics be used effectively today? Explain.
5. HOLISTIC ACTIVITY Students as Musicians
   You are a member of a group of musicians who are often called upon to perform in freedom rallies in the South. Using the "scatting" form, write a song that recounts the triumphs as well as horrors that you have seen in the Civil Rights Movement. Perform for your class.

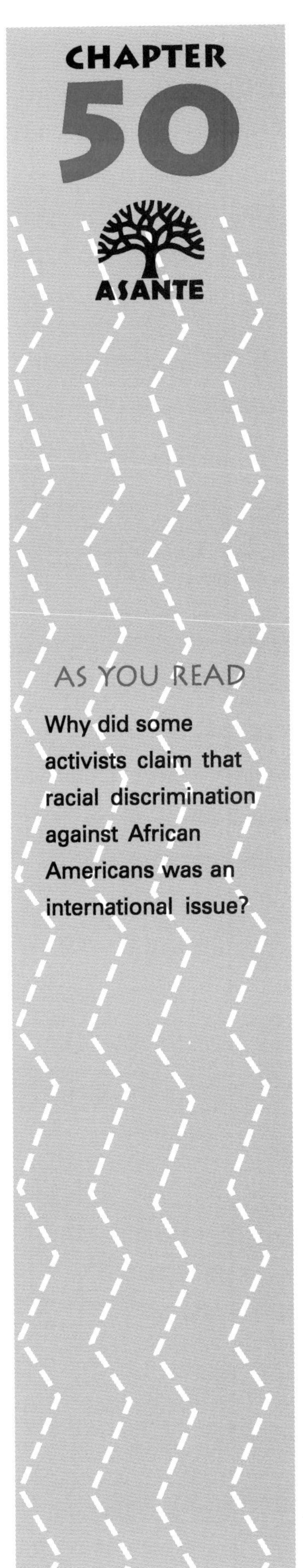

MALCOLM X
"OUR SHINING BLACK PRINCE"

CENTER YOUR VOCABULARY

- ▲ manhood
- ▲ assassinated
- ▲ nationalism
- ▲ eulogized

The same forces that shaped the Montgomery bus boycott and Dr. King's role in the Civil Rights Movement also helped to transform Malcolm Little into Malcolm X. Malcolm X rose like an eagle from the streets of Boston and Detroit to become the most representative voice of the masses of African Americans. Dr. Martin Luther King, Jr., represented a moral ideal, a standard for all people to live up to. Malcolm X represented African American manhood, a deep-seated need in the African American community to determine one's life conditions and opportunities. Malcolm's words created strong feelings of nationalism, unity, and brotherhood among all people of African descent, and these words shook the foundations of the Civil Rights Movement as nothing had before. Malcolm's movement had an even more powerful effect on middle-class African Americans than Marcus Garvey's Universal Negro Improvement Association and African Communities League had had in the 1920s. He encouraged Africans all over the world to work together in unity for their own self-interest and in the interest of their fellow African brothers and sisters. From a philosophical point of view, Malcolm was perhaps the most important leader during the 1960s because he helped to transform and redirect African American consciousness from dependency to self-determination.

▲ Malcolm X

Malcolm Little was born in Omaha, Nebraska, in 1925. He was introduced to the Nation of Islam (NOI), led by Elijah Mohammed, while he was in jail for robbery. He joined NOI in 1952, changed his name to Malcom X, and quickly rose to a high position in the organization because of his outstanding speaking skills, intelligence and leadership abilities.

By 1961, under Malcolm's leadership, there were 69 NOI temples and missions in 27 states, and 100,000 to 200,000 members, compared to about 40,000 when he joined. Malcolm also founded and edited the newspaper, *Mohammed Speaks*.

Using nationalist terms, he identified some of the common elements in the struggle for African American liberation. In his "The Ballot or the Bullet" speech, he says:

"We have the same problem, a common problem—a problem that will make you catch hell whether you're a Baptist, or a Methodist, or a Muslim, or a nationalist . . . . All of us have suffered here, in this country, political oppression at the hands of the white man, economic exploitation at the hands of the white man, and social degradation at the hands of the white man. Now in speaking like this, it doesn't mean that we're anti-white, but it does mean that we're anti-exploitation, we're anti-degradation, we're anti-oppression. And if the white man doesn't want us to be anti-him, let him stop oppressing and exploiting and degrading us . . . ."

Malcolm believed that whites did not have to worry about violence from African Americans if whites did not persecute them.

Malcolm X was suspended from the NOI for an unpopular comment he made about President John F. Kennedy's assassination on November 22, 1963. In 1964, Malcolm X broke away from the Nation of Islam and formed the Organization of Afro-American Unity (OAAU). He set out to bring charges against humanity before the United Nations against the United States. W.E.B. Du Bois had proposed the same tactic as early as 1947. Malcolm said:

". . . Our next move is to expand the civil rights struggle to the level of human rights, take it to the United Nations . . . And let the world

▲ Dr. Martin Luther King, Jr., (left) and Malcolm X (right) were the representative voices of the people.

see that Uncle Sam is guilty of violating the human rights of 22 million Afro-Americans and still has the audacity or the nerve to stand up and represent himself as the leader of the free world."

His words were the fighting words spoken by a thousand African voices before him and felt in the hearts of millions of others.

Malcolm X saw that the issues of racial discrimination against African Americans had to be placed on the international agenda as an assault against humanity. The hypocrisy of the American nation to speak about justice and yet be unjust to the African and Native American peoples within its borders was unbearable for many African American freedom fighters. They had to speak out, and when they could not speak out against injustice, then Malcolm X was the voice they heard. Malcolm X would continue his campaign until he was brutally assassinated in 1965 while speaking at a rally in Harlem.

Malcolm was eulogized by actor Ossie Davis who told African Americans:

". . . if you knew him, you would know why we must honor him: Malcolm was our manhood, our living black manhood! This was his meaning to his people. And in honoring him, we honor the best in ourselves . . . . And we will know him then for what he was and is—a Prince—our own black, shining prince!—who didn't hesitate to die, because he loved us so."

Malcolm's assassination threw the country into a racial uproar. Students were boycotting department stores. Civil rights organizers were targeting movie theaters, amusement parks, supermarkets, and libraries with more acts of civil disobedience.

◆ CENTER YOUR THINKING

1. Explain why Malcolm X was suspended from the Nation of Islam.
2. Why is Malcolm X referred to as "our shining black prince?"
3. Why did Malcolm X set out to place issues of racial discrimination against African Americans as a top priority?
4. According to the author, what were the main points made by Malcolm X in his "The Ballot or the Bullet" speech?
5. HOLISTIC ACTIVITY Students as Film Makers
   You are a group of present-day film makers who have been contacted to make a film about Malcolm X. Make a chart with at least eight boxes, and sketch out a scene for your movie. Write captions and dialogue for each scene.

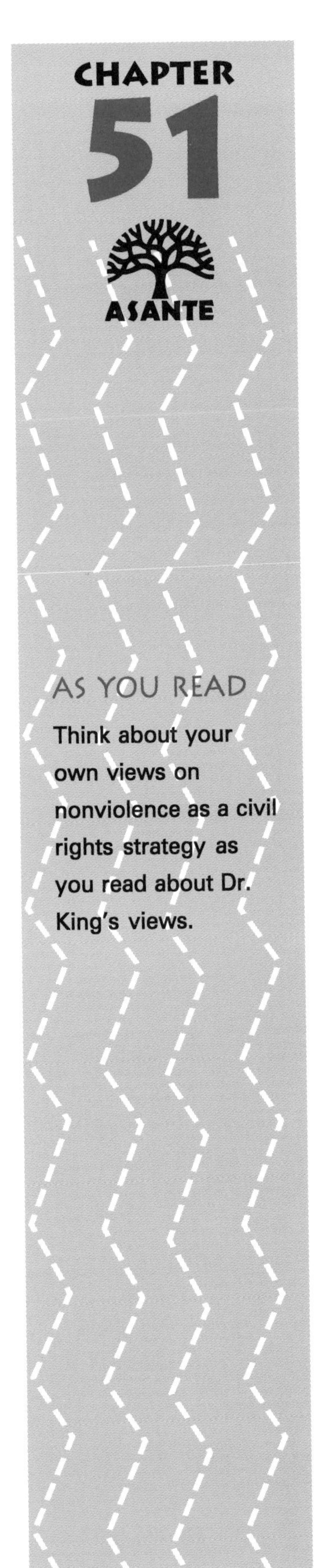

MARTIN LUTHER KING, JR., THE VOICE OF CONSCIENCE

CENTER YOUR VOCABULARY

▲ nonviolent protest

▲ moral character

Thrust to the forefront of the Civil Rights Movement by his success in Montgomery, Dr. Martin Luther King, Jr., took the nation's conscience in his hands and reshaped it with eloquent pleas for justice and righteousness.

Dr. King was born into a comfortable, middle-class activist family in Atlanta, Georgia, in 1929. He received his education at Morehouse College and Boston University. During his studies, Dr. King was introduced to the philosophy of nonviolence put forward by Mahatma Gandhi when he led the Indians against the British colonial settlers in India in the late 1940s. Gandhi taught that nonviolent protest demanded a higher moral character of the protesters, and that one had to be prepared to accept abuse for doing justice.

Dr. King knew that the civil disobedience he and his followers committed would elicit a violent response from white America. The success of nonviolent protest, a form of passive resistance, lay in the very violence committed against the protesters by white Americans. Nonviolence allowed the protesters to assume a moral position higher than that of their oppressors, placing the burden of oppression on the shoulders of the oppressors, who now had to explain *their* position.

At the height of the Civil Rights Movement, Dr. King was not the popular hero he is today. His movement, like Malcolm X's, was seen

▲ Dr. Martin Luther King, Jr.'s policy of nonviolent protest placed him at the forefront of the Civil Rights Movement.

by many as an unjustified attack on U.S. society. Dr. King responded to a statement published by white clergymen who condemned his activities in his famous "Letter from Birmingham Jail" on April 16, 1963. After explaining that he rarely took the time to answer all of his critics, he went on to confront their concerns head-on in what has become the standard statement on nonviolence. King wrote:

"Nonviolent direct action seeks to create such a crisis and foster such a tension that a community which has constantly refused to negotiate is forced to confront the issue . . . . We know through painful experience that freedom is never voluntarily given by the oppressor; it must be demanded by the oppressed . . . . I stand in the middle of two opposing forces in the Negro community. One is a force of complacency . . . . The other is one of bitterness and hatred, and it comes perilously close to advocating violence . . . . If [the Negro's] repressed emotions are not released in nonviolent ways, they will seek expression through violence; this is not a threat but a fact of history."

▲ Dr. Martin Luther King, Jr., delivers one of his most passionate speeches, *I Have a Dream.*

▲ Dr. King offers a word of encouragement to a young protestor.

By challenging the clergy ministers in this way, Dr. King demonstrated his philosphical leadership. A few months later in August, he would give his most famous speech, "I Have a Dream." It would be heard around the world and make him a truly international figure.

Dr. King understood quite clearly his place in the struggle. In 1964, he was awarded the Nobel Peace Prize in Stockholm, Sweden, becoming at the time only the third person of the African descent to receive the award. Two others, Ralph Bunche of the United States and Albert Luthuli of South Africa, had received it earlier.

In April 1968, while supporting a strike of city garbage workers in Memphis, Tennessee, Dr. King was assassinated as he stood on the balcony of the Lorraine Motel talking with some of his aides. While African Americans mourned, whites such as Senator Henry Byrd of Virginia condemned Dr. King for participating in violent activities. He said that African American activists like Dr. King "become the victims of the forces they set in motion. Violence all too often attended his action, and at the last, he himself met a violent end." Senator Byrd seemed neither to have heard Dr. King's message nor to have understood that truth can never be silenced.

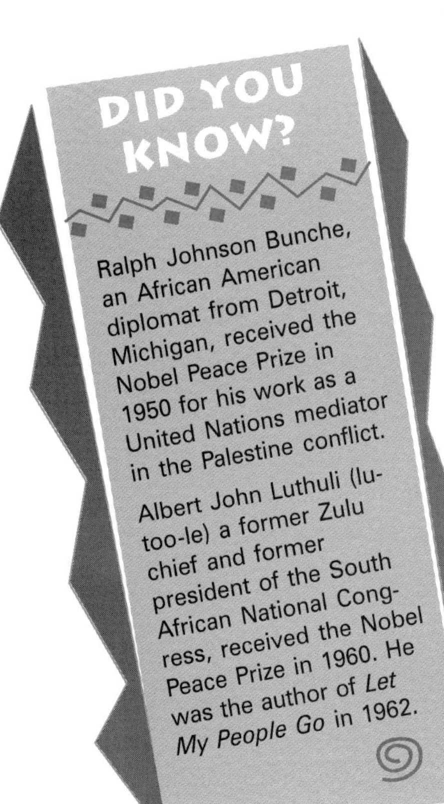

DID YOU KNOW?

Ralph Johnson Bunche, an African American diplomat from Detroit, Michigan, received the Nobel Peace Prize in 1950 for his work as a United Nations mediator in the Palestine conflict.

Albert John Luthuli (lu-too-le) a former Zulu chief and former president of the South African National Congress, received the Nobel Peace Prize in 1960. He was the author of *Let My People Go* in 1962.

◆ CENTER YOUR THINKING

1. Who are the three individuals of African descent who won the Nobel Peace Prize?
2. Define *nonviolent protest.*
3. What justification did Dr. Martin Luther King, Jr., give for adopting nonviolence as a civil rights strategy?
4. Describe some nonviolent ways that were used to protest effectively.
5. HOLISTIC ACTIVITY Students as Bibliographers
   A bibliography is a list of sources of information that have been published on a specific subject. A bibliography may include books, films, videos, tapes, and articles. Work with your group to compile a good bibliography of multimedia sources of information about Dr. Martin Luther King, Jr., and the Civil Rights Movement.

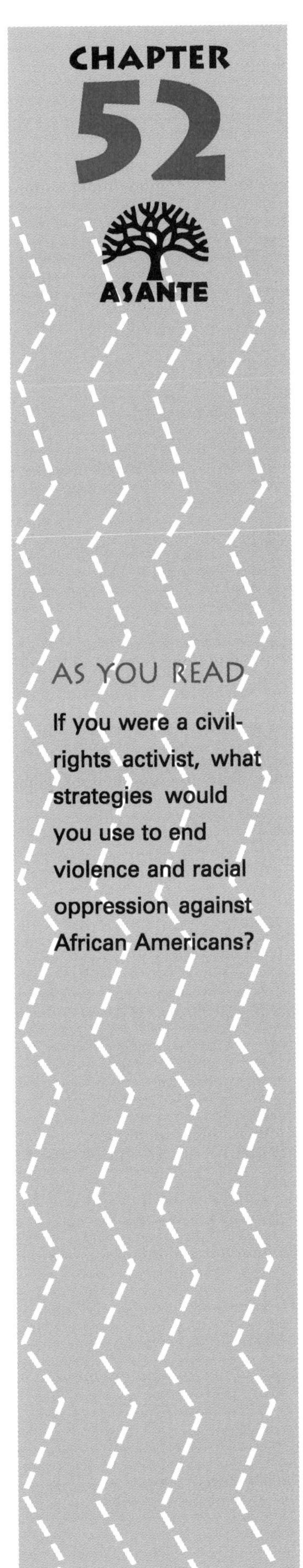

AGENTS FOR CHANGE

CENTER YOUR VOCABULARY

- ▲ sit-ins
- ▲ freedom rides
- ▲ plebiscite
- ▲ integrate
- ▲ desegregation
- ▲ underground

While Dr. Martin Luther King, Jr., and Malcolm X commanded the nation's attention, many other African American leaders and groups were also working for change. Throughout the South, African Americans stirred with the desire to be free from discrimination and injustice. The sit-ins, the occupying of seats in segregated places of business to deny them to white customers, began in 1960 when four African American students from North Carolina Agricultural and Technical College sat down at the all-white lunch counter of the Woolworth's store in Greensboro, North Carolina. They sat for an hour without being served. The technique spread as African American students in other cities conducted other sit-ins, wade-ins at beaches, and kneel-ins at churches where African Americans took over pews in churches that had all-white memberships. Other strategies to demonstrate that the segregationists were wrong were tried by other groups of students and some civil rights organizations.

One individual who was fed up with racism was Robert Williams. He was a Marine Corps veteran who became the president of the Monroe, North Carolina, chapter of the NAACP in 1955. He attempted to integrate the local swimming pool. It had been built with federal funds, but access was denied to African Americans. He brought a legal suit after city officials refused to make the pool

▲ Students stage a sit-in in a "white-only" waiting room in Montgomery, Alabama.

accessible to African Americans or to build one in the African American community.

The Ku Klux Klan had been terrorizing the local African American population, and Williams's work intensified their intimidation efforts. Williams appealed to city officials, the governor, and President Dwight Eisenhower to stop the Klan from shooting up the Monroe community. None of the appeals was successful.

Williams and 60 other NAACP members formed a rifle club and joined the National Rifle Association. They successfully prevented the Klan from attacking one of their member's house in 1957 by displaying their weapons in a show of force.

In 1958, a seven-year-old white girl from Monroe, North Carolina, playfully kissed a nine-year-old African American boy on the cheek. The boy and a friend who was with him at the time were arrested for rape and sentenced to 14 years in a reform school. Robert Williams asked the national office of the NAACP in New York for assistance in handling the case, but they refused because they considered it a

▲ Demonstrators protest outside an F.W. Woolworth store.

"sex case," not a civil rights case. Newspapers in the United States refused to print anything about the case until European newspapers printed the story and embarrassed the United States press by exposing the case to the world. The boys were released a year later after President Eisenhower intervened.

In 1959, an eight-month's pregnant African American woman in Monroe was beaten and raped by a white man. An all-white jury cleared him of all charges. Robert Williams decided that the only sane action for African Americans was to arm themselves for self-defense. When he said this publicly, the NAACP suspended his chapter because they feared the talk of arms and violence. Armed resistance had never been the NAACP's style of resistance because the organization was involved mainly in legal representation.

Williams and his supporters held sit-ins and other demonstrations to protest segregation in Monroe's schools and in the city pool. The NAACP did not support his efforts. Whites fired pistols and rifles over the heads of the protesters while the local police chief looked the other way. Williams sent a telegram to the U.S. Justice Department. They referred him to the FBI, which told him it was the Justice Department's responsibility. There were several assassination attempts on his life.

When civil rights demonstrators, who rode buses all over the South to protest African American injustice (freedom rides), came to Monroe later in 1960, they were arrested and jailed. Shortly after, Robert Williams received a call from a police officer, who warned him that he would be arrested and then hanged in his cell because of his outspoken actions. As the police came down his street, Williams and his family managed to escape. They went to Canada and eventually to Cuba.

Robert Williams's position on self-defense was not any different than the position taken by the American founding fathers, such as Thomas Jefferson and George Washington, and certainly no different from the bold stance of such African American resisters as William Parker. The U.S. Constitution guarantees each citizen's right to self-defense. Williams said in his book, *Negroes With Guns*:

"The stranglehold of oppression cannot be loosened by a plea to the oppressor's conscience. Social change in something as fundamental as racist oppression involves violence . . . . Always the powers in command are ruthless and unmerciful in defending their position and their privileges."

Williams went on to say that, as a veteran who had fought for the United States, he saw every reason to defend his wife, children, and home with weapons because he had gone to war to defend a nation that refused to defend him from the local Ku Klux Klan. Robert Williams inspired hundreds of other people to take their first step, an initiative for liberation.

▼ Children lead a protest against segregated schools.

Various forms of protest emerged during the next few years, yet it seemed that nothing African Americans did could bring justice soon enough. School children remained segregated by race because whites believed that African Americans were inferior. Hundreds of African American children in Topeka, Kansas, had to travel long distances to school, passing perfectly decent white schools that were closer to them than the segregated schools across town. The same situation occurred in Little Rock, Atlanta, Montgomery, and many other places in the South.

▲ Linda Brown's case, *Brown v. Board of Education of Topeka,* was one of five cases against segregation that was argued before the Supreme Court.

Five such cases were brought before the U.S. Supreme Court in 1953. Thurgood Marshall, who was appointed to the Supreme Court in 1967 by President Lyndon B. Johnson, was the NAACP Legal Defense Fund's lead lawyer in 1953 in the case against the Topeka Board of Education. In the documents filed with the Supreme Court in 1953, the NAACP argued that "the substantive question common to all is whether a state can, consistently with the Constitution, exclude children, solely on the ground that they are Negroes, from public schools which otherwise they would be qualified to attend."

In 1954, the Supreme Court ruled in the historic case *Brown v. the Board of Education of Topeka, Kansas,* that racial segregation in public schools was unconstitutional. The court ordered that school districts obey the decision "with all deliberate speed," which meant that they were to start the process of desegregation immediately.

Three years later, in 1957, after numerous marches, demonstrations, and bus boycotts, Arkansas Governor Orval Faubus, previously considered a moderate on race, called out the state-controlled National Guard to prevent nine African American students from entering Central High School in Little Rock. This confrontation over desegregation was the first major clash between a state and the federal government since 1877. Faubus's use of armed force to prevent the state from carrying out a federal law forced President Dwight D. Eisenhower to use federal troops to force the admittance of the nine students.

▲ Daisy Bates

Daisy Bates, a former newspaper editor and the president of the Arkansas state NAACP, was the leading voice against racism in education during this period. She took the nine Arkansas students—Carlotta Walls, Jefferson Thomas, Elizabeth Eckford, Melba Patillo, Ernest Green, Thelma Mothershed, Terrance Roberts, Minnejean Brown, and Gloria Ray—under her political and legal wing on that September 3, 1957.

Two hundred-fifty National Guard troops surrounded the school building when the young students approached. The students must have been frightened of the mob that had assembled outside the school, but they did not show their fear. They were walking into the

▲ Despite the pressures of integration, students give thanks at a pre-Thanksgiving dinner at the home of NAACP State President Daisy Bates.

books for something that was right and honorable. A white mob of women, men, and children jeered at the nine as they were escorted to the school by eight adults, four of the six African American escorts were ministers. The other two escorts were white. The mob shoved and spat upon the students as they entered the schoool but their actions could not turn back the wheels of progress. Segregation was defeated that day at Central High as it was at hundreds of other schools throughout the South.

CAUSE FOR ALARM

In addition to the problems in education, African Americans in the 1950s had other social problems with whites. One example is Emmett Till, a 14-year-old Chicago boy, who visited his relatives in Money, Mississippi. While in Money, he allegedly whistled at a white woman. He was abducted by several white men, driven to a rural area, murdered, and thrown into a swamp. His badly decomposed body was found several weeks later. The two white men who were accused of his death were acquitted by an all-white jury during their trial. Because of its brutality and senselessness, Till's death was a wakeup call for the entire nation on the future of race relations in America.

▲ Thousands of mourners gather outside the Raynor Funeral Chapel in Greenwood, Mississippi, to view the slain body of 14-year-old Emmett Till.

ELLA JO BAKER

Perhaps every organization needs a spark, a charismatic personality, if it is to exist as an inspirational agency. The Southern Christian Leadership Conference (SCLC) had many such individuals, but none stood so solidly as the visionary Ella Jo Baker, the soul and fire of the organization. A long-time activist, Baker worked with the Young Negroes' Cooperative League in New York City, the NAACP, and the SCLC. She was the coordinator of the Atlanta office of the SCLC during the 1960s.

Baker was a behind-the-scenes organizer who planned actions, decided strategy, and arranged the details for demonstrations and other nonviolent campaigns. In the early 1960s, she convinced the SCLC leadership to sponsor a conference of student group leaders involved in civil rights activities for the purpose of charting a mass movement among young people. Once she convened the meeting, she was able to convince the young people that they should organize a separate group to carry the Civil Rights Movement to thousands of students. Out of this came the Student Nonviolent Coordinating Committee (SNCC). It was a child of the SCLC, but most of all, it was the brainchild of Ella Jo Baker.

SNCC

The Student Nonviolent Coordinating Committee was formed by African American college students under the guidance of Ella Jo Baker on April 15, 1960, in Raleigh, North Carolina. SNCC's goal was to coordinate the activities of student groups who had been conducting various acts of civil disobedience throughout the country.

Within a year, the organization had 70,000 students engaged in summer sit-ins in the South. By September 1961, 3,600 students had been jailed, but 300 different businesses had been desegregated.

SNCC also conducted massive voter registration drives and organized political parties in Alabama and Mississippi. John Lewis, now a Georgia state senator, was one of the first leaders of SNCC. He was beaten unconscious four times and arrested at least 40 times. SNCC eventually denounced nonviolence as a civil rights tactic because of the violence many of its members suffered at the hands of white racists.

STOKLEY CARMICHAEL

Stokely Carmichael (now Kwame Toure) succeeded Lewis as National Chairman of SNCC in 1966, but he is better known as the father of black power. Carmichael first used the term *black power* in Greenwood, Mississippi, during James Meredith's march against fear.

▲ Stokley Carmichael

The slogan introduced a new, more militant attitude to SNCC and the civil rights struggle. It became a rallying cry for young African Americans in the 1960s. Carmichael explained the significance of black power:

"For once, black people are going to use the words they want to use—not just the words whites want to hear. And they will do this no matter how often the press tries to stop the use of the slogan by equating it with racism or separatism . . . .

With power, the masses could make or participate in making the decisions that govern their destinies and thus create basic changes in their day-to-day lives. . . .

The concept of black power is not a recent or isolated phenomenon;

Harlem CORE workers support black power. ▶

it has grown out of the ferment of agitation and activity by different people and organizations in many black communities over the years.

"Where Negroes lack a majority, black power means proper representation. Politically, black power means . . . the coming together of black people to elect representatives and to force those representatives to speak to their needs."

The concept of black power was seen in the raised, gloved fists of African American athletes at the Olympic Games in Mexico in 1968. It was seen in the hair, clothing, and attitudes of African Americans during the 1960s and 1970s. It was seen in the use of *black* instead of *Negro* to describe African Americans.

Many whites misunderstood the term. Robert Browne, an African American professor on his way back from a 1967 Black Power Conference in Newark, New Jersey, explained to whites what black power meant to African Americans:

"Black Power may not be the ideal slogan to describe this new self-image which the black American is developing, for to guilt-ridden whites the slogan conjures up violence, anarchy and revenge. To frustrated blacks, however, it symbolizes unity and a newly found pride in the blackness to which the Creator endowed us and which we realize must always be our mark of identification. Heretofore this blackness has been a stigma, a curse with which we were born. black power means that this curse will now be a badge of pride rather than scorn."

JAMES MEREDITH

When James Meredith enrolled in the all-white University of Mississippi in 1962, federal troops had to be called in to control the rioting. In 1966, Meredith decided to see if an African American man could walk from Memphis, Tennessee, to Jackson, Mississippi, during a primary election and not be harmed by white racists. He was shot and injured on the first day of his one-man march against fear. African American activists throughout the country came to his aid. Dr. Martin Luther King, Jr., Stokely Carmichael, Floyd McKissack, Roy Wilkins, and Whitney Young came to Meredith's hospital bedside in Memphis. They decided that they would continue his march.

It was during this march that Stokely Carmichael used the slogan, *black power*. He said, "The only way we're going to stop them white men from whipping us is to take over. We've been saying freedom for six years, and we don't have nothing. What we're going to start saying now is black power."

CORE

The Congress of Racial Equality (CORE) initiated freedom rides under the leadership of James Farmer, an activist who was the director of CORE. In 1961, seven African Americans and six whites rode an interstate bus from Washington, D.C., to various points in the South. They were attacked by whites at the Rock Hill, South

▲ A freedom-ride bus is burned in Anniston, Alabama.

Carolina, bus terminal. One of their buses burned in Anniston, Alabama. Whites in Birmingham, Alabama, beat the riders with metal bars as the police looked on. The white bus drivers refused to continue the rides. The CORE bus riders were then joined by other groups and conducted massive freedom rides and voter-registration campaigns all over the South.

Hundreds of college students went to Mississippi in 1961 to explain voting requirements to African Americans, and to help them register to vote. Many were arrested and beaten; some were murdered. This was the beginning of the end of the ironclad rule of white Southern supremacists. The freedom riders targeted every sector of Southern society where segregation was both the custom and the law, and began to break it down.

FANNIE LOU HAMER

African American women played a leading role in the Civil Rights Movement of the 1960s. One of the most courageous and heroic was Fannie Lou Hamer. The youngest of 20 children, she was born in Mississippi to poor sharecropping parents. She was 44 when she joined the Civil Rights Movement by registering to vote in

Mississippi. Until the young college students came to her town to help African Americans register to vote, she had not known that African Americans had the right to vote in Mississippi.

The owner of the plantation where she and her husband worked as sharecroppers told her she would have to remove her name from the voter rolls or leave his farm. Hamer told him, "I didn't go down there to register for you, I went down to register there for myself." She, her husband who had sharecropped on the same farm for 30 years, and their children, all left the plantation. The family stayed with friends nearby until a group of whites fired 16 shots at the friend's house to force Fannie Lou out. Fannie Lou Hamer moved out and found shelter in a nearby town to save her friends from death.

She became an instructor in a voter-registration program run by SNCC, and actively began to teach African Americans how to read and register to vote. Her work brought her into close contact with African Americans and white civil rights activists from the North. Soon after, Hamer and her friend, Annelle Ponder, were arrested and viciously beaten in jail for attempting to use a "whites-only" restroom in Winona, Mississippi. However, the real reason for their arrest was their association with the civil rights activists.

As a result of the beating, Hamer's kidneys were permanently damaged and she lost her sight in one eye. Fannie Lou Hamer refused to be intimidated. In her speeches she would state:

"I'm sick and tired of being sick and tired. I ain't going no place .... With all my parents and grandparents gave to Mississippi, I have a right to stay here and fight for what they didn't get .... The white man is the scardest person on earth. Out in the daylight he don't do nothing. But at night he'll toss a bomb or pay someone to kill. The white man's afraid he'll be treated like he's been treating Negroes, but I couldn't carry that much hate."

Hamer entered politics and became a delegate to the Mississippi Freedom Democratic Party (MFDP). The party was formed to challenge the racist state Democratic Party which had excluded African Americans. The MFDP tried to be seated at the

1964 Democratic National Convention in Atlantic City, New Jersey, but the convention refused to seat them. However, their actions resulted in a resolution that banned the convention from allowing segregated delegations in the future. Fannie Lou Hamer later served on the Democratic National Committee.

The political and social unrest of the early 1960s was marked by the actions of courageous individuals and groups who were committed to achieving equality for African Americans. Their success in placing civil rights for African Americans at the forefront of the nation's consciousness led to new legislation aimed at bringing about equality under the law. Some politicians even spoke of affirmative-action laws, laws that would be used to erase the long disadvantage that African Americans had suffered because of the enslavement and discrimination. This policy allowed institutions to affirm their commitment to equality by opening their doors to African Americans who had been excluded from the universities, industries, and government agencies. Affirmative action was the nation's best answer at the time to the continuing racism against African Americans.

Unfortunately, most African Americans never benefited from affirmative action. Only those who were prepared for the opportunities that were available could actually be helped by the affirmative action mandate; others continued to operate on their own best initiative, doing as always, their best in a tough situation. Of course, there were new laws that made life somewhat easier and less troublesome.

Civil Rights Act of 1964

The most far-reaching civil rights legislation yet, this law became the 24th Amendment to the U.S. Constitution. It:

- strengthened previous civil rights acts;
- outlawed devices such as the poll tax and literacy tests which were designed to keep African Americans from voting;
- outlawed discrimination in public places such as restaurants, hotels, and theaters;

- ❖ outlawed segregation in parks, stadiums, and swimming pools;
- ❖ gave financial aid to all schools in the process of desegregation;
- ❖ said that federal funds would be withheld from schools or programs that discriminated;
- ❖ extended the life of the Civil Rights Commission for four more years;
- ❖ prohibited discrimination by employers and unions;
- ❖ prevented a federal court from sending a civil rights case back to state or local courts;
- ❖ established the Community Relations Service to arbitrate local race problems;
- ❖ provided the right of a jury trial for any case brought under the protection of the Civil Rights Act of 1964.

THE VOTING RIGHTS ACT OF 1965

This act provided for direct federal examination of voter registration and voting procedures. Prior to this act, a Southern state could argue that it had the right to determine its own procedures and that the federal government could not intervene. This act made it possible for the federal government to intervene directly if it appeared that a problem of discrimination existed. But this act would not end discrimination or protests against discrimination. Numerous organizations appeared to extend the reach for justice and equality. Many of them, such as the Student Nonviolent Coordinating Committee, were led by students, but all of them found the model of SNCC with its youthful energy an organization to be followed. Julian Bond, Stokely Carmichael, Marion Barry, John Lewis, Diane Nash, and H. Rap Brown were just a few of the names of the young students who filled leadership posts in the civil rights era. Several of them would pursue political careers in later decades.

▲ Huey Newton

THE BLACK PANTHERS

SNCC's successes launched the student movement as a force to be reckoned with and gave rise to other student-based organizations. The most prominent was the Black Panthers. The Black Panthers

▲ Bobby Seale

was formed in 1966 by Huey Newton and Bobby Seale, two students at Merritt College in Oakland, California. Both Newton and Seale were influenced by Malcolm X's militant stance and his insistence on self-defense.

Seale became Minister of Defense. The students patterned their organization loosely on the leadership of Mao Tse-tung (MOU-zuh-DOONG), a Chinese communist leader in the 1950s. Bobby Hutton, later martyred, became the first member of the organization. David Hilliard, another student, was chief of staff. From this nucleus, the Black Panthers grew to become a national organization that competed with SNCC for student demonstrators and members. Women such as Elaine Brown and Kathleen Cleaver became prominent members in the organization.

The philosophy of the organization was based on a 1966 platform which included the following:

- We want freedom. We want power to determine the destiny of our black community
- We want full employment for our people
- We want an end to the robbery by the white man of our black community
- We want decent housing, fit for shelter of human beings
- We want education for our people that exposes the true nature of decadent American society
- We want all black men to be exempt from military service
- We want an immediate end to police brutality and murder of black people
- We want freedom for all black men held in federal, state, county and city jails and prisons
- We want all black people, when brought to trial, to be tried in a court by a jury of their peer group
- We want land, bread, housing, education, clothing, justice, and peace.

Members called themselves "children of Malcolm" because Malcolm X influenced their philosophy. Like Malcolm, Minister of Information Eldridge Cleaver spoke of two types of violence: "violence directed at you to keep you in your place, and violence to defend yourself against that suppression and to win your freedom."

▲ Huey Newton appeared in ads like this one to promote the platform of the African People's Socialist Party.

The first is called *oppressive violence,* the second is called *resistant violence.*

The Panthers believed that oppressive violence had to be fought by resistant violence. They encouraged their members to buy and use guns in their defense against the police and others who tried to take away their rights. Because of their insistence on defending themselves, they became the targets of the police and the FBI. The police, the FBI, and other law enforcement agencies harassed the Panthers, further convincing the African American community that it would never have protection from these agencies.

Panther member Bobby Hutton, just 17 years old, was killed by the police on April 6, 1968. The Black Panther newspaper wrote the following about his death:

"The circumstances surrounding the death, the murder, the crucifixion, have often been told. How the pigs (police), in an effort to destroy the leadership of the Black Panther Party, ambushed Eldridge Cleaver and a group of Panthers including Lil' Bobby. How the pigs fired hundreds of rounds of ammunition into the house where Lil' Bobby and Eldridge had sought shelter. . . . How Lil' Bobby and Eldridge emerged from the house and were beaten brutally by the pigs; Lil' Bobby was murdered by a fusillade of fire from the pigs. How Lil' Bobby had his hands in the air and was obeying the pigs's orders when they fired on him. This is all history, not to be forgotten, but to inflame and inspire."

In Chicago, Los Angeles, and Philadelphia, the Black Panthers were attacked by the police. Mark Clark and Fred Hampton, leaders of the Black Panthers in Chicago, were killed on December 4, 1969. Police broke through the door of their house after firing hundreds of rounds of ammunition. Scores of African Americans were jailed as the raids on the Panthers intensified.

▲ Armed members of the Black Panthers stand guard outside their bomb-scarred headquarters.

In 1970, the Philadelphia police, led by then-police chief and later mayor Frank Rizzo, raided the Panthers office in North Philadelphia, lined up the members on the street outside of the office, stripped them naked, and allowed the news media to take pictures of them to humiliate the organization. Despite this, the organization continued to flourish and capture the imagination of young people. The Panthers made international headlines for their courage and independence. Some members of the Black Panther Party found exile in Cuba, Algeria, and France.

The Panthers called for a United Nations-supervised plebiscite to determine the will of African people concerning their national destiny. The plebiscite would have allowed African Americans to stay Americans or form an independent nation. A vote was never held on this issue.

The Panthers excited much fear in whites with their defiant program of self-defense, self-reliance, and independence. However, soon it was possible for all people to see that the Panthers were not supporters of violence; they were simply expressing the American values of self-defense, self-reliance, and self-determination.

▲ Angela Davis

ANGELA DAVIS

Angela Davis was among the close friends and supporters of the Black Panthers. Davis was thrust into the forefront of the student movement for her activism and communist beliefs. Davis was active in all areas of civil rights, including prisoners' rights, capital punishment, and women's rights.

Angela Davis first came to national attention when the University of California at Los Angeles refused to renew her teaching contract because she was a communist. She was active with the Black Panthers and went underground, in hiding, after a 1970 shootout at the Marin County, California, courthouse left four people dead. She was accused of providing the guns used in the shootout. Davis was captured in 1971 and served 16 months in jail until she was tried and acquitted of all charges. In 1980, she was the Communist Party's vice presidential candidate for the general elections.

All of the forces for change and agencies for action would come together at the Lincoln Memorial in Washington, D. C. The work of the organizers, field workers, lawyers, freedom riders, and demonstrators was recognized in a national outpouring for justice.

◆ CENTER YOUR THINKING

1. Name three civil rights organizations.
2. Why did the NAACP suspend the chapter led by Robert Williams?
3. What justification was given by Robert Williams for using weapons in the Civil Rights Movement?
4. Name the civil rights activist with whom you *most* identify and explain why.
5. HOLISTIC ACTIVITY Students as Chartmakers
Organize the information in this chaper into three columns. Label one column LEADER, the second column ORGANIZATION, and the third column FREEDOM AND RESISTANCE ACTIVITIES. Update the chart with modern-day leaders you learn about throughout the school year.

AS YOU READ

What accomplishments achieved by the Civil Rights Movement benefit you today?

THE MARCH ON WASHINGTON

CENTER YOUR VOCABULARY

- ▲ rage
- ▲ Black Studies
- ▲ imperalism
- ▲ capitalism

The March on Washington, August 28, 1963, was the most politically charged demonstration ever mounted by African Americans and supporters of the Civil Rights Movement. More than 250,000 people, the population of a medium-size city, gathered at the Lincoln Memorial to call for racial justice and harmony.

Martin Luther King, Jr., weary from nonviolent campaigning but hopeful because of his mission, came with more than 250,000 others to the March on Washington. Encouraged by the battles he had won and the support of the labor unions and churches, King gave one of the greatest speeches ever recorded in the United States. The "I Have a Dream" speech has become the signature piece of the Civil Rights era. It is quoted thousands of times on all types of occasions. It was considered a masterful speech because it laid out the history of the African American struggle and projected a vision of national unity.

The March on Washington was the crowning moment of the Civil Rights Movement. Arthur Smith, a young 21-year-old African American student and his Asian friend John Lye of Singapore had driven to the march from Oklahoma. Both men stood near the Lincoln Memorial with tears flowing down their faces as King

▲ The nation's capital is filled with marchers carrying signs of protest.

dramatically finished his speech: "Free at last. Free at last. Thank God Almighty, we are free at last!" But African Americans were not free. The struggle would continue and give rise to a growing sense of rage, an extreme anger, that would mushroom in the coming years.

By the mid-1960s, it was clear for all to see that there was both a general rage in the African American community over the slow pace of change and a genuine alarm in the white community at African Americans' fury and determination. Many whites claimed that they did not realize the depth of African Americans' anger and vowed to eliminate segregation and racism in their institutions. Some whites, however, called for more police action to control the rage in the African American community.

Police forces across the country responded by initiating antiriot training tactics. Between 1963 and 1966, images of tear gas, armored cars, and tanks being used against African American demonstrators in large urban areas were commonplace on the the evening news on television.

▲ Dr. Martin Luther King, Jr., speaks to the thousands gathered at the Lincoln Memorial for the March on Washington.

▲ Dr. King and others watch as President Lyndon B. Johnson signs the Kerner Commission Report.

▲ Family and friends mourn Dr. King's death. (*Second from right*, Coretta Scott King with her two sons)

During 1967, there were more riots and rebellions. President Lyndon B. Johnson appointed a National Advisory Commission on Civil Disorders. The commission was chaired by former Illinois Governor Otto Kerner. In a forthright report, the Kerner Commission, as it was known, said that America was ". . . moving toward two societies, one black, one white—separate and unequal." It further argued that to continue the present course of racial strife would mean the destruction of basic democratic values.

On April 4, 1968, Dr. Martin Luther King, Jr., was assassinated in Memphis, Tennessee, as he stood on the balcony of a motel. Riots broke out in more than 100 U.S. cities as African Americans expressed their rage. Washington, Chicago, Cleveland, Philadelphia, Los Angeles, and other major cities were under siege by roving bands of angry people. The National Guard was called out to put down the disturbances. Schools were closed in some cities, and President Johnson declared Sunday, April 6, a day of national mourning. He issued an order for all U.S. flags on government buildings to be flown at half-mast.

A wounded soldier is carried piggyback style by rescuers of the First Cavalry 2 miles from the Cambodian border. ▶

Dr. King's death did little to quiet the agents for change. There were quiet protests that were as powerful as the explosive demonstrations in the large cities. African American students took over administration buildings at several universities and colleges. They demanded Black Studies programs and more African American faculty members. This was a drive to ensure that racism would be confronted with facts because the students believed that racism was based on ignorance.

Overseas, African American athletes John Carlos and Tommie Smith staged their own personal demonstration. They raised their fists in a black power salute at the victory stand after the 200-meter race at the Olympics in Mexico City. Both said they were protesting racism in the United States of America.

THE VIETNAM WAR

The Vietnam War came at the height of civil rights activity and the protests against discrimination. Many African Americans questioned whether or not African Americans should participate in a conflict that they felt was an excuse for U.S. imperialism. They believed that Vietnam was another political hotspot in the tug-of-war among the Europeans to promote capitalism and crush communism in underdeveloped nations. Capitalism is an economic system in which the majority of the goods and services of a country are produced by privately owned companies for a profit.

▲ U.S. patrols wade through the muddy waters of Dong Tam, South Vietnam.

The Vietnamese and French Armies fought each other from 1945 to 1954. The French Army was defeated in the famous battle at Dien Bien Phu (dee-N-BEEN-foo) in 1954 by a supposedly technologically inferior people. In Vietnam, people still carried their goods on their heads over winding country roads. It was a society where a wheelbarrow represented a technological advance; yet, the Vietnamese brought the French Army to its knees. The French withdrew from this supposedly backward country that they could no longer dominate. Their withdrawal brought the United States into the war with the Vietnamese under the administration of President Dwight David Eisenhower in the late 50s.

In the early 1960s, President John F. Kennedy increased the American role in the Vietnam War in order to secure a capitalist South Vietnam in opposition to a communist North Vietnam. In 1963, President Lyndon B. Johnson made the war the main item on the U.S. government's foreign agenda. Vietnam was now involved in another war with another Western nation. African Americans faced the prospect of more discrimination and racism in the U.S. military despite the fact that President Harry Truman had given an executive order in 1948 ending segregation in the armed forces.

Some 274,937 African Americans served in the Vietnam War. That was 11 percent of the total number of persons who served. Nevertheless, African Americans accounted for 23 percent of the American deaths, giving rise to complaints that these soldiers were given the most dangerous assignments and were most frequently made pointmen, soldiers who lead other troops on search-and-destroy missions. White officers' explanations that the African American soldiers sought these missions were unverified. Although the armed services were now integrated, many racial problems still remained.

▲ Julian Bond

The battle against the North Vietnamese communists would prove to be one of the toughest faced by the United States military because of the guerilla nature of the war. The United States government introduced fake money into the North Vietnam economy, sending it into total disarray. The U.S. bombed North Vietnamese dams and dikes, causing severe floods. On December 26, 1971, more than 50 B-52s accompanied by about 50 fighter planes attacked the North Vietnamese city of Hanoi in the most deadly bombing raid of the war.

The North Vietnamese had terrible techniques of their own. Captured Americans were paraded before the Vietnamese people of Hanoi and taunted with insults. Vietnamese women carrying bombs entered clubs where Americans gathered and detonated or discharged their weapons causing considerable injury and death.

Dr. Martin Luther King, Jr., felt that the war was immoral. Julian Bond, SNCC communications director, was denied his elected seat in the Georgia House of Representatives because of his opposition to the war.

▼ Mohammed Ali

Boxing great Mohammed Ali, was stripped of his heavyweight boxing title for four years because he refused to serve in the army. Ali received a five-year sentence and a $10,000 fine for his refusal. He appealed the sentence. Three years later, the decision was reversed.

As a member of the Nation of Islam (NOI), Ali felt that it was against his religion to serve in the army. The leader of the NOI, Elijah Mohammed, had been jailed during the Second Major European War for declining to serve. As a follower of Elijah Mohammed, Mohammed Ali believed that he was doing the right thing by refusing to be involved in a war where Africans had no personal or collective stake. "The Vietnamese have never done anything to black people," he was fond of saying.

◆ CENTER YOUR THINKING

1. What is *capitalism?*
2. What was a finding of the Kerner Commission?
3. Why did many African Americans oppose the Vietnam War?
4. Select one law that was passed in the 1960s, and explain how it protects the rights you enjoy today.
5. HOLISTIC ACTIVITY Students as Researchers
   In African culture and traditions, there is heavy value on oratory, or speaking, and the power of the spoken word. One of the most powerful orators in the United States was Martin Luther King, Jr. Reread his "I Have a Dream" speech or listen to a tape recording. Analyze the distinctly African American aspects of the speech: for example, the use of metaphor, poetic rhythm, audience participation, and repetition for dramatic effect. Summarize your group's analysis for the class.

CHAPTER

54

ASANTE

THE BLACK STUDIES MOVEMENT

CENTER YOUR VOCABULARY

- ▲ relevant education
- ▲ Kawaida
- ▲ Afrocentric idea
- ▲ scholar-activist
- ▲ Kwanzaa
- ▲ agency

AS YOU READ

How did Black Studies programs in colleges and universities provide opportunities for students to learn and study from their own cultural points-of-view?

Coming in the wake of the Civil Rights Movement, the Black Studies movement on campuses around the country sent shock waves through American society. This round of change was most sharply felt in the colleges and universities around the country. *Black Studies* is the name given to the movement in schools and colleges to teach African and African American experiences as a subject in its own right, and not simply as a minor branch of U.S. or American culture and history.

The Black Studies movement began in 1967 when African American students at San Francisco State University began a protest for relevant education. The students were fed up with not seeing themselves or their culture reflected in the subjects they were being taught. It was hard for the students to see how the subjects in the classroom connected with their world. Some African American students went even further. They said that the majority of courses being taught were not relevant, meaning that the courses did not bear upon their lives in an immediate way. For example, students who took courses in American literature were not given the opportunity to study the works of African American writers such as Langston Hughes, Paul Laurence Dunbar, or Zora Neale Hurston. They were angered by the statements of some white professors that there were no African American writers worthy of study. Students demonstrated against such views by boycotting classes and occupying the offices of college administrators.

Nathan Hare, a sociologist and professor was the leading voice in the Black Studies movement in 1967. Hare had been a student of the famous sociologist E. Franklin Frazier at Howard University and had written a book, *The Black Anglo-Saxons*. As a result of the student protest, Hare was brought in by the administrators at San Francisco State College to help ease the tension between the African American students and the administrators. Hare was the most prominent faculty voice in support of the students. His advocacy and the students' persistence led to the opening of the first department of Black Studies in the nation in 1968. Soon after, departments and programs were set up at University of California campuses at Los Angeles (UCLA) and Berkeley, Cornell University, Northwestern, Ohio State, and the University of Wisconsin.

▲ Dr. Leonard Jeffries

The first generation of leaders of the Black Studies field included many scholar-activists, students who were active in the Civil Rights Movement but were now college and university professors. Some of these early leaders had organized student protests on the very campuses where the demonstrations for Black Studies were occurring. Outstanding figures in this first generation included Leonard Jeffries, who began his career at San Jose State; William Nelson at Ohio State; Sonja Stone at the University of North Carolina; Edward Crosby at Kent State; James Turner at Cornell University; Delores Aldridge at Emory University; Talmadge Anderson at Washington State University; and Ewart Guinier at Harvard. They were among the numerous pioneers in organizing African American Studies.

Among the scholars who wrote for this exciting new field were Maulana Karenga, Richard Long, Gerald McWorter, Winston Van Horne, and Linda James Myers. Karenga produced the most widely used text in the field, *Introduction to Black Studies*, which soon became a classic. It explained the need for the study of African Americans and placed the entire movement in the general framework of culture and activism.

Karenga became the embodiment of the Black Studies movement. His philosophy, known as Kawaida (customs), formed the basis of much of the Black Studies discussion on college campuses. He devoted years of study to the historical and cultural roots of African people, both in the Americas and in Africa. This meant that he had to master several languages, including French, Zulu, Kiswahili, Spanish, and the ancient Kemetic language, referred to as medu neter, the sacred writing of the Kemetic people.

▲ Maulana Karenga's work provided a foundation for the Black Studies movement on college campuses.

Karenga has received numerous honors and awards for his work in Black Studies. In 1994 he was honored by the Committee of the Cheikh Anta Diop (SHEK AN-tah JOH-pay) Conference as one of the major contemporary philosophers of Black Studies, and a figure who has contributed, both intellectually and culturally, to the reconstruction of African American values.

Departments of Black Studies began to teach the Kiswahili language in the late 1960s as a direct influence of the Kawaida movement. Karenga argued that Kiswahili was one of the least ethnic languages of Africa and therefore could be used as an international African language without creating tension among the various ethnic groups. The Festival of African People and Culture (FESPAC) proved Karenga's judgment correct when it decided in 1977 in Lagos, Nigeria, to use Kiswahili as the international African language.

According to Karenga, the need for a cultural revolution was so great that African Americans had to rebuild the way they approached religion, health, social welfare, fashions, economics, and politcs. But this could not be done in isolation. This change had to be connected to a new level of consciousness that involved discipline and action. With this in mind, Karenga founded *Kwanzaa* a cultural celebration of African American traditions and values. *Kwanzaa* means "first fruits" in Kiswahili. He adapted the seven principles of Kwanzaa to accommodate the needs of the African American community. Today, Kwanzaa incorporates the seven principles of community: *umoja,* unity; *kujichagulia,* self-determination; *ujima,* cooperative economics; *ujamaa,* collective work and responsibility; *nia*, purpose; *kuumba,* creativity; and *imani,* faith. With these ideas as guiding principles, many Black Studies programs would find a useful philosophical base for their academic curricula.

UCLA's struggle to develop a Black Studies program was typical of the situation on other college campuses. After intense debate in meetings with the chancellor and his staff, African American students were able to get a commitment for the establishment of the first Center of Afro-American Studies in the nation. As a research center, the Center of Afro-American Studies did not have the power of a department to hire faculty. But it had a budget that could be used to support faculty researchers and it could develop library materials. Although a department would have been more traditional and would have placed the Black Studies program more squarely in the power loop of the university, the administration convinced the students that a center could be more quickly developed. Thus, the center was seen as a major victory, given the difficulty the administration had convincing white faculty members of the value of the center. Victory was declared and more than $150,000 was allocated to the center to begin its work.

Robert Singleton, a Ph.D. student in economics, was asked to be the acting director until a search was completed. Arthur L. Smith, now Dr. Molefi Kete Asante and the author of this book, was hired as the first director of the center in 1969. Throughout the nation, at Northwestern, Cornell, Albany, Yale, Temple, Harvard, Ohio State, and numerous other colleges, the same process was unfolding. Students were pressing college administrations for change and winning some victories. There were, however, some institutions that refused to modify their curricula and their programs to accommodate the demands of African American students.

Dr. Molefi Kete Asante (standing) and Dr. John Henrik Clarke ▶

Like most centers and departments, the UCLA Center for Afro-American Studies celebrated African American life and culture and challenged the reigning ideologies of racism by producing scholarly essays to refute them. The center also promoted the integration of African culture on overwhelmingly white campuses by providing African art, dance, and cultural programming as well as political and social seminars. Never had the major colleges and universities had so many opportunities to study and learn about African Americans. In fact, African American scholars such as Arnold Bontemps, St. Clair Drake, Harold Cruse, and John Henrik Clarke were brought to some colleges as distinguished guest professors.

Departments of Black Studies rushed to demonstrate that they were worthy to be academic units by producing conferences, holding symposia, and engaging in debates with their colleagues on campus. On the other hand, students and faculty of the Black Studies departments and programs also taught community people composition, tutored young students, and volunteered with social agencies.

The departments created interracial communication classes, racial-understanding seminars, African American psychology, African religion, and African American dance forums. They hired African

American faculty members in response to the demands of their students. From coast to coast, the entire nation saw changes in colleges and universities. The field would eventually evolve as a strong academic discipline and in 1993 be given the name *Africology* by the African American Studies Department of the University of Wisconsin, Milwaukee. Many journals, articles, books, and other materials about the African world began to surface. This was truly a Black Studies revolution, but it was not without foundations. W.E.B. Du Bois, Martin Delaney, Edward Wilmot Blyden, Carter G. Woodson, Anna Julia Cooper, J. A. Rogers, Arthur Schomburg, Yosef ben-Jochannan, Benjamin Quarles, and many other scholars had already created the groundwork for the new thrust. Everywhere it seemed people were reading, interpreting, and discussing the meaning of the African cultural and social influences in the United States and the Caribbean. The *Journal of Black Studies* and the *Black Scholar* were among the many publications formed to keep the community and colleges involved in the spread of information. Schools were set up with the idea of teaching children literature, art, science, and history from their own cultural point-of-view.

This was to be the beginning of "a black perspective" later identified as the Afrocentric idea, that is, the giving of agency to African people. *Agency* means that African people are studied as subjects rather than as objects, as actors rather than people who are acted upon. This book is an exercise in the Afrocentric idea because it is written from the standpoint of African Americans as doers, builders and achievers: subjects in their own right and not objects on the fringes of others' history.

The National Council for Black Studies was formed in 1974 as the organization committed to advancing and promoting the professional interests of the field. On campuses, students have formed organizations such as the Black Students Union, the African People's Club, and the Pan African Association. By 1988, there were more than 250 colleges with Departments of Black Studies, Africana Studies or Africology in the nation. The Department of African American Studies at Temple University became the first department to establish a Ph.D. program. In 1994, 25 students received their doctorates in African American Studies from Temple University, making them the first to receive a terminal degree from an African American Studies department.

◆ CENTER YOUR THINKING

1. What is the meaning of *Africology?*
2. How do you define *culturally relevant education?*
3. The author states that many African American scholars had created the groundwork for the Black Studies movement. Identify three African American scholars, and describe their contributions to the Black Studies movement.
4. How does the author define *agency?* Give examples of ways that Black Studies programs helped to give agency to African Americans.
5. HOLISTICS ACTIVITY Students as Activists

   Form a small group and imagine that you are African American students at a major university during the 1970s. You have convinced the university administration to establish an African Studies department. What are some of the courses that you would propose to be offered as part of the curriculum? Write brief summaries of these proposed courses, and then write them up as they would be written in a university catalog of new courses. Present the catalog to your classmates, and discuss the merits of each course.

SUGGESTED READINGS

Autobiography of Malcom X

Berry, Mary F. & John Blassingame. *Long Memory: The Black Experience.*

Carmichael, Stokely and Charles Hamilton. *Black Power: The Politics of Liberation in America.* New York: Vintage Books, 1967.

Chambers, Bradford. *Chronicles of Black Protest.*

King, Martin L. *Why We Can't Wait.*

Lincoln, C. Eric. *Black Muslims in America.*

Lincoln, C. Eric. *The Negro Pilgrimate in America.*

Malcolm Speaks

Seale, Bobby. *Seize the Time*

UNIT REVIEW

SUMMARY

The Civil Rights Movement was built on the contributions of earlier African American activists in what became known as the Second Reconstruction. African Americans made great sacrifices to oppose racism and discrimination, organizing boycotts that were effective throughout the South as a civil disobedience strategy to fight segregation. *(Chapter 49)*

Malcolm X inspired a sense of nationalism and unity among people of African descent. He emphasized that African Americans had the right to use violence in response to violent persecution by whites. *(Chapter 50)*

Some African Americans disagreed that violence, even if justified, should be used to fight racial oppression. Dr. Martin Luther King, Jr., who became a major leader in the Civil Rights Movement, advocated nonviolent protest, a form of passive resistance. *(Chapter 51)*

The Civil Rights Movement focused on ending discrimination and injustice against African Americans in the South. The Student Nonviolent Coordinating Committee, Congress of Racial Equality, Southern Christian Leadership Conference, NAACP, and other organizations used the judicial system, sit-ins, and other nonviolent actions to fight segregation. The term *black power* was a rallying cry for young African Americans in the movement. *(Chapter 52)*

Some African Americans defended the use of force to counter violence from others. The Black Panthers, for example, believed that oppressive violence should be fought with resistant violence. *(Chapter 52)*

The ironclad rule of white supremacists began to erode in the South. Still, many African Americans were outraged by the slow pace of change. Some questioned the reasons for African American participation in the Vietnam War. After the assassination of Dr. Martin Luther King, Jr., peaceful and violent demonstrations occurred on college campuses and in cities nationwide. African American activism caused many improvements, including the passage of new legislation to protect the civil rights of all, the creation of Black Studies programs in universities, and the establishment of Kwanzaa as the first distinctly African American holiday. *(Chapter 53)*

Personal Witnessing

REFLECTION

Think about some of the attributes that made the African American leaders in this unit so effective and great. Write your thoughts in your journal.

TESTIMONY

You have been appointed director of a newly formed African American Studies Department in a large university. It is 1960. Write a speech or paper to present on the subject of the need and importance of establishing African American Studies as a discipline in other universities.

Unit 15 Rite of Passage

Review the seven Nguzo Saba principles. Create your own individual or group expression of the seven principles. Design your creative expression in Unit 15, and include a description of it in your Portfolio. Be sure that you include all seven principles. You will perform your expression for your Rite of Passage for Unit 16.

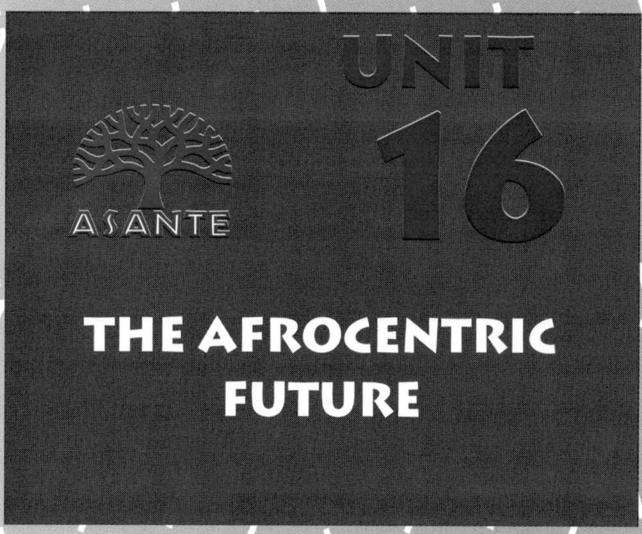

UNIT 16

ASANTE

THE AFROCENTRIC FUTURE

Brainstorm a list of reasons to be proud of African Americans and the new lessons you have learned in this book as you study from an African-centered viewpoint. Now, make a creative presentation in any format your group chooses to demonstrate why the 21st century will be one of triumph for African Americans.

As you read this unit, the triumph of the African American struggle becomes obvious. What goals do you have for the 21st century?

1971
Jesse Jackson founds People United to Save Humanity (P.U.S.H.)

1972
First National Black Political Convention in Gary, Indiana

Shirley Chisholm runs for president

1973
Thomas Bradley is elected mayor of Los Angeles

Coleman Young is elected mayor of Detroit

1974
Maynard Jackson is elected mayor of Atlanta

Over 200 African Americans attend the 6th annual Pan-African Congress in Dar es Salaam

Frank Robinson becomes the first African American manager of a professional baseball team (Cleveland Indians)

1976
Andrew Young is named U.S. Ambassador and Chief Delegate to the United Nations

“ *Who*
can be born black
and not
sing
the wonder of it
the joy
the
challenge
Who
can be born
black
and not exult! ”

MARI EVANS,
WE SPEAK AS BLACK POETS

1977
Alex Hailey's *Roots* airs on network television

1978
Major Frederick D. Gregory, Major Guion S. Bluford and Dr. Ronald E. McNair become the first three African American astronauts

1980
Major race riots occur in Miami, Florida. At least 18 persons are killed and more than 300 injured

1984
Jesse Jackson runs for president of the United States

1989
Nelson Mandela is released from prison.

Colin Powell becomes head of Joint Chiefs of Staff, the highest ranking military position held by an African American

1990
Douglass Wilder is elected as Governor of Virginia

1994
Nelson Mandela is elected president of free South Africa

1995
Dr. Bernard A. Harris, Jr., a physician, is the first African American astronaut to walk in space

CHAPTER 55

ASANTE

THE AFROCENTRIC FUTURE

CENTER YOUR VOCABULARY

- ▲ genres
- ▲ discrimination
- ▲ patrons
- ▲ subtle

AS YOU READ

Who are African Americans? What battles against bias are still being fought?

Counting the battles won and lost, the African American community record book is weighted on the side of victory. All of the strife, tension, pain, suffering, and ill-will can never be fully explained, but one thing is sure: African Americans are respected throughout the world for their consistent and persistent struggle against all forms of racial prejudice and discrimination.

People in other nations use the themes and the songs of the African American freedom movement as their own. The Chinese students who protested against the communist regime in Beijing's Tienanman Square in 1990 sang "We Shall Overcome," a classic African American freedom song. So, yes, African Americans have come a long way when the world now sings the songs their forefathers and mothers sang in their struggle for equality and justice.

As we approach the 21st century, African Americans represent nearly 12 percent of the U.S. population. The diversity of the African American population reflects the energy and dynamism of today's society. There are African people from the Caribbean, Africa, Central and South America, the Middle East, Alaska, Europe, Asia, and many other regions that now comprise the African American community. One of the leading African American cinematographers is Haile Gerima who was born in Ethiopia. Shirley Chisholm, former congresswoman and the first African American female to run for

▲ Former congresswoman Shirley Chisolm is the first African American woman to run for president.

president, is from Barbados. Colin Powell, former chairman of the Joint Chiefs of Staff for the U.S. military, was born in the United States of Jamaican parents. Carlos Moore, a leading African American intellectual is Cuban. Ama Mazama, the distinguished linguist, is from Guadaloupe. Mustafa Hefny, the African educator who fought to have his racial classification changed from white to African, was born in Egypt. Marta Vega, the founder of the Caribbean Cultural Center of New York, is Puerto Rican. Yet all of these individuals participate in the traditional African American community.

Today, African Americans stand firmly on the foundations of struggle laid by a diverse group of committed individuals who were driven by the demands of their community.

But full equality has not been achieved. We have a long way to go. African Americans and whites still come up with different answers to national questions such as, "Does discrimination still exist?" "Are whites given greater opportunities than African Americans?" Different views are expressed by whites and African Americans on many issues. This is seen quite often in politics where opinion polls

▼ General Colin Powell, former chairman, Joint Chiefs of Staff, shakes hands with crew members of the battleship *USS Wisconsin* in the Persian Gulf.

show that whites and African Americans have opposite views on individual freedom and fairplay.

Today, African Americans are gravely concerned about the crisis in Haiti and U.S. treament of Haitian refugees, economic support for Africa, and the creation of a mixed-race category for the upcoming census, among other issues. African Americans are also continuing the struggle against economic discrimination. There is a large number of African Americans who remain outside the economic avenue of power. Sometimes, entire families have been so victimized or abused by the legacies of enslavement that they cannot see themselves ever rising beyond their current circumstances.

History has shown that without government support, there will never be equal opportunity for African Americans stuck at the bottom of the economic ladder. In fact, banks still discriminate in loaning money to African Americans. On home mortgages, for example, many large banks deny mortgages more frequently to African Americans than whites. When mortgage loans are approved, African Americans' are charged a higher rate of interest than whites. African Americans rage, given the incredible sacrifices generations of Africans have made to the United States, is certainly normal and justified. If African Americans did not express any signs of rage, perhaps they would need to have their sanity questioned.

Civil rights legislation created opportunities and made it illegal for whites to discriminate against African Americans. But the law has its limits. Discrimination exists when individuals use every means at their disposal to get around the law. Many people have found new ways to obstruct the law and frustrate justice. This kind of discrimination is so subtle that it is very difficult to prove. For example, if the law says that African Americans must be admitted into public hotels, an owner can chose to turn the hotel into a private club with restrictions that are guaranteed to keep African Americans out. If the law says that it is illegal to deny African Americans access to employment, a company can create artificial requirements such as a recommendation from someone who has worked in the position being filled or some other requirement that has little to do with the

▲ Astronaut Mae Jemison

candidate's ability to perform that job. Failure to meet these and other obscure requirements allows the discriminating company to argue that African Americans do not meet company standards. This kind of reasoning is no different from the logic that 19th century whites used when they created the Grandfather Clause that allowed an African American to vote only if his grandfather had voted before 1867 (See Chapter 37). While civil rights legislation did not change people's prejudices, it did restrict their ability to openly discriminate against African Americans as they had done in the past.

Civil rights legislation has helped to create more African American millionaires, more middle-class professionals, and more avenues for social and economic advancement for those with ambition and

A young Bill Cosby (left) played football at Temple University and worked evenings as a bartender before becoming the first African American to star in a prime time TV series. He is one of the most successful performers and businesspersons in the United States. ▶

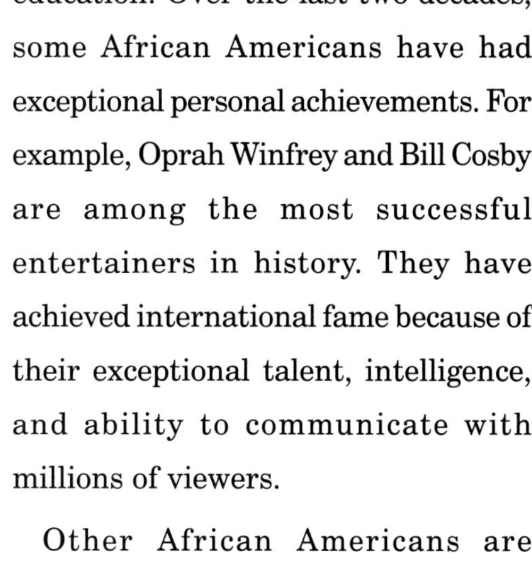

education. Over the last two decades, some African Americans have had exceptional personal achievements. For example, Oprah Winfrey and Bill Cosby are among the most successful entertainers in history. They have achieved international fame because of their exceptional talent, intelligence, and ability to communicate with millions of viewers.

Other African Americans are recognized for their intellectual, scientific and artistic gifts. Mae Jemison, Cornel West, Maulana Karenga, Whoopi Goldberg, Manning Marable, Bell Hooks, and Marimba Ani, among hundreds of others, are now household names. The University of North Carolina in Chapel Hill boasts more African American holders of distinguished chairs than any other university.

▲ Whoopi Goldberg

African American athletes are found in nearly all world-class athletic competitions.

▲ "Mother" Clara McBride Hale and daughter, Dr. Lorraine E. Hale have devoted years of loving service to disadvantaged African American children.

In politics, numerous elected officials attest to the power of the vote and the eagerness with which African Americans have entered the arena of civic responsibility. In science, there are hundreds of active practitioners in every branch of human sciences. In law, African Americans have made steady progress in the legal field. In art and literature, the works of the painters, sculptors, writers and film makers excel in almost all genres or categories. In human service, African Americans are not without their patrons or sponsors of goodwill.

◆ CENTER YOUR THINKING

1. What percentage of the U.S. population is made up of African Americans?
2. Give an example of how individuals are able to get around the civil rights laws in order to discriminate against African Americans.
3. In your opinion, why would African Americans be gravely concerned about the creation of a mixed-race category for the population census?
4. Why do you think that African Americans and whites still come up with different answers to national questions such as "Does discrimination still exist?"
5. HOLISTIC ACTIVITY Students as Newscasters
   You are a group of network newscasters on one of the Sunday morning television news-analysis programs. The question you will be discussing is: "What are the implications of adding the category *mixed-race* to the U.S. census?" Discuss your opinions, and debate them. If time permits, hold your discussion in front of the class as the audience, and let them "call in" their questions to you.

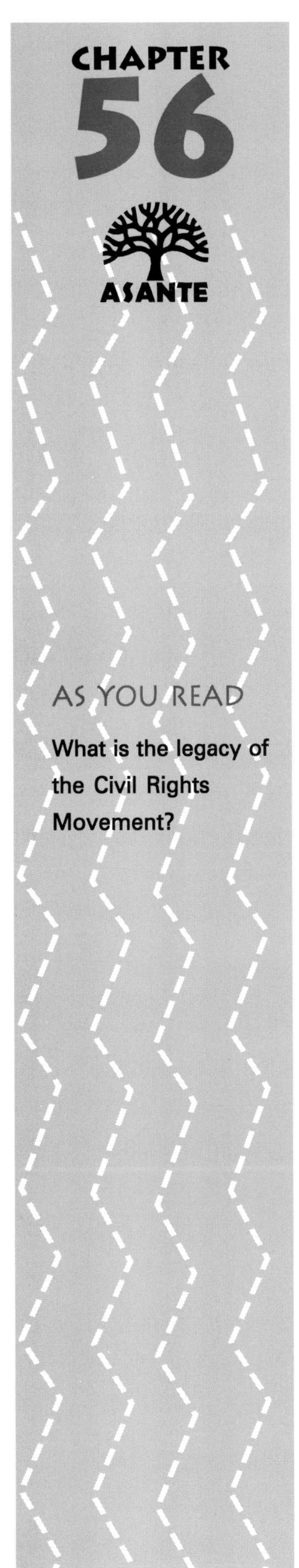

POLITICAL EMPOWERMENT

CENTER YOUR VOCABULARY

- ▲ affirmative action
- ▲ liberal
- ▲ Afrocentricity
- ▲ conservative
- ▲ electorate
- ▲ Pan African

The last three decades have seen the acquisition of some political empowerment as a record number of African Americans gained political office. Their weight is felt in most large cities because the African American vote often means the difference between winning and losing for many candidates.

The political atmosphere during the Republican administrations of Ronald Reagan and George Bush seemed hostile to the advancement of civil rights and to a harmonious relationship between African Americans and whites. In fact, the African American community believed that with the election of Ronald Reagan, the United States was turning its back on an activist past. Several actions on the part of the Republican administrations were seen as harmful to the interests of African Americans. Actions by these two presidents seemed to disregard the historic battles that African Americans have fought for justice. The Republican administrations literally challenged the militant tradition of seeking affirmative action, a program for correcting discrimination in employment and education against African Americans and other groups.

Both Presidents Reagan and Bush appointed judges and other officials who disagreed with affirmative action and other progressive

▲ Members of the Supreme Court

programs for African Americans. President George Bush, for instance, nominated Clarence Thomas, a conservative African American judge to fill Justice Thurgood Marshall's seat on the U.S. Supreme Court. One of the characteristics of someone who is described as a conservative is opposition to established traditions or institutions. Clarence Thomas earned this title for his opposition to affirmative action programs, among others. The majority of African American civil rights leaders and many educators opposed Thomas's appointment on the basis of his weak qualifications and his lack of involvement with seeking justice for women and African Americans. Judge Thomas was seen as a figurehead or symbol for the conservative Republican Party.

▲ Thurgood Marshall

African Americans responded with a great show of support for Democrat President Bill Clinton. They supported Clinton for his liberal or progressive position on issues such as universal health care because many African Americans do not have adequate health coverage. The 1992 election appeared to be a turning point for change.

African American mayors were elected in major cities, such as Washington, New York, Philadelphia, Cleveland, Detroit, Gary, Atlanta, Kansas City, Los Angeles, Newark, Birmingham, and Denver.

▲ Rev. Jesse Jackson

These gains were tempered by the election of a Republican Senate and House in the 1994 election.

Longtime civil rights activist Jesse Jackson, who had sought the Democratic Party nomination for president in 1984 and again in 1988, viewed the 1994 election as a time for deep reflection. What did it mean for the African American community that a conservative electorate bent on stopping the progressive movement ushered in by the Clinton administration had gained its way?

By 1995, African Americans could look back at a long list of African Americans who had demonstrated outstanding skills in government, education, and science. General Colin Powell served well as chairman of the Joint Chiefs of Staff from 1989 to 1993. He was the leading strategist in the Persian Gulf War, and is universally respected as a military leader.

Ron Brown was elected chairman of the Democratic National Committee during a time when the Reagan-Bush Republican coalition was strongest. He succeeded in strategizing to elect Clinton with an overwhelming outpouring of African American votes, enough to give Clinton a fighting chance against Bush, who had a majority of white votes. Brown subsequently became Secretary of Commerce and was the first African American to hold this position in the U.S. government.

In 1990, L. Douglas Wilder became the first elected African American governor in Virginia. P. B. S. Pinchback had acted as governor of Louisiana in 1873 for six weeks after the white governor was removed, but he had been appointed, not elected.

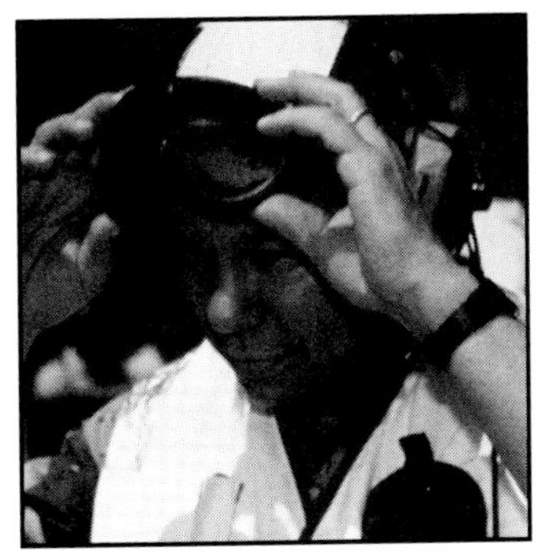

▲ Colin Powell

Carol Moseley Braun from Chicago became the first African American female U.S. Senator. She has championed women's rights and civil rights during her time in office.

The number of congressional Black Caucus members rose from 26 to 43 in 1992. During the 1994 congressional takeover by the Republicans, the Black Caucus lost some of its influence. The Republicans cut the support staffs and budget of the Black Caucus.

THE TORCH IS PASSED

A growing number of African Americans have realized that political and economic influence is not enough to change conditions in their community. Without an awareness of the traditions, culture, and values that have played major roles in their survival, the majority of African Americans will still be lost in America. If an African American politician does not serve the interests of his or her discriminated community, then that person must be seen as a traitor to the interests of the people. If someone becomes an economic success, worth millions of dollars, but does not spend his or her money in a way that creates better living conditions in African American communities, then that person has only succeeded in sucking the life blood out of the community. Therefore, political and economical empowerment is not simply a matter of political or economic power, but also a grounding in social and cultural awareness to influence political and economic decisions.

Modern leaders of the African American community must be committed to changing the thinking of African Americans from the enslavement mentality of the past where Africans expected others to solve all of their problems to the more aggressive, ambitious, and self-reliant position of African Americans helping themselves as much as possible. This is the attitude of the philosophy of Afrocentricity, the most current thinking on the question of African American agency, or the ability to act for oneself.

Afrocentricity is the process of viewing African people as subjects in history rather than as victims operating on the fringes of society. To search for one's center is one way to find the things that are changeable and to change them. This philosophy has been adopted by thousands of people around the world who believe that the concept is applicable within many different cultures. Take, for example, the idea of Latinocentricity as it relates to people of that ethnic background. Members of the Latino community who see themselves as subjects rather than as objects become actors in their own history. But the reason centeredness is especially necessary for African Americans is because the enslavement took them so far away from their cultural, religious, geographical and psychological center that they became displaced and decentered.

The need for Afrocentricity is recognized around the world. An entirely new group of leaders, committed to a Pan African worldview, or the collective uplifting of African people all over the world, has emerged in the African American community. They see the interaction between the Caribbean, South America, Africa, and North America as positive and productive. The Africans in these regions are all Pan-African and all have Afrocentric inclinations. Hundreds of these individuals live in the United States today. They are creating change and consciousness through organizations such as the National Afrocentric Institute, the revived National Association for the Advancement of Colored People, minister Louis Farrakhan's Nation of Islam, the Association for the Study of Classical African Civilizations, and numerous other local institutions.

◆ CENTER YOUR THINKING

1. Who was the first elected African American governor of Virginia? When was he elected?
2. What reasons were given for African American support for President Clinton?
3. How were the administrations of Presidents Reagan and Bush hostile to the advancement of civil rights?
4. What is the relationship between Afrocentricity and a Pan-African worldview?
5. HOLISTIC ACTIVITY Students as Community Leaders Dr. Asante describes Afrocentricity as African people acting, from an inside view, as subjects of their own history rather than as objects acted upon or victims. You are a group of African American community leaders. How will you actively communicate your interpretation of this philosophy in your community? Discuss and write a strategy. As a class, discuss ways to implement in your school and community some of the strategies that the groups create.

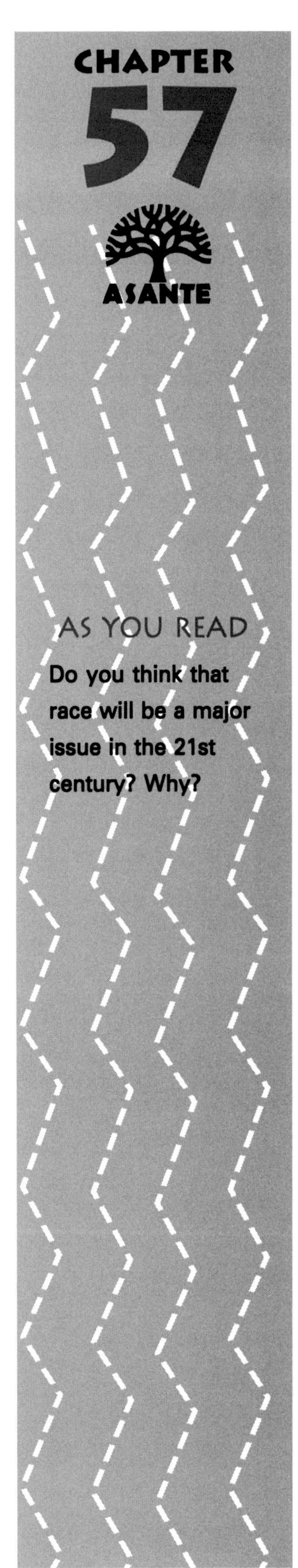

BRING ON THE 21ST CENTURY

CENTER YOUR VOCABULARY

▲ millenium ▲ rites of passage

Perhaps few people in the United States of America are as happy as African Americans to be facing a new century, indeed a new millenium. Everywhere the word is: "Bring on the 21st century and we will see what we will do!" The past battles can only serve now as guides, road maps, and atlases of where we have been and where we must go. The present battles must be framed in the context of new beginnings.

The 20th century opened with the question of race at the top of the U.S. agenda. The century closes without the issue having been resolved. It is still on the agenda, perhaps not so prominently as before, but certainly a thorn in the side of our national progress and unity. Yet, African Americans are an optimistic, hardworking, joyous people and as an African American I join them in saying, "Bring it on!"

Why is this sound of confidence heard among people who have survived the muddy fields of racism, whose very lives have been trapped in a quagmire of prejudice and discrimination? It is because the voices of the ancestors, always present in the ways we approach life and death, can never release us from our sense of justice and destiny. Did not the early fighters for justice believe that African Americans' struggle for equality would humanize the nation and create a sense of harmony from the disharmony? Could this be the

▲ Filmmaker Spike Lee finds inspiration in the dynamic experiences of ordinary and extraordinary African Americans.

source of the old negro spirituals when we knew that victory was possible, or the origin of the Blues when we thought victory was impossible?

Look at the contemporary music in the community. Rap, or hip-hop, has become a modern African American musical form with a powerful political message. Throughout the African world, music has always been used to convey messages. There is no art for art's sake, and there is no music for music's sake. All art is to transform human beings, to bring us closer to the victory over decay and disharmony.

Rap artists urge African American youth to "fight the power" by knowing African and African American history and culture, by avoiding drugs and gangs, by staying in school, but most important, by being militantly opposed to discrimination against gender, race, and color. This militancy must be with purpose, direction, and tradition. These are the key components of a conscious and active political and cultural life.

NEW HEIGHTS

White response to rap music has been equally political. It is the same response that whites have traditionally made to African American activism. African American resistance, including revolts against enslavement, crusades against lynching, challenges to unfair treatment in the military, and agitation for civil rights have all brought the same reaction—that somehow African Americans do not have the right to protest against mistreatment in this country. The irony is that as government officials condemn African Americans for seeking equality and justice, they command them, along with others, to travel to Iraq to engage the Iraqis over the invasion of Kuwait. The African American soldiers who fought in the Persian Gulf War in 1991 did so as members of the same government that was literally kicking us in our history, disrespecting our traditions,

▲ The assembled crew of the *USS Wisconsin* listened to an address by General Colin Powell during the Persian Gulf War.

and refusing to allow our culture and history to be taught in the public schools. Yet, we say bring on the 21st century because we will establish a pattern of human achievement based on our ancient and contemporary experiences that will propel us and this nation to greater heights of glory.

More than 50 percent of the African American community opposed the Persian Gulf War. The 132,300 African Americans who served made up 24.5 percent of the total number of military personnel engaged in the conflict.

Nevertheless, we say, "Bring on the 21st century" because we will be so glad to leave this one. Change has happened, that is a fact. But racism is still here with us and the job for the future is cut out for us, we only have to put the pieces together and bind them with the proper stitching.

▼ Dr. Bernard A. Harris, Jr., the first African American to walk in space, is shown with his partner aboard the space shuttle *Discovery* in February 1995

As we look to the future, we see many wonderful things ahead. Following Dr. Bernard Harris's historic walk in space February 10, 1995, we anticipate a future filled with many more African American astronauts breaking new barriers. Dr. Bernard A. Harris Jr., a

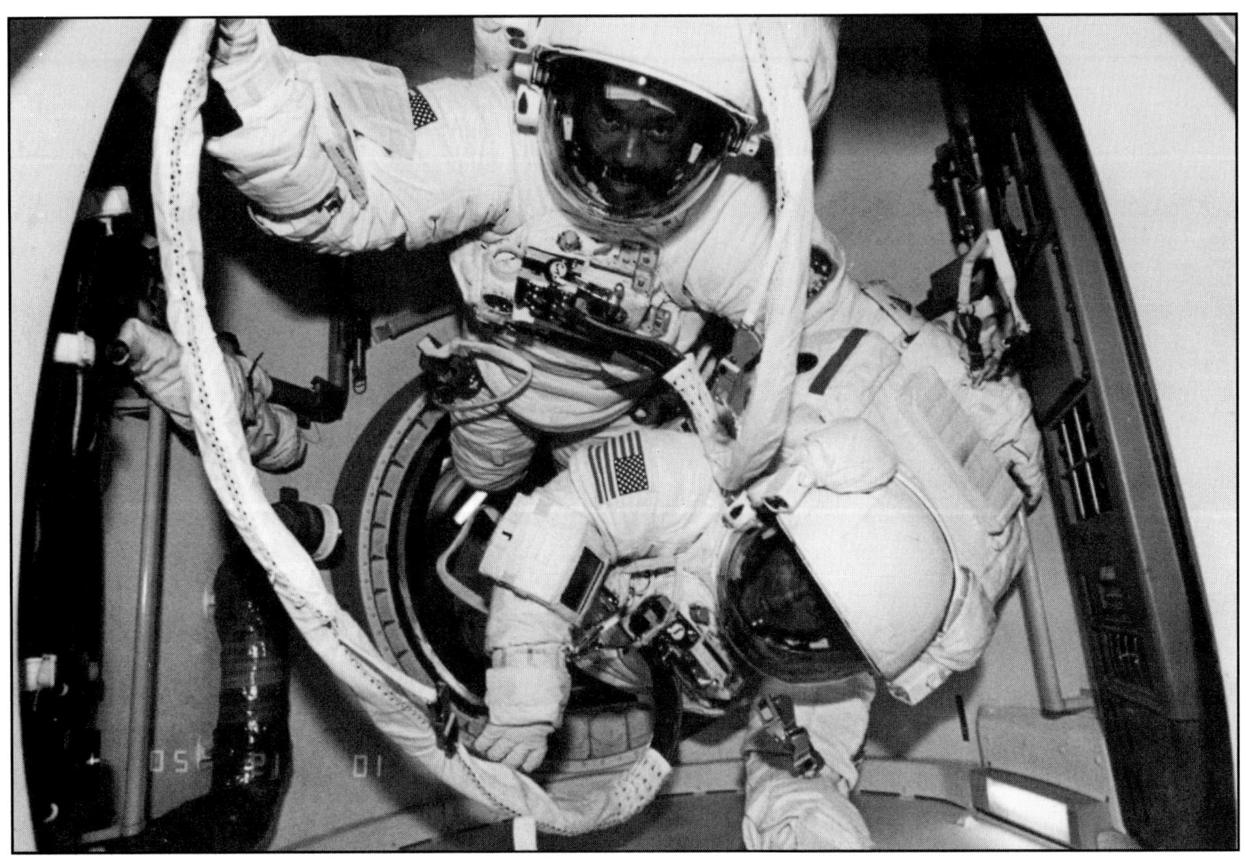

▲ On the forefront of change, the first African American female cadets at Westpoint.

physician and currently one of only two African American astronauts in the National Aeronautics and Space Administration (NASA) program, is the first African American to walk in space. Dr. Harris teamed up with five astronauts aboard the space shuttle *Discovery* to help NASA determine how future space walkers will handle massive objects in the construction of a planned international space station.

In addition to our achievements in science and technology, African people throughout the world will support the movement toward a new reality. The movement toward multiple cultural centers, African, Latino, Asian, and white, among many others, will help to free whites from racism and prejudice. It will also play a key role in liberating women from sexism. Respect and appreciation for our different cultures can only improve understanding and appreciation for our own differences.

▲ African scholar Dr. Asa Hilliard wears traditional African clothes and jewelry.

Being centered in one's own history does not mean ridiculing those of other cultural centers; actually, centeredness is the cornerstone of respect for difference. Those who are not sure of their own culture often show prejudice and bias toward others. The centered person is knowledgeable, sensitive, and open to the many ways human societies evolve. One cannot remain closed to the impact of these forces that are around us.

Change is coming. African Americans are on the forefront of technological change, but we are also holding on to the traditions of the past. Many wear traditional African clothes, jewelry, and hairstyles. We give our children African names and are adopting ancient African traditions such as rites of passage to prepare young African Americans to meet the challenges of a new age. African

Americans will continue to excel in art, science, electronics, literature, sports and communications. A people long oppressed cannot and will not be oppressed forever. As we achieved our physical freedom in the 19th century, and our legal freedom in the 20th century, the 21st century will be the century of our mental and psychological freedom. Bring on the 21st century!

◆ CENTER YOUR THINKING

1. Name one outcome that the author feels will be achieved by African Americans in the 21st century.
2. In your opinion, why did more than half of African Americans oppose the Persian Gulf War?
3. Do you agree with Dr. Asant's outlook on the 21st century? Explain why you agree or disagree.
4. Explain how rap music can be compared with the political activism of past African Americans.
5. HOLISTIC ACTIVITY Students as Rap Artists
   Create a rap expressing your views on discrimination and the solutions for it. Write your rap down in a booklet to share with the class, and perform your rap for the class.

SUGGESTED READINGS

Asante, Molefi. *Afrocentricity;* Africa World Press, Trenton, N.J. 1980.

Asante, Molefi and Mark Mattson. *Historical and Cultural Atlas of African Americans*; Macmillan, N.Y. 1991.

Hornsby, Alton. *Milestones in 20th Century African American History*.

Keto, C. Tsehloane. *Africa–Centered Perspective of History*; K&A Publishers, Blackwood, N.J. 1991.

Tate, Greg. *Flyboy in the Buttermilk: Essays on Contemporary America*.

SUMMARY

Today, African Americans are a diverse group composed of people from many parts of the world. The legacy of enslavement continues to affect many African Americans. While legislation has been passed to protect their rights, discrimination still exists. *(Chapter 55)*

African Americans have exerted a significant influence on the political process. Elected officials have played varying roles in terms of responding to the best interests of African Americans. African American leaders themselves must be committed to an approach of self-help and self-reliance, an approach that recognizes and incorporates the collective uplift of African people throughout the world. *(Chapter 56)*

The close of the 20th century has not been accompanied by the resolution of the problems facing African Americans. Today, whites respond to the political messages of rap music in the same ways as they have traditionally responded to African American activism. The legacy of African people throughout the world will be to maintain a moral voice against racism, prejudice, and discrimination. *(Chapter 57)*

REFLECTION

Reflect on how this book has affected you. How have your views changed? What do you think about an Afrocentric outlook? about the future of America? of African Americans? How do you feel about learning history from a centered perspective, inside a culture?

TESTIMONY

Write an essay expressing your views on the book and on Dr. Asante's philosophy. How do you recommend changing education to help end discrimination?

Perform or share one of your Rites of Passage from a unit. If possible, invite the community, your family, and young children. Include mementos of your performance in your Portfolio.

For all students judged worthy on all 16 Rites of Passage activities, now is the time for a Rites of Passage ceremony. Finalize plans for the ceremony you began designing in Unit 12.

GLOSSARY

A

abolitionist (ah-boh-LIH-shun-ihst) a person who is openly in favor of ending enslavement

abridgment (uh-BRIJ-mehnt) a reduction or shortening

absurd ridiculously unreasonable, unsound, and meaningless

accommodation (uh-kom-moh-DAY-shun) to please a person or group, even if you don't believe or prefer the item or action yourself

accords (ah-CAWRDZ) agreements, usually written and signed

acquitted (uh-KWIH-tehd) discharged completely, as a court would discharge an accused person who has been found not guilty or for reasons of insufficient evidence

activism (AK-tih-vihsm) the practice of direct, vigorous action in support of or in opposition to one side of an often controversial issue

advance man (ad-VANTS) someone who prepares a person, a group of people, an area, or an object for an oncoming event, person, or group of people

advocate (AHD-voh-cayt) the supporter of a person, group, principle, or idea

affirmative action (uh-FUHR-muh-tihv AHK-shuhn) an active effort to improve the employment or education opportunities of minority groups and women

Africalogists (ah-frik-AH-loh-jists) those who teach about ancient Africa

African Americans (AH-frih-kuhn uh-MEH-rih-kihnz) a term used for Africans who lived in the United States after emancipation

African-centered curriculum (AH-frih-kuhn SEHN-tuhrd kuh-RIH-kyoo-luhm) a course of study that focuses on African history, traditions, and customs as its core

Africans' rights (AH-frih-kuhnz REYETZ) the rights of African Americans as granted to all people by the U.S. Constitution

Africology (ah-frik-AH-loh-jee) title given by Black Studies departments to the field of African American studies

Afrocentric ideas (ah-froh-sehn-TRIK eye-DEE-uhs) the idea of African Americans as doers, builders, and subjects in their own rights and not on the fringes of others' history

Afrocentricity (ah-froh-sehn-TRIH-sih-tee) the process of viewing African people as subjects in history rather than as victims who operate on the fringes of society

agency (AY-gehn-see) a person or thing through which power is exerted or an end is achieved

agitate (AH-juh-tayt) to attempt to arouse public feeling by disturbing, troubling, and shaking up the people

agitation (ah-juh-TAY-shun) the arousal of public feeling by disturbing, troubling, and shaking up the people

alleged (uh-LEHJD) statements that are stated but not proven

amended (uh-MEHN-dehd) to have something added to or changed in a spoken or written item such as a book, a document, a statement, or a speech

amendment (uh-MEHND-mehnt) an addition to or a change in a spoken or written item such as a book, a document, a statement, or a speech

Americans (uh-MEH-rih-kehnz) all the races and classes of people who migrated to the Western Hemisphere to live permanently and to become a part of the "melting-pot" concept

Americas (uh-MEH-rih-kuhz) North, Central, and South America, including Mexico

amnesty (AM-neh-stee) the granting of a pardon to a person or group of people

ancestors (AN-ses-terz) those from whom people are descended, such as great grandparents

antebellum (an-tee-BEHL-luhm) before the war, usually in reference to the Civil War

anthropologist (an-throh-PAH-loh-jist) one who studies the origin, nature, and destiny of human beings

apartheid (uh-PAHR-teyed) the system of racial separation that served to oppress the African population in South Africa

architecture (are-kih-TEHK-tyoor) the science of designing and building

aristocracy (ah-rihs-TOK-ruh-see) the elite class; the wealthiest class

Asiento (ah-SYEHN-toh) the contract, created by the Spanish rulers, that gave traders the exclusive right to take Africans from Africa to the Spanish colonies for a 30-year period; the contract was bought and sold to the highest bidder many times over.

assassinated (uh-SAH-sih-nay-ted) murdered, usually for political reasons

assumption (ah-SUMP-shun) an underlying thought that is promoted as fact

autobiography (aw-toh-beye-AH-gruh-fee) a life story written by the subject of it

autonomy (aw-TAH-noh-mee) self-leadership

B

B.C.E. before the Common Era

Black Codes a series of 19th-century laws and practices used to control the activities of free Africans in both the North and the South; their movements, choice of professions, education, and social life were severely restricted; enslaved Africans, of course, had no rights whatsoever.

Black Cross Arthur Moziah Garvey's version of the Red Cross, part of his work to establish a higher self-image and self-esteem for African Americans and more self-reliance

blacklisted (BLAHK-lihs-tihd) to be boycotted when considered for work; to be refused work because of one's supposed unpopular political, social, or ethnic position

Black Studies (BLAK STUH-deez) a concentration in education on African history, culture, psychology, religion, traditions, and ethics; later, the field was called *Africology* by Black Studies departments.

bonds (BAHNDZ) money that is posted to guarantee the good behavior of someone; in Chapter 25, this refers to the bond that free Africans had to post, guaranteeing that they be mild mannered, respectful of white domination, and nonpolitical.

boycott (BOI-kaht) the refusal to use a certain facility (such as public transportation) or to buy a certain product ion protest against a policy connected with that item

bribes (BREYEBZ) valuable goods or amounts of money that were paid to people to commit crimes

C

C.E. in the Common Era

capitalism (KAP-uh-tuhl-ihsm) an economic system, based on belief in the individual—that individuals should own the means of producing wealth—in which the majority of goods and services are produced by privately owned companies for a profit

censored (SEHN-suhrd) examined in order to suppress or delete anything that is considered objectionable

centering (SEHN-tuh-ring) giving central focus to a parti-cular idea or position

chattel (CHAT-tuhl) personal property to be bought or sold according to the owner's wishes; enslaved Africans were consid-ered to be chattel by their enslavers and by the law

chronology (krah-NAH-loh-gee) an arrangement or listing of events in the order in which they happened

citizen (SIH-tih-zihn) a person who lives in a certain region, is entitled to all the rights and privileges of a freeman, owes allegiance to a government, and is entitled to protection by it

civil disobedience (SIH-vihl dihs-oh-BEE-dee-ehnts) the challenging of particular laws by breaking them or by refusing to obey government demands in order to effect change in the laws or in policy; perhaps the most well-known case was the refusal of the Southern states' governments to integrate public schools in the 1950s and 1960s.

civil libertarian (SIH-vihl lih-buhr-TAIR-ee-uhn) a person who advocates and fights for individual rights

civil rights (SIH-vihl REYETZ) the nonpolitical rights of a person—in particular, the right to personal liberty

Civil War (SIH-vihl) the war between the federal union and the seceded confederacy of states (1861-1865)

collateral (coh-LAH-tuhr-uhl) a pledge that something will happen, or a token of security against damage

collective economics (kuh-LEHK-tihv eh-coh-NOM-iks) the belief on the part of Marcus Moziah Garvey that African Americans would pool their resources to set up their own businesses

colonialism (kuh-LOH-nee-uhl-ihsm) one power establishes control of a group of people, making them dependent on them and, usually, giving them feelings of inferiority

color line an imaginary boundary that separates people of different races

common labor ordinary work of the most menial kind

communism (KAH-myoo-nihsm) the theory that said that all means of producing wealth should be owned by the government

comply (kuhm-PLEYE) to conform or adapt one's activity to someone's authority, to a rule or law, or to a directive

compromise (KOM-proh-meyez) a settlement of differences by arbitration or mutual consent following the giving up on either side of some parts of their demands in order to reach agreement

condemn (kuhn-DEHM) to declare to be wrong or evil

condescending (kahn-duh-SEHN-ding) characterized by an attitude of superiority or of patronizing

confederacy (kon-FEH-duh-ruh-see) an alliance for a common purpose, mutual support, or common action; in Chapter 32, it (the Confederacy) refers to the group of Southern states that seceded from the United States over their insistence on the continuation of enslavement

conservative (kuhn-SUHR-vuh-tihv) tending to or favoring the maintaining of existing views, policies, conditions, or institutions; traditional

conspirators (kuhn-SPIH-rah-tawrz) people who plot together against a person or a group of people

conspire (kuhn-SPEYER) to plan or act together with a group of people against a person or group of people

contagious (kon-TAY-jus) exciting similar emotions or reactions in others

contest (kuhn-TEST) to challenge

continent (KON-tih-nent) a large, continuous mass of land

contrabands (KON-truh-bandz) illegal or prohibited, usually smuggled goods

contradiction (kon-trah-DIHK-shun) a situation in which items in a statement, factors, or actions are inconsistent or contrary to one another

convict labor system the system of using unpaid convicts to work on a farm or in a mill, factory, mine, or some other commer-cial operation

cultural patterns (KUL-tyoo-ruhl PAT-turnz) the customs, traditions, and characteristics of people of a common background

D

deceit (duh-SEET) dishonesty

decentering (dee-SEH-tuh-ring) taking central focus away from a particular idea of position

de facto (DAY FAHK-toh) in reality

defiance (dee-FEYE-ehnts) the act of boldly challenging someone or something

dehumanization (dee-hyoo-mih-neye-ZAY-shun) the idea of reducing humans to things by treating them as nonhuman objects

depression (dee-PREH-shun) an economic downturn in a region or a country

desegregation (dee-seh-greh-GAY-shun) the act of ending the exclusion of people from a group or organization based on racial, ethnic, sexual, or political bias; the opening of such a group to all people, regardless of race, ethnicity, sex, or political affiliation

deserted (dee-ZUR-tehd) to have quit the armed services without leave; to have left the service illegally

destiny (DEH-stih-nee) fate

detonated (DEH-toh-nay-ted) caused a situation or an item to explode; the explosion of a force—either a figurative one such as a particularly controversial issue or a literal one such as dynamite—that causes open antagonism, devastation, and injury of some kind

diaspora (dee-AZ-poh-rah) See *mfecane.*

dinqnesh (DEENK NEHSH) so-called by Ethiopians; the famous 3.2-million-year-old female fossil found in Africa; known in America as *Lucy*

discriminatory (dihs-KRIH-mih-muh-taw-ree) applying or favoring prejudice in outlook, treatment, or action toward someone, a group, or even an issue

dislocation (dihs-loh-CAY-shun) the psychological and physical shift of a people from their home, history, values, customs, and traditions

double standards (DUH-bluhl STAN-duhrdz) the system of hav-ing two sets of rules—one for each group—that are unequal, unfair, or unjust in some way, shape, or form

draft (DRAFT) the calling of people to serve involuntarily in the armed service

draft riots (DRAFT REYE-uhts) outbreaks of violoence by those who refused to serve in the armed forces

***Dred Scott* decision** the Supreme Court ruling that enslaved Africans could not be citizens, even if they traveled north of the Missouri Compromise line, as Dred Scott had; the Supreme Court justices were divided on the issue of whether a freed African could become a citizen, though they agreed that Scott, who was never freed, was not a citizen.

durante vita (doo-RAHN-tay VEE-tah) for life

dzimbabwes (dzihm-BAHB-weez) stone cities built between the 9th and 15 centuries all over the southern region of Africa

E

Ebonics (eh-BAHN-iks) a language that was formed by a mix-ture of English words and African structures that served the Af-rican population in the colonies in communicating with each other and with whites

economic depression (eh-coh-NOM-ik dee-PREH-shun) a great or even total loss of financial stability in one area, state, or country that causes the collapse of the economy of that locale

economics (eh-coh-NOM-iks) the principles by which a society produces goods and services and then distributes and consumes those goods and services

electorate (uh-LEHK-toh-rayt) a body of people who are enti-tled to vote

emancipated (ee-MAHN-sih-pay-ted) freed

Emancipation Proclamation (ee-mahn-sih-PAY-shun prah-cluh-MAY-shun) a proclamation issued by President Abraham Lincoln in 1862 that freed all the enslaved Africans in the seceded states

eminent (EH-mih-nent) standing out above others in some qual-ity or position

empire (EHM-peyer) a major territory of great extent (or a number of territories or peoples) under a single ruler

enfranchisement (ehn-FRAN-cheyez-mehnt) the act of giving rights, especially the right to vote, to a person or group of people

enlightened (ehn-LEYE-tehnd) educated; aware of both sides of an issue

enlist (en-LIHST) to sign up for or join the armed services of one's own free will

enslavement (ehn-SLAYV-mehnt) dehumanizing treatment of people who are taken by force to work for others, usually for the rest of their lives, for no other reason than for the profit of the enslavers

enterprising (EHN-tuhr-preye-zing) readiness to undertake or experiment in a new project or idea

entrepreneurs (AHN-truh-prehn-OORZ) people who organize and manage business with the sole purpose of making money

equality (ee-KWAH-luh-tee) on the same level in every way, shape, and form

equitable (EH-kwti-uh-bul) equal; fair

eulogized (YOO-loh-jeyezd) to speak or write in high praise of someone, usually who is dead

exodus (EKS-oh-duhs) a departure; the act of exiting; leaving someplace

Exodusters (EGS-oh-duhs-tuhrz) African Americans who—to escape pseudoslavery—bought land in Kansas between 1779 and 1881 and who considered themselves to be making an exodus out of bondage

expatriate (eks-PAY-tree-ayt) to banish or send into exile

expedient (ex-PEE-dee-ehnt) advantageous; suitable for achiev-ing a given end in a given circumstance

exploited (ex-PLOY-tehd) taken unfair advantage of

extended family (eks-TEHN-dehd FAM-uh-lee) a household that includes near relatives—such as aunts, uncles, grandparents, and cousins—in addition to the immediate family

F

figurehead (FIH-gyoor-hehd) the head or chief in name only; one who has the important title but not the power

franchise (FRAN-cheyez) to have rights, especially the right to vote; to *disenfranchise* means to remove one's rights, usually from a person.

freedom fighters (FREE-duhn FEYE-turz) people who risk betrayal and death to organize and fight oppressors for their freedom

freedom rides (FREE-duhm reyedz) the travels of civil rights demonstrations to locations all over the South, usually in buses, to protest African American injustice

frock coat a man's knee-length coat, usually double breasted

Fugitive Slave Law (FYOO-jih-tihv) law passed in 1850 that gave the federal government full power to deny rights to Africans forcefully: being denied their testimony, runaway enslaved people were placed in custody without a warrant or a hearing, were de-nied hearings and an investigation of their case, and could not testify on their own behalf; all Africans were assumed to be guilty rather than innocent. Federal marshals who failed to car-ry out the law could be fined $1,000; if a fugitive escaped from their custody, the marshals were liable for the full value of the fugitive. People who blocked a fugitive's arrest, assisted a fu-gitive's escape, or harbored or concealed a fugitive face a fine of up to $1,000 and six months' imprisonment; anyone found guilty of breaking this law was also fined $1,000 for each escaping fugitive.

Funga (FOON-gah) traditional West African dance of welcome, made popular in the United States by African American dancer Pearl Primus

G

Garveyite (GAHR-vee-eyet) members of Marcus Moziah Gar-vey's Universal Negro Improvement Association and his African's Communities League

genre (ZHAHN-ruh) a category; usually, a type of litera-ture (e.g., short story, novel, biography, play, poem)

Grandfather Clause a law that excused anyone from the harsh voting requirements if his grandfather had voted before 1867; needless to say, African Americans were excluded completely because in 1867 they were not even allowed to vote

Great Depression (dee-PREH-shun) the period in United States history from 1929, when the stock market crashed, until the early 1940s, when the United States econony was revitalized by its shift to wartime status

Great Migration (meye-GRAY-shun) during the first two decades of the 1900s, the mass movement of African Americans in the United States to the North

griots (GREE-ohs) storytellers who record people's past as oral history

H

harassed (huh-RASD) to be annoyed continually and persis-tently

homogeneous (hoh-moh-GEE-nyus) having the same or a similar type of structure, such as culture, heritage, tradition, and so forth

humanity (hyoo-MAH-nih-tee) the quality or state of being compassiomnate, sympathetic, and considerate toward people or animals

hypocrisy (hih-PAH-cruh-see) the pretense of being more sincere than you really are

I

ideals (eye-DEE-uhlz) standards of perfection that become one's goal or as a model for imitation

illiterate (ih-LIH-tuh-riht) having little or no education, especially being unable to read or write

impeach (ihm-PEECH) to bring charges against a public official in an effort to remove the official from office

imperialism (ihm-PEE-ree-uhl-ihsm) the policy or practice of taking over a nation, usually by force, to gain direct control over that nation's political and economic life

indentured (in-DEN-tyoord) a type of servant who works for another person for a period of time, usually to pay off a debt

indentureship (in-DEN-tyoor-shihp) the European practice that allowed a person to enter into a contract or bond to work for someone else, usually for a period of seven years; at the end of the indentureship, the servant or bondsperson was released; how-ever, indentured Africans eventually served for life as enslaved Africans.

indigenous (in-DIH-jih-nis) native-born people of a region, or something produced or grown in a region

indiscriminate (ihn-dihs-CRIH-mih-niht) haphazard; random

industrialization (in-DUHS-tree-uh-eye-zay-shun) the change from small types of work—usually small farms—to large-scale work—such as factories or, in this case, the enslavement of African peoples to make a huge profit

infanticide (ihn-FAN-tuh-seyed) the murder of children

innunendo (ih-nyoo-EHN-doh) a hint; an insinuation

inspiration (ihn-spih-RAY-shun) someone or something that influences or moves a person emotionally toward a certain opinion or action

insurrection (ihn-suh-REK-shun) resistance and revolt against someone or something, usually by force

integrated (in-tuh-GRAY-tehd) having members of various groups in equal membership in a society or group

integrate (in-tuh-GRAYT) the act of bringing members of different races, ethnicities, sexes, or political persuasions into equal membership in a society or group

internalized (ihn-TUHR-nuh-leyezd) to have incorporated values and the like within oneself as conscious or subconscious guiding principles through learning or experience

intimidate (ihn-TIH-mih-dayt) to control through the use of fear or threats

J

jales (JAYLS) praise singers, storytellers, and historians of West Africa

Jim Crow an enslaver whose name is associated solely with laws that whites passed legislating segregation and discrimination

K

Kawaida (kah-wah-EE-dah) [literal translation: "customs"] Maulana Karenga's philosophy which had the historical and cul-tural roots of the African people, both in Africa and the Amer-icas, as its core and Kiswahili as its official language

Kemet (keh-MET) the African name of ancient Egypt before the Greeks changed it to *Aigyptos* (eye-GYP-tos)

Kiswahili (kee-swah-HEE-lee) considered to be one of the least ethic of African tongues, this African language was adopted as the international African language

Kwanzaa (KWAHN-zah) [Kiswahili for "first fruits"] a cultural celebration of African American traditions and values, this festival is held in late December.

L

legacy (LEH-guh-see) a gift from an ancestor or a ruler to a person, a people, or a nation; for example, the ancient Africans by their early achievements, inventions, and discoveries left a legacy of knowledge for all people; in modern day, the gift is usually left in a will to someone.

legend (LEH-jehnd) a story that comes down from the past; a person or thing that inspires people

liberal (LIH-buh-ruhl) associated with the ideals of the indi-vidual—especially greater individual participation in govern-ment—and the consitutional, political, and administrative re-forms that are designed to secure these objectives; nontraditional

liberation (lih-buh-RAY-shun) freedom

linsey (LIHN-zee) a coarse cloth made of cotton and wool

literacy test (LIH-tuh-ruh-see) a test to prove that the prospective voter could read and write

lynching (LIHN-chihng) the murder—usually by hanging—of individuals by mob action without a lawful trial

M

maimings (MAY-mihngz) crippling; beating with intent to cripple

majority (muh-LAW-ruh-tee) one more than half

mandate (MAN-dayt) to order, direct, or require

manhood the condition of being a human being

Manifest Destiny (MAH-nuh-fehst DEH-stih-nee) the belief that United States territorial expansion to the Pacific Ocean was inevitable and fated to happen

manumission (mah-nyoo-MIH-shun) the act or process of releasing someone from slavery

marauder (mah-RAW-dehr) a person who roams about and raids in search of plunder

maroon communities (muh-ROON kuh-MYOO-nih-teez) villages or groups of runaway enslaved Africans and Native Americans in Hispaniola who raided sugar plantations to free other enslaved people and take the supplies they needed

Maroon (muh-ROONZ) a runaway enslaved African in Hispaniola who raided sugar plantations to free other enslaved people and take the supplies they needed

Mason and Dixon Line (MAY-sehn, DIHK-sehn) an imaginary boundary between Pennsylvania and Maryland that divided the slaveholding states from the relatively free states

massacre (MAH-suh-kuhr) a large-scale slaughter of people

medu netr (MEH-doo NAY-tur) the language of ancient Africa and the "sacred writing" of the Kemetic people

menial (MEE-nyuhl) of or relating to a lowly, humble, servant's type of work; servile; lacking interest or dignity

mental enslavement (MEHN-tuhl ehn-SLAYV-mehnt) the adop-tion of a negative self-image into one's mind until one believes it, thereby becoming a "slave" to the belief of one's inferiority

mfecane (MEF-eh-kayn) a southern African word that means "a great scattering;" the forced removal of African people from their own communities in Africa and their dispersion over most of the Americas and the Caribbean; also called the *African diaspora*

Middle American referring to the people or land of Mexico and Central America

Middle Passage the journey by enslaved Africans aboard a slave ship across the Atlantic from Africa to the Americas

militancy (MIH-lih-tihn-see) an extremely careful watchfulness or study—to the point of being almost soldierlike—of a situation for any change

militant (MIH-lih-tihnt) engaged in actively opposing or even physically fighting for a cause

millenium (mih-LEH-nee-uhm) The turn of a century to a year that is in round thousands, such as the year 2000

minority (meye-NAW-rih-tee) less than half

misdemeanor (mihs-duh-MEE-nuhr) minor offenses against the law

mixed heritage (MIKSD HEH-rih-tihj) the background of children who result from an African and white union

mob violence (MAHB VEYE-uh-lunts) outbreaks of violence by organized groups of by groups who are unified in a point of view against the established rule

moral character (MAW-ruhl KAH-ruhk-tuhr) a person's adherence to the principles of right and wrong in his or her behavior

moral suasion (MAW-ruhl SWAY-zhun) an abolitionist position that favored a nonviolent approach to persuade whites to end enslavement; fostered by Willian Lloyd Garrison

mosque (MOSK) temple

N

narratives (NAH-rah-tihvz) true-life stories

Nation of Islam (NA-shun, IH-slahm) religion founded by W.D. Fard and Elijah Poole (later known as Elijah Mohammed) whose mem-bers declared themselves Muslims and called for a total separation of African Americans from whites; many gave up their "slave" names and adopted the unknown X as a surname, symbolizing that African names that were lost during the *mfecane.*

nationalism (NAH-shun-uhl-ism) love of country or heritage

"Negro spirituals" (NEE-groh SPIH-rih-tyoo-uhls) hymns of encouragement and faith that African Americans sang for more than 100 years—and still continue to sing

New Negro a term created by Alain Locke to describe the new confidence and pride that many African Americans had in themselves

nonviolent protest (nahn-VEYE-oh-lehnt PROH-tehst) a form of passive resistance in which a position against an established policy or law is stated by peaceful methods, using no forms of violence whatsoever; Mahatma Ghandi (muh-HAT-muh GAHN-dee) was the prime exponent of this method in the 1940s in India; Martin Luther King, Jr., was the same in the United States during the 1960s Civil Rights Movement.

O

Oklahoma Grandfather Clause (oh-klah-HOH-mah) law that said that only those people who grandfathers had voted in the previous election could vote; the Supreme Court declared this law illegal in 1915.

oppressor (ah-PREH-sur) a person or a group who keeps others down by cruel and unjust use of power

optimism (AHP-tih-mihsm) an inclination to see only the favorable side of actions or events or to anticipate the only best possible outcome

oral tradition (AW-ruhl truh-DIH-shen) the passage of sto-ries from generation to generation by speaking or telling of the past

orator (ARE-uh-tuhr) a great speaker

overseer (OH-vur-see-ur) a plantation manager

overt (oh-VUHRT) open; in full view; apparent to the viewer

P

pagan (PAY-gun) one who has little or no religious life and values only physical pleasures and materialistic values

paleontologist (pay-lee-un-TAH-oh-jist) one who learns about the history of the world by studying fossil remains

Pan-African of, relating to, or involving all the countries in Africa

passes special permission, usually in writing, to enlisted personnel from a commanding officer

passive resistance (PAH-sihv ree-SIHS-tehnts) nonviolent resistance

patronizing (PAH-troh-neye-zihng) insultingly condescending

patrons (PAY-truhnz) sponsors, usually financial, of an artist, movement, or foundation

peonage (PEE-yuh-nihj) African Americans were forced to work on farms as hired hands or domestic servants for whites; other-wise, they were charged with vagrancy. If so, they had to take the same jobs for no pay. This law did not apply to whites.

perspective (purh-SPEHK-tihv) viewpoint

petition (peh-TIH-shun) a formal request

Philadelphia clubwoman (fih-luh-DEHL-fee-ah KLUHB-wuh-mihn) the subject of Langston Hughes's profile of a 1920s elite woman who represented a class of wealthy urban African American women who were trying desperately to distance themselves from things African

philanthropist (fih-AN-throh-pihst) one who dispenses funds that have been set aside for humanitarian purposes

plebiscite (PLEH-buh-seyet) a vote by which the people of a country of a district express an opinion for or against a propo-sal, especially in the choice of a government or a ruler

Plessy v. Ferguson (PLEH-see VUHR-sihs FUHR-guh-suhn) a Supreme Court decision that said that if a person's system has even one drop of African blood, that person is African and will be treated like other Africans; this decision established the separate-but-equal doctrine, which meant that African Americans and whites could have separate public facilities as long as they were equal.

poignant (POY-nyant) touching; painfully affecting the feelings

poll tax a fee that had to be paid by African Americans so that they could vote

polyrhythmic (pah-lee-RITH-mihk) having many different rhythms or beats, usually in music

postscript (POHST-skrihpt) a note or series of notes added to the end of a completed letter, a book, or article

prejudice (PREH-joo-dihs) bias or hatred of a person that is founded on racial, religious, ethnic, or some other unreasonable basis

progressive (proh-GREH-sihv) making use of or interested in new ideas, findings, or opportunities

pseudonym (SOO-doh-nihm) a name that one uses instead of one's own; a pen name; an alias

pseudoslavery (SOO-doh-slay-vuh-ree) the practice by farm owners of renting land and equipment to African Americans at such high rates that, at the end of the growing season, the African Americans were still in debt to the farm owners

punitive laws (PYOO-nuh-tihv) laws that prescribed specific punishment for certain crimes

Q

Quakers (KWAY-kurz) a religious group, also called the Reli-gious Society of Friends, that showed an early moral interest in freeing Africans from enslavement; Quakers believe in passive resistance, or suasion, and denounced violence, war, and other uses of force.

queen mother the mother of a reigning king or queen

R

racial discrimination (RAY-shul dihs-krih-mih-NAY-shun) an act of prejudice directed at a particular group of people because of their race

racism (RAY-sizm) hatred that is based on the belief that race is the primary decider of a person's traits and capacities and that racial differences produce the inborn superiority of a particular race

rage (RAYJ) fury; anger that is so intense as to lead to possible or actual violence

rebellion (ree-BEHL-yun) opposition to one in authority or command, usually violent

recompense (REH-kuh-pehns) payment

reconcile (REH-kun-seyel) to adapt to something; to settle or adjust to something

reconstruction (ree-kun-STRUK-shun) the act of rebuilding or putting something back together

recourse (REE-cawrs) the right to turn to someone or something (such as the law) for help or protection

redemption (ree-DEHMP-shun) the paying of a ransom or fee to free someone from captivity

redemptive violence (dee-DEHMP-tihv VEYE-oh-lents) violence that will supposedly atone, repay, or repair a bad situation

redress (ree-DREHS) compensation for a wrong or a loss

regiment (REH-juh-mehnt) a military unit usually consisting of a number of batallions

relevant education (REH-luh-vehnt eh-dyoo-KAY-shun) courses that bear in an immediate way upon the lives of those who take them

renaissance (REH-nug-sahns) a rebirth, usually of learning about history, culture, or some other aspect of heritage

resilience (ree-ZIH-lyents) the strength to endure and survive

resistance (ree-ZIHS-tenhts) opposition against something

retaliation (ree-tah-lee-AY-shun) revenge; the act of paying someone back in the same way that they treated you

revoke (ree-VOHK) to take back, to cancel

revolt (ree-VOHLT) an uprising, usually violent, against something or someone

rites of passage (REYETZ, PAH-sij) a ritual associated with a crisis or a change of status (such as marriage, illness, or death) for an individual

S

sanction (SANK-shun) official approval of or consent to do something

sanctuary (SANK-tyoo-ay-ree) a place of protection

sarcastic (sare-CAS-tik) marked by bitterness, taunting, and ridiculing in order to sting or hurt the victim's feelings

scatting (SKAH-ting) meaningless words or syllables that are strung together and sung very rapidly; while the words in them-selves mean nothing, they verbalize the emotions of the singer and became a highlight in the performance of the best jazz singers, such as Ella Fitzgerald and Cab Callaway.

scholar-activist (SKAH-luhr AK-tih-vihst) a student who was active in the Civil Rights Movement and is now college or university professors

secede (see-SEED) to withdraw from; to quit; to separate from

segregation (seh-greh-GAY-shun) a system of legal separation of two or more groups or people

self-actualization (SEHLF ak-choo-ul-ih-ZAY-shun) the freedom to be the best a person can be

self-determination (SEHLF dee-tehr-mih-NAY-shun) the free choice of one's own acts or lifestyle without external force or pressure

self-reliance (SEHLF ree-LEYE-uns) to be dependent on oneself

sharecropping system (SHAIR-krah-peeng) a person farms some-one else's land for a share of profits when the crops are sold

sit-ins the occupying of space by sitting either in regular seats or on the floor so as to disrupt orderly operation; this action grew out of the actions of early African Americans when, in such segregated places of business as lunch counters, they occupied seats to deny them to white customers.

slave-hunter a person who hunted and caught runaway Africans for the money paid in reward; also known as *slave-catcher*

slavery (SLAY-vuh-ree) a system of punishment for crime or for nonpayment of debts, voluntary servitude by people who could not provide for themselves, or handling of prisoners of war

socialism (SOH-shuh-lism) a belief that the means of pro-ducing wealth should be owned by the community as a group

sojourn (SOH-jurn) to travel

states' rights the right of states to pass laws that over-ride unconstitutional federal laws

statute (STAH-tyoot) a law

stereotype (STEH-ree-oh-teyep) a mental picture that is held in common by members of a group and that represents an oversim-plified opinion, a prejudiced attitude, or an unreasonable judg-ment; when the picture is negative, it causes bias against the subject.

stigma (STIHG-mah) a mark, usually figurative, against a person who is accused or convicted of something that is considered wrong

stock market (STAHK MAHR-kut) a place where shares of owner-ship in companies are bought and sold

stringent (STRIGN-jehnt) harsh

submissive (suhb-MIH-sihv) obedient to someone or something in a humble way

submission (suhb-MIH-shun) the act of yielding to the authority or control of another

subtle (SUH-tuhl) difficult to understand or to see clearly; obscure; elusive

suffrage (SUH-frihj) the right to vote

suicide (SOO-uh-seyed) the act of killing oneself

superficial (soo-puhr-FIH-shuhl) shallow; without depth; on the surface

supplement (SUH-pluh-mehnt) to add to

T

tariff (TAH-rihf) a tax on goods that come into the country

tenets (TEH-nehtz) a principle, belief, or doctrine that is generally held to be true

token (TOH-kehn) something small or a small number of people included in a much larger group to show the absence of discrimi-nation; the smallness of the included number will have no affect on the final group's goal, therefore pointing out the presence of discrimination in any event

treason (TREE-zehn) the attempt to overthrow the government to which the traitor owes allegiance or to injure or kill the head of that state or a member of that person's family; the betrayal of one's country; the crime is punishable by death.

tragedy (TRAH-juh-dee) a disastrous event; a calamity; a great misfortune

Triangular Trade (treye-ANG-yoo-lahr) the im-port/export component of the European Slave Trade; basically, the system was similar to this: Europeans exported goods and guns manufactured in Europe via slaver traders; the latter traded these in Africa for captured Africans, who were taken to the colonies and traded for raw materials; the raw materials were taken to Europe and traded for the manufactured goods.

U

unconstitutional (ugn-kon-stih-TOO-shun-ul) against the laws of a constitution, usually the U.S. Constitution

underground a movement or group organized in strict secrecy among people in order to maintain communcations, provide solidar-ity, and organize and carry out disruptive action against a civil order or government

Underground Railroad a network of people who helped enslaved Africans to reach freedom in safe territory and of churches, taverns, private homes, and the like—called *stations* —where the Africans hid on their route to freedom

undermine (UHN-duhr-meyen) to discredit

unwavering (un-WAY-vuh-ring) to give an opinion about or to stand by a person or an issue without hesitation, faltering, or swaying

uprising (UHP-reye-zihng) an act of defiance against estab-lished authority, usually violent

V

vagrancy (VAY-grehn-see) the state of having no established place to live or no lawful or visible means of support (job); loitering

vagrant (VAY-grehnt) a person who has no established place to live or no lawful or visible means of support (job); a loiterer

valor (VAH-lawr) bravery

victimized (VIHK-tih-meyezd) to be cheated; to be subjected to deceit or fraud

waistcoat (WEHST-kit) a vest

wanton (WAHN-tihn) merciless; inhumane; without check, lim-itation, or boundaries

Z

zeal (ZEEL) intense enthusiasm and passionate eagerness in the pursuit of a certain goal

PRONOUNCIATION KEY FOR PROPER NAMES

Abubakari II (ah-boo-bah-KAH-ree) early 13th-century leader of the Malian people

Agadja (ah-GAH-jah) Dahomean king who successfully combated the English Slave Trade

Ahmed Baba (AH-mehd BAH-bah) Noted author and professor at the University of Sankore in the late 1500s C.E. who taught about the origins of the Songhay Empire

Ansah (AHN-sah) ruler of the Fante people (1472-1484) who tried to prevent Europeans from coming ashore from their ships in his territory

Asantehene (ah-SAHN-tay-hay-nay) paramount king of the Asante people

Askia Mohammed (ahs-KEE-ah moh-HAH-med) Songhay emperor (circa 1530s C.E.) under whom the religion of Islam and African arts and culture were allowed to flourish in freedom; his use of a cabinet of advisors made him the first modern ruler of what is today Sudan.

Attucks, Crispus (AH-tukz, KRIHS-puhs) the first person killed in the Revolutionary War, in the Boston Massacre

Banneker, Benjamin (BAH-neh-kur) an African who lived in the colonies; an astronomer, clockmaker, farmer, almanac writer, and surveyor

Beckwourth, James (BEHK-wurth) a trader for the American Fur Company who discovered the lowest point across the Sierra Nevada; this point is now called Beckwourth Pass.

Belley, Jean-Baptiste (behl-LAY, ZHAN bahp-TEEST) Haitian volunteer who fought first in the American Revolution and then in his own country's revolution

Besse, Martial (BEHS, MAHR-shul) Haitian volunteer who fought first in the American Revolution and then in his own country's revolution; later, Haitian ambassador to the United States

Boah Tafo (BOH-ah TAH-foh) a queen mother of a Ghanaian king

Boukman (BOOK-mahn) religious leader in Haiti who, with Mother Marie (another religious leader), plotted a revolt against French enslavers on the island of Haiti; Toussaint L'Ouverture finally carried out the plot and led the enslaved people to freedom.

Cassuneuve, John (kah-sah-NAY-oov) captain of the slave ship, *Don Carlos*

Cato (KAY-toh) led the ill-fated Stono Rebellion (1739) in South Carolina

Christophe, Henri (kree-STOHF, ahn-REE) Haitian volunteer who fought first in the American Revolution and then in his own coun-try's revolution; later became king of Haiti

Cimarrones (see-mah-ROH-nehs) special Spanish police force organized (1532) to try to recapture Africans who had run away to escape enslavement in the Americas

Cinque, Joseph (SANK) a Mandingo African prince who led en-slaved Africans to steal the ship *L'Amistad* in Cuba and sail to the United States in 1839; abolitionists led by John Quincey Adams defended him, and the Supreme Court set him free; he became a business agent for European slave traders.

Deslandes, Charles (day-LAHND) led an ill-fated uprising (1811) in Louisiana

Dias, Bartolomeu (DEE-as, bahr-toh-loh-MAY-yoo) Portuguese explorer (1450-1500)

Du Bois, W.E.B. (doo BOYZ) author and African American spokesman whose clear perception allowed him to praise the achievements of Booker T. Washington while firmly rejecting Washington's philosophy of accommodation

Dunham, Katherine (DUHN-um, KAH-thuh-rihn) choreographer and dancer who provided her versions of Jamaican and Haitian dances for the stage and African dances for the Metropolitan Opera's production of the opera *Aida*

Ellington, Duke (eh-LEENG-tuhn) African American composer, bandleader, and performer who, it is said, wrote more than 1,000 compositions, including "Mood Indigo" and "Take the 'A' Train"

Equiano, Olaudah (eh-kwee-AH-noh, oh-LOW-dah) enslaved Afri-can who was able to buy his freedom; later wrote of the differ-ences between African enslavement and slavery in Africa

Frederiksted (FREH-duh-rihk-stehd) town on the island of St. Croix that was set afire during a labor revolt by African laborers

Gama, Vasco Da (GAH-mah, VAHS-koh dah) Portuguese naviga-tor and explorer (1460-1524)

Garvey, Marcus Moziah (GAHR-vee, MAHR-cuhs moh-ZEYE-uh) African American mass leader who determined to uplift the African American people to pride of race, self-reliance, self-determina-tion, and world leadership

Gottlieb, General Moses Buddhoe (GAHT-leeb, BUHD-hoh) Danish general who, in the early 1800s, forced the government of the Virgin Islands to free enslaved Africans

Hessians (HEH-shenz) German soldiers who fought on the British side in the Revolutionary War only for the money

Karenga, Maulana (kah-REHN-gah, mah-oo-LAH-nah) the embodi-ment of the Black Studies movement whose philosophy, Kawaida, formed the basis of much of the Black Studies discussion on college campuses; he fostered the adoption of Kiswahili as the in-ternational African language

Leutze, Emanuel (LOYT-zuh, ee-MAH-nyoo-ehl) famous artist who painted the portrait of Washington and his men crossing the Delaware River

Liberia (leye-BEE-ree-ah) a colony set up in the 1820s by the American Colonization Society to settle free Africans

Loguen, Jermain (LOH-gwehn, jehr-MAYN) a preacher who favored violence to liberate enslaved Africans

L'Ouverture, Toussaint (LOO-vair-toor, TOO-san) led successful revolt of enslaved people against the French enslavers in Haiti

Mansa Musa (MAN-sah moo-SAH) descendent of Sundiata Keita and emperor of Mali around the early 1330s C.E.; conquered the Songhay Empire, expanded trade, and supported education and the arts

Maremba, Nzenga [Mbemba, Nzinga] (muh-REHM-bah, en-ZEHN-gah) [ehm-BEHM-bah, en-ZEHN-gah] African king who took the name Affonso [Afonso I]

Nzinga (en-GIHN-gah) queen of Angola who waged a 50-year war against slave traders; the Portuguese finally negotiated a treaty with her in 1636, which remained in effect until her death in 1663.

Okomfo Anokye (oh-KUM-foh uh-NYOH-kyeh) supreme priest of seven villages in 16th-century Africa

Osei Tutu (oh-SAY-ee TOO-too) a young king in 16th-century Africa

Primus, Pearl (PREE-muhs PUHRL) celebrated African American dancer-choreographer-teacher

Rillieux, Norbert (rihl-YUH) invented a vacuum cup that revolutionized the sugar-refining industry

St. Croix (SAYNT CROY) one of the Virgin Islands, in the Caribbean Sea

Scholten, Peter von (SKOHL-ten) Danish governor of the Virgin Islands who was forced by General Moses Buddhoe Gottlieb, in the early 1800s, to free enslaved Africans

Sierra Leone (see-EH-rah lay-OH-nee) colony in Africa for free Africans; set up by the British in 1787

Sundiata Keita (soon-JAH-tah KAY-tah) founder and first king of the Malian Empire (around 1255 C.E.)

Sunni Ali Ber (SOO-nee AH-lee BER) Emperor of Songhay (late 15th century C.E.); reestablished the presence of African culture in religion, education, and traditions

Susquehanna (suhs-kwee-HAH-nah) a river in Pennsylvania

Van Vechten, Carl (VAHN VEHK-tehn) a financier and avid sup-porter of African American literature in the 1930s and 1940s

Vesey, Denmark (VEE-see) led an ill-fated rebellion (1822) in South Carolina

BIBLIOGRAPHY

Alexis, Stephen. *Black Liberator: The Life of Touissaint Louverture*. New York: 1949.

Ani, Marimba. *Yurugu: An Africa-Centered Analysis of European Thought and Behavior*. Trenton, NJ: Africa World Press, 1994.

Aptheker, Herbert. *American Negro Slave Revolts*. New York: International Publishers, 1963. The classic work on the major slave revolts in America. Aptheker examines slave revolts from the earliest presence of Africans in North America. His conclusion is that there were more revolts than usually admitted by historians.

Asante, Molefi K. *Afrocentricity*. Trenton, NJ: Africa World Press, 1988. This is the first book written on the concept of Afrocentricity. The author defines the idea of Afrocentricity and discusses its implication for social and political consciousness.

Asante, Molefi K. *Classical Africa*. Maywood, NJ: Peoples Publishing Group, 1993. This is a survey of the six principal African civilizations from 3000 B.C.E. to 1590. Beginning with the ancient Egyptian civilization and ending with the decline of Songhay, this text covers the origins, evolution, and achievements of six significant civilizations.

Asante, Molefi K. and Mark Mattson. *Historical and Cultural Atlas of African Americans*. New York: Macmillian, 1991. A very comprehensive guide to the history and spatial representation of the culture and population of the African American community.

Asante, Molefi K., *Kemet, Afrocentricity, and Knowledge*. Trenton: Africa World Press, 1990. This is an essay in Afrocentric research methodology.

Asante, Molefi K. *The Afrocentric Idea*. Philadelphia: Temple University Press, 1987.

Ball, Charles. *Fifty Years in Chains*. New York: Dover Publications, 1970.

Ben-Jochannon, Y. *Black Man of the Nile*. Trenton, NJ: Africa World Press, 1990.

Bennett, Lerone. *Before the Mayflower*. Chicago: Johnson Publishing Company, 1990. A comprehensive introduction to African American history. Written in a popular style and using numerous allusions from the African American culture, this book is one of the most widely referred to histories of the African American people.

Blackshire, C. Aisha, ed. *Language and Literature in the African American Imagination*. Westport, CT: Greenwood Press, 1992.

Blassingame, John. *The Slave Community in the Plantation South*. New York: Oxford University Press, 1972. This is the classic study of the enslaved communities in the antebellum South. It discusses religion, society, and labor conditions on the plantations.

Bradford, Sarah H. Harriet. *The Moses of Her People*. Auburn: 1897.

Brawley, Benjamin. *The Negro Genius*. New York: 1937.

Broderick, Francis L. *W. E. B. Du Bois, Negro Leader in a Time of Crisis*. Stanford, CA: Stanford University Press, 1959.

Butcher, Margaret Just. *The Negro in American Culture*. New York: 1956. A rare treatment of the historical roots of African American art, literature, dance, and religion.

Carmichael, Stokely, and Charles, Hamilton. *Black Power*. New York: 1967.

Clarke, John Henrik, ed. *Marcus Garvey and the Vision of Africa*. New York: 1963.

Cronon, Edmund. *Black Moses*. Madison, WS: University of Wisconsin, 1968.

Davidson, Basil. *The Lost Cities of Africa*. Boston: 1959. The best discussion of the historical cities of Africa. Davidson writes of the cities that contributed to the expansion and development of trade and commerce throughout the continent. For anyone who seeks to understand the complexity of African urban cultures, this is the classic work.

Davis, David Brion. *The Problem of Slavery in Western Culture*. Ithaca, NY: Cornell University Press, 1966.

Diop, Cheikh Anta. *The African Origin of Civilization*. New York: Lawrence Hill, 1974.

Diop, Cheikh Anta. *The Cultural Unity of Black Africa*. Chicago: Third World Press, 1978. This book shows the cultural unity of African cultures. Starting from the position that all African cultures are interrelated, Diop examines the commonalities in language, social institutions, and kinship patterns.

Drake, St. Clair, and Horace, Clayton. *Black Metropolis*. New York: 1945.

Du Bois, W. E. B. *The Souls of Black Folk*. New York: Bantam Books, 1989. Du Bois's great classic on the life and experiences of the African American people. This book demonstrates the resilience of the oppressed Africans during the first part of the 20th century. It is in this book that Du Bois discusses the failure of Booker T. Washington's ideas.

Fauset, Arthur Huff. *Sojourner Truth*. Chapel Hill: 1938.

Fisher, Miles Mark. *Negro Slave Songs in the United States*. Secaucus, NJ: Carol Publishing Group, 1990. This book shows the uniqueness of the songs of the African people. Spirituals and songs of the antebellum South are described as more than musical expressions.

Franklin, John Hope. *Emancipation Proclamation*. Garden City, NY: Doubleday, 1963. A brilliant exposition of Abraham Lincoln's proclamation giving freedom to the enslaved Africans in states that were in revolt against the United States.

Harding, Vincent. *There is a River*. New York: Harcourt, Brace, Jovanovich, 1981. This is a penetrating and eloquent testimony of the nobility of the African American people in the face of many odds. Harding writes of the streams of ideas and the streams of struggle that have created character in the African American people.

Harlan, Louis. *Booker T. Washington*. New York: 1972.

Hodges, Norman. *Breaking the Chains of Bondage*. New York: Simon and Schuster, 1972.

Karenga, Maulana. *Introduction to Black Studies*. Los Angeles: University of Sankore Press, 1990. This is the most comprehensive treatment of the issues and topics usually covered in the field of black studies. As the first text of its kind, this book has become a classic in the introductory classes in African American Studies.

Keto, C. T. *The Africa-Centered Perspective of History*. C and A Publishers, 1992.

King, Martin Luther, Jr. *Stride Toward Freedom*. New York: 1958.

King, Martin Luther, Jr. *Why We Can't Wait*. New York: 1964.

Levine, Lawrence. *Black Culture and Black Consiousness*. New York: Oxford University Press, 1977. A major analysis of the manner in which African Americans have responded to the challenges of racism and discrimination.

Malcolm X. *The Autobiography of Malcolm X*. Edited by Alex Haley. New York: 1964. The autobiography of one of the most colorful and creative African American social leaders of the 20th century. This book shows how a man who had gotten on the wrong path as a teenager grew to become a conscious and knowledgeable leader.

Nell, William. *The Colored Patriots of the American Revolution*. Boston: 1855.

Quarles, Benjamin. *Frederick Douglass*. Washington, D.C.: 1948.

Quarles, Benjamin. *The Negro in the Making of America*. New York: 1964. This is the classic history of African Americans by one of the most distinguished historians of all time. Quarles takes the position that the influence of Africa has been seen throughout the African American's experiences and that the response to oppression has made the people stronger and more resilient.

Raboteau, Albert. *Slave Religion*. New York: Oxford University Press, 1981.

Reddings, J. Saunders. *They Came in Chains: Americans from Africa*. New York: Doubleday, 1950. Reddings's comprehensive treatment of the history of African Americans. This book was one of the first attempts to discuss the role of Africans who came in chains to the special meaning of being American.

Redkey, Edwin. *Black Exodus*. New Haven, CT. Yale University Press, 1969.

Rogers, J. A. *Sex and Race*. 3 vols. New York: 1940-44.

Sertima, Ivan van. *They Came Before Columbus*. New York: Random House, 1976. Discusses the African presence in the Americas before the coming of Columbus. Sertima writes in a journalistic style that gives this book an accessibility that is often missing in books of this importance.

Stuckey, Sterling. *Slave Culture*. New York: Oxford University Press, 1987. Written by one of the leading historians of the African American community, this book delves into the making of the contemporary culture. What is the basis of the intellectual ideas, the groups of the music, and the assumptions of the present religions on the African American community?

Washington, Booker T. *Up From Slavery*. New York: 1901.

Welsh-Asante, Kariamu, ed. *The African Aesthetic*. Westport, CT.: Greenwood Press, 1993. Articles in this powerful collection deal with various aspects of the aesthetic ideals of African Americans.

Wesley, Charles H. *Prince Hall*. Washington: 1977.

White, Charles. *A Man Called White*. New York: 1948.

Williams, Chancellor. *The Destruction of Black Civilzation*. Chicago: Third World Press, 1974. A pioneering work to explain the destruction of African civilizations and the degeneration of African culture at the hands of the invaders of Africa. This book discusses the subsequent enslavement of African people in both physical and psychological ways.

Wilmore, Gayraud. *Black Religion and Black Radicalism*. Garden City, NY: Doubleday, 1972. A masterful discussion of African American spirituality and its relationship to the empowerment of the African American community. This is the best work on the subject.

Wood, Peter H. *Black Majority: Negroes in Colonial South Carolina from 1670 through the Stono Rebellion*. New York: 1974.

Woodson, Carter. *The Miseducation of the Negro*. Trenton: Africa World Press, 1989. An examination of the problems with the education of the African American.

INDEX

A

B

C

D

Continued on page 480

E

F

G

Continued on page 481

Continued on page 482

Lincoln Continued from page 481

M

N

O

P

Continued on page 483

P CONTINUED FROM PAGE 482

Continued on page 484

T CONTINUED FROM PAGE 483

U

V

W

Y

PHOTOGRAPH AND ART CREDITS

UNIT 1

pp. 3, 6 (top), Courtesy of the Ghana Embassy; pp. 3, 6, 25, PPG Photo Archives; pp. 3, 19, Dirk Bakker, The Detroit Institute of the Arts; pp. 3, 25, Mexican Government Tourism Office; pp. 19, 23, National Museum of African Art, Eliot Elisofon Archives, Smithsonian Institution.

UNIT 2 & UNIT 3

pp. 38, 39, 40, 46, 56, 60, PPG Photo Archives; pp. 32,44,51,56,57,58,63, North Wind Picture Archives; pp. 49,50, National Museum of African Art, Eliot Elisofon Archives, Smithsonian Institution.

UNIT 4

pp. 69 (bottom), 71, 90, 91, 95, North Wind Picture Archives; pp.68 (top & bottom), 78, 91, 96, 98, 99(top & bottom), PPG Photo Archives; pp. 95, The Library of Congress.

UNIT 5 & UNIT 6

pp. 104, 105, 109, 113, 117, 124, 125, 128, 134, 138, PPG Photo Archives.

UNIT 7

pp. 144, 145, 147, 153, 154, 161, 167, 168, 169, 170, 179, 181, PPG Photo Archives; pp. 148, The Library of Congress; pp. 144, 162, The Underground Railroad, C. Webber, Cincinnati Art Museum; pp. 163, North Wind Picture Archives.

UNIT 8

pp. 186, 187, 189, 199, 201, 202, PPG Photo Archives; pp. 186, 196, Photographs and Prints Division Schomberg Center for Research in Black Culture, The N.Y. Public Library, Astor,Lenox & Tilden Foundation.

UNIT 9 & UNIT 10

pp. 208, 229, 256, Lincoln University; pp. 209, 213, 215, 227(top), 233, 238, 242, 243, 244, 249 , 250, PPG Photo Archives; pp. 219, 239, 246, North Wind Picture Archives; pp. 227, Bettmann Archives; pp. 257, The Library of Congress; pp. 258, National Archives.

UNIT 11

pp. 264, 268, 270, 275, 290, North Wind Picture Archives; pp. 264, 293, Bettmann Archives; pp. 265, 285, Photographs and Prints Division Schomberg Center for Research in Black Culture, The N.Y. Public Library, Astor, Lenox & Tilden Foundation; pp. 269 (top), 272, 281, 291, 292, PPG Photo Archives; pp. 269 (bottom) , Courtesy of Mississippi Department of Archives and History; pp. 274, Courtesy of South Carolina Department of Archives and History; pp. 286, Courtesy of the U.S. Supreme Court; pp. 294, Chicago Historical Society.

UNIT 12

pp. 303, 304, 311, 316, 321, 325, PPG Photo Archives; pp. 301, 315, The Philip Collection, Washington D.C.; pp. 309, The Library of Congress; pp. 320, Tuskegee Institute, Frances B. Johnson; pp. 323, Courtesy of Kenneth Miller.

UNIT 13 & UNIT 14

pp. 333, 344, 351, 352, 353, 355, 358(top), 362 , 371, 373, 381, 383 (top), PPG Photo Archives; pp. 336 (top), 337, 338 (top) , The United States Military Academy Archive; pp. 336(bottom), 338(bottom), 339, 372, 374, Bettmann Archives; pp. 340, 354 , 355 (top center), 358 (bottom), 359, 361, 383 (bottom), AP/Wide World Archives.

UNIT 15

pp. 391 (top), 398, 402, 412, 418, 419, 420, 425 (bottom), 426, 429 (top), 433, 435, PPG Photo Archives; pp. 391 (bottom), 392, 409, 410, 411, 421, 424, 425 (top), AP/Wide World Archives; pp. 393, Lincoln University; pp. 406, 427, 428, Bettmann Archives; pp. 317, Photographs and Prints Division Schomberg Center for Research in Black Culture, The N.Y. Public Library, Astor, Lenox & Tilden Foundation; p. 429, Courtesy of Muhammad Ali Educational & Humanitarian Foundation; p. 432, Courtesy of Budd Williams.

UNIT 16

pp. 443, 450 (bottom), 456 (top), Courtesy of the U.S. Navy, Department of Defense, Scott Allen; pp. 444, 450 (top), 455, 457 (bottom), 458, PPG Photo Archives; pp. 445, 446 (bottom), Courtesy of NASA; pp. 446, Courtesy of Bragman Nyman Catarelli; pp. 449, National Graphic Society; pp. 457 (top), The United States Military Academy Archives.